Connecting Ethics & Practice: A Lawyer's Guide to Professional Responsibility

ASPEN SELECT SERIES

Connecting Ethics & Practice: A Lawyer's Guide to Professional Responsibility

Katerina P. Lewinbuk
Professor of Law
South Texas College of Law Houston

Wolters Kluwer

Published by Wolters Kluwer in New York.

Wolters Kluwer Legal & Regulatory U.S. serves customers worldwide with CCH, Aspen Publishers, and Kluwer Law International products. (www.WKLegaledu.com)

To contact Customer Service, e-mail customer.service@wolterskluwer.com, call 1-800-234-1660, fax 1-800-901-9075, or mail correspondence to:

    Wolters Kluwer
    Attn: Order Department
    PO Box 990
    Frederick, MD 21705

Printed in the United States of America.

1 2 3 4 5 6 7 8 9 0

ISBN 978-1-4548-8773-7

About Wolters Kluwer Legal & Regulatory U.S.

Wolters Kluwer Legal & Regulatory U.S. delivers expert content and solutions in the areas of law, corporate compliance, health compliance, reimbursement, and legal education. Its practical solutions help customers successfully navigate the demands of a changing environment to drive their daily activities, enhance decision quality and inspire confident outcomes.

Serving customers worldwide, its legal and regulatory solutions portfolio includes products under the Aspen Publishers, CCH Incorporated, Kluwer Law International, ftwilliam.com and MediRegs names. They are regarded as exceptional and trusted resources for general legal and practice-specific knowledge, compliance and risk management, dynamic workflow solutions, and expert commentary.

—To the Privilege and Responsibility of Serving Others...

Summary of Contents

Contents

Acknowledgments

This book, along with all of my academic work, is dedicated to the precious memory of my father, Dr. Vladimir Z. Parton, who will always remain my inspiration. Special thanks go to my husband Dan, my children Alexandra and Michael, and to my mother for their endless love and support. I also would like to extend my deep appreciation and gratitude to Karey Sopchak, my student, research assistant, and friend, for her invaluable assistance and collaboration in the preparation of this book. After having taken my Professional Responsibility course, Karey served as inspiration and vehicle for turning my class materials into this manuscript; I would not have done it without her support. Further, I wish to thank Erin DeBooy, Teresa Lakho, and Sarah Tejada for their help with various aspects of the preparation and publication of this book. I am especially grateful to Sarah Tejada for putting my vision into mind map drawing format and to Teresa Lakho for her exceptional technological skills and ability to inspire others on a daily basis.

Introduction
to Professional Responsibility:
A Course Overview

A. SEQUENCE OF RULES

Understanding how the Model Rules of Professional Conduct (Model Rules) are set out will help in the preparation for each class, the final exam, and the Multistate Professional Responsibility Exam (MPRE). However, understanding the sequence of the rules will also provide guidance to anyone in the legal profession, including prospective lawyers or senior lawyers, who is confronted with a new task and is unsure of ethical guidelines. The sequence should confirm the point made throughout this textbook: rules are everywhere, but the diligent attorney will know which rule to look to in any situation. As a result, the rules are set out in an order that creates a pathway of checkpoints that must be considered and sometimes checked off before opening a small private practice, becoming a partner in a large firm, joining in-house counsel at a corporation, or even entering the legal profession altogether.

Chapter 1 of this book, History and Theory of Professional Responsibility—Where We Started and Who We Are Today, offers an overview of the discipline and a brief history and current status of the legal profession. The majority of those reading this book are currently in law school with hopes of being admitted to their respective state bars. Chapter 2, The Importance of Integrity—Before and After Entrance into the Profession, studies the first step in this process. This chapter will give an overview of the rules regulating admission to the bar, the application process, and which behaviors are not permissible for admission. However, the rules and regulations for bar admission do not end once a lawyer is admitted to the bar. The other rules highlighted in this chapter focus on ways in which the legal profession maintains integrity amongst those who are both newly admitted to the bar and those who are considered senior lawyers. These additional rules shall follow any lawyer into all aspects of her legal career.

After admission to the bar, a new lawyer will be eager to put her hard-earned law degree to the test. To do this, she will need to find clients. Therefore, Chapter 3, Obtaining Clients Through Advertising and Solicitation, addresses obtaining clients through advertising and solicitation. Although advertising seems like a straightforward topic, the Model Rules provide certain restrictions on both the form of advertising and when direct solicitation is permissible. However, despite the popularity of advertising and solicitation, lawyers can also gain clients through pro bono work or by judicial appointments. Chapter 4, Obtaining Clients Through Pro Bono Work, Judicial Appointment, and Other Ways of Creating the Attorney-Client Relationship, focuses on the rules for client relationships for both voluntary pro bono work and judicial appointments. These methods for obtaining clients are growing in popularity and have become a heavily utilized process for obtaining clients.

Through advertising her services, the new lawyer is contacted by a person interested in hiring her as his attorney. It may be the lawyer's first client, and it may also be the start of her first attorney-client relationship. It is next important to address the duties that a lawyer owes her client. Some of these duties are very standard, including competence, diligence, and sufficient communication. However, the scope of representation is not always straightforward; it may depend upon the type of client or whether he can even be considered a "current client." A diligent and competent lawyer will also need to be aware of other critical aspects of the attorney-client relationship, including fees and confidential information. These topics are addressed next, in Chapter 5, Confidentiality and Attorney's Fees, and in Chapter 6, Reality Check—Waiving Confidentiality and Applicable Exceptions.

Before a lawyer can agree to enter into an attorney-client relationship, she must consider a number of matters in addition to fees and the scope of her representation. For instance, a lawyer must always consider whether representing a particular client will spark a conflict of interest. A number of standard conflicts are to be considered, such as conflicts for current clients or former clients, but there are also specialized conflicts to take into account, including whether a lawyer has worked for the government or as a judge. In some instances, the conflict cannot be overcome even with sufficient screening measures, which might lead to a lawyer declining or terminating representation. These topics are discussed in Chapter 7, Conflict of Interest, and Chapter 8, The Prosecutor's Rule, Declining Representation and Sale of Law Practice.

After the scope of representation is set, attorneys' fees are agreed upon and there are no conflicts of interest to be concerned with, the next step along the path is the actual client representation. Chapter 9, Working on the Case—Responsibilities in Representing Clients, addresses these responsibilities. A lawyer is required to be both a counselor and an advocate for her client to ensure that the client is represented in the most effective manner possible. However, the lawyer should always be conscious of third parties and uphold the same level of integrity in her communications to those who are not under her representation. Chapter 10, You Can't Work This Client's Case Alone—What Are Your Duties in a Law Firm?, addresses these specific considerations.

Although a lawyer might feel invincible at times, the reality is the lawyer usually cannot possibly effectively represent her client by herself. This is where Chapter 10, which focuses on other lawyers and non-lawyers in a firm, becomes critical. In many instances, a new lawyer will need to confide in her superiors for legal advice and rely on her paralegals to take care of some of the behind the scenes work. The rules and duties under these types of scenarios are addressed next, including instances in which a lawyer has to go beyond her jurisdiction where she is licensed to represent a client.

However, there is another important member of the legal profession that lawyers will interact with frequently: a judge. Chapter 11, The Role of Judges and the License to Practice Law, discuss this topic. The canons of judicial ethics only apply to judges, but understanding them is an essential part of not only the MPRE, but also practicing law. For some, becoming a judge is the milestone of her legal career and thus these canons are critical. For those who do not wish to become judges, it is still beneficial to know the boundaries of judicial conduct, when a judge can and must recuse himself, and how to interact with a judge over a pending matter in the lawyer's case.

In addition to disciplinary proceedings, lawyers may also find their conduct regulated by judicial decisions over legal malpractice claims filed in civil courts. Chapter 12, Malpractice Liability—Regulating from Outside the Disciplinary System, focuses on the issues of attorney exposure and liability. Next, Chapter 13, Lawyers and Their Role in the Protection of Human Rights, addresses numerous issues relating to lawyers and human rights, including the level of responsibility a lawyer should take for the actual, real-life consequences of her legal decisions. Finally, Chapter 14, Balance in the Legal Profession—Contemplative Law and Mindfulness, discusses many challenges that lawyers face as they struggle to maintain balance between various aspects of their professional and personal lives. It then specifically focuses on using mindfulness practices as one possible solution.

B. HOW TO PREPARE FOR CLASS

Most students who enroll in professional responsibility will discover very quickly that while the Model Rules can initially appear straightforward, the details and specifics turn out to be not the easiest to understand. The language used in the rules can be very ambiguous. There are a lot of "ands" and "ors" scattered throughout the rules, meaning some requirements are conjunctive while others are disjunctive. Some of the rules are also lengthy and contain a number of exceptions, meaning there are multiple steps to consider for a given situation. Due to the nature of the rules, this course offers additional resources to utilize each week to get a better grasp on what the rules actually mean and how they have been specifically applied in practice.

As the sequence indicates, each chapter focuses on a different rule or a part of a rule. Every week, students should begin preparation by reading the featured rule or rules very carefully. Sometimes the rule will be better understood after reading the official corresponding comments. The comments are all very important, but students should be sure to focus on the comments highlighted at the beginning of each chapter that accompany a certain rule. These comments will sometimes provide a more specific explanation of the rule or describe certain scenarios that are often encountered and fall within the rule's scope. Because of the helpful nature of the comments, not to mention that they are often tested on the MPRE, reading and understanding them is a critical part of class preparation.

Sometimes the key to understanding one of the Model Rules involves actually applying it to a certain set of facts. The next step in class preparation is reading the articles and case examples in each chapter that apply the Model Rules to real life situations encountered in the legal profession. When reading the cases, pay close attention to how the court applies the rule. Consider what the case stands for and illustrates. The discussion questions after each case example and article are there to guide students to discover and comprehend what the case stands for. Some of the questions will also challenge the students to consider how the outcome of the case might have changed if the lawyer (or other individual) took a different course of action. The questions will also prompt students to consider how the rule might change as certain advancements, such as technology and social media, continue to thrive in the legal profession. The purpose of these questions is not just to challenge the students in the area of legal reasoning and analysis, but also to help them better understand what the rule stands for.

An additional resource available to students in preparing for class each week is studying a visual map, also known as a "mind map," which establishes how certain aspects of the rules fit together. A mind map is like a flow chart in that it depicts how different rules or parts of the same rule fit together and relate to each other. The center of the mind map is the main subject, such as the rule that is being dissected. The lines that flow from the center are the main topics or focus points of the main subject. In this class, these lines may consist of the rules within one particular rule.

For instance, if Rule 8 is the main subject, Rule 8.4 might be one of the lines that flows from the center subject. In some mind maps, there will be secondary lines that stem from the main lines. In this course, it might be the requirements within one of the rules. For instance, the secondary lines could be the requirements or guidelines within Rule 8.4.

The mind map is beneficial not only to visual learners, but to anyone who wants to understand how the rules all fit together. Along with reading the rule, the comments, and the case examples and articles, the mind maps should be utilized for additional understanding of the parts of the rules and staying organized with the structure of the course. For those who miss utilizing their creative side in law school, drawing out one's own mind map by hand for the rules or the course structure can also be very beneficial. Drawing a mind map challenges the creator to understand how the rules fit together and it also is meant to maintain organization throughout the course. Creative learners might prefer making a mind map as a form of preparing for the exam in addition to writing out an outline, because a mind map accomplishes the similar goal of organizing and connecting the concepts, except it does so on a visual level.[1]

C. PURPOSE OF THE COURSE

This course is the first step in achieving mastery on the MPRE because it covers all of the rules tested on the MPRE. For most law school classes, once the final exam is over students are not tested over the subject again until they take the state bar exam. However, professional responsibility is unique because students do not have to wait until the bar exam to confront legal ethics again.

The MPRE is a section of the state bar exam that students can take before they take the actual state bar exam. The MPRE is designed to test one's understanding of legal ethics by applying the concepts learned in professional responsibility course to multiple-choice questions. Students will have a total of 2 hours to answer 60 multiple-choice questions dealing with not only the Model Rules, but also the official comments and the ABA's Model Code of Judicial Conduct. Each state has a specific score that students must get in order to pass the MPRE. If a student passes, the score will be reported to the state the student plans to practice law in and will count towards getting licensed by the state bar.

Although answering 60 multiple-choice questions in 2 hours does not seem any more difficult than the average law school exam, the MPRE is

---

[1] *See generally* Tony Buzan & Barry Buzan, *The Mind Map Book: Unlock Your Creativity, Boost Your Memory, Change Your Life* (BBC Active 2002) (providing instructions and ideas on how to create a mind map).

known as a very challenging test. The multiple-choice questions can be very lengthy and like most exams, there might be 2 or 3 answer choices that seem correct. That is why adequate preparation is critical in order to pass.

Taking this professional responsibility course and preparing the material each week is a great starting point. Also, many professional responsibility professors will practice MPRE-type questions with their students. However, students should also consider practicing multiple-choice questions within a certain time limit leading up to the MPRE. Additionally, many bar-prep companies offer a special preparation course for the MPRE. Students should consider taking the course and answering the practice exams offered afterward. It is also very important to read over the rules and comments multiple times, highlighting the disjunctive and conjunctive requirements or any other part of the rule that is important to remember when answering a question. Because of the extensive preparation, students should give themselves a few weeks at the very least to focus primarily on the MPRE preparation.

After the MPRE, however, legal ethics does not go away. The purpose of this course is also to provide students with a better understanding of what to do if they are confronted by an ethics-related issue while in practice. In this course, we will explore various ethical scenarios and learn how to properly handle them, a skill that will come handy when one has to face numerous real life ethical situations head on. It is important to realize that, unlike many other law school courses, professional responsibility applies to each and every lawyer and the rules learned in this course (or their state equivalent) will follow every member of the bar no matter which road she decides to take in her legal career.

*Connecting Ethics & Practice: A Lawyer's Guide to
Professional Responsibility*

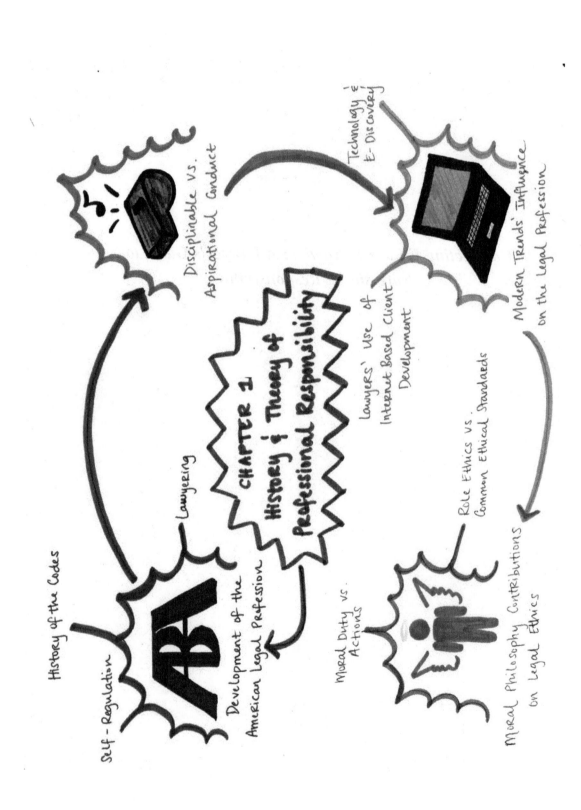

History of the Codes

Self-Regulation

Lawyering

Development of the
American Legal Profession

CHAPTER 1
History & Theory of
Professional Responsibility

Disciplinable vs.
Aspirational Conduct

Technology &
E-Discovery

Lawyers' Use of
Internet Based Client
Development

Role Ethics vs.
Common Ethical Standards

Modern Trends' Influence
on the Legal Profession

Moral Duty vs.
Actions

Moral Philosophy Contributions
on Legal Ethics

CHAPTER 1:
HISTORY AND THEORY OF PROFESSIONAL RESPONSIBILITY—WHERE WE STARTED AND WHO WE ARE TODAY

A. INTRODUCTION

Rules are everywhere. They are introduced to young children when they enter pre-school and they remain a part of people's lives as they advance to higher education and eventually into their professional life. Although difficult to keep up with sometimes, rules are what help maintain honesty, integrity, and professionalism in some of the distinguished fields in the world. For legal professionals, these rules are found in the Model Rules of Professional Conduct (Model Rules). The Model Rules set out the basic standards that those in the legal profession should abide by in order to remain in good professional standing. These rules combine both mandatory, as well as aspirational standards for lawyers. The Model Rules are not binding, but many states have adopted them (with some frequently minor changes) as their own rules of professional conduct, which then become the basis for lawyer regulation in a specific state.

There are a total of eight rules in the Model Rules of Professional Conduct, but each rule has a number of subparts that encompass the entire rule and each subpart may have multiple components to it. The accompanying comments are also important in that they provide interpretation of various parts of each rule. The state version of the rules applies to all lawyers that are members of that state's bar (including some rules being applicable to bar applicants) no matter what stage of their career they are in. Thus, a lawyer with one day's worth of experience is expected to abide by the rules in the same way as a lawyer with 20 years of experience. This is why it is so important to learn and understand the rules early on in one's legal career. This book, along with a copy of the Model Rules of Professional Conduct, is a great start to thoroughly learn the rules that will govern the remainder of one's law practice.

This introduction chapter provides an example of how this book will tackle the rules. Each chapter will contain articles from newspapers, as well as legal journals, and cases that will provide a real life example of how the rules addressed in that chapter (or, more specifically, the applicable state's version of the same) apply to the legal profession. It is important to note how each article or case explains the rule at issue and applies it to the facts of the real life situation. At the end of each chapter, questions will be provided to prompt student discussions about the rule that was covered. The questions will prepare students to handle these rules if confronted on an exam and in the real world as a legal professional.

As an example, this first chapter begins with an article about the tobacco lawyers and how one of the most important confidentiality rules in the Model Rules allowed these lawyers to withhold vital "scientific" information. This situation provides an example of how following the rules may often lead to public scorn and create a distasteful image of the legal profession. Many believe the tobacco lawyers acted fraudulently. This caused a negative perception of lawyers both in and outside the legal profession. The article is a great example of how the Model Rules differ from the public's view of morality and how it can lead to controversy surrounding the legal profession.

B. RULES

Please briefly look over each rule to get acquainted with the language and terminology used in the Model Rules of Professional Conduct.

- Rule 1: Client-Lawyer Relationship (See Rule 1.1-Rule 1.18)
- Rule 2: Counselor (See Rule 2.1-Rule 2.4)
- Rule 3: Advocate (See Rule 3.1-Rule 3.9)
- Rule 4: Transactions with Persons Other than Clients (See Rule 4.1-Rule 4.4)
- Rule 5: Law Firms and Associations (See Rule 5.1-Rule 5.7)
- Rule 6: Public Service (See Rule 6.1-Rule 6.5)
- Rule 7: Information About Legal Services (See Rule 7.1-Rule 7.6)
- Rule 8: Maintaining the Integrity of the Profession (See Rule 8.1-Rule 8.5)

C. CASES AND ADDITIONAL READINGS

TOBACCO LAWYERS SHAME THE ENTIRE PROFESSION
The National Law Journal, Vol. 1, May 18, 1998, A22
By Geoffrey C. Hazard

The disclosure of the confidential files of the tobacco industry in the Minnesota trials reveals facts that will haunt the legal profession for a long time. The files show perversion of the lawyer's role in counseling business clients and exploitation of the attorney-client privilege to conceal deception.

These abuses are not merely suggested by political agitators against business but also are demonstrated in industry documents. They were not casual or aberrant, but were systematic and sustained over decades. They were the work not of fringe or rogue practitioners, but of lawyers holding themselves out as reputable members of our profession.

They evidence what amounts to fraud on the public, conducted under the mantle of legitimate law practice. It requires some analysis to see why this is so, but there is no escaping that conclusion.

What these confidential papers disclose is that, going back at least 30 years, the tobacco companies were concerned about two aspects of the effects of tobacco on human beings.

One aspect was the effect of nicotine, a natural ingredient of tobacco. Did nicotine contribute to the pleasure of smoking and, if so, what was the correlation between the concentration of nicotine and the pleasure sensation? A related issue was whether nicotine also induced heightened yearning for further use-in other words, whether it was addictive.

The second effect that concerned the companies was whether the ingestion of "tars" or other ingredients of tobacco was correlated with cancer. Each of these issues was potentially explosive.

Moreover, if tobacco was both addictive and correlated with cancer, then cigarettes were a product that tended to hook people into a habit that could cause slow death. The tobacco companies were understandably concerned about answers to these questions and, one might say, rightly so.

Opening Pandora's Box

A fundamental problem, however, was the necessary ambivalence of the tobacco companies toward the answers that might be forthcoming. If nicotine induced heightened yearning and could be more or less controlled, that would be a terrific marketing factor. On the other hand, if it was "addictive," that would be a basis for regulation and, perhaps, suppression on the same basis as marijuana.

A correlation with cancer would be a disastrous marketing factor and a basis for regulation and suppression, just as radium has long been prohibited as an illuminant. There was, however, some possibility that nicotine could be found to be only mildly addictive and not significantly correlated with cancer.

The tobacco companies cooperated to sponsor and finance sustained research into these questions. To the extent the studies negated or were inconclusive, the companies could say that there was no scientific evidence indicating these effects. But the investigations might indicate otherwise. How to handle the situation so that good findings could be made public, but bad findings kept secret?

The salutation adopted by the tobacco companies was to have their "scientific" research conducted under the close consultation, and sometimes under the management, of their lawyers. The idea was that bad findings could be held back as lawyer-client confidences, whereas good findings could be described as the product of scientific inquiry.

Different Industry Norms

The heart of the problem is the radical differences in the professional norms and legal rules governing the activity of scientists and lawyers.

In science, the professional norms are that inquiry has no predisposition as to the social or political significance of the conclusion. This norm would apply to scientific findings about tobacco, asbestos, breast implants or whatever. A second scientific norm is that scientists must share their findings and how they arrived at them. This transparency allows challenges of the conclusions, verification through replication and extension to related issues. Transparency is the basis of legitimacy of scientific conclusions. For this reason, mere silence concerning an inquiry purporting to be scientific is itself a violation of scientific norms.

The professional norms in law are quite different. First, our predisposition is to our client—the duty of loyalty. Second, we are required to keep secret information whose disclosure would not be advantageous to our client—the duty of confidentiality.

There are important exceptions to these norms. A notable one is when a lawyer is engaged to do "due diligence" on which a third party is to rely —for example, in connection with a securities issue or an environmental evaluation. Here, the governing norms are similar to those applying in scientific inquiry. In doing due diligence for a report issued to a third party, we must disclose our methods and our findings, whatever they might be— or else make no report.

The lawyers for the tobacco companies were employed so that the companies could have it both ways. The companies never said that the "scientific" findings they were publishing were not really scientific. The lawyers never acknowledged that they were not preserving client confidences, but were helping to manufacture data that would be clothed in the mantle of science. It seems not unfair to characterize that activity as assisting in fraud on the public. Until the tobacco litigation of recent years, neither the companies nor the lawyers were called on to disclose and define what the lawyers had been doing. But a day of reckoning has arrived.

Many members of the public will conclude that other respectable lawyers for other well-known companies are also engaged in fraud. All of use in the legal profession will pay the price. Disrespect for the legal profession, indeed.

Reprinted with permission from the 1998 edition of the "National Law Journal" © 2016 ALM Media Properties, LLC. All rights reserved.

Questions and Comments

1. Do you believe the tobacco lawyers disrespected the legal profession as a whole? Why or why not?

2. Do you think actions of attorneys are frequently misunderstood by the public and, if so, in what ways? Does the misunderstanding make it difficult for all attorneys to portray a positive professional image and be respected?

3. The lawyers in the article were able to keep certain information from disclosure because it was covered by the attorney-client privilege. As such, they argued they were properly following the rules by withholding this information. In your view, what should have been more important in this case: following the rules and protecting one's client or disclosing the information about nicotine to the public?

LOVE FOR TRADE: ETHICAL ISSUES IN ATTORNEY FEE ARRANGEMENTS
The Texas Bar Journal, Vol. 77, No. 7, July 2014, 606
By William Herrscher

Preema, a suburban housewife (whose name has been changed), allegedly earned extra spending money by acting as a "personal service provider" for male clients. Paul, her husband, was suspicious of her behavior. During their divorce proceedings, Paul's private investigator—on stakeout at the local apartment brothel—watched Preema's attorney arrive at her room wearing shorts, a T-shirt, and sunglasses, but carrying no briefcase. He left exactly one hour later. During Preema's deposition, she explained that her lawyer came that day to pick up payment for his legal services. She testified that she paid her lawyer in cash but had no receipt. Paul's attorney sought a motion to compel the opposing lawyer's deposition. The court denied the request, suggesting that the lawyer refer the matter to a State Bar of Texas grievance committee. Would you file a grievance against this opposing counsel?

Comment 17 to Texas Disciplinary Rule of Professional Conduct 1.06 (b)(2) concerning conflicts of interest provides the following:

> Raising questions of conflict of interest is primarily the responsibility of the lawyer undertaking the representation.... Where the conflict is

such as clearly to call in question the fair or efficient administration of justice, opposing counsel may properly raise the question. Such an objection should be viewed with great caution, however, for it can be misused as a technique of harassment.

The preamble to our ethics rules provides the following:

"... Compliance with the rules, as with all law in an open society, depends primarily upon understanding and voluntary compliance, secondarily upon reinforcement by peer and public opinion, and finally, when necessary, upon enforcement through disciplinary proceedings." Furthermore, "...the client has a reasonable expectation that information relating to the client will not be voluntarily disclosed...."

Understanding these cautions, the lawyer—in acting true to the Texas Lawyer's Creed—would report such conduct only when the opposing lawyer is clearly interfering with the fair or efficient administration of justice. This requires us to think and care about the legal rights of the person litigating against our client. Unfortunately, as lawyers we tend to see the delinquencies of our opposing counsel as opportunities for success, rather than giving rise to a duty to protect.

Assuming Preema's lawyer was paid with sexual services, we have no specific rule prohibiting such conduct because a State Bar of Texas membership referendum voted to reject the no-sex-with-client proposed rule in 2011. Furthermore, without clear evidence to the contrary, it is possible that the lawyer was Preema's client prior to legal representation; in fact, his knowledge and acceptance of her trade may be the reason she hired him in the first place.

Comment 13 to Rule 1.06 provides further guidance:

... Relevant factors in determining whether there is potential for adverse effect include the duration and intimacy of the lawyer's relationship with the client ... the functions being performed by the lawyer, the likelihood that actual conflict will arise, and the likely prejudice to the client from the conflict if it does arise. The question is often one of proximity and degree.

Preema has an expectation that her sexual services—illegal under current law—will not be disclosed incidental to her attorney relationship. In addition, it is perfectly legal for a lawyer to barter and accept the services of a client in satisfaction of the lawyer's fees. The prudent lawyer will understand, however, that sexual relationships outside of marriage are often rife with conflict. When a conflict of interest arises such that representation of the client is adversely limited by the lawyer's own interests, then Texas Rules of Professional Conduct require that the lawyer decline or withdraw from representation. Therefore, a sexual relationship with a client, although not per se unethical, should be undertaken only with mutual understanding—preferably in writing—that if an irreconcilable conflict is created by the sexual relationship, the lawyer will withdraw from the legal representation.

In 2002, the American Bar Association passed a flat ban against lawyer-client sexual relationships that occur after the legal representation begins. As of 2011, 28 states had adopted this ban. Four other states adopted a modified approach, finding that a sexual relationship with a client creates a rebuttable presumption of unethical conduct when it causes the lawyer to render incompetent services.

Along with the stories of women being forced to engage in unwanted sexual relationships with their lawyers are stories of jilted lovers filing grievances against their lawyer-lover to exact revenge. The lawyer who takes on the representation of a lover may soon find the legal relationship burdensome and difficult to end.

Lawyers violate the public trust by sexually abusing the client. When these situations occur there is one successful cause of action that the client can bring: breach of fiduciary duty. But suits against consensual lawyer-lovers based upon fraud or intentional infliction of emotional distress are difficult to prove and may be barred as a matter of law. In the case of *Gaspard v. Beadle*, the lawyer had an extended affair with the client during representation in a usury matter and did not bill the client. When the affair ended, the lawyer sent the former client-lover a bill for the legal services and then sued to collect. The former client-lover countersued. The court held that while the lawyer's behavior was socially inappropriate, as a matter of law, the conduct was not so extreme and outrageous to constitute intentional infliction of emotional distress.

Similarly, in the case of *Kahlig v. Boyd*, a lawyer representing a husband in a divorce matter had an affair with his client's wife and, after a fee dispute, was sued by the former client for fraud. The court stated, "While we find Boyd's private behavior during his professional representation of Kahlig abhorrent for a member of our profession, ... the evidence is legally insufficient to support" the finding of fraud.

The lesson from these two cases is to pay attention to your choice of action. Fraud is not found where the lawyer's actions of non-disclosure are motivated simply by a desire to surreptitiously continue an affair for personal gratification.

On the other hand, a grievance filed for violation of conflict of interest rules and a lawsuit based upon a breach of fiduciary duty have been successful. In the Texas case of *Piro v. Sarofim*, the lawyer had an affair with a client while representing her in a divorce. The jury found that the lawyer had violated his fiduciary duty when he engaged in an inappropriate "romantic" relationship that *impaired the client's ability to make rational decisions*. Result? A fee forfeiture of $3 million.

In Texas, we have some unique notions about sex and conflicts of interest. Almost every jurisdiction except the Lone Star State has found that a sexual relationship between a judge and an attorney who appears before him or her is a conflict of interest and undermines the integrity of the legal proceeding. Of all the courts in the country to have considered the issue, only the Texas Court of Criminal Appeals has failed to recognize this imperative.

In the 2009 Texas death penalty case of *Charles Dean Hood v. The State of Texas*, attorneys filed a TRCP Rule 202 civil discovery suit to take the depositions of the former Collin County judge and prosecutor whose prior affair had been kept secret during the capital murder trial in 1990. Upon finally documenting the extra-marital sexual relationship between the judge and prosecutor 18 years later, Hood filed his ninth appeal based upon judicial bias and denial of due process. The U.S. Supreme Court dismissed the appeal on Texas's procedural filing deadline grounds. The merits of the case were never considered. Did Texas courts uphold justice or uphold a conviction?

Practice tip: serve interrogatory requesting disclosure of personal relationships between the opposing party, including their attorneys, and any other party, lawyer, judge, or witness to the case. Lawyers should strive to remember tenants of the U.S. Constitution: "…The ordinary administration of criminal and civil justice" is the "great cement of society," and "contributes, more than any other circumstance, to impressing upon the minds of the people, affection, esteem, and reverence towards the government."

Reprinted with permission from the July 2014 edition of the "Texas Bar Journal" © Texas Bar Journal 2016. All rights reserved.

Questions and Comments

1. In the case regarding the suburban housewife, Preema, why do you think the court denied the request to compel the opposing lawyer's deposition? If you were the opposing counsel, would you take the court's advice and file a grievance with the State Bar of Texas? Explain why or why not.

2. The article refers to the case of *Gaspard v. Beadle*, where the lawyer had an extended affair with the client and did not bill the client until after their affair ended. The court referred to his conduct as "socially unacceptable," but did not find him guilty of a violation because the "conduct was not so extreme and outrageous to constitute intentional infliction of emotional distress." Why do you think the court ruled in the lawyer's favor? What are instances where an attorney's conduct would become a violation?

3. The sexual relationship between an attorney and client certainly is not the only type of unethical conduct frowned upon in the legal

profession. Almost all jurisdictions find sexual relationships between judges and attorneys that appear before them as a conflict of interest. However, *Charles Dean Hood v. The State of Texas* is cited in the article to give a different example. Did Texas courts uphold justice or uphold a conviction with its ruling in *Hood*? Explain. What benefits, if any, would Texas have in implementing this rule?

THE POWER OF PROFESSIONALISM: CIVILITY AS A STRATEGY FOR EFFECTIVE ADVOCACY
The Texas Bar Journal, Vol. 79, No. 6, June 2016, 432
By Kevin Dubose and Jonathan E. Smaby

For 27 years, the Texas Lawyer's Creed has encouraged Texas attorneys to practice law with civility and professionalism. Yet some lawyers continue to express concern that being polite and agreeable is inconsistent with their duty to zealously advocate for their clients. Who's right? You may be surprised, but there is good reason to believe that a lawyer who behaves with civility is a more effective advocate.

Zealous and Professional Advocacy

Nothing in the Texas Disciplinary Rules of Professional Conduct contemplates that *zealous* means discourteous or disrespectful. The word *zealously* appears twice in the Preamble: in paragraph 2, which says "a lawyer zealously asserts the client's position *under the rules of the adversary system*"; and in paragraph 3, which says "a lawyer should zealously pursue clients' interests *within the bounds of the law*" (emphasis added). Paragraph 4 adds that lawyers should "use the law's procedures only for legitimate purposes and not to harass or intimidate others. A lawyer should demonstrate respect for the legal system and for those who serve it, including judges, other lawyers, and public officials."

So, rather than suggest uncivil behavior, *zealous* in the rules of professional conduct merely envisions *zeal*, a passionate and enthusiastic manner designed to achieve a favorable *outcome* for the client. Thus, zealousness should not be judged by its stridency but by the result.

Outcomes Depend Upon Impressions

Favorable outcomes depend on favorable responses by the decision-makers. Accordingly, the focus should not be on whether an advocacy technique or attitude gratifies your ego, or appeals to your client's bloodlust, or rattles opposing counsel. It should be on which behaviors and attitudes are likely to favorably influence the decision-making process.

Daniel Kahneman's 2011 book, *Thinking, Fast and Slow*, synthesizes two decades of academic research and has some insights about human nature that can illuminate our understanding of advocacy. The research discussed in the book shows that decision-making happens in two ways, which are labeled System 1 and System 2. System 1 ("thinking fast") is intuitive, emotional, and unconscious. System 2 ("thinking slow") is rational, rule-based, and deliberative. Neither system is good nor bad, and we all go back and forth between the systems. Different types of decision-making are appropriate for different types of decisions.

These studies also demonstrate that the human brain is inherently lazy, and because thinking fast is easier, the brain constantly pushes us in that direction. Perhaps more alarming, even when we consciously strive to be in System 2—which most decision-makers in the legal process do—the brain subverts that process by intruding with System 1 influences.

Research suggests that the data we use to make rational and rule-based decisions has already been screened and shaped by our intuitive and emotional judgments. As Kahneman observes, "System 2 is more of an apologist for the emotions of System 1 than a critic of those emotions—an endorser rather than an enforcer. Its search for information and arguments is mostly constrained to information that is consistent with existing beliefs, not with an intention to examine them."

In other words, despite the rules and deliberative processes built into the legal system, legal decision-makers—like all humans—are genetically predisposed to form early impressions and then subconsciously seek and retain information supporting gut reactions while simultaneously blocking contrary information. Because this process occurs outside our awareness, we are all subject to its influence.

Therefore, prudent attorneys should not undermine substantive arguments by allowing themselves to behave uncivilly and create a negative initial impression. A positive first impression provides the subconscious brain with a subliminal incentive to reach an outcome consistent with that favorable first feeling. This is not to suggest that lawyers and judges do not make rational decisions; instead, it is a recognition that our decision-making process is subject to the same scientifically documented shortcomings of the brain that afflict all decision-makers.

Decision-makers Respond to Professionalism

While the strength of the evidence and supporting arguments is critical, the demeanor of the advocate while making an argument has a significant impact on how it is perceived. For a variety of reasons, decision-makers are more likely to be impressed by an advocate who is courteous and respectful to the decision-maker, opposing counsel, the litigants, and the legal process.

First, most decision-makers see themselves as participants in a dignified process of resolving disputes in a civilized way. They do not want to be reduced to refereeing fights between childish and churlish lawyers. It demeans the role of the decision-maker.

Second, many decision-makers feel like they are overworked and undercompensated, and they often are. When they have to spend more time reading insults and personal attacks than they do reading about the merits of the case, it squanders their most precious resource.

Third, unprofessional conduct damages credibility. When an advocate behaves in a way that causes the decision maker to believe that the advocate will say or do anything to win, the advocate is no longer seen as reliable.

Finally, unprofessionalism is unpleasant. When lawyers are nasty to each other, it makes everyone in the room uncomfortable and embarrassed for them. Creating this kind of discomfort in the decision-maker is not conducive to a favorable outcome.

Guidelines for Professionalism

Behaving professionally means more than just following minimum codified rules of conduct. It means following standards of behavior and attitude, the violation of which may not result in court-ordered penalties and sanctions, but which nonetheless have adverse consequences.

Two helpful sets of guidelines are available: the Texas Lawyer's Creed and the Standards for Appellate Conduct, promulgated in 1989 and 1999, respectively. Both acknowledge that lawyers have duties to the legal system, their clients, other lawyers, and the court. They also recognize that these duties may conflict, but that one should not be elevated to the exclusion of all others. There must be a balance. The Preamble to the Texas Lawyer's Creed says:

> I must abide by the Texas Disciplinary Rules of Professional Conduct, *but I know that professionalism requires more than merely avoiding the violation of laws and rules.*

Likewise, the Standards for Appellate Conduct Preamble notes:

> Problems that arise when duties conflict can be resolved through understanding the nature and extent of a lawyer's respective duties, avoiding the tendency to emphasize a particular duty at the expense of others.

Behaving Professionally Demands an Attitude of Respect

Using civility to improve advocacy begins by embracing the attitude that underlies all of these rules: respect for the justice system and the people who play a role in it.

Respect for the system. It is a system for fairly resolving disputes in an equitable manner. Aggressively manipulating it for personal gain, or even overreaching for your client, does not show respect for a process that is supposed to work for everyone.

Respect for judges. Judges are human beings who almost invariably try to be fair. While they have their own worldviews and life experiences, they rarely consciously pursue ideological agendas or predetermined outcomes when deciding cases. They do not appreciate being insulted or told what they have to do. A reasoned and rational approach that respects their intelligence and judgment will serve you better.

Respect for opposing counsel and parties. Opposing counsel are not your enemy; they are simply other lawyers trying to do their job of representing their clients. You should always treat them as worthy adversaries who deserve your respect and who raise the level of your game.

Opposing parties—in most cases—are good-faith participants in the justice system, exercising their legal rights. That they view the facts differently does not mean they are untruthful. Their subjective view of what happened may be as valid as yours or your client's. If you accept and embrace that concept, your ability to respect opposing parties will increase dramatically.

Respect for your client. A desire to win does not excuse overreaching and unprofessional conduct. Respecting your client means believing that they have a right to a fair result—and nothing more. It also means they have a right to be represented by a lawyer who behaves with class and dignity.

Respect for yourself. You should conduct yourself in a way that makes you feel good about yourself; that makes decision-makers want to find reasons to decide in your favor; that makes opposing counsel look forward to dealing with you; and that makes clients want to hire you again and tell friends about you.

When you unfailingly show respect for yourself and others, those others will, in turn, respect you. And a respected attorney is a successful attorney.

Questions and Comments

1. Though the Texas Lawyer's Creed encourages civility and professionalism, some lawyers express their concern that "being polite and agreeable is inconsistent with their duty to zealously advocate for their client." Why do you think this is? Can a lawyer act with passion and enthusiasm for their client and still remain collegial with an opposing party and counsel? Explain.

2. The article notes respect as a crucial element for effective advocacy. Thus, a lawyer should not focus on gratifying his/her ego, appeal to a client's "bloodlust," or "rattle" opposing counsel. What behaviors and attitudes should be used, then, to obtain a favorable outcome and influence the decision-making process?

3. It is common knowledge first impressions carry the most weight. As the article states, having a respectable first impression of professionalism may work in your favor because a "positive first impression provides the subconscious brain with a subliminal incentive to reach an outcome consistent with that favorable first feeling." If an attorney confuses zealousness with being overly aggressive, judges may be inclined to favor the other party. Keep this mind as your read the following case. Do you think the judge would have ruled differently had the attorney acted in a different manner?

The Ethical Limits of Attorney Social Media Investigations
Law 360 (Online), New York, July 7, 2015
By Michael A. Kolcun and Craig Weiner

Over a billion. That is the number of people who interact on social media. Last quarter alone, Facebook boasted over 1.4 billion users. LinkedIn has 347 million members, Instagram has 300 million, and Twitter has nearly 290 million. YouTube acclaims more than a billion users.

Given these figures across a variety of different social media outlets, it did not take long for the legal profession and social media to intersect, and attorneys are catching on. Indeed, attorneys are increasingly turning to social media for investigative purposes and as an informal discovery tool. But while Rule 1.1 of the New York Rules of Professional Conduct ("NYRPC") requires competent representation of a client, nowhere has an attorney's aptitude in social media been specifically delineated. But as social media continues to thrive, and ethics opinions proliferate regarding an attorney's use of social media, this is beginning to change.

Just last month, the Commercial and Federal Litigation Section of the New York State Bar Association ("NYSBA") revised its nationally recognized social media ethics guidelines. Notably, the NYSBA updated its guidelines to include a section on attorney competency, opining that a "lawyer has a duty to understand the benefits and risks and ethical implications associated with social media, including its use as a mode of communication, an advertising tool and a means to research and investigate matters." Continuing, the NYSBA opines that attorneys "need to be conversant with, at a minimum, the basics of each social media network that a lawyer or his or her client may use." Given the undisputed popularity of social media, the NYSBA's analysis is certainly a step in the right direction. In addition to clients, it will not be long before the social media networks of adversaries, jurors, and witnesses are similarly mandated grounds for investigation as well.

Given attorneys' taking to social media, it is also predictable that the ethical rules will further expand to mandate an attorney's active engagement in social media as well. Indeed, NYRPC 1.1(c) provides that an attorney shall not intentionally "fail to seek the objectives of the client through reasonably available means permitted by law and these Rules." With access to nearly every social media network by computer, tablet and smart phone, it can hardly be disputed that a plethora of free information is easily accessible and at an attorney's fingertips. Instances of attorney admonishment and sanctions for failing to do so are well documented.

And what information is reasonably available? The examples of evidence and information to be obtained from social media are nearly limitless. In nearly any practice area, social media may reveal juror biases, provide material for impeachment or assist in identifying a witness. More specifically, social media may benefit a client in a case where physical, mental or emotional state are at issue, it may impact an Fair Labor Standards Act matter where nonwork-related activity is shared, business marketing may evidence breach of a noncompete, and infringing music or videos may be captured and preserved as evidence. The willingness of individuals to volunteer such information should hardly be surprising, since it is now commonplace for social media users to post content, comment, and share opinions on nearly anything and everything.

But while the legal profession is rightfully taking to social media for investigative purposes, attorneys must simultaneously caution themselves to maintain compliance with the ethics rules when doing so. In most instances, the prohibitions against attorney deceit and the "no-contact" rule with respect to represented parties and jurors are of most prominent implication. It must also be remembered that attorneys' ethical obligations are imputed to their agents, investigators and even clients under NYRPC 5.3 and 8.4. As many ethics opinions recognize, such considerations primarily turn on whether a person's social media webpage is public or private and, accordingly, when contact with the social media user is prohibited.

In the case of investigating a person's public social media webpage, attorneys may rest assured that the review and use of evidence from a person's public social media webpage is permissible under the ethics rules. Specifically, the NYSBA has opined that viewing the public portion of a person's social media page, like any other public information, is entirely permissible. And so should it be, as social media is no different than other source of public information that an attorney can and should comb through on a client's behalf. And given the intentionally public nature of such social media profiles or posts, concerns of breaches of privacy are not implicated. Indeed, one court has gone so far as to liken posting a tweet to screaming out of a window.

The same may also be said with respect to viewing a potential or sitting juror's public social media webpage. The NYSBA, New York City Bar Association ("NYCBA"), and the New York County Lawyers' Association ("NYCLA") all extend an attorney's investigative reach to public social media pages of potential and sitting jurors, the benefit of which continues even after a juror has been sworn in and throughout trial. In doing so, the NYCBA goes so far as to opine that social media has "expanded an attorney's ability to conduct research on potential and sitting jurors, and clients now often expect that attorneys will conduct such research. Indeed, standards of competence and diligence may require doing everything possible to learn about the jurors who will sit in judgment on a case."

Attorneys are even granted wide investigative latitude when viewing and using evidence from private or restricted social media webpages in some instances. Indeed, both the NYSBA and NYCBA opine that an attorney may contact an unrepresented party to request access to their restricted social media webpage, so long as the attorney uses their full name and an accurate profile, and does so in a manner that does not create false profile to mask their identity so as to avoid implicating NYRPC 4.3 and 8.4. In this instance, the active engagement of social media can be an invaluable tool for obtaining information. This is particularly the case if it is an attorney's agent or investigator who contacts an unrepresented party. Even still, many social media users are not adverse to accepting online connection requests even if they do not know who the person is. However, should the unrepresented party request information of the attorney in response to such a request, the NYSBA opines that an attorney has the option to either accurately provide such information or withdraw. The NYCBA, on the other hand, opines that such disclosures are unnecessary.

The liberal interaction between the benefits of social media and attorney investigations significantly constricts, however, in the instance of a private social media page of a represented party or juror. This is primarily due to the no-contact rule that attorneys must be diligent in observing. The NYSBA has specifically opined that an attorney cannot contact a represented person to request access to their restricted site unless an express authorization to do so has been given. But this should come as no surprise under NYRPC 4.2. That said, however, attorneys may find solace in the emerging trend of courts to permit disclosure of some, if not all, of a restricted or private social media webpage. But while attorneys may endeavor to adhere to the no-contact rule to the letter, competence in social media platforms is of utmost importance to avoid any unintended communications. Specifically, great caution must be taken in that some social media sites, such as LinkedIn, may send automatic notifications to the owner or operator of a webpage when it is viewed. This can be problematic in that contact may be deemed to have occurred with a represented party upon receipt of such notification, or if the subject of investigation is alerted to the fact that opposing counsel viewed his social media webpage.

Attorneys should be especially wary of such automatic notifications in the context of sitting or potential jurors, as such contact may be similarly prohibited under NYCRP 3.5. In fact, the NYCBA and the NYCLA have both opined that even such inadvertent contact by automatic messages or notifications may be considered an ethical violation. As is clear from the proliferation of judicial decisions and ethical opinions on the issue, social media is becoming an integral part of the legal profession, and it is here to stay. But while social media is undoubtedly another weapon in an attorney's investigative arsenal, attorneys must continue to be vigilant in abiding by all applicable ethical obligations when diligently representing their clients.

Reprinted with permission from the 2015 edition of the "Law 360"

Questions and Comments

1. This article introduces a rule concerning social media and the legal profession that places an ethical guideline on an attorney's use of social media. Are you surprised to learn this? Do you think social media is something that should be regulated by the Model Rules (or, more specifically, their state equivalent)? On the contrary, do you think social media use is something personal to the attorney and should not be regulated?

2. The article discusses an attorney's ability to get information about a client, juror, defendant, or pretty much anyone through social media. Do you think social media is an effective tool to get this type of information? Consider what is posted on social media and how one questionable post or photograph can taint someone's representation.

3. As the article states, most people have some sort of social media account. The article also points out that many lawyers use social media to do various duties of their legal profession, such as advertise, investigate, or simply get the word out about a victory in court. In your opinion, does the increased use of social media have a positive or negative influence on our profession? You might consider the ease that social media gives lawyers to advertise their services or discover helpful information; however, also consider how some lawyers (and judges) have used social media in an unethical way.

D. DISCUSSION QUESTIONS

1. How do you feel about the tobacco lawyers' actions? Do you believe the lawyers acted in a truly ethical manner or were they merely complying with the rules of confidentiality and doing what was expected of them?

2. Reflect upon how the rules of disclosure are different between the legal profession and the scientific field. Do you think that the legal profession should be more like the scientific field? Why do you think there is a difference in the first place?

3. The *Power of Professionalism* article focuses on advocacy and how to maintain professional etiquette even while zealously representing one's client. In light of the saying that goes "actions speak louder than words," how might one's professionalism in a courtroom come across more positive and persuasive than the behavior of someone who is not as professional, but an aggressive and driven advocate? In other words, which one is more likely to influence the jury?

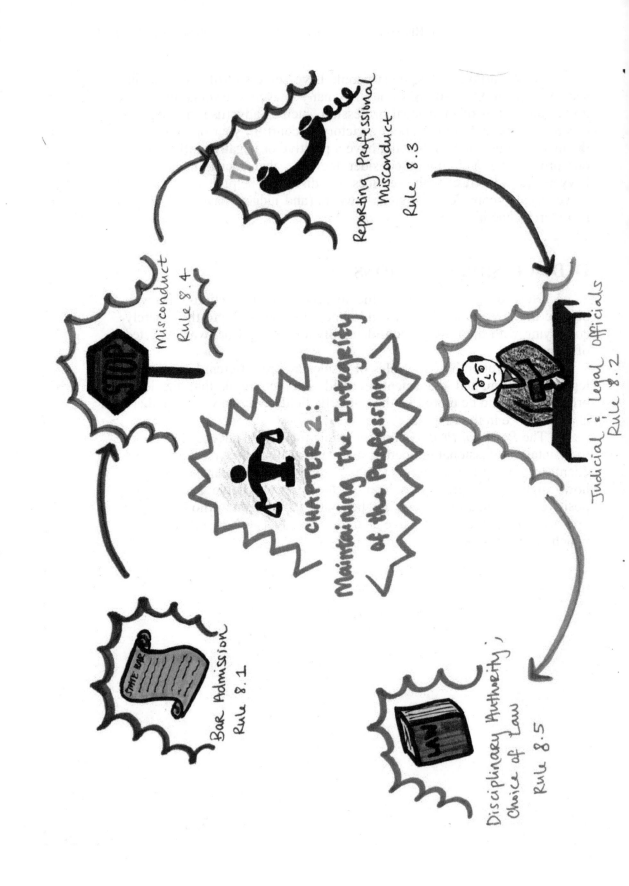

Reporting Professional Misconduct
Rule 8.3

Misconduct
Rule 8.4

CHAPTER 2:
Maintaining the Integrity of the Profession

Judicial & legal officials
Rule 8.2

Bar Admission
Rule 8.1

STATE BAR

Disciplinary Authority; Choice of Law
Rule 8.5

CHAPTER 2:
THE IMPORTANCE OF INTEGRITY—
BEFORE AND AFTER ENTERING INTO THE
PROFESSION

A. INTRODUCTION

It is difficult to imagine that two people who are licensed to practice law would threaten their own professional integrity by sending insulting emails to each other. It is also difficult to believe that a prospective legal professional in law school would create a controversy in his class by continuously harassing and insulting his fellow colleagues and professors. As hard as it is to comprehend a legal professional exhibiting this type of behavior, these scenarios are actually true stories. That is why Rule 8 of the Model Rules of Professional Conduct is such a critical part of maintaining the integrity of the legal profession. This rule provides a vehicle for enforcement of the standards of integrity and may subject its violators to face the consequences of their professional misconduct.

Rule 8 is likely one of the first rules that legal professionals encounter because it governs the bar admission process that begins before a student graduates from law school. It is expected that all legal professionals—both prospective and current—are honest about their own behavior and the behavior of others, including lawyers, judges, and legal officials. This expectation begins early when a law student applies to take the state bar exam. The state bar will conduct a character and fitness examination governed by Rule 8. The rule states the prospective law student must not fail to disclose anything requested by the licensing board. The student must also ensure she does not intentionally leave out information that is false or misleading and if she accidently omits an important relevant fact, she must correct that misrepresentation as soon as possible. This same standard applies to all bar members when providing information to the state bar about a prospective lawyer.

The legal profession is unique in the sense that Rule 8.3 requires a lawyer to report her fellow colleague if she knows that her colleague is exhibiting professional misconduct. Although reporting a fellow colleague can sometimes create an uncomfortable situation, this requirement is key to maintaining the integrity of the legal profession. We are a self-regulated profession and the state bar cannot keep an eye on every legal professional, which is why it is so important that lawyers both pay attention to their own actions and ensure that other lawyers are exhibiting professional behavior. It is important to keep in mind not every questionable step needs to be reported. It is only the type of misconduct amounting to an actual or attempted ethics rule violation, thus challenging the integrity of the profession and impacting a lawyer's ability to effectively represent her clients that a lawyer who actually knows about it has to report to the appropriate authority.

Rule 8.4 sets forth what is considered professional misconduct in the legal profession. At first glance, it may seem the type of behavior set forth in Rule 8.4 would almost never occur, but consider what a heavy workload and stress can do to a person's attitude and behavior. If a lawyer does violate Rule 8.4 or any of the Model Rules, Rule 8.5 governs the conflicts of law issue, i.e. which jurisdiction(s) can become the disciplinary authority and which law would govern the situation. The practice of law is a privilege and not a right with Rule 8.1 setting forth the criteria for bar admission.

B. RULES

In preparation, read carefully the following sections of the Model Rules of Professional Conduct along with any relevant comments listed below.

- Rule 8.1: Bar Admission and Disciplinary Matters
  - Comment [1]
- Rule 8.2: Judicial and Legal Officials
- Rule 8.3: Reporting Professional Misconduct
  - Comments [2], [3]
- Rule 8.4: Misconduct
  - Comments [1], [2], [3]
- Rule 8.5: Disciplinary Authority; Choice of Law
  - Comments [2], [3], [5]

C. CASES AND ADDITIONAL READINGS

THE MENTALLY ILL ATTORNEY
Nova Law Review, Vol. 27, Issue 1, Art. 6, 2002
By Len Klingen

I. Introduction

ABC Excavating is a small construction firm specializing in site preparation work. The company has been successful for a number of years on a small scale, providing a comfortable existence for the company's shareholders, Jack Brown and his wife. Early in 1999, the firm orally contracted to perform some work in a South Florida county. As is sometimes the case, the property owner paid the general contractor, and the general contractor did not pay ABC Excavating. ABC Excavating filed a lien against the property and, failing any response from either the owner or the general contractor, ABC Excavating sought to foreclose. With that in mind, the owners of ABC Excavating turned over all of their meager paperwork to their attorney, Mike Pfenning of Rodriguez, Marko & Pfenning, P.A. A year went by, and the statute of limitations for lien foreclosure expired. Another year went by, and the statute of limitations for suing on an oral contract expired. During this period, ABC Excavating was regularly assured by Pfenning that he was filing pleadings and that everything was going well.

However, nothing was going well. As Pfenning later said in his letter to the Florida Bar, he was afflicted with a mental disorder that made him put all of his work into various desk drawers and then forget about it. Pfenning would spend the remainder of his days staring out of the windows of his office, or would simply not show up for work. His partners were aware of his behavior but were reluctant to intervene. They were even more reluctant to inform his clients. Pfenning's partners let their malpractice insurance lapse. Ultimately, they dissolved the partnership. Since then, Pfenning has been disbarred. All three partners have liquidated their assets or moved them into the names of others. Two of the three partners have filed for bankruptcy and the third is not far behind. ABC Excavating is now seeking to recover from the attorneys personally, but the bankruptcy actions have all but eliminated their chances for recovery.

Although the incidence of mental illness and drug abuse among attorneys is far from negligible, stories this egregious are, fortunately, not played out every day. Several questions raised by this case include the following:

- What could the Browns have done to mitigate the damage caused by their attorney?

- What could the attorney have done to mitigate or prevent the damage his illness has caused?
- What were the responsibilities of the partners to the clients, to the mentally ill partner, and to the Florida Bar?

***

B. Duty to Report Another Attorney's Misconduct

While there is some latitude and interpretation permitted concerning the duty to prevent misconduct, there is none at all regarding its reporting once misconduct has been found. Cases such as *Himmel* and *Skolnick v. Altheimer & Gray* are an indication of the gravity with which the courts regard the reporting of misconduct. The courts have consistently held that the requirement to report misconduct is absolute, leaving attorneys to wander about in a minefield where reporting is required, but where the determination of what constitutes misconduct remains open for interpretation. Comments to the *Model Rules of Professional Conduct* Rule 8.3 read as follows:

> If a lawyer were obliged to report every violation of the Rules, the failure to report any violation would itself be a professional offense. Such a requirement existed in many jurisdictions but proved to be unenforceable. This Rule limits the reporting obligation to those offenses that a self-regulating profession must vigorously endeavor to prevent. A measure of judgment is, therefore, required in complying with the provisions of this Rule. The term "substantial" refers to the seriousness of the possible offense and not the quantum of evidence of which the lawyer is aware.

Generally speaking, the type of misconduct to be reported is no surprise: misappropriation of client funds, bribery, blatant violations of confidentiality, fraud, forgery of a client's signature, and so on. Difficulties arise when the misconduct is not so clearly defined, where the reporting attorney notices a pattern of incidents that as a group are reportable but individually are not, and particularly, where the reporting attorney must make a judgment call and knows he or she could be mistaken. This is further exacerbated by the feeling that reporting is "squealing." To quote Campbell: "Few rules... stir more emotion and potential controversy than the 'squealer' or 'snitch' rule .... [t]he 'schoolyard' refrain of tattletale still rings... in our minds." Tattletale or not, failure to "squeal" can be costly. A Texas attorney was suspended for thirty-nine months for violating "rules regarding candor toward the tribunal [for failing] to report another lawyer's misconduct."

If one covers for a partner at a hearing once because the partner was still intoxicated from the previous night's activities, does the intoxication raise a substantial question as to the partner's fitness? If one covers for the partner a second, a third, or a fourth time? Who decides when conduct becomes reportable misconduct? An attorney confronted with such a situation may consult the state's ethics committee for guidance, but the final determination rests with the state's highest court of appeal. If the ethics committee and the court differ in an interpretation, the court prevails and the attorney may face sanctions despite his reliance on the ethics committee's opinion. Reporting misconduct is a two-edged sword. Those who fail to report run afoul of the state's disciplinary authorities. Those who report run the risk of expulsion from the partnership, and with it, attendant loss of work, financial hardship, and dubious reputation as a whistleblower. Although a fiduciary duty exists between partners in a law firm, such a duty "does not encompass a duty to remain partners. Despite arguments that such an extension of a partner's duty is necessary to prevent retaliation against a partner who in good faith reports suspected misconduct, the court in *Bohatch* held that "[j]ust as a partner can be expelled... over disagreements about firm policy... a partner can be expelled for accusing another partner of [misconduct] without subjecting the partnership to tort damages." The court's majority understood the dissent's concern that "retaliation against a partner... virtually assures that others will not take these appropriate steps in the future, but stated that a lawyer's "duties sometimes necessitate difficult decisions ..." and that "[t]he fact that the ethical duty to report may create an irreparable schism between partners [does not] excuse the failure to report."

A mentally disordered attorney may be in a difficult professional position, but failure to take action on his or her own behalf places partners in a more difficult position. The partners will likely agonize over decisions forced on them when the illness or addiction reaches the point where it impairs the ability to practice. The firm may, as mentioned above, suggest counseling or threaten expulsion, but once the illness manifests itself by misconduct, it will be forced to report him or her. The interpersonal difficulties that such action poses may well be fatal to the survival of the firm, especially in a small partnership where the principals share something more than just a professional relationship.

The partnership discussed in the opening anecdote chose to do nothing. It stood by, wringing its collective hands, as Pfenning's cases dissolved into a collection of nonactionable disputes, whose statutes of limitations had long since passed. There is plenty of blame to go around here. Although Pfenning had ultimate responsibility for his conduct, illness or not, the inaction of his partners exacerbated an arguably correctible situation. Their inaction ruined them and, more importantly, ruined the cases of their clients and made a mockery of the judicial process.

V. Conclusion

Although the incidence of malpractice due to mental illness is statistically not high, such a revelation is of small comfort to those clients forever prevented from pursuing their claims because of unanticipated attorney misconduct. Of the three parties to an attorney's mental illness—the client, the attorney, and the law firm—the client is least able to protect him or herself, and the most likely to suffer damage in the professional setting.

***

It is understood that attorneys have a duty to abide by the *Rules of Professional Conduct,* and to seek treatment or removal when they are unable to do so. It is also clear that no attorney works in utter isolation—even solo practitioners generally have family or friends. The attorney's employers or partners are the next line of defense, and they have a moral and ethical duty to protect the interests of *all* of their clients. They also have a duty to protect their mentally disordered colleague from further damage to self and to the profession.

Mental illness rarely gives rise to the same measure of compassion as physical illness or damage. A diagnosis of influenza or a broken leg in a partner elicits compassion; a diagnosis of paranoid schizophrenia may still elicit suspicion, fear, and flight. This must change for two reasons: moral and pragmatic. The moral question is deeply personal, but the pragmatic question points straight to the *Rules of Professional Responsibility.* Failure to address the existence of a mental disorder in a colleague leads to disaster for clients, for the attorney, and quite rightly, for the law firm. The spineless response of Pfenning's partners hurt them all.

Appropriate action by the law firm at the first substantial hint of a problem or misconduct may be painful, but the consequences of cowardice are so great that a de facto decision to do nothing is impossible to justify.

Endnotes omitted (See Len Klingen, The Mentally Ill Attorney, Nova Law Review, Volume 27, Issue 1 (2002) for full article version). Reprinted with permission from the 2002 edition of the "Nova Law Review" © 2016 Len Klingen. All rights reserved.

Questions and Comments

1. The article makes it clear that it is an absolute requirement that if an attorney is aware of a fellow attorney's violation of the Model Rules, she must report that attorney. Despite the requirement imposed by the Model Rules, what are other reasons the attorney should report the behavior of her colleague? Why do you think the Model Rules makes the reporting aspect of the rule absolute and not discretionary?

2. As the article indicates, reporting another attorney's behavior related to a mental illness is often difficult. Why do you think this aspect of reporting is so complex? Where does one draw the line between mental illness that does not require reporting compared to mental illness that does?

3. Let's brainstorm about ways that could make reporting mental illness to the state bar easier for both the attorney experiencing the mental illness and the attorney who wants to report it. Should the Model Rules set specific guidelines on when to report? Should the state bars provide more resources for attorneys battling with mental illness?

CONVERSE V. NEBRASKA STATE BAR COMMISSIONER
Supreme Court of Nebraska (1999)
602 N.W.2d 500

Per Curiam. Paul Raymond Converse appeals a decision of the Nebraska State Bar Commission (Commission) denying his request to take the July 1998 Nebraska bar examination. Converse claims that the decision of the Commission should be reversed because the Commission rested its denial of Converse's application, at least in part, upon conduct protected by the First Amendment to the U.S. Constitution and, in the alternative, that Converse's conduct did not constitute sufficient cause under Nebraska law for denying his application on the ground of deficient moral character. For the reasons that follow, we affirm the decision of the Commissioner.

Factual Background

In 1998, Converse applied for permission to sit for the Nebraska bar examination. On June 29, 1998, Converse was notified by letter that the Commission had denied permission for him to take the July 1998 Nebraska bar examination because it had determined that Converse lacked the requisite moral character for admission upon examination to the Nebraska State Bar Association. On July 7, the Commission received notice that Converse was appealing the Commission's initial determination. Converse's appeal was heard on September 15, after which the Commission reaffirmed its initial determination and notified Converse on December 18 that he would not be allowed to sit for the Nebraska bar examination at that time.

The evidence at the Commission hearing revealed that as part of the application process, Converse was required to request that the dean of his law school submit a form certifying completion of Converse's law school studies. That form contained a question asking, "Is there anything concerning this application about which the Bar Examiners should further inquire regarding the applicant's moral character of fitness to practice law?" The question was answered, "Yes," and the dean also noted, "Additional information will be provided upon request." The Commission followed up on this notation by conducting an investigation which ultimately revealed certain facts regarding Converse.

After the completion of his first semester at the University of South Dakota (USD) Law School, Converse sent a letter to then assistant dean Diane May regarding certain issues not relevant to this appeal that he had had with the law school during fall classes, closing that letter with the phrase, "Hope you get a full body tan in Costa Rica." Subsequent to that note, Converse had several more encounters with May, beginning with his writing letters to May about receiving grades lower than what he believed he had earned in an appellate advocacy class.

After he received a grade he believed to be unjustified by his performance in the appellate advocacy course, Converse wrote letters to May and to the USD law school dean, Barry Vickrey, requesting assistance with an appeal of that grade. In addition to writing letters to Vickrey and May, Converse also sent a letter to the South Dakota Supreme Court regarding the appellate advocacy course professor's characterization of his arguments, with indications that carbon copies of the letter were sent to two well-known federal court of appeals judges. The letter was written to suggest the professor believed her stance on certain issues was more enlightened than that of judges. Converse sent numerous correspondence to various people regarding the grade appeal against the specific professor. Despite all such correspondence, Converse testified at the hearing that no formal appeal of the grievance was ever filed. Converse's grade was never adjusted.

The evidence showed that following the grade "appeal," Converse prepared a memorandum and submitted it to his classmates, urging them to recall an "incident" in which yet another professor lashed out at him in class, and to be cognizant of the image that incident casts "on [that professor's] core professionalism" prior to completing class evaluations. Converse also wrote a letter to a newspaper in South Dakota, the Sioux Falls Argus Leader, regarding a proposed fee increase at the USD law school. Converse immediately began investigating the salaries of the USD law professors and posted a list of selected professors' salaries on the student bulletin board, as well as writing a letter that accused Vickrey of trying to pull a "fast one."

Converse's next altercation at the USD law school involved a photograph of a nude female's backside that he displayed in his study carrel in the USD law library. The picture was removed by a law librarian. In response to the removal of this photograph, Converse contacted the American Civil Liberties Union (ACLU) and received a letter indicating that his photograph might be a protected expression under the First Amendment. Once again, Converse went to the student newspaper to alert the student body of the actions of the law school authorities, accusing them of unconstitutional censorship.

Converse redisplayed the photograph once it was returned by the law librarians. Vickrey received several complaints about the photograph from other students, classifying Converse's behavior as "unprofessional and inappropriate." Upon Converse's redisplay of the photograph, Vickrey sent him a memorandum explaining that the picture would not be removed only because Vickrey did not want to involve the school in controversy during final examinations. Converse testified that he redisplayed the photograph in order to force the alleged constitutional issue.

The evidence also revealed that Converse filed an ethics complaint with the North Dakota Bar Association regarding certain correspondence between Vickrey and a retired justice of the North Dakota Supreme Court. The complaint was dismissed. Converse went to the USD student newspaper, claiming that a letter from a retired North Dakota justice to the ACLU, in response to questions from Vickrey, was a violation of professional ethics (apparently Model Rules of Professional Conduct Rule 4.2 (1999), which precludes a lawyer from discussing matters with opposing parties the lawyer knows to be represented by counsel). In addition to going to the press, Converse also contacted the president of USD, referring to Vickrey as an "incompetent" and requesting that Vickrey be fired. In addition to this incident, Converse reported his suspicions about USD's student health insurance policy to the student newspaper under the title of "Law Student Suspects Health Insurance Fraud," as well as in a separate article alleging that USD had suppressed an investigation of its insurance carrier.

The Commission also heard testimony regarding Converse's attempt to obtain an internship with the U.S. Attorney's office in South Dakota. Converse arranged for the internship on his own, only to have his request subsequently rejected by the law school. Upon receiving his denial, Converse sent a complaint to all of USD's law school faculty members. Vickrey testified that Converse's internship was rejected because he failed to comply with the law school's procedures regarding internships. Converse then contacted the chairperson of the law school committee of the south Dakota State Bar Association with his complaint, expressly referring to Vickrey as being "arrogant." There is no indication of a response from the chairperson on record.

The issue next considered by the Commission was that of various litigation threatened by Converse. Converse indicated that he would "likely" be filing a lawsuit against Vickrey for violations of his First Amendment rights. Converse was also involved in a dispute with other law students, in which he threatened to file a lawsuit and warned the students that all lawsuits in which they were involved would need to be reported to proper authorities when they applied to take a bar examination.

Further, Converse posted signs on the bulletin board at the law school denouncing a professor, in response to the way in which Converse's parking appeal was handled, and then went to the student newspaper to criticize the process and those involved in that appeal.

One of the final issues addressed by the Commission in its hearing was that of a T-shirt Converse produced and marketed on which a nude caricature of Vickrey is shown sitting astride what appears to be a large hot dog. The cartoon on the shirt also contains the phrase "Astride the Peter Principle," which Converse claims connotes the principle that Vickrey had been promoted past his level of competence; however, Converse admits that the T-shirt could be construed to have certain sexual overtones. Converse admitted the creation of this T-shirt would not be acceptable behavior for a lawyer.

In response to not being allowed to post signs and fliers at the law school, Converse sent a memo to all law students in which he noted to his fellow students that his "Deanie on a Weanie" T-shirts were in stock. In that same memo, Converse included a note to his schoolmates:

> So far 4 causes of action have arisen, courtesy Tricky Vickrey. [He then listed what he believed the causes of actions to be.] When you pass the SD Bar, if you want to earn some atty [sic] fees, get hold of me and we can go for one of these. I've kept evidence, of course.

Vickrey asked Converse not to wear his T-shirt to his graduation ceremony, and Converse decided that "it would be a better choice in [his] life not to go to that commencement." Converse acknowledges that Vickrey's request was made in a civil manner.

The evidence also revealed that prior to law school, Converse, in his capacity as a landlord, sued a tenant for nonpayment of rent and referred to the tenant as a "f****** welfare b****." At the hearing, in response to questioning from the Commission, Converse testified at great length as to how he tends to personally attack individuals when he finds himself embroiled in a controversy.

After the Commission notified Converse on December 18, 1998, that he would not be allowed to sit for the Nebraska bar examination, Converse appealed the adverse determination to this court pursuant to Neb. Ct. R. for Adm. of Attys. 15 (rev 1996).

Assignment of Error

Converse claims, restated and renumbered, that the Commission erred in (1) basing its decision, in part, upon conduct and speech arguably protected by the First Amendment; (2) not making Converse aware of all of the "charges" against him in the proceedings in violation of the 14th Amendment; and (3) determining that Converse's conduct gave rise to sufficient cause under Nebraska law for the Commission to deny his application to sit for the Nebraska bar examination.

***

Analysis

Converse first assigns as error that the Commission's determination should not stand because it is based in large part upon speech that is protected by the First Amendment. Thus, the threshold question we must answer is whether conduct arguably protected by the First Amendment can be considered by the Commission during an investigation into an applicant's moral character and fitness to practice law. We answer this question in the affirmative.

***

We conclude that the Commission properly considered Converse's conduct as it reflects upon his moral character, even if such conduct might have been protected by the First Amendment. Converse's first assignment of error is therefore without merit.

Converse next contends that the Commission violated his due process rights by not making him aware of all of the "charges" against him in these proceedings. This argument is basically that when the Commission determined that he lacked the requisite moral character and gave some examples as to why they reached such a determination, they should have provided an all-inclusive list delineating every reason on which their decision was based. We conclude that such a procedure is not required.

By alleging that he has not been made fully aware of the "charges" against him, Converse has confused this inquiry into his moral character with a trial. Such is not the case. An inquiry regarding an application to the bar is not a lawsuit with the formalities of a trial, but, rather, is an investigation of the conduct of an applicant for membership to the bar for the purpose of determining whether he shall be admitted. *See In re Doss,* 367 Ill. 570, 12 N.E.2d 659 (1937). No charges have been filed against Converse, and he has been advised of the reasons for which his application was denied. Converse's assignment of error that he has been denied due process of the law is therefore without merit.

Converse's third assignment of error alleges that the Commission erred by determining there was sufficient cause to deny his application to sit for the Nebraska bar exam. Much of his argument centers around his conduct being protected by the First Amendment, as discussed previously. However, the question presented is not the scope of Converse's rights under the First Amendment, but whether Converse's propensity to unreasonably react against anyone whom he believes opposes him reveals his lack of professional responsibility, which renders him unfit to practice law. *See In re Martin-Trigona,* 55 Ill. 2d 301, 302 N.E.2d 68 (1973).

There is no question that "[a] state can require high standards of qualification, such as good moral character or proficiency in its law, before it admits an applicant to the bar . . . ." *Schware v. Board of Bar Examiners,* 353 U.S. 232, 239, 77 S. Ct. 752, 1 L. Ed. 2d 796 (1957). The Court has also stated that it must be "kept clearly in mind . . . that an applicant for admission to the bar bears the burden of proof of 'good moral character' a requirement whose validity is not, nor could well be, drawn into question here." *Konigsberg v. State Bar,* 366 U.S. 36, 40-41, 81 S. Ct. 997, 6 L. Ed. 2d 105 (1961). "If at the conclusion of the proceedings the evidence of good character and that of bad character are found in even balance, the State may refuse admission . . . ." 366 U.S. at 42. Nebraska does, in fact, require a bar applicant to show that the applicant is of good moral character. See, *In re Application of Majorek,* 244 Neb. 595, 508 N.W.2d 275 (1993); Neb. Rev. Stat. § 7-102 (Reissue 1997). Therefore, the burden is upon Converse to adequately prove his fitness to practice law in Nebraska, and the evidence will be viewed in this light.

The legal reality is that this court, and only this court, is vested with the power to admit persons to the practice of law in this state and to fix qualifications for admission to the Nebraska bar. *In re Application of Collins-Bazant,* 254 Neb. 614, 578 N.W.2d 38 (1998); *In re Application of Majorek, supra.* With that in mind, we commence our analysis with the standards for moral character required for admission to the Nebraska bar as set out in our rules and governing the admission of attorneys. Neb. Ct. R. for Adm. Of Attys. 3 (rev. 1998) governs this situation, which provides in pertinent part:

> An attorney should be one whose record of conflict justifies, the trust of clients, adversaries, courts, and others with respect to the professional duties owed to them. A record manifesting a significant deficiency by an applicant in one or more of the following essential eligibility requirements for the practice of law may constitute a basis for denial of admission. In addition to the admission requirements otherwise established by these Rules, the essential requirements for admission to the practice of law in Nebraska are:
>
> a) The ability to conduct oneself with a high degree of honesty, integrity, and trustworthiness in all professional relationships and with respect to all obligations;
> b) The ability to conduct oneself with respect for and in accordance with the law and the Code of Professional Responsibility;
> c) The ability to conduct oneself professionally and in a manner that engenders respect for the law and the profession.

Under rule 3, Converse must prove that his past conduct is in conformity with the standards set forth by this court, and the record in this case compels the conclusion that he has failed to do so.

***

We explained in *In re Appeal of Lane*, 249 Neb. at 511, 544 N.W.2d at 375, that the "requisite restraint in dealing with others is obligatory conduct for attorneys because 'the efficient and orderly administration of justice cannot be successfully carried on if we allow attorneys to engage in unwarranted attacks on the court [or] opposing counsel . . . . Such tactics seriously lower the public respect for . . . the Bar.'" (Emphasis supplied.) (Quoting *Application of Feingold*, 296 A.2d 492 (Me. 1972)). Furthermore, "'an attorney who exhibits [a] lack of civility, good manners, and common courtesy . . . tarnishes the . . . image of . . . the bar . . . .'" *Id.* (Quoting *In re McAlevy*, 69 N.J. 349, 354 A.2d 289 (1976)). We held *In re Appeal of Lane*, 249 Neb. At 512, 544 N.W.2d at 375, that "abusive, disruptive, hostile, intemperate, intimidating, irresponsible, threatening, or turbulent behavior is a proper basis for the denial of admission to the bar." *Id.*

***

The evidence in this case shows that Converse's numerous disputes and personal attacks indicate a "pattern and a way of life which appears to be [Converse's] normal reaction to opposition and disappointed." See *In re Appeal of Lane*, 249 Neb. 499, 512, 544 N.W.2d 367, 376 (1996). The totality of the evidence clearly establishes that Converse possesses an inclination to personally attack those with whom he has disputes. Such inclinations "are not acceptable in one who would be a counselor and advocate in the legal system." *Id.* at 510, 544 N.W.2d at 374.

In addition to Converse's tendency to personally attack those individuals with whom he has disputes, his pattern of behavior indicates an additional tendency to do so in arenas other than those specifically established within the legal system. This tendency is best exemplified by observing Converse's conduct in situations where there were avenues through which Converse could have and should have handled his disputes, but instead chose to mount personal attacks on those with whom he had disputes through letters and barrages in the media.

One such incident occurred when Converse received the below average grade in the appellate advocacy course, and he wrote letters to various individuals regarding his arguments. Converse testified that he wrote letters to members of the South Dakota Supreme Court, Judge Richard Posner, Judge Alex Kozinski, and others, but filed no formal appeal. Moreover, upon return of the nude photograph, Converse testified that he redisplayed the photograph to force the issue with the university, but chose not to pursue any action regarding the alleged violation of his rights. There was also the incident regarding Converse's internship with the U.S. Attorney's office, where Converse went outside established procedures, arranged for the internship on his own, and then complained to all faculty and to members of the South Dakota bar when his request was denied for not complying with established procedures. Finally, there was Converse's production and marketing of the T-shirt containing a nude depiction of Vickrey on a hot dog as a result of the ongoing tension between Vickrey and himself. Converse is 48 years old, and his actions cannot be excused as isolated instances of youthful indiscretions.

Taken together with other incidents previously discussed, the evidence clearly shows that Converse is prone to turbulence, intemperance, and irresponsibility; characteristics which are not acceptable in one seeking admission to the Nebraska bar. See *In re Appeal of Lane, supra.* In light of Converse's admission that such conduct would be inappropriate were he already an attorney, we reiterate that we will not tolerate conduct by those applying for admission to the state bar that would not be tolerated were the person already an attorney. See *id.* Furthermore, Converse has consistently exhibited a tendency to cause disruption and then go to some arena outside the field of law to settle the dispute, often to an arena not specifically designed for dispute resolution. [***]

The record before us reflects that the Commission conducted such an inquiry and, at the conclusion thereof, correctly determined that Converse possessed a moral character inconsistent with one "dedicated to the peaceful and reasoned settlement of disputes," see 401 U.S. at 166, but, rather, more consistent with someone who wishes to go outside the field of law and settle disputes by mounting personal attacks and portraying himself as the victim and his opponent as the aggressor. Such disruptive, hostile, intemperate, threatening, and turbulent conduct certainly reflects negatively upon those character traits the applicant must prove prior to being admitted to the Nebraska bar, such as honesty, integrity, reliability, and trustworthiness. *See In re Appeal of Lane,* 249 Neb. 499, 544 N.W.2d 367 (1996). *See also* Rule 3.

The result might have been different if Converse had exhibited only a "single incident of rudeness or lack of professional courtesy," *see In re Snyder,* 472 U.S. 634, 647, 105 S. Ct. 2874, 86 L. Ed. 2d 504 (1985), but such is simply not the case. The record clearly establishes that he seeks to resolve disputes not in a peaceful manner, but by personally attacking those who oppose him in any way and then resorting to arenas outside the field of law to publicly humiliate and intimidate those opponents. Such a pattern of behavior is incompatible with what we have required to be obligatory conduct for attorneys, as well as for applicants to the bar.

Converse has exhibited a clear lack of self-restraint and lack of judgment, and our de novo review of the record leads us to independently conclude that Converse has exhibited such a pattern of acting in a hostile and disruptive manner as to render him unfit for the practice of law in Nebraska. We conclude that the Commission's determination to deny Converse's application was correct, and Converse's third assignment of error is therefore without merit.

Conclusion

The commission correctly determined that Converse possessed insufficient moral character and was unfit to practice law in the State of Nebraska. This determination was based on an inquiry into Converse's moral character that was both proper and constitutionally permissible. Finding no error in the Commission's determination or the process used to reach that determination, we affirm the Commission's denial of application.

Questions and Comments

1. Do you think the court made the right decision in affirming the Commission's determination to deny Converse's application? Do you agree with the court that Converse's behavior exhibited his moral character as being inconsistent with one "dedicated to the peaceful and reasoned settlement of disputes?" If you agree with the court's decision, which incident(s), in particular, made Converse seem unfit to practice law?

2. The facts of the case establish that Converse was 48 years old when he engaged in the behavior described. Do you think it would have made any difference in the court's decision if Converse were a young adult in his early 20s and perhaps fresh out of his undergraduate lifestyle? Can you think of any other factors that could have mitigated the court's decision?

3. Nebraska holds prospective lawyers to the same behavioral standards and guidelines as those who are already admitted to the bar. Do you think this is fair considering most prospective lawyers are young adults, fresh out of college, and perhaps not in tune with what it means to be a professional? Can you think of any behavior that could arguably be permissible for a prospective lawyer, but not permissible for someone who has been in the profession for years? Should there be a distinction?

MATTER OF ANONYMOUS
Supreme Court of New York, Appellate Division, Third Department (2009)
875 N.Y.S.2d 925

Per Curiam. Applicant passed the February 2008 New York State bar exam and the State Board of Law Examiners certified him for admission to this Court (*see* 22 NYCRR 520.7). The Committee on Character and Fitness has completed its investigation of his application for admission, including an interview of applicant (*see* NYCRR 805.1).

Applicant has disclosed various student loans with balances now totaling about $430,000. He has stated that the loans are currently delinquent but professes good faith intentions to pay them. He has attributed his nonpayment to the downturn of the economy and bad faith negotiations on the part of some of the loan servicers. Our review of the application indicates that the disbursement dates of the loans cover a 20-year period, from as early as 1985. Applicant has not made any substantial payments on the loans. He has not been flexible in his discussions with the loan servicers. Under all the circumstances herein, we conclude that applicant has not presently established the character and general fitness requisite for an attorney and counselor at law (*see Judiciary Law § 90 [1][1]*).

Cardona, P.J., Spain, Malone Jr., Kavanagh and McCarthy, JJ., concur. Ordered that this application for admission is denied.

Questions and Comments

1. In that case, the applicant has loans that cover a 20-year period, he has not made any substantial payments on the loans, and he has not been flexible in discussions with loan servicers. Do you think this behavior is indicative of possible future behavior or should define one's moral character and fitness to practice law?

2. If you were representing the applicant, what argument would you make on his behalf? Do you think if he had made more of an effort to repay his loans over the years, the case outcome would have been different?

3. The applicant's loans here date back 20-years. Does this fact hurt his case as compared to an average law student who potentially has loans dating back 8 to 10 years?

In re James H. Himmel
Supreme Court of Illinois (1988)
533 N.E.2d 790

STAMOS, J.: This is a disciplinary proceeding against respondent, James H. Himmel. On January 22, 1986, the Administrator of the Attorney Registration and Disciplinary Commission (the Commission) filed a complaint with the Hearing Board, alleging that respondent violated Rule 1–103(a) of the Code of Professional Responsibility (the Code) (107 Ill. 2d R.1-103(a)) by failing to disclose to the Commission information concerning attorney misconduct. On October 15, 1986, the Hearing Board found that respondent had violated the rule and recommended that respondent be reprimanded. The Administrator filed exceptions with the Review Board. The Review Board issued its report on July 9, 1987, finding that respondent had not violated a disciplinary rule and recommending dismissal of the complaint. We granted the Administrator's petition for leave to file exceptions to the Review Board's report and recommendation. 107 Ill. 2d R.753(e)(6).

We will briefly review the facts, which essentially involve three individuals: respondent, James H. Himmel, licensed to practice law in Illinois on November 6, 1975; his client, Tammy Forsberg, formerly known as Tammy McEathron; and her former attorney, John R. Casey.

The complaint alleges that respondent had known John Casey's conversion of Forsberg's funds and respondent failed to inform the Commission of this misconduct. The facts are as follows.

In October 1978, Tammy Forsberg was injured in a motorcycle accident. In June 1980, she retained John R. Casey to represent her in any personal injury or property damage claim resulting from the accident. Sometime in 1981, Casey negotiated a settlement of $35,000 on Forsberg's behalf. Pursuant to an agreement between Forsberg and Casey, one-third of any monies received would be paid to Casey as his attorney fee.

In March 1981, Casey received the $35,000 settlement check, endorsed it, and deposited the check into his client trust fund account. Subsequently, Casey converted the funds. Between 1981 and 1983, Forsberg unsuccessfully attempted to collect her $23,233.34 share of the settlement proceeds. In March 1983, Forsberg retained respondent to collect her money and agreed to pay him one-third of any funds recovered above the $23,233.34.

Respondent investigated the matter and discovered that Casey had misappropriated the settlement funds. In April 1983, respondent drafted an agreement in which Casey would pay Forsberg $75,000 in settlement of any claim she might have against him for the misappropriated funds. By the terms of the agreement, Forsberg agreed not to initiate any criminal, civil, or attorney disciplinary action against Casey. This agreement was executed on April 11, 1983. Respondent stood to gain $17,000 or more if Casey honored the agreement. In February 1985, respondent filed suit against Casey for breaching the agreement, and a $100,000 judgment was entered against Casey. If Casey had satisfied the judgment, respondent's share would have been approximately $25,588.

The complaint stated that at no time did respondent inform the Commission of Casey's misconduct. According to the Administrator, respondent's first contact with the Commission was in response to the Commission's inquiry regarding the lawsuit against Casey.

In April 1985, the Administrator filed a petition to have Casey suspended from practicing law because of his conversion of client funds and his conduct involving moral turpitude in matters unrelated to Forsberg's claim. Casey was subsequently disbarred on consent on November 5, 1985.

***

Before retaining respondent, Forsberg collected $5,000 from Casey. After being retained, respondent made inquiries regarding Casey's conversion, contacting the insurance company that issued the settlement check, its attorney, Forsberg, her mother, her fiancé, and Casey. Forsberg told respondent that she simply wanted her money back and specifically instructed the respondent to take no further action. Because of respondent's efforts, Forsberg collected another $10,400 from Casey. Respondent received no fee in this case.

The Hearing Board found that respondent received unprivileged information that Casey converted Forsberg's funds, and that respondent failed to relate the information to the Commission in violation of Rule 1-103(a) of the Code. The Hearing Board noted, however, that respondent had been practicing law for 11 years, had no prior record of any complaints, obtained as good a result as could be expected in this case, and requested no fees for recovering the $23,233.34. Accordingly, the Hearing Board recommended a private reprimand.

Upon the Administrator's exceptions to the Hearing Board's recommendation, the Review Board reviewed the matter. The Review Board's report stated that the client had contacted the Commission prior to retaining the respondent and, therefore, the Commission did have knowledge of the alleged misconduct. Further, the Review Board noted that respondent respected the client's wishes regarding not pursuing a claim with the Commission. Accordingly, the Review Board recommended that the complaint be dismissed.

The Administrator now raises three issues for review: (1) whether the Review Board erred in concluding that respondent's client had informed the Commission of misconduct by her former attorney; (2) whether the Review Board erred in concluding that respondent had no violated Rule 1-103(a); and (3) whether the proven misconduct warrants at least a censure.

As to the first issue, the Administrator contends that the Review Board erred in finding that Forsberg informed the Commission of Casey's misconduct prior to retaining respondent. In support of this contention, the Administrator cites to testimony in the record showing that while Forsberg contacted the Commission and received a complaint form, she did not fill out the form, return it, advise the Commission of the facts, or name whom she wished to complain about. The Administrator further contends that even if Forsberg had reported Casey's misconduct to the Commission, such an action would not have relieved respondent of his duty to report under Rule 1-103(a). Additionally, the Administrator argues that no evidence exists to prove that respondent failed to report because he assumed that Forsberg had already reported the matter.

Respondent argues that the record shows that Forsberg did contact the Commission and was forwarded a complaint form, and that the record is not clear that Forsberg failed to disclose Casey's name to the Commission. Respondent also argues that Forsberg directed respondent not to pursue the claim against Casey, a claim she had already begun to pursue.

We begin our analysis by examining whether a client's complaint of attorney misconduct to the Commission can be a defense to an attorney's failure to report the same misconduct. Respondent offers no authority for such a defense and our research had disclosed none. Common sense would dictate that if a lawyer has a duty under the Code, the actions of a client would not relieve the attorney of his own duty. Accordingly, while the parties dispute whether or not respondent's client informed the Commission, that question is irrelevant to our inquiry in this case. We have held that the canons of ethics in the Code constitute a safe guide for professional conduct, and attorneys may be disciplined for not observing them. (*In re Yamaguchi* (1987), 118 Ill. 2d 417, 427*, citing *In re Taylor* (1977), 66 Ill. 2d 567.) The question is, then, whether or not respondent violated the Code, not whether Forsberg informed the Commission of Casey's misconduct.

As to respondent's argument that he did not report Casey's misconduct because his client directed him not to do so, we again note respondent's failure to suggest any legal support for such a defense. A lawyer, as an officer of the court, is duty-bound to uphold the rules in the Code. The title of Canon 1 (107 Ill. 2d Canon 1) reflects this obligation: "A lawyer should assist in maintaining the integrity and competence of the legal profession." A lawyer may not choose to circumvent the rules by simply asserting that his client asked him to do so.

As to the second issue, the Administrator argues that the Review Board erred in concluding that respondent did not violate Rule 1-103(a). The Administrator urges acceptance of the Hearing Board's finding that respondent had unprivileged knowledge of Casey's conversion of client funds, and that respondent failed to disclose that information to the Commission. The Administrator states that respondent's knowledge of Casey's conversion of client funds was knowledge of illegal conduct involving moral turpitude under *In re Stillo* (1977)*, 68 Ill. 2d 49, 54. Further, the Administrator argues that the information respondent received was not privileged under the definition of privileged information articulated by this court in *People v. Adam* (1972), 51 Ill. 2d 46, 48, cert. denied (1972), 409 U.S. 948, 34 L. Ed. 2d 218, 93 S. Ct. 289. Therefore, the Administrator concludes, respondent violated his ethical duty to report misconduct under Rule 1-103(a). According to the Administrator, failure to disclose the information deprived the Commission of evidence of serious misconduct, evidence that would have assisted in the Commission's investigation of Casey.

Respondent contends that the information was privileged information received from his client, Forsberg, and therefore he was under no obligation to disclose the matter to the Commission. Respondent argues that his failure to report Casey's misconduct was motivated by his respect for his client's wishes, not by his desire for financial gain. To support this assertion, respondent notes that his fee agreement with Forsberg was contingent upon her first receiving all the money Casey originally owed her. Further, respondent states that he has received no fee for his representation of Forsberg.

Our analysis of this issue begins with a reading of the applicable disciplinary rules. Rule 1-103(a) of the Code states:

> (a) A lawyer possessing unprivileged knowledge of a violation of Rule 1–102(a)(3) or (4) shall report such knowledge to a tribunal or other authority empowered to investigator or act upon such violation." 107 Ill. 2d R. 1-103(a).

Rule 1–102 of the Code states:

> A lawyer shall not . . .
> (1) violate a disciplinary rule;
> (2) circumvent a disciplinary rule through actions of another;
> (3) engage in illegal conduct involving moral turpitude;
> (4) engage in conduct involving dishonesty, fraud, deceit, or misrepresentation; or
> (5) engage in conduct that is prejudicial to the administration of justice." 107 Ill. 2d R. 1-102.

***

This court has also emphasized the importance of a lawyer's duty to report misconduct. In the case *In re Anglin* (1988), 122 Ill. 2d 531, because of the petitioner's refusal to answer questions regarding his knowledge of other persons' misconduct, we denied a petition for reinstatement to the roll of attorneys licensed to practice in Illinois. We stated, "Under Disciplinary Rule 1–103 a lawyer has the duty to report the misconduct of other lawyers. (107 Ill. 2d Rules 1-103, 1-102(a)(3), (a)(4).) Petitioner's belief in a code of silence indicates to use that he is not at present fully rehabilitated or fit to practice law." (*Anglin*, 122 Ill. 2d at 539). Thus, if the present respondent's conduct did violate the rule on reporting misconduct, imposition of discipline for such a breach of duty is mandated.

***

We agree with the Administrator's argument that the communication regarding Casey's conduct does not meet this definition. The record does not suggest that this information was communicated by Forsberg to the respondent in confidence. We have held that information voluntarily disclosed by a client to an attorney, in the presence of third parties who are not agents of the client or attorney, is not privileged information. (*People v. Williams* (1983), 97 Ill. 2d 252, 295, cert. denied (1984), 466 U.S. 981, 80 L. Ed. 2d 836, 104 S. Ct. 2364.) In this case, Forsberg discussed the matter with respondent at various times while her mother and fiancé were present. Consequently, unless the mother and fiancé were agents of respondent's client, the information communicated was not privileged. Moreover, we have also stated that matters intended by a client for disclosure by the client's attorney to third parties, who are not agents of either the client or the attorney, are not privileged. (*People v. Werhollick* (1970), 45 Ill. 2d 459, 462.) The record shows that respondent, with Forsberg's consent, discussed Casey's conversion of her funds with the insurance company involved, the insurance company's lawyer, and with Casey himself. Thus, under *Werhollick* and probably *Williams*, the information was not privileged.

Though respondent repeatedly asserts that his failure to report was motivated not by financial gain but by the request of his client, we do not deem such an argument relevant in this case. This court has stated that discipline may be appropriate even if no honest motive for the misconduct exists. (*In re Weinberg* (1988), 119 Ill. 2d 309, 315; *In re Clayter* (1980), 78 Ill. 2d 276, 283.) In addition, we have held that client approval of an attorney's action does not immunize an attorney from disciplinary action. (*In re Thompson* (1963), 30 Ill. 2d 560, 569. *People ex rel. Scholes v. Keithley* (1906), 255 Ill. 30, 41.) We have already dealt with, and dismissed, respondent's assertion that his conduct is acceptable because he was acting pursuant to his client's directions.

***

We conclude, then, that respondent possessed unprivileged knowledge of Casey's conversion of client funds, which is illegal conduct involving moral turpitude, and that respondent failed in his duty to report such misconduct to the Commission. Because no defense exists, we agree with the Hearing Board's finding that respondent has violated Rule 1-103(a) and must be disciplined.

The third issue concerns the appropriate quantum of discipline to be imposed in this case. The Administrator contends that respondent's misconduct warrants at least a censure, although the Hearing Board recommended a private reprimand and the Review Board recommended dismissal of the matter entirely. In support of the request for a greater quantum of discipline, the Administrator cites to the purposes of attorney discipline, which include maintaining the integrity of the legal profession and safeguarding the administration of justice. The Administrator argues that these purposes will not be served unless respondent is publicly disciplined so that the profession will be on notice that a violation of Rule 1-103(a) will not be tolerated. The Administrator argues that a more severe sanction is necessary because respondent deprived the Commission of evidence of another attorney's conversion and thereby interfered with the Commission's investigative function under Supreme Court Rule 752 (107 Ill. 2d R.752). Citing to the Rule 774 petition (107 Ill. 2d R.774) filed against Casey, the Administrator notes that Casey converted many clients' funds after respondent's duty to report Casey arose. The Administrator also argues that both respondent and his client behaved in contravention of the Criminal Code's prohibition against compounding a crime by agreeing with Casey not to report him, in exchange for settlement funds.

In his defense, respondent reiterates his arguments that he was not motivated by his desire for financial gain. He also states that Forsberg was pleased with his performance on her behalf. According to respondent, his failure to report was a "judgment call" which resulted positively in Forsberg's regaining some of her funds from Casey.

***

[W]e agree with the Administrator that public discipline is necessary in this case to carry out the purposes of attorney discipline. While we have considered the Boards' recommendations in this matter, we cannot agree with the Review Board that respondent's conduct served to rectify a wrong and did not injure the bar, the public, or the administration of justice. Though we agree with the Hearing Board's assessment that respondent violated Rule 1-103 of the Code, we do not agree that the facts warrant only a private reprimand. As previously stated, the evidence proved that respondent possessed unprivileged knowledge of Casey's conversion of client funds, yet respondent did not report Casey's misconduct.

This failure to report resulted in interference with the Commission's investigation of Casey, and thus with the administration of justice. Perhaps some members of the public would have been spared from Casey's misconduct had respondent reported the information as soon as he knew of Casey's conversions of client funds. We are particularly disturbed by the fact that respondent chose to draft a settlement agreement with Casey rather than report the misconduct.

***

Both respondent and his client stood to gain financially by agreeing not to prosecute or report Casey for conversion. According to the settlement agreement, respondent would have received $17,000 or more as his fee. If Casey had satisfied the judgment entered against him for failure to honor the settlement agreement, respondent would have collected approximately $25,588.

We have held that fairness dictates consideration of mitigation factors in disciplinary cases. (*In re Yamaguchi* (1987), 118 Ill. 2d 417, 428, citing *In re Neff* (1980), 83 Ill. 2d 20.) Therefore, we do consider the fact that Forsberg recovered $10,400 through respondent's services, that respondent has practiced law for 11 years with no record of complaints, and that he requested no fee for minimum collection of Forsberg's funds. However, these considerations do not outweigh the serious nature of respondent's failure to report Casey, the resulting interference with the Commission's investigation of Casey, and respondent's ill-advised choice to settle with Casey rather than report his misconduct.

***

Questions and Comments

1. Do you agree with the decision to suspend Himmel from law practice based on the circumstances of the case? Would a less severe punishment have been sufficient? Do you believe the court was trying to send out a certain message in ruling against Himmel?

2. The court states that even if Forsberg would have filed a complaint against Casey based on his conduct, Himmel would have still had a duty to report Casey to the proper authority. Do you agree with this requirement? The client was ultimately the one impacted by Casey's actions thus, could it be argued the client filing suit would be sufficient to address the issue at hand? Why or why not?

3. If you were a judge in that court, would you have given any consideration to Himmel's argument that he was abiding by what his client wanted in not reporting Casey? Should the court have considered the fact that Himmel was successful in recovering his client's money?

FLORIDA SUPREME COURT SANCTIONS LAWYERS ENGAGED IN TOXIC E-MAIL FEUD
Posted in Ethics & Malpractice Claims, Musings on the Practice of Law
By Juan C. Antúnez

The histrionics we see on television are almost never allowed in a real courtroom. If something truly appalling is going to happen, it's going to happen outside of the courtroom. **Prime example: toxic e-mail feuds.**

Sooner or later we all run into opposing counsel who try to provoke us into some kind of angry e-mail exchange. **My policy: do NOT engage.**

These sorts of soul crushing e-mail feuds do nothing to help the clients, move the focus of the case away from the substance of the matter (where it should be) to the lawyers (where it shouldn't be), and are ultimately demeaning as well as psychologically damaging for all concerned.

The *St. Petersburg Times* recently reported on an e-mail feud between two litigators that resulted in sanctions for **both** sides. Here's an excerpt from Court punishes bay area lawyers who called each other 'hack' and 'loser'—and worse:

> TAMPA—The e-mail messages show two lawyers trying to schedule hearings and depositions for a lawsuit. They can't agree on dates, or much of anything else.
>
> Then it gets ugly.
>
> Tampa lawyer Nicholas F. Mooney calls his opponent a jerk and a "junior lawyer." Palmetto lawyer Kurt D. Mitchell questions Mooney's mental health. The name-calling continues over six months.
>
> **Now the Florida Supreme Court has weighed in, issuing sanctions for both lawyers.**
>
> After two complaints by the Florida Bar, Mitchell was suspended for 10 days and was ordered to attend an anger management class. Mooney gets a public reprimand and must take a class on professionalism.
>
> **All because the men refused to be civil.**
>
> ***
>
> In October, the insults got truly personal. Mitchell said he was looking online for a mental disability based on Mooney's "symptoms," such as "closely spaced eyes, dull blank stare, bulbous head, lying and inability to tell fiction from reality." Mooney, who said his son has a birth defect, called Mitchell a jerk and suggested he look in the mirror for signs of mental disability. **"Then check your children (if they are even yours. ... Better check the garbage man that comes by your trailer to make sure they don't look like him)."**
>
> Mitchell's reply: **"While I am sorry to hear about your disabled child; that sort of thing is to be expected when a retard reproduces. ... Do not hate me, hate your genetics. However, I would look at the bright side, at least you definitely know the kid is yours."**

If you're dealing with opposing counsel that just doesn't get it, you may want to send him or her a copy of the Florida Bar Complaints filed against the lawyers in this case, and note that toxic e-mails can actually get them sanctioned, as noted in the concluding paragraph of both Florida Bar Complaints:

> By reason of the foregoing, the Respondent has violated the following Rules Regulating The Florida Bar: Rule 3-4.3 (commission of any act

that is unlawful or contrary to honesty and justice); and Rule 4-8.4(d) (a lawyer shall not engage in conduct in connection with the practice of law that is prejudicial to the administration of justice, including to knowingly, or through callous indifference, disparage, humiliate, or discriminate against litigants, jurors, witnesses, court personnel, or other lawyers on any basis, including, but not limited to, on account of race, ethnicity, gender, religion, national origin, disability, marital status, sexual orientation, age, socioeconomic status, employment, or physical characteristic).

Endnotes omitted (See Juan C. Antúnez, Florida Supreme Court Sanctions Lawyers Engaged in Toxic E-mail Feud, Florida Probate & Trust Litigation Blog (2011) for full article version). Reprinted with permission from the 2011 edition of the "Florida Probate & Trust Litigation Blog" © 2016 Juan C. Antúnez. All rights reserved.

Questions and Comments

1. Both lawyers received relatively small sanctions, including a brief suspension and taking anger management and professionalism classes. Do you believe the lawyers should have received more punishment or less punishment? Would "stress" constitute a mitigating factor or excuse?

2. In a situation such as this involving name-calling and immature behavior, should the disciplinary authority take into consideration mitigating factors, such as a lawyer's clean history, years of experience, or good reputation before imposing a sanction? In other words, are there scenarios that are so ridiculous that there should not even be a consideration of a lawyer's prior "positive" behavior and clean record?

In the Era of Social Media, What's a Facebooking Judge to Do?
Texas Lawyer (Online), August 6, 2015
By John G. Browning

Imagine preparing for an important hearing or trial and learning that the presiding judge is a Facebook "friend" of the opposing counsel. Or more, that the judge had tweeted or posted about the upcoming trial. The issue of judicial use and misuse of social media continues to perplex lawyers, judges and judicial ethics authorities alike. Consider these examples:

- In April, Louisville Judge Olu Stevens stirred up controversy by criticizing on Facebook a victim impact statement made in his court. The judge, who is African-American, deplored the claim in the statement that a home invasion and robbery committed by two African-

American males had left a 3-year-old girl traumatized with fear of black men. While Judge Stevens initially made this emotional reaction to the statement during a sentencing hearing for one of the defendants, it was his Facebook post about the "generalized stereotyped and racist opinions" that drew fire, not only from members of the public who have called for Steven's removal from office, but also from legal ethics scholars critical of the judge's remarks.

- In May, Florida Judge Linda Schoonover resigned her bench in the midst of a judicial ethics inquiry into a series of misconduct allegations, including the claim by one woman who accused Schoonover of retaliating against her in a divorce case after she refused the judge's Facebook "friend" request.
- In Alabama, Walker County District Judge Henry P. Allred was reprimanded and censured in 2013 for making public comments on his Facebook page and in an email sent to all state court judges about then-pending contempt proceedings against a specific lawyer, and requesting that Facebook friends "spread" the posting "far and wide."

Texas judges have not been immune from criticism for their social media activities, either. Earlier this year, Denton County Judge Steve Burgess was recused from presiding over a lawsuit brought by the Texas Ethics Commission against prominent conservative political strategist Michael Quinn Sullivan. Judge Burgess "offense" was not for any posts or tweets made, but for merely being one of Sullivan's over 7,000 "followers" on Twitter and having "access" to tweets by Sullivan. The TEC accused Judge Burgess of having "ex parte access" to Sullivan despite the fact that Sullivan was not a Twitter follower of the judge, and for "back-channel" messages to occur between Twitter users, both must be followers of each other.

In a widely-reported case, Judge Michelle Slaughter of Galveston County appealed a public admonition issued by the State Commission on Judicial Conduct in April 2015 (her trial de novo was held in July, and a ruling is expected by late September). Judge Slaughter was accused of violating applicable Canons of Judicial Conduct by "commenting" about a case pending in her court, and thereby calling into question her impartiality. In an attempt to fulfill a campaign pledge to promote transparency and to connect with public she serves, Judge Slaughter posted to Facebook brief statements about goings on in her court. The Facebook posts, innocuous or not, prompted motions to recuse and for mistrial (both of which were granted), as well as the Commission on Judicial Conduct's action.

Cases like these illustrate the need for guidance for judges and lawyers alike on where the ethical boundaries are for judges engaging on social media. Canon 3B (10) of the Texas Code of Judicial Conduct explicitly envisions that judges may make "public statements, in the course of their official duties" or may explain "for public information the procedures of the court;" however, judges must abstain from commenting publicly about a pending or impending proceeding "in a manner which suggests to a reasonable person the Judge's probable decision on any particular case." And in a more sweeping pronouncement, Canon 4A of the Texas Code of Judicial Conduct reminds judges to conduct their extrajudicial activities in a manner that doesn't "cast reasonable doubt on the judge's capacity to act impartially as a judge" or "interfere with the proper performance of judicial duties."

But the Code of Judicial Conduct's pronouncements have to be understood in the context of our modern, wired world in which 74 percent of online adults have at least one social networking profile. According to national surveys of judges by groups like the Conference of Court Public Information Officers, judicial use of social media has been on the rise, particularly in jurisdictions where judges are elected, like Texas. No less a figure than Texas Supreme Court Justice Don Willett, the state "Tweeter Laureate" with more than 17,000 followers, has called it "political malpractice" not to use social media. He noted in a recent *Washington Times* op-ed that "Harnessing technology is indispensable to openness" and praised social media as "another fruitful way for the judiciary to engage citizens." The American Bar Association agrees, observing in its 2013 Formal Opinion 462 that there was nothing wrong with judges using social media and calling it "a valuable tool for public outreach." And in the only Texas appellate opinion addressing judicial use of social media, 2013's *Youkers v. State*, the Dallas Court of Appeals similarly blessed the practice.

This is consistent with the dozen or so states that have issued judicial ethics opinions on the subject. Most of these ethics bodies, such as those in New York and Ohio, have concluded that it is generally permissible for judges to have a social networking presence and connect online with attorneys as long as they are careful to avoid the appearance of impropriety, avoid ex parte communications, and otherwise comply with applicable ethical rules. In the most restrictive states like Florida and California, judges cannot be "friends" with attorneys appearing before them. Most jurisdictions are quick to remind us that interactions involving judges via social media must be evaluated in the same way as other interactions using more traditional avenues of communications. Avoiding ex parte communications or the implication of special influence is just as critical in cyberspace as it is on the golf course, a restaurant, or any other setting.

Punishing judges for connecting on social media with the community that they serve isn't the answer, unless we truly want philosopher-priests cloistered in jurisprudential temples. Providing education and guidance, particularly as we apply existing rules of judicial ethics to scenarios involving technology that wasn't envisioned when those rules were created, is the answer.

Reprinted with permission from the August 2015 edition of the "Texas Lawyer" © 2016 ALM Media Properties, LLC. All rights reserved.

Questions and Comments

1. Do you believe any of the examples of judges using social media in inappropriate ways would constitute misconduct under Rule 8.4 in the Model Rules of Professional Conduct? Why or why not?

2. Do you agree with the message urged by the article that instead of not allowing judges (and lawyers) to use social media for promoting and discussing legal issues, the proper approach would be to provide education and guidance to legal professionals on how to use social media properly? What would be some efficient ways of educating legal professionals on this subject or do you think they are professionals and should "know better," so to speak?

3. Imagine a scenario where Lawyer A sees multiple posts on Facebook from Lawyer B that shows Lawyer B at night clubs and holding alcoholic beverages on multiple days during the week when Lawyer A knows that Lawyer B is supposed to have client engagements and important court dates. Looking back on Rule 8.3 and the duty of one lawyer to report another lawyer's misconduct, do you believe these photos would reach the level of impairment or misconduct that would require Lawyer A to report Lawyer B to the proper authority?

D. DISCUSSION QUESTIONS

1. Rule 8.3 places the duty on the legal profession to be a self-regulating profession—hence why a duty to report other lawyers exists in instances of misconduct or a material impairment in the ability to represent clients. After reading the cases and other materials, do you believe this is the best way to regulate the legal profession? Overall, should the burden rest on lawyers to report misconduct amongst themselves?

2. In an example discussed, a prospective lawyer was denied admission to the bar because of debt. In your view, how will other state bars handle situations regarding outstanding student debt as the years go on? Will they likely continue to consider it before admission? Or do you believe since tuition and student loans continue to grow, it will no longer be important when reviewing an applicant's character and fitness? Finally,

would preventing a prospective lawyer from bar admission make it impossible for him to pay off the debt and thus such decisions just make matters worse?

3. As indicated by the readings, one of the newest controversies amongst the legal profession is social media and how the Model Rules or their state equivalent should regulate lawyers' postings on Facebook, Twitter and other types of social media. In your opinion, should the Model Rules include a separate rule or expand on Rule 8 to add specific language addressing posting on social media? In other words, should be there be specific guidelines on what would be considered acceptable, or desired, professional conduct online in response to the growing number of lawyers posting personal as well as professional information on social media websites? If so, what guidelines do you propose? Alternatively, do you believe the general principles of the Model Rules are clear and can be easily applied to social media postings?

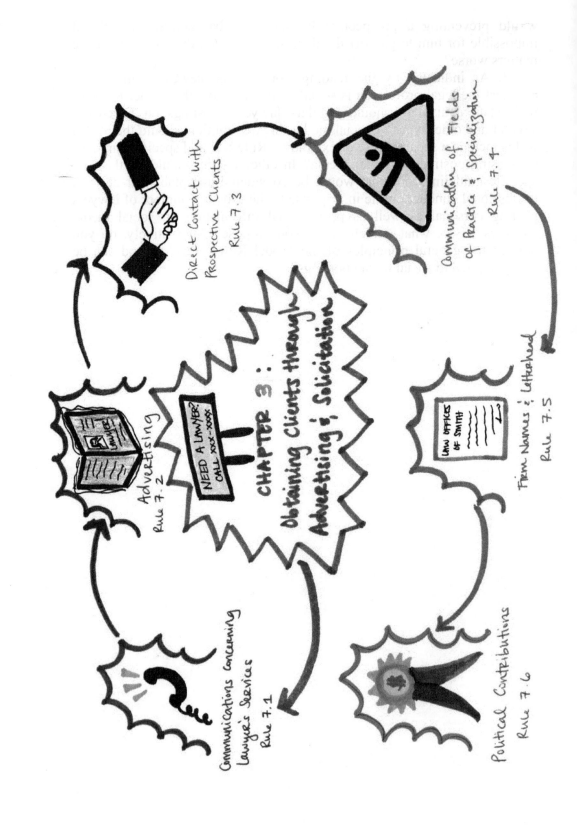

CHAPTER 3:
Obtaining Clients through
Advertising & Solicitation

Direct Contact with
Prospective Clients
Rule 7.3

Communication of Fields
of Practice & Specialization
Rule 7.4

Advertising
Rule 7.2

NEED A LAWYER?
CALL XXX-XXXX

Firm Names & Letterhead
Rule 7.5

Communications concerning
Lawyer's Services
Rule 7.1

Political Contributions
Rule 7.6

LAW OFFICES
OF SMITH

Chapter 3:
Obtaining Clients Through Advertising and Solicitation

A. Introduction

Whether it is a short drive down the local highway or a brief flip through a magazine, advertisements are sure to be an everyday sight for the average person. Like doctors' offices, retail stores, and real estate agents, lawyers also utilize the benefits offered by modern advertising. As technology has taken the world by storm, more lawyers have turned to professional and sometimes witty advertising as a way to promote their legal services and hopefully catch the eye of someone who is seeking legal help. A lawyer is free to advertise as she pleases, but she must comply with the specific guidelines set forth by Rule 7 of the Model Rules of Professional Conduct.

Rule 7.1 presents the basic guidelines for communications concerning a lawyer's services. The basic message of Rule 7.1 is that a "lawyer shall not make a false or misleading communication" about the lawyer herself or the services she offers. The communication is considered false or misleading if it contains a material misrepresentation of fact or law, or omits a fact necessary to avoid making the whole statement misleading. The objective is not to create "unjustified expectation" on the part of prospective clients.

The coverage of Rule 7.1 extends into Rule 7.2, which governs lawyer advertising. Advertising involves a lawyer's quest for clients, but the quest must be limited to the guidelines in Rule 7.2. A lawyer is allowed to advertise her services through basic communications—including written, recorded, electronic, or through public media. As long as the lawyer's advertisement is not false or misleading and accurately lists the name and address of at least one lawyer in the firm, the rules of advertising are not particularly stringent.

The rules get stricter when it comes to client solicitation. Solicitation is different from advertising because solicitation involves targeted communication directed at a specific person or persons that the lawyer knows are in need of legal services, whereas advertisement is more of a broad communication. Rule 7.3 governs client solicitation and states that a lawyer shall not solicit professional employment when the lawyer's primary motive for doing so is pecuniary gain by in-person, live telephone or real-time electronic contact. The exceptions to this rule involve instances when the lawyer contacts another lawyer or someone who has a familial, personal or prior professional relationship with the lawyer. In the reading that follows, pay special attention to the rule instituted by Florida's State Bar and some of the free speech arguments and concerns raised in *Florida Bar v. Went For It.*

If a lawyer is involved in a particular field of practice or specializes in a certain type of law, she needs to properly communicate in accordance with Rule 7.4. A lawyer must also ensure the firm name advertised to prospective clients and the letterhead in which advertisements may be sent out, comply with Rule 7.5 and ultimately are not false and misleading communication.

This chapter also addressed the new challenges that have emerged in the field of lawyer advertising as a result of the increasing use of social media. Social media enables attorneys to advertise and post information about legal services with more ease than traditional methods of advertising. All a lawyer has to do is write a few sentences about her legal services and hit the "post" button and suddenly the services are advertised to a substantial pool of "friends," which can reach thousands of readers. As such, consider how social media has influenced the world of attorney advertising and whether the state bar should make more of an effort to regulate lawyers on social media. If so, how specifically should the state bar do so?

B. RULES

In preparation, read carefully the following sections of the Model Rules of Professional Conduct along with any relevant comments listed below.

- Rule 7.1: Communications Concerning Lawyer's Services
  - Comment: [2]
- Rule 7.2: Advertising
  - Comments: [5], [6], [7], [8]
- Rule 7.3: Solicitation of Clients
  - Comments: [1], [5], [7], [8]
- Rule 7.4: Communication of Fields of Practice and Specialization
  - Comment: [1]
- Rule 7.5: Firm Names & Letterheads
  - Comments: [1]
- Rule 7.6: Political Contributions
  - Comments: [1], [2], [6]

C. CASES AND ADDITIONAL READINGS

ENDLESS PURSUIT: CAPTURING TECHNOLOGY AT THE INTERSECTION OF THE FIRST AMENDMENT AND ATTORNEY ADVERTISING

Journal of Technology & Policy, Vol. 17, No. 1, June 2012
By Jan L Jacobowitz & Gayland O. Hethcoat II

I. Introduction

The elusive Roadrunner flashes past Wile E. Coyote as Coyote ceaselessly pursues the bird, undaunted by Roadrunner's trademark "Beep! Beep!" In one episode of the cartoon featuring the two characters, Coyote convinces Roadrunner to reverse course, back through a long pipe. At long last, it appears, Coyote will catch Roadrunner. When Roadrunner emerges from the pipe, though, it is a giant incarnation of itself, dwarfing Coyote in size. Staring at the audience in frustration, Coyote holds up two signs: "Okay, wise guys—you always wanted me to catch him—"; "Now what do I do?"

Coyote and Roadrunner first appeared in 1949, long before the "beeping" of today's technology. The phenomenon of endless pursuit to control that which continues to evolve and elude capture, however, renders these characters a compelling metaphor to describe the legal profession's ongoing attempts to revise its professional code of conduct to incorporate technological and cultural changes.

The law sometimes compels society forward and at other times lags behind a rapidly changing aspect of society. The Internet, for example, has revolutionized communication and created a global community, impacting international relations, commerce, education, and politics—generally every sphere. The law, no less, has tried to "catch up" with these changes. Copyright and privacy are just a couple of areas that are morphing to adjust to a different set of circumstances.

The legal profession itself is no exception. Technology and globalization have fueled the long-running debate whether the practice of law is a profession or business. Laurel Terry's astute observations as to the inception of the term "service providers" as applied to lawyers in international agreements, and Christopher Whelan's description of the revamping of England's approach to the legal profession in the Legal Services Act lend credence to the argument that the practice of law has become, at a minimum, a business that maintains aspirational goals.

Regardless of whether a "winner" may be declared in the profession versus business debate, legal advertising indisputably has grown with the advent of firm websites and social media. Since 1977, when the U.S.

Supreme Court deemed attorney advertising constitutionally protected commercial speech in *Bates v. State Bar of Arizona*, the American Bar Association (ABA) and its state counterparts have debated and enacted various regulations of attorney advertising. The tension between the First Amendment's protection of advertising for the "business" of law and the view of advertising as demeaning to the "profession" of law and exploitive of the public often has driven the regulatory process.

This tension has heightened since the days when most advertising appeared in the Yellow Pages, on benches and billboards, or on the more costly media of radio and television. Now, the Internet and social media provide virtually unlimited avenues for low-cost, far-reaching advertising. The 2010 ABA Legal Technology Survey found that approximately 87% of attorneys in the United States have a website, and 56% of attorneys in private practice have a presence on an online social network as compared to 15% in 2008. The general user statistics reported by social-networking sites are perhaps more compelling: Facebook claims more than 400 million users; LinkedIn, more than 65 million users; and Twitter, more than 105 million users. As these figures suggest, a state bar association attempting to stay abreast of technology to regulate attorneys in its jurisdiction is much like Coyote in pursuit of Roadrunner: Even if the bar association corrals the current technology, the technology is always changing and therefore eluding ultimate capture. The regulators are left to ponder Coyote's query: "Now what do I do?"

***

Even if the proposed rules become law and overcome legal challenge, the process by which the Bar enacted them is one that other bars may want to learn from and avoid. Bureaucratic obfuscation and paternalism have been staple features of this process—at the cost of certainty, time, and resources. A better approach to follow is one where constitutional principles play a prominent role early on in regulators' efforts to respond to the public policy challenges that accompany new innovations in society.

II. Florida: A Case Study in Attorney Advertising Regulation

Florida is a terrific case study of a state bar's striving to navigate the tension between the First Amendment's protection of attorneys' freedom of speech and the legal profession's desire to regulate attorney advertising. A close look at the history of regulation in the state reveals that as Florida has exceeded many other states in the extent to which it has addressed attorney advertising, it has invited major constitutional challenge.

After the *Bates* decision in 1980, the Florida Bar amended its advertising rules to allow advertising in accordance with the Supreme Court's opinion to prohibit fraudulent, deceptive, or misleading advertising. Because computers and the Internet were not yet considerations, the Bar premised its rules on traditional media, such as newspapers, television, and radio. The Florida Board of Governors voted in 1985 to maintain its regulatory jurisdiction over advertising, and the Bar continued to study and amend its advertising rules throughout the 1980s and 1990s.

Fast forward to 1999. That year, the Florida Supreme Court adopted rule 4-7.6, governing "computer accessed-communications," to acknowledge and regulate Internet advertising. Rule 4-7.6 provides that an attorney has to provide some basic information about office location and licensure, but generally deems a website "information upon request." The comment to the rule elaborates:

> The specific regulations that govern computer-accessed communications differ according to the particular variety of communication employed. For example, a lawyer's Internet web site is accessed by the viewer upon the viewer's initiative and, accordingly, the standards governing such communications correspond to the rules applicable to information provided to a prospective client at the prospective client's request.

When the Supreme Court adopted rule 4-7.6 in 1999, the rule was understood by reference to then rule 4-7.9, which defined information upon request as information subject to the general advertising rules with the exception of the prohibitions of statements characterizing the quality of legal services and referring to past results.

As the use of new technology proliferated, the Bar petitioned the Supreme Court in 2005 to delete rule 4-7.9 and exempt "information upon request" from the advertising rules by amendment of rule 4-7.1. The court adopted that proposal and declined to address rule 4-7.6 because the Bar informed the court that a committee was studying proposals for future website regulation. As a result of the deregulation of "information upon request," websites were no longer subject to the general advertising rules; an attorney remained bound only to the specific provisions of rule 4-7.6 and the general prohibition of dishonesty, fraud, deceit, and misrepresentation in rule 4-8.4. Consequently, websites could presumably contain testimonials and references to past results on the theory that the attorney was not reaching out to the client, but rather the client was seeking and requesting the information.

***

In 2008, based upon the recommendation of the Special Committee, the Bar filed a petition with the Supreme Court that offered a compromise. The Bar proposed that the homepage of an attorney's website be governed by the advertising rules but that limited exceptions exist for the rest of the website. Under these exceptions, statements characterizing the quality of legal services, references to past results, and testimonials would be permissible if truthful and, in regard to the latter two exceptions, if accompanied by a disclaimer. The court, however, rejected the Bar's proposal in February of 2009. Rule 4-7.6, therefore, was unchanged; websites remained virtually unregulated. The Bar then filed a motion for clarification in which it emphasized that the court's rejection of the Bar's proposal left websites subject to minimal regulation.

The court granted the Bar's motion for clarification and in November of 2009 issued a revised opinion in which it held that information on attorney websites would be governed by all the advertising rules, including those prohibiting statements containing past results, references to the quality of legal services, and testimonials. The court noted that these types of statements are "extremely troubling" because they have the highest ability to mislead consumers. Moreover, according to the court, these statements have the greatest potential for "further denigrating the justice system and the legal profession in the minds of the public." The court saw no convincing rationale for effectively loosening the rules for a medium that the Bar could not adequately monitor or control.

The flashpoint now gave birth to a firestorm. Only days before the court issued its November 2009 opinion, the Bar reached a settlement with attorney Joel Rothman, who sued to challenge on First Amendment grounds the Bar's application of the advertising rules with respect to his profile on avvo.com, a website that rates attorney services using client testimonials. The stipulation stated that the Bar:

> [W]ill consider a lawyer's online profile to be a communication at the prospective client's request under rule 4-7.1(f) if it appears on a Web site that allows creation of public or private profiles as part of a legal or business directory, or ratings site, and if the lawyer's profile may be reached by searching for or selecting the lawyer's name under circumstances where it is reasonably clear that the user is accessing information about the lawyer. This stipulation is not intended to cover information that would otherwise be prohibited by rules if that information is automatically displayed within the result of a general search inquiry not designed to produce information about the particular advertising lawyer.

Rothman bemoaned his triumph as fleeting because the Supreme Court's November 2009 opinion was to take effect on January 1, 2010. The court's opinion did not go into effect, however, because of an initial moratorium on enforcement and then a stay. More study, additional proposals, and considerable discussion and debate ensued.

As these developments occurred, the economic stakes became enormous. Many Florida law firms with websites would be in violation of the court's November 2009 order if it became effective and enforceable. In fact, eight large law firms that invested considerable funds into their websites filed a sixty-page comment arguing, based upon their First

Amendment rights, against any amendments to the rules that the Bar proposed to effectuate in the November 2009 opinion. The conflict between the economic impact of the court's opinion and the state interest in protecting the public thus caused the discussion to refocus on the First Amendment as the Bar proposed an entirely revamped set of advertising rules. It now appears that perhaps the Bar's efforts have concluded where they might have more properly begun in 2005: with an analysis of the constitutional safeguards that protect attorney advertising.

III. Recent Federal Court Cases Regarding Attorney Advertising

As pressures from the practicing bar have compelled the Florida Bar to reevaluate the constitutionality of its advertising rules, cases in the federal courts have further raised the stakes in regulatory reform. Two federal circuit courts of appeals, the Second and Fifth Circuits, recently revisited the First Amendment jurisprudence governing attorney advertising and overturned several rules in New York and Louisiana, respectively, the latter of which drew heavily from the rules in Florida. Meanwhile, following an opinion by the Eleventh Circuit that focused largely on justiciability issues, a Florida district court held that a number of the Florida Bar's advertising rules are unconstitutionally vague and infringe attorneys' commercial speech rights.

The Second and Fifth Circuit cases—*Alexander v. Cahill* and *Public Citizen v. Louisiana Attorney Disciplinary Board*, respectively—are markedly similar in their holdings and rationales. Among the various rules the courts analyzed, both courts invalidated prohibitions of references to or testimonials about attorneys' services—advertising techniques that, as Joel Rothman's experience demonstrates, have considerable potential in the new media landscape. To this end, both courts applied the test to access the constitutionality of a regulation on commercial speech, which the Supreme Court articulated in *Central Hudson Gas & Electric Corp. v. Public Service Commission of New York*:

> [The regulation] at least must concern lawful activity and not be misleading. Next, we ask whether the asserted governmental interest is substantial. If both inquiries yield positive answers, we must determine whether the regulation directly advances the governmental interest asserted, and whether it is not more extensive than is necessary to serve that interest.

Rejecting arguments proffered by the regulatory bodies that testimonials are "inherently misleading" and therefore not entitled to any constitutional protection, both courts concluded that testimonials could be protected commercial speech under *Central Hudson*. The courts reasoned that testimonials could encompass verifiable facts, which are protected by the First Amendment. As the Fifth Circuit pointed out, "[a] statement that a lawyer has tried 50 cases to a verdict, obtained a $ 1 million settlement, or procured a settlement for 90% of his clients . . . are objective, verifiable facts," as opposed to "statements such as 'he helped me,' 'I received a large settlement,' or 'I'm glad I hired her' . . . ." Consequently, because testimonials were only "potentially misleading," the courts held that they were due some protection, which an outright ban did not afford.

The Second and Fifth Circuits, furthermore, were skeptical toward paternalism as an undercurrent of Louisiana's and New York's respective rules. In its analysis of Louisiana's testimonial rule, the Fifth Circuit explained that "[e]ven if, as [the Louisiana Attorney Discipline Board] argues, the prohibited speech has the potential for fostering unrealistic expectations in consumers, the First Amendment does not tolerate speech restrictions that are based only on a 'fear that people would make bad decisions if given truthful information.'" Ultimately, the court reasoned, the First Amendment reflects a greater concern about suppression of information than poor decision-making.

The Second Circuit expressed a similar rationale in scrutinizing a New York rule that prohibited advertisements that relied on "irrelevant techniques"—that is, "techniques to obtain attention that demonstrate a clear and intentional lack of relevance to the selection of counsel, including the portrayal of lawyers exhibiting characteristics clearly unrelated to legal competence." The court acknowledged that the rule advanced "an interest in keeping attorney advertising factual and relevant" but rejected this interest as sufficiently substantial under Central Hudson. Further, the court distinguished this interest from "an interest in preventing misleading advertising" and noted that no evidence showed that the "irrelevant techniques" prohibited by the rule were, in fact, "misleading and so subject to proscription." The court seemed to appreciate that as media has evolved, so too have notions of what the legal profession is, or should be, in the public's view.

***

The foregoing developments have crystallized the need for state bars to reconsider long-held assumptions about media and consumers as they embark on overhauling their advertising rules to respond to new technology. The threat of litigation over constitutionally questionable rules is real: Public Citizen—a pro-consumer advocacy group that was a party to all the above cases—has showed that it will file suit across the country to object to overreaching regulations of attorney advertising. While the Florida Bar in particular has endeavored to construct a new, comprehensive code of advertising rules, whether those rules themselves could become the target of litigation depends on an important question: Has the Bar given constitutional considerations their due?

IV. An Early Analysis of the Florida Bar's Proposed Advertising Rules

***

The question remains: Do the proposed rules constitutionally suffice? At least facially, it seems that the rules are an improvement. Recognizing that the First Amendment protects accurate statements of facts, proposed rule 4-7.3 allows advertisements that contain references to past results unless such information is not "objectively verifiable" and also allows advertisements that contain testimonials that comply with certain enumerated criteria. On the other hand, this rule deems advertisements with references to past results that are not objectively verifiable "deceptive or inherently misleading advertising" and accordingly subject to proscription. This rule similarly disallows "comparisons of lawyers or statements, words or phrases that characterize a lawyer's or law firm's skills, experience, reputation or record, unless such characterization is objectively verifiable." Additionally, it limits testimonials from qualified individuals (*e.g.*, clients) to comments "on matters such as courtesy, promptness, efficiency, and professional demeanor."

In these instances, the Bar effectively proposes to prohibit or restrict advertisements that address the quality of an attorney's legal services in a way that cannot be factually substantiated. The proposed comments try to illustrate. The comment on past results explains that a statement that, for example, "a lawyer has obtained acquittals in all charges in 4 criminal defense cases" is objectively verifiable and therefore permissible if true. By contrast, "general statements such as 'I have successfully represented clients' or 'I have won numerous appellate cases' may or may not be sufficiently objectively verifiable" because the average prospective client may understand "successful" and "won" in absolute terms whereas an attorney may understand them in more nuanced terms. Such statements thus may mislead the average prospective client to unjustifiably expecting similar results from a previous case. Likewise, the comment on characterization of skills, experience, reputation, or record explains that the statement "our firm is the largest firm in this city that practices exclusively personal injury law" is objectively verifiable and thus permissible if true. But descriptive statements such as "the best," "second to none," or "the finest" are not objectively verifiable and consequently are prohibited because they are "likely" to mislead prospective clients as to the quality of an attorney's services. The rule also has the effect of prohibiting client testimonials about the quality of an attorney's legal abilities, regardless of the client's legal insight or understanding to render such an opinion. Thus, for example, a client could seemingly testify that an attorney provided "prompt and courteous advice," but not that an attorney "was prompt and courteous in providing cutting-edge legal advice."

***

Public Citizen and *Harrell* beg whether the Bar has met its burden of showing why objectively unverifiable references to past results, comparisons, and certain characterizations (which may be in the form of a testimonial) are "deceptive and inherently misleading," and susceptible to prohibition in the proposed rules. Like the Louisiana Bar, the Florida Bar conducted a survey of Floridians' attitude toward attorney advertising, which it included in support of the proposed rules. Although the survey appears to have ambitiously polled the public on many aspects of attorney advertising, the results may offer only limited support for restricting speech not subject to objective verification. For example, about 22% of the respondents thought that advertisements for professional services are misleading; on the other hand, the same percentage thought that such advertisements are accurate. Additionally, more than half of the respondents indicated that their view of the Florida court system did not change after seeing attorney advertising on television and the Internet, while about a quarter of the respondents said that the advertisements negatively affected their view, and about 10% reported an improved view of the system. The vast majority, however, did not rate advertisements as one of the most important factors in deciding upon whom to retain as counsel. By contrast, 61% rated client endorsements as an important attribute to consider when hiring an attorney. A plaintiff challenging the proposed rules, in sum, may assert that the survey results are inconclusive and thus fail to show a real harm to the public, as is required to restrict commercial speech.

Even if the Bar could meet its legal burden with the survey data, it remains to be seen whether the proposed rules' proscription of unsubstantiated, qualitative statements are truly "clear and simple . . . ." The proposed ban on characterizations of an attorney's skills, experience, reputation, or record, for example, explains that "[s]tatements of a character trait or attribute," "[d]escriptive statements that are true and factually verified," and "[a]spirational statements" are permissible; yet descriptive statements that "cannot be objectively verified" and descriptive statements that are misleading are impermissible. Thus, based on the illustrations in the rule, it seems that an attorney could advertise that "I have obtained acquittals in all ten criminal cases that I have taken" and that "My legal philosophy is guided by careful reasoning and aggressive advocacy," but not that "I have obtained acquittals in all ten criminal cases that I have taken because of my careful reasoning and aggressive advocacy."

***

Despite implying that the proposed rules governing qualitative statements would at least survive vagueness attack, *Harrell* does indicate that one other proposed rule, rule 4-7.5, may be unconstitutionally vague and chill protected speech. That rule bans "unduly manipulative or intrusive advertisements," such as the use of "an image, sound, video or dramatization in a manner that is designed to solicit legal employment by appealing to a prospective client's emotions rather than to a rational evaluation of a lawyer's suitability to represent the prospective client." The rule is similar to the prohibitions of manipulative radio or television advertisements in current rules 4-7.2 and 4-7.5, which the *Harrell* district court concluded are impermissibly vague. As the court reasoned, "almost every television advertisement employs visual images or depictions that are designed to influence, and thereby 'manipulate,' the viewer into following a particular course of action, in the most unexceptional sense." Advertising, in other words, by definition aims to "manipulate" or "intrude" a consumer's decision-making; it thus seems implausible that such manipulation or intrusion could be "undue," at least in any way that attorneys could discern and regulators could measure. Therefore, *Harrell* suggests the proposed rule may not withstand a vagueness attack.

Insofar as the "undue manipulation" rule further would restrict the kind of advertising techniques at issue before the Second Circuit in *Alexander*—"wisps of smoke, blue electrical currents, and special effects"—the rule also may constrain attorneys' First Amendment commercial speech rights. As the court explained there, *Central Hudson* demands that regulators put forward more than "an interest in keeping attorney advertising factual and relevant" to limit advertising they may find tasteless, and show through convincing evidence that such advertising actually misleads the public. But, the court opined, meeting the latter requirement may be impossible in an era in which advertisements that push the envelope are the norm and may have the most communicative impact on the public.

In sum, the proposed rules mark an ambitious attempt to regulate, in a constitutional manner, the continually changing means that attorneys use to advertise to the public. To the Bar's credit, the rules are an improvement over the comparatively rigid rules that are still in effect as of this writing, especially when juxtaposed with recent case law. Nevertheless, the foregoing points show that the proposed rules are not foolproof to constitutional challenge. If the Florida Supreme Court adopts the rules as they are, the history of attorney advertising in Florida indicates that such a challenge is likely, if not inevitable.

V. Observations and Conclusion

The Florida Bar has built its reputation as an aggressive regulator of attorney advertising, particularly as it has evolved with new technology. Even with its less restrictive proposed advertising rules, the Bar endeavors to regulate, in great detail, advertising that it determined corrodes the public interest and the veracity of the legal system. Given the scope of this regulatory regime, attorneys are bound to test its constitutionality if the Florida Supreme Court enacts it.

The Bar's proposed rules are not the only template for regulating attorney advertising. The American Bar Association's latest policy position offers an alternative, suggesting that a "less is more" approach is better. In revealing proposals governing attorney "use of technology-based client development tools," the ABA Commission on Ethics 20/20 recently declined to amend or qualify the basic prohibition of false and misleading communications that is cross-referenced in ABA Model Rule of Professional Conduct 7.2." Though the Model Rules were written before these technologies had been invented," explained Commission Co-Chair Jamie Gorelick, "their prohibition of false and misleading communications apply just as well to online advertising and other forms of electronic communications that are used to attract new clients today." The Commission proposed changes only to the comment to rule 7.2, which distinguishes the ABA's policy from more restrictive policies:

Some jurisdictions have had extensive prohibitions against television and other forms of advertising, against advertising going beyond specified facts about a lawyer, or against "undignified" advertising. Television, the Internet, and other forms of electronic communication are now among the most powerful media for getting information to the public, particularly persons of low and moderate income; prohibiting television, Internet, and other forms of electronic advertising, therefore, would impede the flow of information about legal services to many sectors of the public. Limiting the information that may be advertised has a similar effect and assumes that the bar can accurately forecast the kind of information that the public would regard as relevant.

Whichever approach a jurisdiction adopts, the decision-making process that it employs should be guided centrally by the constitutional principles that set the outer bounds of regulatory authority. Although the recent opinions of the Second, Fifth, and Eleventh Circuits reaffirm the validity of the state's interests in protecting the public and the trustworthiness of the legal system by regulating deceptive and misleading advertising, the opinions also highlight the constitutionally slippery slope that emerges when regulations contain restrictions for which there is inadequate evidence of a nexus to harm. Additionally, when these

State interest

restrictions are subject to inconsistent, subjective interpretation, a void for vagueness challenge may arise.

Though the innovations of the day may warrant regulators to exercise the power with which they have been publically entrusted, these principles should not be lost in the bureaucratic fray, as they have been in Florida as regulators delegated tasks to advisory bodies whose policy prescriptions at times clashed. Constitutionally dubious rules create uncertainty for the practicing bar and the public that depends upon its services, and expose regulatory responses to criticisms of overreaction and shortsightedness. In sum, a bar association fares better if it ensures from the onset that its rules are constitutional and possess the flexibility to remain so in the face of evolving technology—considerations that reduce the risk of returning to the drawing board to wonder, "Now what do I do?"

Endnotes omitted (See Jan L. Jacobowitz & Gayland O. Hethcoat II, Endless Pursuit: Capturing Technology at the Intersection of the First Amendment and Attorney Advertising, Journal of Technology Law & Policy Volume 17, No.1 (June 2012) for full article version). Reprinted with permission from the June 2012 edition of the "Journal of Technology Law & Policy" © 2016 Journal of Technology Law & Policy. All rights reserved.

Questions and Comments

1. In the *Endless Pursuit* article, the authors indicate that the legal profession has struggled to keep up with the world of evolving technology and advertising. Why do you think it has been such a challenge for the legal profession to keep up with regulating evolving technology and online advertising? Do you think there is anything the legal profession can do (such as have more CLEs on technology and advertising, for example) to make it easier for the regulatory authorities to keep up with how to regulate online advertising?

2. The rules instituted by the Florida Bar seem to indicate that descriptive statements of the attorney's skill, experience, record, and reputation are not permissible, but aspirational statements, which can be verified, are allowed. The article gives the example that an advertisement that says "I have obtained acquittals in all ten criminal cases that I have taken" and "My legal philosophy is guided by careful reasoning and aggressive advocacy," are okay but "I have obtained acquittals in all ten criminal cases that I have taken because of my careful reasoning and aggressive advocacy" is not okay. Do you see a difference between the messages of these two statements? Does the latter statement seem misleading in anyway? If so, why do you believe it is misleading? Why do you think the Bar saw the latter statement as more misleading?

3. According to *Endless Pursuit*, some jurisdictions have instituted rules limiting lawyers to only advertising very specific facts about the lawyer and prohibiting advertisements on television and similar media. Do you think the state bar's approach—telling lawyers exactly what they can say about themselves—is the most effective? Could this be a violation of First Amendment rights? Are these jurisdictions prohibiting attorneys from advertising through certain media? Do you think these prohibitions help or hurt lawyer advertising?

4. Based on your reading and understanding of the article and the rule Florida has instituted on advertising, do you believe the rules pass constitutional muster? If not, do you think appropriate change can be made? If so, which ones?

FLORIDA BAR V. WENT FOR IT

Supreme Court of the United States (1995)
515 U.S. 618

Justice O'Connor delivered the opinion of the Court.

Rules of the Florida Bar prohibit personal injury lawyers from sending targeted direct-mail solicitations to victims and their relatives for 30 days following an accident or disaster. This case asks us to consider whether such Rules violate the First and Fourteenth Amendments of the Constitution. We hold that in the circumstances presented here, they do not.

In 1989, the Florida Bar (Bar) completed a 2-year study of the effects of lawyer advertising on public opinion. After conducting hearings, commissioning surveys, and reviewing extensive public commentary, the Bar determined that several changes to its advertising rules were in order. In later 1990, the Florida Supreme Court adopted the Bar's proposed amendments with some modifications. *The Florida Bar: Petition to Amend the Rules Regulating the Florida Bar—Advertising Issues,* 571 So. 2d 451 (Fla. 1990). Two of these amendments are at issue in this case. Rule 4-7.4(b)(1) provides that "[a] lawyer shall not send, or knowingly permit to be sent, ... a written communication to a prospective client for the purpose of obtaining professional employment if: (A) the written communication concerns an action for personal injury or wrongful death or otherwise relates to an accident or disaster involving the person to whom the communication is addressed or a relative of that person, unless the accident or disaster occurred more than 30 days prior to the mailing of the communication." Rule 4-7.8(a) states that "[a] lawyer shall not accept referrals from a lawyer referral service unless the service: (1) engages in no communication with the public and in no direct contact with prospective clients in a manner that would violate the Rules of

Professional Conduct if the communication or contact were made by the lawyer." Together, these rules create a brief 30-day blackout period after an accident during which lawyers may not, directly or indirectly, single out accident victims or their relatives in order to solicit their business.

In March 1992, G. Stewart McHenry and his wholly owned lawyer referral service, Went For It, Inc., filed this action for declaratory and injunctive relief in the United States District Court of the Middle District of Florida challenging Rules 4-7.4(b)(1) and 4-7.8 as violative of the First and Fourteenth Amendments to the Constitution. McHenry alleged that he routinely sent targeted solicitations to accident victims or their survivors within 30 days after accidents and that he wished to continue doing so in the future. Went For It, Inc., represented that it wished to contact accident victims or their survivors within 30 days of accidents and to refer potential clients to participating Florida lawyers. In October 1992, McHenry was disbarred for reasons unrelated to this suit, *Florida Bar v. McHenry,* 605 So. 2d 459 (Fla. 1992). Another Florida lawyer, John T. Blakely, was substituted in his stead.

The District Court referred the parties' competing summary judgment motions to a Magistrate Judge, who concluded that the Florida Bar had substantial governmental interests, predicated on a concern for professionalism, both in protecting the personal privacy and tranquility of recent accident victims and their relatives and in ensuring that these individuals do not fall prey to undue influence or overreaching. Citing the Florida Bar's extensive study, the Magistrate Judge found that the Rules directly serve those interests and sweep no further than reasonably necessary. The Magistrate recommended that the District Court grant the Florida Bar's motion for summary judgment on the ground that the Rules pass constitutional muster.

The District Court rejected the Magistrate Judge's report and recommendations and entered summary judgment for the plaintiffs, 808 F. Supp. 1543 (MD Fla. 1992), relying on *Bates v. State Bar of Ariz.,* 433 U.S. 350, 53 L.Ed 2d 810, 97 S. Ct. 2691 (1997), and subsequent cases. The Eleventh Circuit affirmed on similar grounds, *McHenry v. Florida Bar,* 21 F.3d 1038 (1994). The panel noted, in its conclusion that it was "disturbed that *Bates* and its progeny require the decision" that it reached, 21 F.3d at 1045. We granted certiorari, 512 U.S. 1289 (1994), and now reverse.

II

A

Constitutional protection for attorney advertising, and for commercial speech generally, is of recent vintage. Until the mid-1970's, we adhered to the broad rule laid out in *Valentine v. Chrestensen,* 316 U.S. 52, 54, 86 L.

Ed 1262, 62 S. Ct. 920 (1942), that, while the First Amendment guards against government restriction of speech in most contexts, "the Constitution imposes no such restraint on government as respects to purely commercial advertising." In 1976, the Court changed course. In *Virginia Bd. Of Pharmacy v. Virginia Citizens Consumer Council, Inc.,* 425 U.S. 748, 48 L. Ed. 2d 346, 96 S. Ct. 1817, we invalidated a statue statute barring pharmacists from advertising prescription drug prices. At issue was speech that involved the idea that "I will sell you the X prescription drug at the Y price." Id., at 761. Striking the ban as unconstitutional, we rejected the argument that such speech "is so removed from 'any exposition of ideas,' and from 'truth, science, morality, and arts in general, in its diffusion of liberal sentiments on the administration of Government,' that it lacks all protection." Id., at 762 (citations omitted).

***

One year later, however, the Court applied the *Virginia Bd.* principles to invalidate a state rule prohibiting lawyers from advertising in newspapers and other media. In *Bates v. State Bar of Arizona, Supra,* the Court struck a ban on price advertising for what it deemed "routine" legal services: "the uncontested divorce, the simple adoption, the uncontested personal bankruptcy, the change of name, and the like." 433 U.S. at 372. Expressing confidence that legal advertising would only be practicable for such simple, standardized services, the Court rejected the State's proffered justification for regulation.

Nearly two decades of cases have built upon the foundation laid by *Bates.* It is now well established that lawyer advertising is commercial speech and, as such, is accorded a measure of the First Amendment protection. (citations omitted) Such First Amendment protection, of course, is not absolute. We have always been careful to distinguish commercial speech from a speech at the First Amendment's core. "'[C]ommercial speech [enjoys] a limited measure of protection, commensurate with its subordinate position in the scale of First Amendment values,' and is subject to 'modes of regulation that might be impermissible in the realm of noncommercial expression.'" *Board of Trustees of State Univ. of N.Y. v. Fox,* 492 U.S. 469, 477, 106 L. Ed. 2d 388, 109 S. Ct. 3028 (1989), quoting *Ohralik v. Ohio State Bar Assn.,* 436 U.S. 447, 456, 56 L. Ed. 2d 444, 98 S. Ct. 1912 (1978). We have observed that "'[t]o require a party of constitutional protection for commercial and noncommercial speech alike could invite dilution, simply by a level of process, of the force of the Amendment's guarantee with respect to the latter kind of speech.'" 492 U.S. at 481, quoting *Ohralik, supra,* at 456.

Mindful of these concerns, we engage in "intermediate" scrutiny of restrictions on commercial speech, analyzing them under the framework set forth in *Central Hudson Gas & Elec. Corp. v. Public Serv. Comm'n of*

intermediate scrutiny/central Hudson

N.Y., 477 U.S. 557, 65 L. Ed. 2d 341, 100 S. Ct. 2343 (1980). Under *Central Hudson,* the government may freely regulate commercial speech that concerns unlawful activity or is misleading. *Id.* at 563–564. Commercial speech that falls into neither of those categories, like the advertising at issue here, may be regulated if the government satisfies a test consisting of three related prongs: First, the government must assert a substantial interest in support of its regulation; second, the government must demonstrate that the restriction on commercial speech directly and materially advances that interest; and third, the regulation must be "narrowly drawn." *Id.* at 564–565.

B

***

We have little trouble crediting the Bar's interest as substantial. On various occasions we have accepted the proposition that "States have a compelling interest in the practice of professions within their boundaries, and . . . as part of their power to protect the public health, safety, and other valid interests they have broad power to establish standards for licensing practitioners and regulating the practice of professions." *Goldfarb* v. *Virginia State Bar,* 421 U.S. 773, 792, 44 L. Ed. 2d 572, 95 S. Ct. 2004 (1975); see also *Ohralik, supra,* at 460; *Cohen* v. *Hurley,* 366 U.S. 117, 124, 6 L. Ed. 2d 156, 81 S. Ct. 954 (1961). Our precedents also leave no room for doubt that "the protection of potential clients' privacy is a substantial state interest." See *Edenfield, supra,* at 769. In other contexts, we have consistently recognized that "[t]he State's interest in protecting the well-being, tranquility, and privacy of the home is certainly of the highest order in a free and civilized society." *Carey* v. *Brown,* 447 U.S. 455, 471, 65 L. Ed. 2d 263, 100 S. Ct. 2286 (1980). Indeed, we have noted that "a special benefit of the privacy all citizens enjoy within their own walls, which the State may legislate to protect, is an ability to avoid intrusions." *Frisby* v. *Schultz,* 487 U.S. 474, 484–485, 101 L. Ed. 2d 420, 108 S. Ct. 2495 (1988).

Under *Central Hudson's* second prong, the State must demonstrate that the challenged regulation "advances the Government's interest 'in a direct and material way.'" *Rubin* v. *Coors Brewing Co.,* 514 U.S. 476, 487, 131 L. Ed. 2d 532, 115 S. Ct. 1585 (1995), quoting *Edenfield, supra,* at 767. That burden, we have explained, "'is not satisfied by mere speculation or conjecture; rather, a governmental body seeking to sustain a restriction on commercial speech must demonstrate that the harms it recites are real and that its restriction will in fact alleviate them to a material degree.'" 514 U.S. at 487, quoting *Edenfield, supra,* at 770–771.

***

The direct-mail solicitation regulation before us does not suffer from such infirmities. The Florida Bar submitted a 106-page summary of its 2-year study of lawyer advertising and solicitation to the District Court. That summary contains data—both statistical and anecdotal—supporting the Bar's contentions that the Florida public views direct-mail solicitations in the immediate wake of accidents as an intrusion on privacy that reflects poorly upon the profession. As of June 1989, lawyers mailed 700,000 direct solicitations in Florida annually, 40% of which were aimed at accident victims or their survivors. Summary of the Record in No. 74,987 (Fla.) on Petition to Amend the Rules Regulating Lawyer Advertising (hereinafter Summary of Record), App. H, p. 2. A survey of Florida adults commissioned by the Bar indicated that Floridians "have negative feelings about those attorneys who use direct mail advertising." Magid Associates, Attitudes & Opinions Toward Direct Mail Advertising by Attorneys (Dec. 1987), Summary of Record, App. C(4), p. 6. Fifty-four percent of the general population surveyed said that contacting persons concerning accidents or similar events is a violation of privacy. *Id.,* at 7. A random sampling of persons who received direct-mail advertising from lawyers in 1987 revealed that 45% believed that direct-mail solicitation is "designed to take advantage of gullible or unstable people"; 34% found such tactics "annoying or irritating"; 26% found it "an invasion of your privacy"; and 24% reported that it "made you angry." *Ibid.* Significantly, 27% of direct-mail recipients reported that their regard for the legal profession and for the judicial process as a whole was "lower" as a result of receiving the direct mail. *Ibid.*

***

In light of this showing—which respondents at no time refuted, save by the conclusory assertion that the rule lacked "any factual basis," Plaintiffs' Motion for Summary Judgment and Supplementary Memorandum of Law in No. 92-370-Civ. (MD Fla.), p. 5—we conclude that the Bar has satisfied the second prong of the *Central Hudson* test. […] After scouring the record, we are satisfied that the ban on direct-mail solicitation in the immediate aftermath of accidents, unlike the rule at issue in *Edenfield,* targets a concrete, non-speculative harm.

In reaching a contrary conclusion, the Court of Appeals determined that this case was governed squarely by *Shapero* v. *Kentucky Bar Assn.,* 486 U.S. 466, 100 L. Ed. 2d 475, 108 S. Ct. 1916 (1988). Making no mention of the Bar's study, the court concluded that "'a targeted letter [does not] invade the recipient's privacy any more than does a substantively identical letter mailed at large. The invasion, if any, occurs when the lawyer discovers the recipient's legal affairs, not when he confronts the recipient with the discovery.'" 21 F.3d at 1044, quoting *Shapero, supra,* at 476. In many cases, the Court of Appeals explained, "this invasion of privacy will involve no more than reading the newspaper." 21 F.3d at 1044.

***

We find the Court's perfunctory treatment of privacy in *Shapero* to be of little utility in assessing this ban on targeted solicitation of victims in the immediate aftermath of accidents. While it is undoubtedly true that many people find the image of lawyers sifting through accident and police reports in pursuit of prospective clients unpalatable and invasive, this case targets a different kind of intrusion. The Florida Bar has argued, and the record reflects, that a principal purpose of the ban is "protecting the personal privacy and tranquility of [Florida's] citizens from crass commercial intrusion by attorneys upon their personal grief in times of trauma." Brief for Petitioner 8; cf. Summary of Record, App. I(1) (citizen commentary describing outrage at lawyers' timing in sending solicitation letters). The intrusion targeted by the Bar's regulation stems not from the fact that a lawyer has learned about an accident or disaster (as the Court of Appeals notes, in many instances a lawyer need only read the newspaper to glean this information), but from the lawyer's confrontation of victims or relatives with such information, while wounds are still open, in order to solicit their business. In this respect, an untargeted letter mailed to society at large is different in kind from a targeted solicitation; the untargeted letter involves no willful or knowing affront to or invasion of the tranquility of bereaved or injured individuals and simply does not cause the same kind of reputational harm to the profession unearthed by the Florida Bar's study.

Nor do we find *Bolger* v. *Youngs Drug Products Corp.,* 463 U.S. 60, 77 L. Ed. 2d 469, 103 S. Ct. 2875 (1983), dispositive of the issue, despite any superficial resemblance. In *Bolger,* we rejected the Federal Government's paternalistic effort to ban potentially "offensive" and "intrusive" direct-mail advertisements for contraceptives. Minimizing the Government's allegations of harm, we reasoned that "recipients of objectionable mailings . . . may "'effectively avoid further bombardment of their sensibilities simply by averting their eyes."' *Id.,* at 72, quoting *Consolidated Edison Co. of N. Y.* v. *Public Serv. Comm'n of N. Y.,* 447 U.S. 530, 542, 65 L. Ed. 2d 319, 100 S. Ct. 2326 (1980), in turn quoting *Cohen* v. *California,* 403 U.S. 15, 21, 29 L. Ed. 2d 284, 91 S. Ct. 1780 (1971). We found that the "'short, though regular, journey from mail box to trash can . . . is an acceptable burden, at least so far as the Constitution is concerned.'" 463 U.S. at 72 (ellipses in original), quoting *Lamont* v.*Commissioner of Motor Vehicles,* 269 F. Supp. 880, 883 (SDNY), summarily aff'd, 386 F.2d 449 (CA2 1967). Concluding that citizens have at their disposal ample means of averting any substantial injury inhering in the delivery of objectionable contraceptive material, we deemed the State's intercession unnecessary and unduly restrictive.

Here, in contrast, the harm targeted by the Florida Bar cannot be eliminated by a brief journey to the trashcan [sic]. The purpose of the 30-day targeted direct-mail ban is to forestall the outrage and irritation with the state-licensed legal profession that the practice of direct solicitation only days after accidents has engendered. The Bar is concerned not with citizens' "offense" in the abstract, see *post,* at 638-639, but with the demonstrable detrimental effects that such "offense" has on the profession it regulates. See Brief for Petitioner 7, 14, 24, 28. Moreover, the harm posited by the Bar is as much a function of simple receipt of targeted solicitations within days of accidents as it is a function of the letters' contents. Throwing the letter away shortly after opening it may minimize the latter intrusion, but it does little to combat the former. We see no basis in *Bolger,* nor in the other, similar cases cited by the dissent, *post,* at 638–639, for dismissing the Florida Bar's assertions of harm, particularly given the unrefuted empirical and anecdotal basis for the Bar's conclusions.

Passing to *Central Hudson's* third prong, we examine the relationship between the Florida Bar's interests and the means chosen to serve them. See *Board of Trustees of State Univ. of N. Y.* v. *Fox,* 492 U.S. at 480. With respect to this prong, the differences between commercial speech and noncommercial speech are manifest. In *Fox,* we made clear that the "least restrictive means" test has no role in the commercial speech context. *Ibid.* "What our decisions require," instead, "is a 'fit' between the legislature's ends and the means chosen to accomplish those ends," a fit that is not necessarily perfect, but reasonable; that represents not necessarily the single best disposition but one whose scope is 'in proportion to the interest served,' that employs not necessarily the least restrictive means but . . . a means narrowly tailored to achieve the desired objective." *Ibid.* (citations omitted).

***

Respondents levy a great deal of criticism, echoed in the dissent, *post,* at 642–644, at the scope of the Bar's restriction on targeted mail. "By prohibiting written communications to all people, whatever their state of mind," respondents charge, the rule "keeps useful information from those accident victims who are ready, willing and able to utilize a lawyer's advice." Brief for Respondents 14. This criticism may be parsed into two components. First, the rule does not distinguish between victims in terms of the severity of their injuries. According to respondents, the rule is unconstitutionally over inclusive [*sic*] insofar as it bans targeted mailings even to citizens whose injuries or grief are relatively minor. *Id.,* at 15. Second, the rule may prevent citizens from learning about their legal options, particularly at a time when other actors—opposing counsel

3. OBTAINING CLIENTS THROUGH ADVERTISING AND SOLICITATION | 71

and insurance adjusters-may be clamoring for victims' attentions. Any benefit arising from the Bar's regulation, respondents implicitly contend, is outweighed by these costs.

We are not persuaded by respondents' allegations of constitutional infirmity. . . . Unlike respondents, we do not see "numerous and obvious less-burdensome alternatives" to Florida's short temporal ban. *Cincinnati, supra,* at 417, n. 13. The Bar's rule is reasonably well tailored to its stated objective of eliminating targeted mailings whose type and timing are a source of distress to Floridians, distress that has caused many of them to lose respect for the legal profession.

Respondents' second point would have force if the Bar's Rule were not limited to a brief period and if there were not many other ways for injured Floridians to learn about the availability of legal representation during that time. Our lawyer advertising cases have afforded lawyers a great deal of leeway to devise innovative ways to attract new business. Florida permits lawyers to advertise on prime-time television and radio as well as in newspapers and other media. They may rent space on billboards. They may send untargeted letters to the general population, or to discrete segments thereof. There are, of course, pages upon pages devoted to lawyers in the Yellow Pages of Florida telephone directories. These listings are organized alphabetically and by area of specialty. See generally Rule 4-7.2(a), Rules Regulating The Florida Bar ("[A] lawyer may advertise services through public media, such as a telephone directory, legal directory, newspaper or other periodical, billboards and other signs, radio, television, and recorded messages the public may access by dialing a telephone number, or through written communication not involving solicitation as defined in rule 4-7.4"); *The Florida Bar: Petition to Amend the Rules Regulating The Florida Bar—Advertising Issues,* 571 So. 2d at 461. These ample alternative channels for receipt of information about the availability of legal representation during the 30-day period following accidents may explain why, despite the ample evidence, testimony, and commentary submitted by those favoring (as well as opposing) unrestricted direct-mail solicitation, respondents have not pointed to—and we have not independently found—a single example of an individual case in which immediate solicitation helped to avoid, or failure to solicit within 30 days brought about, the harms that concern the dissent, see *post,* at 643. In fact, the record contains considerable empirical survey information suggesting that Floridians have little difficulty finding a lawyer when they need one. See, *e. g.,* Summary of Record, App. C(4), p. 7; *id.,* App. C(5), p. 8. Finding no basis to question the commonsense conclusion that the many alternative channels for communicating necessary information about attorneys are sufficient, we see no defect in Florida's regulation.

III

Speech by professionals obviously has many dimensions. There are circumstances in which we will accord speech by attorneys on public issues and matters of legal representation the strongest protection our Constitution has to offer. See, *e.g.*, *Gentile* v. *State Bar of Nevada*, 501 U.S. 1030, 115 L. Ed. 2d 888, 111 S. Ct. 2720 (1991); *In re Primus*, 436 U.S. 412, 56 L. Ed. 2d 417, 98 S. Ct. 1893 (1978). This case, however, concerns pure commercial advertising, for which we have always reserved a lesser degree of protection under the First Amendment. Particularly because standards and conduct of state-licensed lawyers have traditionally been subject to extensive regulation by the States, it is all the more appropriate that we limit our scrutiny of state regulations to a level commensurate with the "subordinate position" of commercial speech in the scale of First Amendment values. *Fox,* 492 U.S. at 477, quoting *Ohralik,* 436 U.S. at 456.

[handwritten margin note: ✗ this case = pure commercial advertising]

We believe that the Bar's 30-day restriction on targeted direct-mail solicitation of accident victims and their relatives withstands scrutiny under the three-pronged *Central Hudson* test that we have devised for this context. The Bar has substantial interest both in protecting injured Floridians from invasive conduct by lawyers and in preventing the erosion of confidence in the profession that such repeated invasions have engendered. The Bar's proffered study, unrebutted by respondents below, provides evidence indicating that the harms it targets are far from illusory. The palliative devised by the Bar to address these harms is narrow both in scope and in duration. The Constitution, in our view, requires nothing more.

[handwritten margin note: Holding]

[handwritten margin note: Interests]

The judgment of the Court of Appeals, accordingly, is *Reversed.*

Questions and Comments

1. In *Florida Bar v Went For It*, the majority held that the 30-day ban on client solicitation after an accident or disaster was not a violation of the First or Fourteenth Amendment. Do you agree with the decision? Do you think that the state bar had the stronger argument that the direct solicitation was intrusive to the victims of disaster and this was an interest that the bar was permitted to protect?

2. Do you think that there was another method the Florida Bar could have adopted besides the 30-day ban on solicitation? In other words, do you agree with the court that this was the least restrictive means of serving their purpose of protecting these prospective clients? Do you think 30-days is a reasonable time span or do you believe it should be shortened or lengthened?

3. In his dissent in this case, Justice Kennedy argues the Florida Bar's concern that a lawyer's communication to an accident victim within 30 days of the accident would undermine the reputation and dignity of the legal profession, is based on only a select few, and this behavior in itself does not necessarily overstep any boundaries. Do you agree with Kennedy's argument that direct contact with an accident victim within 30 days of the accident does not necessarily undermine the reputation of the legal profession? *See Florida Bar v. Went For It,* 515 U.S. 618, 639 (1995). Do you agree with the majority that this behavior does tend to undermine the reputation of the legal profession? Take into consideration the statistics offered by the majority that many Floridians viewed direct mail solicitation as annoying and intrusive.

safe route

Advertising in the Electronic Age: Maintain a Thriving Practice and a Clean Discipline Record Using Applicable Ethical and Legal Advertising Rules
California Bar Journal (Online), November 2010
By Wendy L. Patrick

For many attorneys, catchy and effective advertising is of paramount importance to a successful legal career. One look at the Google results you will get when you search for a lawyer will display the enormous time and effort expended to persuade potential clients that a particular attorney is a better choice than his or her competition. What ethical rules, however, must you keep in mind when crafting those brilliant ads? And how has the technology revolution impacted attorney advertising?

- what ethical rules surround ads?

General Principles

While attorneys may truthfully advertise routine legal services (*Bates v. State Bar of Arizona* (1977) 433 U.S. 350), such advertising is subject to California Rule of Professional Conduct 1-400 as well as potentially the rules of other states in which you market your services. Given the worldwide reach of your website or postings on social networking sites, disclaimers are critical regarding in which jurisdictions you are licensed to practice law. Lawyers must be careful not to post anything on their social networking page that could arguably constitute the practice of law in jurisdictions in which they are not licensed. Many lawyers include disclaimers to this effect right on their site, specifying the states in which they are licensed.

- jurisdx

California Rule of Professional Conduct 1-400

Rule 1-400 defines both "communication" and "solicitation." A communication for purposes of the rule refers to "any message or offer made by or on behalf of a member," regarding employment, that is directed to a prior, current or potential client. Communications include the use of the attorney's name or firm name, letterhead or business cards, advertisements directed to the general public and unsolicited correspondence (Rule 1-400(A)). A solicitation is defined as any communication regarding legal employment where "a significant motive is pecuniary gain," which is either delivered in person or by telephone, or directed towards someone known by the sender to be represented by counsel in the matter (Rule 1-400(B)). Rule 1-400(C) prohibits making solicitations to prospective clients with whom an attorney has no prior professional or family relationship unless the solicitation is constitutionally protected.

Both communications and solicitations are subject to a list of restrictions, enumerated in Rule 1-400(D). These restrictions prohibit the use of false statements as well as deceptive, confusing or misleading information, or the omission of information necessary to place the message in context (Rule 1-400(D)(1)-(3)). They also require the advertisement to indicate its nature "clearly, expressly or by context," and prohibit any message that is "transmitted in any manner which involves intrusion, coercion, duress, compulsion, intimidation, threats or vexatious or harassing conduct" (Rule 1-400(D)(4)-(5)). Subsection (6) prohibits attorneys from referring to themselves as "certified specialists" unless they actually have the current requisite certificate and list the agency or entity that granted such certification. Rule 1-400(D)(3) states that a communication shall not omit any fact necessary to make the statements non-misleading.

Rule 1-400(E) contains standards regarding communications that are presumptive violations of the rule. The rule currently lists 16 presumptive violations. These include communications that guarantee or predict the outcome of the representation, those that contain a testimonial about or endorsement of an attorney without an express disclaimer explaining that such does not guarantee or predict the outcome of the potential client's case, and those targeting potential clients that the attorney knows or should know cannot exercise reasonable judgment about retaining counsel due to their current physical, emotional or mental condition (Rule 1-400(E)(1)-(3)).

The New Millennium: Attorneys in Cyberspace

Modern lawyers frequently use the Internet to showcase their practices. Flash movies, testimonials and instant attorney profiles are just a click away in cyberspace. Attorney websites have become more common as an increasing number of lawyers are discovering the ease with which they can communicate their services and the potential scope of their brilliant advertisements. So which regulations govern the wording and graphics of internet attorney advertising? The answer is: the same regulations that govern print advertising, and more. In California, State Bar Formal Ethics Opinion 2001-155 addressed the emerging issue of advertising online.

Print rules & regs also to online

Online Advertising: Communication or Solicitation?

Formal Opinion 2001-155 concludes that attorney website information relating to employment availability qualifies as a communication under California Rule 1-400(A), but not as a solicitation under Rule 1-400(B). This is the case even if the website offers an electronic mail option facilitating direct correspondence with the attorney. As a communication, the website information must comply with the restrictions governing permissible content of communications. The applicable regulations govern not only the words on the website, but also the sounds and images.

Regarding website e-mail, in concluding that a website is not a solicitation, Formal Opinion 2001-155 described the "delivered in person or by telephone" requirement as very specific and thus intended as an easy to understand "bright line" test. The opinion further explained that "[a]lthough e-mail communication as part of website technology permits faster responses and more interaction than is possible with other forms [of] written communication, it does not create the risk that the attorney might be able to use her persuasive ability and experience to influence unduly the potential client's thoughtful decision to hire her." Regarding the fact that a computer e-mail uses a "telephone" line, the opinion recognized that "its resemblance to a telephone discussion ends with the mechanism of transmission." The opinion compared e-mail to regular mail in the sense that potential clients are afforded the time to analyze and reflect upon the content of the communication.

Also covered was the fact that a website communication is not directed "to a person known to the sender to be represented by counsel in a matter which is a subject of the communication" as is prohibited by Rule 1-400(B)(2)(b), because it is not specifically directed to anyone, but instead, is available to all who choose to visit the site.

Also see COPRAC Formal Op. 2004-166 regarding a lawyer's communication with a prospective fee-paying client in an Internet chat room for victims of mass disaster. According to the opinion, such communication is not a prohibited solicitation but an improper communication because it is delivered to a prospective client whom the attorney knows may not have the requisite emotional or mental state to make a reasonable judgment about retaining counsel. Note, however, that other states may very well view chat room technology as a "real time" communication that would fall within the definition of a solicitation. See ABA Rule 7.3(a).

The savvy lawyer also will have a disclaimer on his or her site in order to guard against false expectations of creating an attorney-client relationship. Regarding website disclaimers, California Formal Op. no. 2005-168 opined that a lawyer who provides his or her website visitors with a means by which they can communicate with the lawyer on the site may effectively disclaim owing a duty of confidentiality "only if the disclaimer is in sufficiently plain terms to defeat the visitors' reasonable belief that the lawyer is consulting confidentially with the visitor." The opinion goes on to specify that "[s]imply having a visitor agree that an 'attorney-client relationship' or 'confidential relationship' is not formed" would not defeat a visitor's reasonable belief that the information transmitted to the lawyer on his or her site will be kept confidential.

Regarding an unsolicited e-mail that is not in response to an invitation on a website, despite containing what one might otherwise consider confidential information, unsolicited e-mail—just like an unsolicited detailed message on an answering machine—normally will not constitute a confidential communication between lawyer and client. See San Diego County Bar Assn. Legal Ethics Committee Opinion 2006-1 (*http://www.sdcba.org/ethics/ethicsopinion06-1.htm*).

And remember, even though a lawyer is advertising online, he or she is not exempt from complying with Rule 1-400(F), which requires the attorney to retain recordings or copies of their communications for two years to make available upon request to the State Bar of California. As cumbersome as this sounds, Formal Opinion 2001-155 states that this mandate applies "to each page of every version and revision of the website."

The Reach of Your Website

If you maintain a website, you must ask yourself: Who is looking at it and where are they? Even if your website complies with all applicable California regulations, all attorneys must be aware that their site is available to viewers worldwide. Multijurisdictional practice is increasingly common, and legal websites are accessible via a broad range of search engines. Links and "Contact Us" buttons on your home page may expose you to potential clients located in remote jurisdictions. Ethics opinions have begun to address this phenomenon and the problems encountered in attempting to regulate interstate legal business. State Bar Formal Ethics Opinion 2001-155, for example, although its main focus is online advertising, recognizes that an attorney's website may have to comply with the regulations of other jurisdictions and might be construed as the unauthorized practice of law. California Rule of Professional Conduct 1-300(B) states that a lawyer shall not practice law in any jurisdiction where such practice would violate the regulations of legal practice in that jurisdiction.

California Rule of Professional Conduct 1-100 states the purpose and function of the rules, the definitions of terms used throughout the rules, the purpose of the discussion sections following the rules, and the scope of the rules. Rule 1-100(D)(1) defines the geographic scope of the California rules as applied to California lawyers. It states that "these rules shall govern the activities of members in and outside this state, except as members lawfully practicing outside this state may be specifically required by a jurisdiction in which they are practicing to follow rules of professional conduct different from these rules." Regarding out-of-state lawyers, 1-100(D)(2) states that "[t]hese rules shall also govern the activities of lawyers while engaged in the performance of lawyer functions in this state; but nothing contained in these rules shall be deemed to authorize the performance of such functions by such persons in this state except as otherwise permitted by law."

ABA Model Rule of Professional Conduct 8.5 Disciplinary Authority; Choice of Law

Where might you be subject to discipline if you are practicing multijurisdictionally? Rule 8.5 provides in paragraph (a) that a lawyer who is practicing in a certain jurisdiction will be subject to discipline in that jurisdiction, regardless of where his or her conduct occurs. A lawyer not admitted in the specific jurisdiction will nonetheless also be subject to discipline in that jurisdiction if he or she provides or offers to provide legal services within the jurisdiction. The rule even explains that "a lawyer may be subject to the disciplinary authority of both this jurisdiction and another jurisdiction for the same conduct."

Regarding choice of law, paragraph (b) explains that when the jurisdiction is exercising disciplinary authority, it will apply the rules of professional conduct in the following manner:

> "(1) for conduct in connection with a matter pending before a tribunal, the rules of the jurisdiction in which the tribunal sits, unless the rules of the tribunal provide otherwise; and (2) for any other conduct, the rules of the jurisdiction in which the lawyer's conduct occurred, or, if the predominant effect of the conduct is in a different jurisdiction, the rules of that jurisdiction shall be applied to the conduct." The rule does, however, state that "a lawyer shall not be subject to discipline if the lawyer's conduct conforms to the rules of a jurisdiction in which the

lawyer reasonably believes the predominant effect of the lawyer's conduct will occur."

Conclusion

Advertising remains the life source for many modern attorneys. Whether it is done through the Yellow Pages or through cyberspace, it remains a valuable way for lawyers to maintain competition and keep a successful practice. By abiding by the applicable ethical and legal rules, lawyers will be able to have a thriving practice, as well as a spotless disciplinary record

Endnotes omitted (See Wendy L. Patrick, Advertising in the Electronic Age: Maintain a Thriving Practice and a Clean Discipline Record Using Applicable Ethical and Legal Advertising Rules, California Bar Journal (2010) for full article version). Reprinted with permission from the November 2010 edition of the "California Bar Journal" © 2016 The State Bar of California. All rights reserved.

Questions and Comments

1. In this article, the author discusses the rule governing advertising in California. The article discusses the different mediums that attorneys use to advertise their services to the public. Do you agree that the same rule should apply to attorneys who use electronic media—such as videos, pictures, and social media—rather than paper advertisements—such as brochures or letters describing their service?

2. The rule in California is that attorney websites with a direct email feature is considered communication and not solicitation. Do you agree with this conclusion? Consider the ease of a direct email and how a client can communicate personally with the attorney using this feature. Is this really different than a lawyer calling a client on a telephone?

3. As the article indicates, more attorneys are now turning to social media sources, such as Facebook and Twitter, to advertise their services. Are there any postings on social media that a lawyer should absolutely not be able to make? Do you find any merit in the argument that lawyers should not post anything about the practice of law on their personal social media pages? Why or why not?

PROPOSED CALIFORNIA BAR OPINION SEEKS TO CLARIFY ADVERTISING RULES FOR LAWYER BLOGS
Holland and Knight Blog, March 31, 2015
By Peter R. Jarvis, Trisha Rich, & Colin P. Smith

Highlights:

- Commentators and ethics boards have generally agreed that comments by a blogging law firm or lawyer are subject to truthfulness requirements; however, it has been less clear whether or not these blogs amount to lawyer advertising subject to applicable restrictions on such communications. California's proposed opinion is the latest attempt by a state to regulate lawyer blogs.

  Are blogs advertising?

- The State Bar of California Standing Committee on Professional Responsibility and Conduct has issued Proposed Opinion 12-0006 that provides guidelines as to what types of blog content would constitute advertising in California, and would thus be subject to California RPC 1-400.

- Under the proposed opinion, where blogs contain some posts that would arguably constitute advertising appear alongside posts that would not constitute advertising, the continuous nature of the blog publication itself requires a finding that the entire blog is classified as advertising material.

There has been some confusion in recent years regarding how state disciplinary boards would—or should—treat lawyer and law firm blogs. While commentators and ethics boards have generally agreed that comments by a blogging lawyer are subject to truthfulness requirements, it has been less clear whether or not these blogs amount to lawyer advertising subject to applicable restrictions on such communications. While Proposed Opinion 12-0006 is the latest attempt to clarify regulations for lawyer blogs, other states have also faced difficulty on the proper way to address this issue. For instance, in 2013, Virginia's supreme court tackled this issue in *Hunter v. Virginia State Bar*, where it decided that a lawyer's blog that primarily discussed his successful outcomes constituted commercial speech subject to regulation under the state's professional conduct code for lawyers. Florida too has attempted to regulate lawyer blogs, which has resulted in a slew of litigation.

In an attempt to clarify lawyer and law firm blog issues in California, the State Bar of California Standing Committee on Professional Responsibility and Conduct (the "committee") has issued Proposed Opinion 12-0006. The proposed opinion provides guidelines as to what types of blog content would constitute advertising in California, and thus be subject to Rule 1-400 of the Rules of Professional Conduct of the State

Bar of California. The committee notes in the proposed opinion that most blogs are maintained, at least in part, to enhance the authority, credibility and visibility of the author in a particular subject area. However, the committee also notes that just because a blog is economically motivated does not always mean that the blog is "commercial speech" that is subject to state bar advertising regulations.

The proposed opinion gives examples of four types of blogs:

1. [A] stand-alone blog in which the author writes about his successful cases and extols the author, for example, as one of the state's "premier criminal defense lawyers"

2. [A] blog embedded in a law firm's website in which the blog's contents include articles written by firm lawyers on various topics of interest to the firm's clients, and every article has a statement that directs the reader to contact the author for additional information about the subject of a given post

3. [A] blog authored by a solo practitioner relating to the subject area of the author's practice, which consists primarily of short articles, and in some cases posts articles that include language to contact the author with questions, but does not include information about the attorney's practice or qualifications, and does not have any overt statements about the author's availability for professional employment

4. [A] blog authored by an attorney that focuses solely on a non-legal area of interest (the opinion uses the example of a jazz blog), but contains a link to the attorney's professional website

The committee starts its analysis by noting that a post in a lawyer's blog is subject to bar regulation if it is a "communication" or "advertisement" under the applicable rules. To qualify as a "communication," a message has to satisfy a three-part test. The communication must:

1. be made by or on behalf of a California attorney
2. concern the attorney's availability for professional employment
3. be directed to a former, present, or prospective client

The committee concludes that because every blog post will meet the first and third parts of the test, the analysis regarding whether any particular blog post will be a "communication" or an "advertisement" will necessarily turn on whether or not it concerns the attorney's availability for professional employment.

In examining the four examples, the committee concludes that the first three would be subject to the state bar's advertising rules, while the fourth blog likely would not, so long as that blog is not used to solicit business. In making its conclusions, the committee notes that some important factors include:

- **The non-interactive nature of the blog.** Blogs that do not allow comments and discourse among readers are more likely to be advertising material.
- **Inclusion of self-promotional material.** Blogs that include material to promote the author are more likely to be advertising material.
- **Providing contact information.** Blog posts that provide information to contact the author with any questions about the post's topic are more likely to be found to be soliciting business.
- **Encouraging lawyer contact.** Blogs that encourage contact with the lawyer about law-related issues are highly likely to be regarded as subject to bar rules.

The committee also notes that in cases where a blog contains some posts that would arguably constitute advertising alongside posts that would not constitute advertising, the continuous nature of the blog publication itself requires finding that the entire blog is classified as advertising material.

The California Draft Opinion's Problems Include Constitutional Issues

While the committee's attempt to create a bright line rule will ultimately provide clarity to some authors, the draft opinion is not without problems. First, it does little to tackle the thorny constitutional issues that can arise in discussions about attorney advertising. Second, the committee's position that a blog containing some posts that are communications or advertising and some that are not renders the entire blog to be commercial speech is likely to be hotly debated, as many lawyers will see this as too broad. Finally, the committee's proposed opinion does not contemplate a common blog scenario where, instead of containing a link with an attorney's contact information, the blog itself actually contains the attorney's contact information. On this last point, however, it seems likely that the committee would treat the inclusion of actual contact information no differently than the inclusion of a link.

The California Standing Committee on Professional Responsibility and Conduct accepted comments from the public about the proposed opinion through March 23, 2015. Following the review of the submitted comments, the committee will publish its final opinion.

Questions and Comments

1. Do you think the California Bar is taking steps in the right direction to keep the Model Rules for advertising in sync with the current trends in social media by clarifying which content counts as advertising and which does not? Do you believe other states should move in a similar direction?

2. The last paragraph of the article indicates that the proposed California rule is not without flaws as it does not address any of the First Amendment Constitutional issues raised in the past. Do you think this will cause an issue based on the past cases and articles you have reviewed? Is California's rule too broad?

D. DISCUSSION QUESTIONS

1. Think of the different standards and regulations for advertising compared to those for solicitation. While considering the arguments made in *Florida Bar v. Went For It* as to the opinions and general feelings about lawyer solicitation, why do you think the bar tries to regulate solicitation on a more stringent level than advertising?

2. These articles provided multiple examples of state bar associations' attempts to regulate lawyer advertising and lawyers defending their methods of advertising by using the First Amendment to support their argument. Using the knowledge gained through these readings and your understanding of the First Amendment, do you think there will ever be a regulation that invades the protection on commercial speech? If not, do you think the current regulations actually impose any obstruction on commercial speech?

3. As social media and the Internet continue to become a medium for attorney advertising, do you think any changes will need to be made to the Model Rules to encompass the new challenges that arise in advertising on social media? In particular, do you think the state bar associations need to make additional efforts to ensure that Rule 7 is complied with, even when advertising is done on social media?

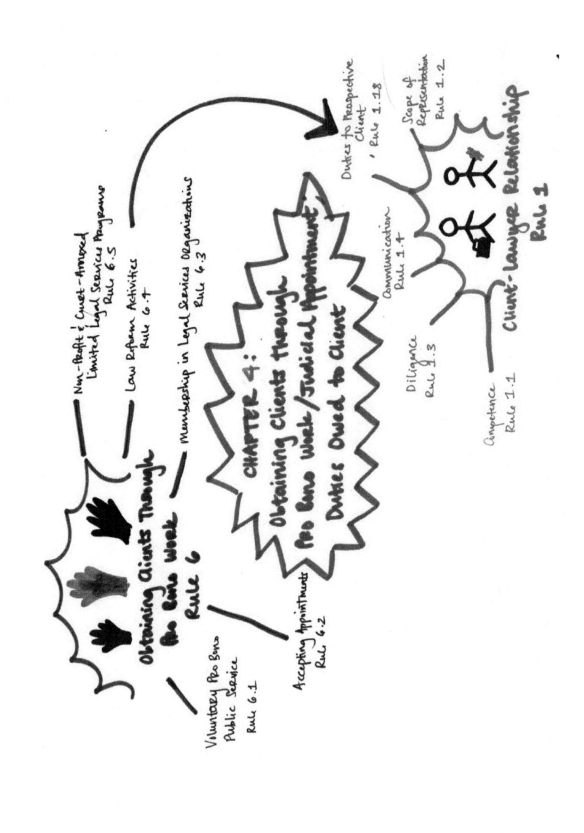

Non-Profit & Court-Annexed
Limited Legal Services Programme
Rule 6.5

Law Reform Activities
Rule 6.7

Membership in Legal Services Organizations
Rule 6.3

Obtaining Clients Through
Pro Bono Work
Rule 6

CHAPTER 4:
Obtaining Clients through
Pro Bono Work / Judicial Appointment
Duties Owed to Client

Voluntary Pro Bono
Public Service
Rule 6.1

Accepting Appointments
Rule 6.2

Duties to Prospective
Client
Rule 1.18

Scope of
Representation
Rule 1.2

Communication
Rule 1.4

Diligence
Rule 1.3

Competence
Rule 1.1

Client-Lawyer Relationship
Rule 1

CHAPTER 4:
OBTAINING CLIENTS THROUGH PRO BONO WORK, JUDICIAL APPOINTMENT, AND OTHER WAYS OF CREATING THE ATTORNEY-CLIENT RELATIONSHIP

A. INTRODUCTION

From an outsider's perspective, one might think lawyers obtain clients by a client showing up in a lawyer's office and, after a brief meeting, the lawyer agrees to represent the client. Although this may be the case in some instances, Rule 6 of the Model Rules of Professional Conduct sets forth the many ways a lawyer may be retained by a client. Once the representation begins, a lawyer is now subject to the multiple duties owed to the client under the Model Rules of Professional Conduct, including Rule 1.

Rule 6.1 sets out the rule for the new hot topic in the legal profession: pro bono work. A lawyer is not required to take part in providing pro bono service, but the rule recommends that lawyers provide at least 50 hours every year. A lawyer can also retain clients through appointments by a tribunal as set out by Rule 6.2. Typically, a lawyer cannot refuse to take on an appointed client, but the rule lists the very limited reasons when such refusal would be appropriate. The rule additionally provides guidelines for a lawyer taking part in legal services organizations, law reform activities affecting a client, and limited legal service programs.

Once a lawyer obtains a client through one of many ways described in Rule 6, the lawyer must exercise her duty to the client with competence and diligence as described by Rules 1.1 and 1.3. The lawyer must also maintain a steady and informative line of communication with her client as set out in Rule 1.4. A continuous communication between the lawyer and the client will often lead to an overall better lawyer-client relationship. The lawyer and client together must set and understand the scope of the lawyer's representation as defined in Rule 1.2, with the lawyer mainly determining the means of representation, while deferring to her client's objectives and requests. Also, note that the lawyer's duties vary depending on whether she is dealing with a current, former, or prospective client (*see* Rule 1.18 re lawyer's duties to a prospective client, Rule 1.7 re duties to current client, and Rule 1.9 re duties to former client).

Pro bono work is merely aspirational and is not currently required by the Model Rules. This chapter will explore the question of whether pro bono work should be done on a volunteer basis or become mandatory for all practicing lawyers. The final part of the chapter looks at real life examples involving the lawyer-client relationship. When reviewing the readings, think about why the Model Rules provide extensive duties for lawyers to follow as part of the lawyer-client relationship. Also, consider steps lawyers can take to ensure that despite a heavy workload, they can adhere to the rules and provide competent and diligent service to their clients.

B. RULES

In preparation, read carefully the following sections of the Model Rules of Professional Conduct along with any relevant comments listed below.

- Rule 6.1: Voluntary Pro Bono Public Service
  - Comments [1], [2], [4]
- Rule 6.2: Accepting Appointments
  - Comments [1], [2], [3]
- Rule 6.3: Membership in Legal Services Organizations
- Rule 6.4: Law Reform Activities Affecting Client Interests
- Rule 6.5: Non-Profit and Court-Annexed Limited Legal Service Programs
  - Comments [1], [2], [3], [4]
- Rule 1.1: Competence
  - Comments [1], [2], [3], [6], [8]
- Rule 1.2: Scope of Representation
  - Comments [2], [3], [7], [9], [10]
- Rule 1.3: Diligence
  - Comments [1], [2], [3]
- Rule 1.4: Communication
  - Comments [1], [3], [4], [5], [6], [7]
- Rule 1.14: Clients with Diminished Capacity
  - Comments [3], [5], [6], [8]
- Rule 1.18: Duties to Prospective Client
  - Comments [1], [2], [3], [4]. [5], [6]

C. Cases and Additional Readings

Pro Bono Publico: Issues and Implications
Loyola University Chicago Law Journal, Vol.26, Issue 1, A4, 61, 1994
By Debra Burke, Reagan McLaurin, James W. Pearce

The lawyer is standing at the gate to Heaven and St. Peter is listening to his sins . . . the list goes on for quite awhile. The lawyer objects and begins to argue his case. He admits all these things, but argues, "Wait, I've done some charity in my life also." St. Peter looks in his book and says, "Yes, I see. Once you gave a dime to a panhandler and once you gave an extra nickel to the shoeshine boy, correct?" The lawyer gets a smug look on his face and replies, "Yes." St. Peter turns to the angel next to him and says, "Give this guy 15 cents and tell him to go to hell."

I. Introduction

***

General complaints concerning attorneys include that attorneys lack caring and compassion, and that the profession fails to promote and police ethical behavior. Another common complaint relates to tasteless advertising by attorneys, a situation that many bar associations are attempting to remedy through regulation. In response to questions about what the profession could do to promote a more positive perception, forty three percent of the people surveyed by the A.B.A. said that providing free legal services to the poor, in other words, providing pro bono services, would improve the public image of the legal profession. Indeed, one attorney characterizes pro bono work as the vaccine which renders him immune to lawyer jokes and claims it provides an opportunity for the profession to counteract the negative, distorted image thrust upon it.

***

B. Constitutional Justifications for Pro Bono Obligations

The Sixth Amendment to the United States Constitution guarantees criminal defendants the right to counsel in federal prosecutions. The right to counsel has been made applicable to the states through the Due Process Clause of the Fourteenth Amendment. Because the right to counsel in criminal cases is fundamental, an attorney must be provided whether or not the accused has an ability to pay for the services to be rendered. While the government must provide an attorney for an indigent defendant, the government does not have a commensurate obligation to pay the attorney to represent the defendant.

No constitutional right to have the assistance of counsel exists in civil cases. In addition, it is still far from settled whether attorneys may be constitutionally required to serve in civil disputes without compensation. In 1892, Congress passed the *In Forma Pauperis* Act (the "Act") to open federal courts to indigent civil plaintiffs. The Act allows indigents to sue without liability for costs and allows judges to assign counsel. In *Mallard v. United States District Court,* the Supreme Court was asked to interpret the Act to determine whether or not federal district courts could compel appointment in civil cases. A bare majority of five held that the use of the word "request" by Congress to describe the authority of courts negated any suggestion that compulsory appointment was intended. By limiting its holding to the statutory interpretation issue, however, the Court did not rule on the constitutionality of compulsory assignments generally. Therefore, while the government's interest in providing counsel under the Sixth Amendment may be compelling and may outweigh the rights of the individual attorney appointed in criminal cases, on balance the government's interest in providing counsel to represent indigents in civil suits may not be as compelling.

C. Practical Justifications for Pro Bono Obligations

***

Another practical consideration centers on the complexity of the legal system. Some lawyers argue that the complexities of today's procedural and substantive laws can be neither understood nor applied effectively by a layperson; therefore, the absence of legal assistance is equivalent to a denial of equal access to justice. While lawyers may not hold the keys to the courthouse doors exclusively, lawyers do help preserve the rights of individuals, primarily because such rights are adjudicated in an adversarial system in which effective representation is of paramount importance. Therefore, lawyers are obligated to assist those who cannot afford legal assistance in gaining access to the legal system, both to vindicate individual rights and to advance the system itself.

An additional rationale for conscripting attorneys into pro bono service lies in the inherent authority of the court itself to order such service as a condition of practice. The state judiciary has the authority to regulate the professional conduct of attorneys. In *In re Hunoval,* an attorney was appointed to represent an indigent defendant charged with a capital offense. The defendant was convicted and the attorney petitioned the state supreme court for a stay of execution so that a writ of certiorari could be filed with the United States Supreme Court. The stay was granted, but the attorney refused to perfect the appeal. The attorney wrote the North Carolina Supreme Court, stating that he was not "an eleemosynary institution" and that some judicial official in the state needed to promise him compensation on a reasonable basis in order for him to continue with the case because he could not "justify working for nothing or at a rate less than that received by a garage mechanic." The court, however, had no problem justifying the attorney's obligation to continue providing legal services in the case or the court's inherent authority to discipline attorneys for unprofessional conduct. The court suspended Mr. Hunoval from the practice of law for a year.

The United States Supreme Court has tentatively suggested that federal courts also might possess inherent authority to compel lawyers to serve; and that attorneys might be under a strong ethical obligation to render assistance as well. Arguably, the officer of the court and related implied consent rationales, coupled with the legal monopoly theory and the recognition of an ethical obligation, afford courts with more than enough inherent authority to compel uncompensated appointment.

D. Ethical Justifications for Pro Bono Obligations

Indeed, the final argument in support of compulsory pro bono rests upon the ethical duty owed by attorneys to perform public service. The Model Rules of Professional Conduct (Model Rules) provide that "[a] lawyer should aspire to render at least (50) hours of pro bono publico legal services per year" and that "[a] lawyer shall not seek to avoid appointment by a tribunal to represent a person except for good cause ... The predecessor to the Model Rules, the Model Code of Professional Responsibility (Model Code), also recognized that lawyers owe a duty to provide legal services to those who cannot afford to pay. Thus, quite apart from other legal foundations, lawyers owe a modem ethical obligation to provide pro bono services. Nevertheless, the ethical duty embraced by both the Model Rules and the Model Code is aspirational in nature. Neither authority mandates pro bono, nor provides disciplinary sanctions for failure to perform pro bono work.

E. Need

The primary justification for requiring pro bono of practitioners, overshadowing the historical, constitutional, practical, and ethical justifications discussed above, is quite simply need. In the mid-1970s, Congress passed the Legal Services Corporation Act which established a central corporation to disburse federal funds for the legal needs of the poor to community-based centers. Unfortunately, in the 1980s the Reagan administration drastically cut funding to the corporation, causing a trickle-down effect upon the community delivery systems. As a result of the Reagan administration's cutbacks, it is now estimated that only fifteen to twenty percent of the civil legal needs of the poor are being met, even though their legal problems often involve questions concerning access to the necessities of life. The bar has responded to this problem by establishing Interest on Lawyer's Trust Account (IOLTA) programs in which the interest paid is used to help fund legal services programs, and by intensifying voluntary pro bono efforts. Although such efforts are certainly commendable, they are currently insufficient to meet the increasing need for legal representation.

In sum, a duty may be owed by the legal profession based upon historical, constitutional, practical, ethical, and need-based justifications. Nevertheless, the exact parameters of that duty, as well as the absoluteness of a court's ability to compel the performance of the duty, may be weaker in cases not implicating Sixth Amendment rights.

III. Opposition to Mandatory Pro Bono

The response by many members of the bar to the question of whether pro bono should be required is: "Why should lawyers in particular be expected to donate their professional services?" These critics argue that even though lawyers are granted a privilege to practice by the State, this does not imply a requirement to assume pro bono obligations, because other practitioners also licensed by the State are not required to donate their services. Furthermore, they assert that it is not as if lawyers hold the keys to the courthouse doors; just as property owners can secure construction permits and build without contractors, litigants can proceed pro se. Finally, opponents of mandatory pro bono express concerns about whether pro bono services infringe upon the duties owed by lawyers to their other clients, and on a more personal level, their own families.

Opponents of mandatory pro bono also raise constitutional concerns about such proposals. For example, opponents argue that even if there are good reasons why attorneys should volunteer their services, state action compelling such service may violate the Equal Protection Clause of the United States Constitution. Singling out attorneys may, however, bear a rational relationship to a legitimate governmental interest. Critics of mandatory pro bono also assert that requiring an unconsenting lawyer to serve may violate the Thirteenth Amendment's prohibition against involuntary servitude. Most courts would reject such a proposition, although the fact that some attorneys would raise that issue may call into question the wisdom of coercive appointments. Critics of mandatory pro bono also argue that uncompensated, compelled service could constitute a taking of property without just compensation or due process in violation of the Fifth and Fourteenth Amendments. While most courts again would probably answer in the negative, that issue is more debatable particularly with respect to compelled appointment in civil cases.

Opponents further argue that mandatory pro bono programs could violate the First Amendment guarantees of freedom of speech and the right of association. Although such rights are recognized with respect to the practice of law, mandatory pro bono probably would not constitute a violation so long as the system of appointment was sufficiently flexible. Finally, critics assert that if an attorney was compelled to represent an indigent client with respect to a criminal matter with which the attorney had no experience, such an action could violate the client's Sixth Amendment right to have the effective assistance of counsel. That attorneys who are required to serve are not immune from malpractice suits should lessen the likelihood of this possibility occurring; yet, it is precisely that lack of immunization which causes many attorneys to fear mandatory pro bono proposals. Aside from these constitutional concerns, there are practical objections to mandatory pro bono proposals. Opponents of these proposals note that poverty law is a specialized field in which the average attorney may not possess sufficient expertise; therefore, the quality of the legal services rendered under a mandatory system may be less than effective. Critics further assert that it is questionable whether or not the implementation of a system of compulsory service is an economically efficient allocation of resources.

***

IV. Pro Bono Today

Currently no federal or state bar association mandates pro bono as a condition of membership. The A.B.A. recently adopted a model rule which urges lawyers to perform fifty or more hours of pro bono work a year, and to devote a substantial majority of that time to the legal needs of the poor. Many state bar associations also have set such aspirational goals. For example, Michigan adopted a voluntary standard of thirty hours or $300 in contributions to non-profit programs which deliver civil legal services to the poor. The Board of Governors of the Washington State Bar passed a resolution which also suggested an annual thirty hour commitment to servicing the unmet civil legal needs of low income people. Some state bar associations encourage attorneys to meet the voluntary quota by offering vouchers for free or reduced admission to continuing legal education seminars. For instance, the State Bar of Texas Board of Directors established a goal of fifty hours and adopted a voluntary reporting requirement. Additionally, the Texas Board established a Pro Bono College to recognize attorneys who perform seventy-five hours or more of eligible pro bono service a year. Thus far, Florida is the only state to adopt a mandatory reporting requirement for the state's aspirational goal of twenty hours of service or a cash contribution of $350 yearly. Under the Florida bar's program, nonresident attorneys are not exempt, while government attorneys who are prohibited from doing pro bono work are exempt.

***

VI. Conclusion

For a variety of reasons, there are rumblings that state bar associations in the future may require its members to perform a set number of hours of pro bono service annually. Although attorneys may owe duties to perform pro bono service for indigent litigants which are historically, constitutionally, practically, and ethically based, as well as need-based, mandating that such service be made available to indigent civil litigants may raise legitimate concerns.

No matter what you call it, the issue is hot—and getting hotter.

Endnotes omitted (See Debra Burke, Regan McLaurin, James Pearce, Pro Bono Publico: Issues and Implications, Loyola University Chicago Law Journal, (1994) for full article version). Reprinted with permission from the Fall 1994 edition of the "Loyola University Chicago Law Journal" © 2016 Loyola University Chicago Law Journal. All rights reserved.

Questions and Comments

1. As the article indicates, there are people on both sides of the argument for making pro bono work mandatory for lawyers. Some argue that mandatory pro bono requirement defeats the purpose of the ethical obligation of pro bono work and the term "mandatory" carries a negative connotation. On the other side, some argue pro bono work should be mandatory based on the enormous difference it makes to clients who cannot afford an attorney. Which side of the argument do you most agree with? Do you think pro bono work should remain an ethical obligation that is purely aspiration or do you believe mandatory pro bono work is necessary?

2. The Model Rules suggest a lawyer doing at least fifty hours of pro bono work every year, although this provision is not mandatory. If pro bono hours become mandatory, do you believe fifty hours per year is a reasonable expectation? Should it be more or less? Consider the workload of many attorneys, including young associates who take on large workloads. What do you think would be best for the profession?

3. How persuasive are the arguments that a mandatory pro bono program would be inefficient and difficult to enforce? Do you agree with the argument that by participating in pro bono work a lawyer is simply donating her services? Is there a better way to approach pro bono work?

Louisiana State Bar Ass'n v. Amberg
Supreme Court of Louisiana (1991)
573 So.2d 1093

***

The three consolidated proceedings present nine specifications of misconduct involving five separate matters.

***

Proceeding 89-B-0421 (The Betz Matter)

This proceeding concerns respondent's handling of a divorce and a malpractice matter for his client, Mrs. Pauline Betz. The first specification of misconduct alleges that respondent neglected to perform the necessary services to complete the divorce matter and to furnish any refund to the client in violation of DR 1-102(A) (lawyer misconduct), DR 6-101(A)(3) (neglect of a legal matter), DR 7-101(A)(2)(3) (zealous representation) and Rule 8.4 (lawyer misconduct), Rule 1.1 (lawyer competency), Rule 1.3 (lawyer diligence), Rule 1.4 (lawyer communication with client) and Rule 1.16 (declining or terminating representation). The second specification of misconduct alleges that respondent neglected to communicate with his client and to perform the necessary services on behalf of her in the malpractice matter in violation of DR 1-102(A), DR 6-101 (A)(3), DR 7-101(A)(2)(3), and Rules 8.4, 1.1, 1.3, and 1.4. The third specification of misconduct alleges that respondent failed to cooperate with the committee in violation of Rule 8.4 (g).

Mrs. Betz testified at the investigatory hearing that she gave respondent $350 to file and secure a divorce from her husband. She also signed an employment contract with respondent to bring a medical malpractice action against the physician who treated her prior to the loss of her unborn child. Although respondent did file suit for divorce in March of 1986, and Mrs. Betz and a witness went to court to secure the divorce, because of an irregularity in service on the husband, the divorce was not completed. Mrs. Betz left town shortly thereafter. She testified that she attempted to reach respondent by phone and by mail and she left her daughter's address in New Orleans with respondent, but she never heard from him and still did not know at the time of the investigatory hearing whether her divorce was complete. In the malpractice matter, Mrs. Betz signed a contingent fee contract on July 17, 1985. Thereafter, she attempted to follow up with respondent regarding the status of her case. Although at times she did reach respondent's secretary, respondent never returned her calls. Finally, Mrs. Betz wrote to the bar association and lodged this complaint.

Respondent testified that he intended to complete the divorce matter but he was unable to contact Mrs. Betz because she moved to Florida and did not leave a forwarding address. When Mrs. Betz did telephone his office it was to find out the status of the malpractice claim and she failed to leave a telephone number or address at which she could be reached. Respondent testified that he presented the malpractice claim to a medical review panel and the claim was dismissed in May of 1987. He could not get in touch with Mrs. Betz to inform her of the panel decision and to determine if she wanted to pursue the claim in court.

We agree with the commissioner that respondent was guilty of failing to communicate with his client and keep her aware of the progress of her cases and failing to use due diligence in handling the matters entrusted to him. Moreover, we agree with the commissioner that respondent failed to cooperate with the committee. Hence, we find that respondent has violated the disciplinary rules and rules of professional conduct set forth in the specifications of misconduct above.

Proceeding 89-B-0422 (The Fleet Finance, Donaldson and Franklin Matters)

This proceeding involved three clients in three separate matters. The first three specifications of misconduct allege that respondent neglected to perform legal services on behalf of each client, neglected to issue a refund of retainers in the Fleet Finance and Donaldson matters and refused to communicate with each client and to furnish the clients with their files in violation of DR 1-102(A) (lawyer misconduct), DR 6-101(A)(3) (neglect of a legal matter), DR 7-101(A)(2)(3) (zealous representation) and Rule 8.4 (lawyer misconduct), Rule 1.1 (lawyer competency), Rule 1.3 (lawyer diligence) and Rule 1.4 (lawyer communication with client) in all three matters and Rule 1.16 (declining or terminating representation) in the Fleet Finance and Franklin matters. The fourth specification of misconduct alleges that respondent refused to cooperate with the committee in all three matters in violation of DR 1-102(A)(1)(4)(5)(6) and Rule 8.4.

The Fleet Finance Matter

In the Fleet Finance matter, Mr. John Adams, the assistant collection manager for Fleet Finance, testified that he hired respondent in a collection matter in March of 1986 and paid him a $265 retainer. After not getting a response and after numerous attempts to contact respondent by phone, in June of 1986, Mr. Adams wrote a letter to the bar association requesting the return of the file and the $265 retainer. At the time of the investigatory hearing, the $265 had not been refunded. Respondent testified that he did not personally do collection work but another attorney in his office would have handled the file. When respondent was contacted by the bar association regarding the initial complaint, he responded by phone that he did not have a client by the name of John Adams and only later in the investigatory process with the committee did he realize that his file was under the name of All State Credit Plan or Credico (Credico having purchased Fleet Finance and All State Credit Plan). According to respondent's letter of December 18, 1989, to the commissioner, the retainer of $265 has been returned to Fleet Finance.

The Donaldson Matter

Mrs. Donaldson testified that in 1983 she met with respondent concerning an injury she incurred while on the premises at Hazel Park School. Mrs. Donaldson paid respondent $110 in February of 1984 and he filed suit against Jefferson Parish instead of the Jefferson Parish School Board and the case was dismissed against the parish on an exception. Mrs. Donaldson testified that she was unaware that her suit had been dismissed and that she called respondent approximately every two or three weeks about the status of her case but he never returned her calls. She filed a complaint with the committee in December of 1986. Respondent testified that he attempted to settle the claim with an attorney for the school board but the attorney refused to settle because he found the claim to be without merit. Respondent admitted that the suit was filed and dismissed on an exception and that he never informed Mrs. Donaldson of the dismissal.

The Franklin Matter

Mrs. Franklin testified that she hired respondent in May of 1984 to handle a malpractice case for her on a contingent fee basis. She filled out an information sheet and told respondent's secretary that she could not pay the $50 consultation fee. She testified that after reviewing her records, respondent told her that he would take the case and obtain a doctor and a nurse to review her medical records and Mrs. Franklin was to call him back in two weeks. She repeatedly called him but could not reach him personally. Some of the calls were answered by his secretary and some by an answering machine. According to Mrs. Franklin's testimony, respondent finally returned her call and told her that proceedings were filed and he was waiting for a medical review panel to be convened. She subsequently called the insurance commissioner's office and found no record of her case being filed. She hired an attorney to pursue a malpractice claim against respondent and to retrieve her file which she testified respondent would not return to her. Mrs. Franklin then wrote a complaint to the bar association. Respondent testified that he would not sign a contract with Mrs. Franklin and take her case until she came up with some advance money to hire medical personnel to review her records. He told Mrs. Franklin to get another lawyer to handle her case. The next thing he knew he was the subject of a potential malpractice claim. Respondent also testified that he told Mrs. Franklin on more than one occasion to pick up her papers and sign a release for them which she never did.

The bar association complained that respondent failed to cooperate with the committee in all three matters. Respondent admitted that he never responded to the committee despite repeated requests and despite his promises to respond. He explained that he was overwhelmed by emotional and personal problems he was experiencing including a divorce, a fire at his office, and an attempt by his ex-wife to commit suicide.

The commissioner found that the cumulative testimony of the witnesses in the three matters had the effect of establishing a neglect and disregard by respondent of his legal responsibilities. The commissioner further concluded that respondent failed to cooperate with the committee. We agree with the commissioner that respondent violated the disciplinary rules and rules of professional conduct in all three matters as set forth in the four specifications of misconduct above.

Discipline

Having found respondent guilty of misconduct, we must consider whether disciplinary action is warranted. The purpose of lawyer disciplinary proceedings is not primarily to punish the lawyer but rather to maintain appropriate standards of professional conduct to safeguard the public, to preserve the integrity of the legal profession and to deter other lawyers from engaging in violations of the Code of Professional Responsibility and the Rules of Professional Conduct. The discipline to be imposed depends upon the seriousness of the offense involved and the facts and circumstances of each case. The court will take aggravating and mitigating circumstances into account. *Louisiana State Bar Association v. Pasquier*, 545 So. 2d 1014 (La. 1989).

We agree with the disciplinary board that respondent is guilty of failing to account for funds in the Sevin matter, neglect of five matters involving five clients, failure to refund advance deposits in three matters and a failure to cooperate with the committee. Respondent is presently suspended from the practice of law for three years for the mishandling of a client's funds, failing to account for the funds and neglect of a legal matter in *Louisiana State Bar Association v. Amberg*, 553 So. 2d 448 (La. 1989). Link to the text of the note Respondent's conduct in the five matters resulting in the present disciplinary violations occurred from about 1983 until 1987, approximately the same time or shortly after the conduct resulting in the prior disciplinary action of respondent. Thus, there appears to be a pattern of general neglect of respondent's professional matters during this period of time.

Respondent explained that during the time that the professional misconduct occurred he was overwhelmed by personal problems including a divorce, the loss of his house in the divorce proceedings, and an attempt by his ex-wife to commit suicide. During this period of time he was forced out of his law office in Harahan and then moved to an office in Kenner which burned down forcing him to move in with another attorney. Many of his files were destroyed or misplaced as a result of the fire. He stated that he was too wrapped up in his own personal affairs to reply to the calls of his clients or to the bar association communications, and, in any event, he knew that he would be appearing before the committee and could explain or reply to the complaints at that time. A totality of the circumstances reflects a pattern of general neglect of respondent's legal matters during the period of time when his personal affairs were in disarray.

We find that respondent's cumulative misconduct in the five matters to be of sufficient gravity to warrant disciplinary action. If respondent's misconduct had been considered at the time of the prior disciplinary proceeding, we do not believe that disbarment would have been warranted. Nor do we find that respondent should be disbarred at this time. Rather, we consider a further suspension from the practice of law for a period of six months to be the appropriate penalty. Additionally, respondent must furnish proof that the outstanding medical bills ($2,068.43) in the Sevin matter have been paid and that he has returned $350 to Mrs. Betz, $265 to Fleet Finance and $110 to Mrs. Donaldson before he will be considered for reinstatement.

Decree

It is ordered, adjudged and decreed that Joseph B. Amberg, Jr. be suspended from the practice of law in Louisiana for six months to run consecutively with the three year suspension presently being served by him in the matter of *Louisiana State Bar Association v. Joseph B. Amberg, Jr.*, 553 So. 2d 448 (La. 1990). Additionally, respondent must furnish proof that the outstanding medical bills ($2,068.43), in the Sevin matter have been paid and that he has returned $350 to Mrs. Betz, $265 to Fleet Finance and $110 to Mrs. Donaldson before he will be considered for reinstatement. Respondent is to bear all costs of these proceedings.

Questions and Comments

1. The lawyer in this case violated multiple rules when working with several clients. Some of the violations include the rules explicitly dealing with the lawyer-client relationship, such as competence (Rule 1.1), diligence (Rule 1.3), and communication (Rule 1.4). The court imposed a penalty of six months suspension against the respondent for violating these rules. Do you think this is a justified penalty for the lawyer's repeated

violations? Consider the nature of these violations and how these rules specifically protect the client.

2. Rule 1.3 sets out the rule for diligence. The rule simply states, "A lawyer shall act with reasonable diligence and promptness in representing a client." Comment 2 to this rule emphasizes how a lawyer's workload should be controlled to provide diligence to each client. Based on what you know about the legal profession and the heavy workload, do you think a single violation of this rule would be grounds for discipline? If not, how many times of failing to act diligently should be considered "too many?"

3. One of the respondent's consistent violations in this case is a failure to effectively communicate with his clients and a failure to communicate to the Louisiana Bar. Why do you think communication with a client, as set out in Model Rule 1.4, is so important to maintaining a good relationship with a client? If the respondent actually communicated with the bar and his clients, do you think this case would have had a different outcome?

BE SURE CLIENTS KNOW THE SCOPE OF REPRESENTATION
Texas Lawyer (Online), October 8, 2001
By Jim McCormack

After our last meeting, I wasn't certain if my client would come back. The client had talked a lot about fiduciary duty and uberima fides—which she claimed meant the same thing. I had played along, hoping that she would get off of that kick and onto something I understood—like what she wanted from me in simple English. I should have known better.

Client: Now that I understand our relationship, we need an agreement in writing.

Me: Sure, I have a standard contract here. Just sign at the bottom and we're on our way.

Client: Don't we need to define the scope of representation first?

Me: The scope? Well, sure. I thought you said it was a civil matter, a commercial dispute or something, something you needed a lawyer for. This is my all-purpose contract; it has the fees and everything I need all spelled out.

Client: Yes, but what about me? This is a big step. What does this mean to me? I mean, I need more than this.

Me: Like what?

Client: Could we define just what we are doing here first? I want this to be special. Defining the scope would really help me.

Me: Why don't you tell me what you want me to do?

Fade out.

Mutual Understanding

For lawyers and clients, defining the scope of representation is like the old saying attributed to carpenters: Measure twice, cut once. The lawyer and client need to understand what the lawyer is hired to do and what the client's expectations are. The two go hand-in-hand.

We, lawyers, have a disciplinary rule that talks about the scope and objectives of representation. Rule 1.02 says that, with exceptions, an attorney must abide by a client's wishes with respect to the following:

- the objectives and general methods of representation;
- whether to accept an offer of settlement of a matter (except as otherwise authorized by law); and
- the plea to be entered, whether to waive a jury trial, and whether the client will testify—all in criminal cases and after consultation with the attorney.

But Rule 1.02 also says that a lawyer may limit the scope, objectives and general methods of the representation if a client consents after consultation.

For our hypothetical client above, the lawyer needs to know what she wants and what she expects. Then she should decide what the legitimate scope and objectives of representation can be. A good contract will define the general subject matter of the representation and make clear—to the client and the attorney—any limitations on the scope and objectives at the outset. For example, the client wishes representation in a commercial dispute. What kind of commercial dispute? Who are the parties? What is the probable venue? What are the client's goals? How far is the attorney willing to reasonably pursue those goals? How far is the client willing to reasonably or unreasonably pursue those goals? What cost is likely to be associated with pursuing those goals?

This reminds me of a story: I once knew an accomplished family attorney in Austin who was a specialist in motions to modify child custody. A typical prospective client would visit my friend and regale him with tales of his or her ex-spouse and various alleged Satan-worshipping, drug-using, sexually abusing activities to which the client's children were subjected daily while in the ex-spouse's custody. In other words, the ex was unfit.

The lawyer listened patiently and said if these allegations were true, custody modification was possible, and then said the cost would be about $20,000—this was a few years back—and he needed a hefty retainer to begin work. After mulling over the cost, many prospective clients decided that a few of the aforementioned character flaws alone shouldn't deprive an ex-spouse of the solace and comfort of continued custody. The lawyer defined the scope—and the cost—with a single number.

The Limits

My point is that helping a client crystallize what the representation is all about—from the beginning—helps the client understand the limits of what the lawyer can and will do. Sophisticated clients who hire lawyers regularly usually understand that the lawyer is hired for X project only or X area of expertise only.

Less sophisticated clients look to us to help them decide what they want us to do. To someone who never has hired an attorney before, a lawyer is a man or woman for all seasons—and for potentially all cases and problems. We better make it clear from the start that we didn't sign on to represent our clients against all life's challenges.

One little phrase in a contract can help, something like: I have been hired to represent John Smith in the matter of X, Y and Z only. I have not been hired for any other case, matter or purpose, unless a separate written agreement for that case, matter or purpose is signed by me. Or: I have been hired only to represent John Smith through the trial or settlement of X, Y and Z claim, but have not been hired to handle the appeal, if any, of these matters. In the event an appeal is filed by any party, John Smith will need to hire an attorney who handles appeals to represent Mr. Smith in those appeals.

But be careful not to hide your limitations in the fine print. The client needs to be pointed specifically to any limits on the scope of your services.

Sounds overly simple? To the sophisticated client, maybe. But even sophisticated clients have been known to misunderstand the scope and limits of an attorney's representation. The "I thought you were taking care of that for me" phone call from client to attorney is one that not a few lawyers have received over the years.

Reprinted with permission from the October 2001 edition of the "Texas Lawyer" © 2016 ALM Media Properties, LLC. All rights reserved.

Questions and Comments

1. This article emphasizes how clients will often look to their lawyer for both legal services and personal support during the time they are facing legal challenges. What steps can a lawyer take in order to ensure this misunderstanding of the lawyer's scope of representation does not occur? Should a lawyer have a standard agreement setting out the scope of representation or do you think the scope should vary on a case-by-case basis depending on each specific client's expectation?

2. Rule 1.2 puts the majority of the power in the client's hands to set forth the scope of representation. The rule specifies when the client's decision should be adhered to. The lawyer has the narrow role of being able to limit the scope of representation. Why do you think the rule gives

so much deference to the client? Are there situations in which the lawyer should absolutely be able to determine the scope of representation?

3. The article discusses the possible difference between sophisticated clients who have dealt with lawyers in the past and unsophisticated clients who have never even spoken to a lawyer before. Do you think the level of a lawyer's control over the scope of representation should be different for the unsophisticated client? The article notes that unsophisticated clients may look to their lawyer for all purposes outside of the scope of representation. How can a lawyer ensure that she does not go too far and take charge of an unsophisticated client's case? How would you go about limiting the scope of representation for these or any other clients?

ATTY. GRIEV. COMM'N V. LEE
Court of Appeals of Maryland (2006)
890 A.2d 273

Opinion by Greene, J.

The Attorney Grievance Commission of Maryland, the petitioner, by Bar Counsel acting pursuant to Maryland Rule 16-751, filed a Petition For Disciplinary Or Remedial Action against Norman Joseph Lee, III, the respondent. The petition charged that respondent violated Rules 1.3 (Diligence), 1.4 (Communication), and 1.16 (Declining or terminating representation) of the Maryland Rules of Professional Conduct (MRPC), as adopted by Rule 16-812.

We referred the case, pursuant to Rule 16-752 (a), to the Honorable Lawrence R. Daniels, of the Circuit Court for Baltimore County, to conduct a hearing and to make Findings of Fact and Conclusions of Law. When respondent did not answer the petition, an order of default was entered against him on April 14, 2005. Pursuant to the Order of Default, a hearing was set for June 30, 2005, at 9:30 a.m. Prior to the June hearing, respondent filed a motion to vacate the Order of Default and an answer to the Petition for Disciplinary Action. Petitioner responded to the motion to vacate and respondent's answer to the Petition for Disciplinary or Remedial Action, requesting that the court deny the motion to vacate the Order of Default and permit the case to proceed, as scheduled, upon the default order on June 30, 2005. The court agreed with petitioner and denied respondent's motion. At the hearing on June 30, 2005, respondent argued that the court should vacate the order of default. He conceded that there is no court record acknowledging the timely receipt of his response to the petition for disciplinary action. Respondent contended, however, that his office records reveal that he sent the court a timely response. Notwithstanding the absence of a timely response, respondent reargued that the court should vacate the Order of Default. The hearing court responded by pointing out that any motion to vacate should have been filed within thirty days after entry of the Order of Default and was not, and that respondent did not, pursuant to Rule 2-613(d), "state the reasons for the failure to plead and the legal and factual basis for the defense of the claim." The hearing court further stated:

Again, I just interrupt because I want the record to be clear that though Mr. Lee did in fact enter his motion to set aside the default or vacate the default, he did not give a reason why there was failure to plead, he did not offer any legal or factual basis.

In addition, pursuant to Rule 16-757 (c), the court found facts by the clear and convincing standard and concluded that respondent violated Rule 1.3 of the Maryland Rules of Professional Conduct.

The record shows that Norman Joseph Lee, III, was admitted to the Maryland Bar on March 31, 1981. Bobby D. Coleman, complainant, retained respondent to seek post-conviction relief in the Circuit Court for Washington County. The retainer agreement was dated July 8, 2002, and signed by respondent and witnessed by his secretary. Respondent accepted a fee of $ 3,500, paid by Mr. Coleman's mother on behalf of her son, as a retainer for services to be rendered in the matter. Thereafter, on August 2, 2002, Mr. Lee entered his appearance in the Circuit Court for Washington County on behalf of Mr. Coleman. In Mr. Coleman's letter to the Attorney Grievance Commission, dated July 10, 2003, he complained that, "as yet he had never met [Mr. Lee] nor had the ability to discuss the job I'm hiring him to perform." Following Mr. Coleman's complaint to the Commission, Mr. Lee scheduled an appointment to interview Mr. Coleman at the prison facility and met with Mr. Coleman on August 23, 2003. This meeting occurred more than a year after Mr. Coleman retained respondent to represent him.

[handwritten note in margin: paid 3,500 & took 1 yr to meet w/ Lawyer]

Specifically, the hearing court found that it took respondent almost one year after he received payment of the retainer to visit Mr. Coleman, who was then incarcerated in Washington County. Further the hearing court noted, from the evidence, that "there's no indication that [respondent] either took action on Mr. Coleman's behalf to file some sort of pleading or indicate that there was no basis to do so and make an accounting to Mr. Coleman of the monies that had been spent out of the retainer and then refund anything that remained if there was a remainder." Based upon these findings of fact, the hearing court concluded that respondent displayed a lack of diligence in violation of Rule 1.3 of the MRPC.

[handwritten note in margin: lack of diligence]

With respect to the violation of Rule 1.4, the hearing court found that respondent attempted to keep in contact with his client and his client's mother. The hearing court made no other specific findings, even though the testimony and documentary evidence in the record shows that Mr. Coleman wrote, approximately in July or early August 2002, to Mr. Lee and had requested that his attorney communicate about any new developments or discoveries in his case and asked Mr. Lee to advise as to what the chances were of having his "conviction reversed in the post-conviction proceeding." In addition, Mr. Coleman pointed out that "he had been experiencing difficulties getting the respondent's phone number on the prison's institutional phone list and that's why he did not call him personally" (Paragraph 10. Petition For Disciplinary Action). This additional information was offered, apparently, to explain why Mr. Coleman's mother was acting as a conduit for her son with regard to specific questions to Mr. Lee about the progress on her son's case. On August 21, 2002, she wrote to respondent and inquired "as a matter of a status report on any research and legal preparation conducted for Bobby's case." Within her letter she made reference to her own legal research in New York, and inquired whether her son's case involved issues relating to wrongful conviction, mistaken eye-witness testimony, admissibility of any prior crimes, search and seizure violations, and evidence disclosure and warrants. Mr. Coleman's mother also "questioned respondent about the pre-sentence report containing false or misleading statements that it would have otherwise impacted the sentence imposed as well as whether or not Maryland Rule 4-342 could apply to her son's case." Moreover, she wanted to know whether "Bobby's case [was] effected [sic] by the recent Supreme Court rulings applying Apprendi?" Further, she questioned how much time she could expect Mr. Lee to take in performing research and copied the letter to Mr. Coleman.

Approximately 2 months later, by letter dated October 16, 2002, Mr. Lee wrote to Mr. Coleman and apologized to Mr. Coleman and his mother "for the delay in the prosecution of your case." Additionally, "he acknowledged that Mrs. Coleman's August 21 letter referenced four cases but that he had 'not had the benefit of reviewing these cases but [was] in the process of reviewing same and [would] advise her accordingly." There is no evidence in the record, however, that Mr. Lee ever followed up on his promise either to review the cases referenced or to give any advice. Averment number 12 of the petition for disciplinary action was that, "other than the meeting [with Mr. Coleman at the prison facility in August 2003, Mr. Lee] performed no substantive legal services on behalf of Bobby D. Coleman."

In finding no violation of Rule 1.4, the hearing court observed that

the court notes that the client is Mr. Coleman and not his mother. I don't believe there is any requirement under the Canons of Professional Ethics that the lawyer keep in touch with the person who paid the fee. It's the client who is and should be the centerpiece of all the attorney's efforts.

Petitioner takes exception to the hearing court's failure to find a violation of Rule 1.4. The respondent did not file exceptions either to the hearing court's findings of facts or conclusions of law. Because exceptions were filed by Bar Counsel, we determine whether the findings of fact have been proven in accordance with the applicable burdens of proof. See Rules 16-759 (b) (2) (B) and 16-757 (b).

In the present case, the hearing court entered a default order. The court should have treated the averments as established pursuant to Rules 16-754(c) and 2-323(e). Rule 16-754(c) permits the court to treat failure to file a timely answer as a default, and Rule 2-323(e) permits the court to treat the averments in a pleading as admitted unless denied. Because the averments were not denied, we treat them as admitted.

Further, in the exercise of our supervision over attorney disciplinary proceedings, we conduct an independent review of the record, accepting the hearing judge's findings of fact unless clearly erroneous. See *Attorney Grievance Comm'n v. Garfield*, 369 Md. 85, 97, 797 A.2d 757, 763-64 (2002). We review de novo the hearing judge's conclusions of law. See Rule 16-759(b)(1); *Attorney Grievance Comm'n v. McLaughlin*, 372 Md. 467, 493, 813 A.2d 1145, 1160 (2002).

The hearing judge concluded that there was no violation of Rule 1.4 because "there is [no] requirement under the [MRPC] that the lawyer keep in touch with the person who paid the fee." We disagree as to the judge's factual findings and conclusion of law as to Rule 1.4. After an unnecessarily protracted evidentiary hearing, it appears that the court eventually adopted the averments contained in the petition for disciplinary action as established facts. The hearing judge, however, did not consider those facts in making his conclusion of law with respect to Rule 1.4. The unchallenged facts, which the hearing court apparently overlooked, are that after execution of the retainer agreement and payment of the fee, Mr. Coleman notified respondent that he (Mr. Coleman) "had been experiencing difficulties getting the respondent's phone number on the prison's institutional phone list and that's why he did not call him personally." Previously, respondent replied to Mr. Coleman about inquires made by Mr. Coleman's mother. In addition, respondent acknowledged, in his letter, dated October 16, 2002, that he had received communication from Mrs. Coleman concerning four cases she had researched. That letter was copied to Mr. Coleman's mother, as well as other correspondence. By letter, dated August 21, 2002, Mrs. Coleman requested a status report on legal research and legal preparation conducted for her son's case. She raised specific questions to Mr. Lee within her letter and copied the letter to her son. Respondent acknowledged receiving the August 21, 2002, letter and, in his delayed response, promised to follow up with an answer. There is no evidence in the record that as of the date of the hearing in this matter—June 30, 2005—respondent ever communicated a response to the inquires made by Mrs. Coleman on behalf of her son other than his letter dated October 16, 2002.

Certainly, if respondent did not wish to communicate with Mrs. Coleman that was his prerogative. There is no evidence that Mr. Lee ever told Mr. Coleman that he would not communicate with Mrs. Coleman regarding her son's case. In accordance with the MRPC, respondent's obligation is to keep Mr. Coleman reasonably informed about the status of his case and to promptly comply with his reasonable requests for information. Thus, the focus is on what, if anything, Mr. Lee did to carry out this obligation under the circumstances of this case.

Respondent did not meet with his client until almost one year after payment of the fee. He acknowledged receipt of the trial transcripts of Mr. Coleman's criminal case, copied them, and returned the originals to the client. After execution of the retainer agreement and payment of the retainer fee, all communication on the part of Mr. Lee essentially stopped. There were inquiries from Mrs. Coleman on behalf of her son, but the only response from Mr. Lee was a delayed response that was not very meaningful. If Mr. Lee did not intend to communicate with his client through his mother, he could have explained that to the client. Having failed to do so, the course of dealings with Mr. Coleman suggested that Mr. Lee would respond to Mr. Coleman through his mother. Therefore, we sustain the petitioner's exceptions and conclude that violation of Rule 1.4 was proven by clear and convincing evidence.

With respect to the Rule 1.3 violation, neither the petitioner nor the respondent has taken exceptions to the hearing court's findings of fact and conclusions of law. As to the appropriate sanction petitioner recommends a reprimand, while respondent recommends that we dismiss the disciplinary proceedings. We agree with petitioner that a reprimand is the appropriate sanction. All that is required of respondent is that he act with reasonable diligence and promptness in representing his client. Under the circumstances of this case, respondent's representation of his client was unreasonable in that for almost one year respondent neglected his client's legal matter. The hearing judge found no mitigating factors and, likewise, we find no mitigating factors. *See Attorney Grievance Comm'n v. Tolar*, 357 Md. 569, 585, 745 A.2d 1045, 1054 (2000) (holding that a public reprimand would "serve the purpose of protecting the public just as well as a short suspension"). Consistent with our view that Mr. Lee's violation of Rule 1.4 warrants a public reprimand, we conclude that his violation of Rule 1.3 also warrants a public reprimand. Our goal is not to punish the respondent, but to impose a sanction that will deter other attorneys from engaging in similar misconduct. *See Attorney Grievance Comm'n v. Mooney*, 359 Md. 56, 96, 753 A.2d 17, 38 (2000) (citing *Attorney Grievance Comm'n v. Ober*, 350 Md. 616, 631-32, 714 A.2d 856, 864 (1998) (citations omitted)). In this case, a reprimand will serve the purpose of protecting the public. It serves as notice to the respondent and other attorneys that this Court considers an attorney's lack of diligence and lack of communication with his or her client, serious matters.

Because the fee paid to Mr. Coleman has not been returned and Mr. Lee remains counsel of record, it appears that he intends to continue his representation of Mr. Coleman. This opinion is limited to the allegations of misconduct which predated the petition for disciplinary action filed in this case. If respondent continues his representation in this case and wishes to avoid any further disciplinary action, he is duty bound to follow the MRPC.

 # public reprimand

Questions and Comments

1. In this case, Mr. Lee failed to diligently perform his duties to the client and to effectively communicate with his client and his mother who was communicating on behalf of her incarcerated son. This case demonstrates a violation of the Model Rules in a criminal case. Can any argument be made that adhering to the rules of diligence and effective communication is even more critical in a criminal than in a civil case, especially if the client is incarcerated?

2. Mr. Lee failed to not only communicate with his client, but he also did not communicate effectively with the client's mother, who sent him multiple requests and inquiries on behalf of her son. Although Mr. Lee's obligation was to his client, he failed to explain to his client that he would only communicate with him and not his mother. Do you think Mr. Lee's communication with Mr. Coleman would have been better if he was able to explain and ensure that Mrs. Coleman understood his lawyerly duty was to communicate solely with her son?

3. It appears that Mr. Lee's failure to communicate with his client and his client's mother was intentional as he received multiple requests to communicate, but each time failed to respond to the requests and did not meet his client until after a year of representation. However, in an instance where the failure to communicate is not intentional, would the rule violation involving a failure to communicate effectively be possibly excused for appointed criminal defense counsel who may have hundreds of clients at a time? Consider a criminal defense lawyer with a handful of homicide cases all going to trial around the same time. If during that time, the lawyer fails to communicate with a client who is charged with petty theft within the proper amount of time, do you think the behavior would still rise to a violation of Rule 1.4?

D. Discussion Questions

1. Rule 1.1 requires a lawyer to provide competent representation to her client. Comment 2 explains that a newly admitted lawyer is considered just as competent as a lawyer who has been practicing for several years. As a future newly admitted attorney, do you agree with this standard? Do you think the rule rightfully holds a new lawyer to the same standard as a lawyer who has been practicing for twenty years? Do you think this standard should be dependent upon the subject matter of the legal issue (i.e. very complex issue compared to a relatively simple issue)?

2. Rule 6.2 governs accepting appointments from a tribunal. The rule makes it clear that a lawyer may only avoid these appointments for "good cause." One of the examples of "good cause" is that the client or cause is so "repugnant" to the lawyer that the lawyer-client relationship may suffer as a consequence. Can you think of an example of when a client or cause would be so repugnant to the lawyer that the lawyer must refuse the appointment? Consider criminal defense lawyers who are appointed to represent people who have committed heinous crimes. Do you think this "good cause" rule should apply to these lawyers?

3. The readings provide examples of lawyers who have violated the rules governing competence, diligence, and, communication. Consider the increasing availability of technology to the legal community. Many lawyers have cell phones allowing them to send emails without having to log on to their computer. Legal research is available on the Internet in multiple forms and many lawyers have phones, iPads, and tablets with Internet access readily available. Do you think the increase in technology should make violations of these rules less excusable?

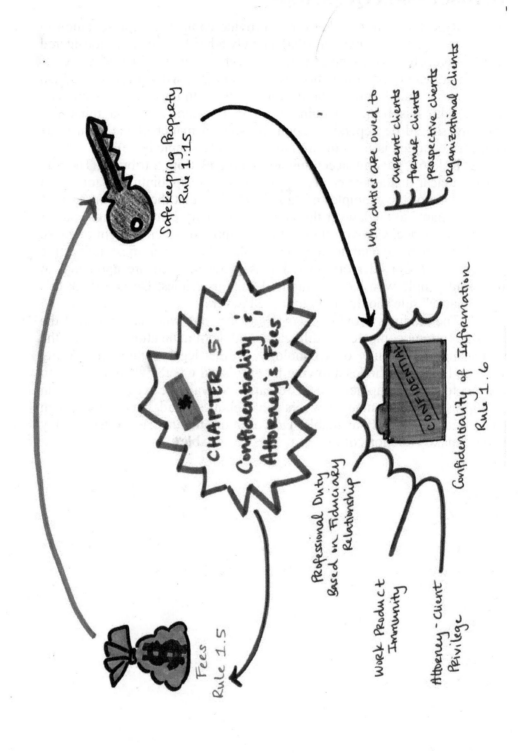

CHAPTER 5:
Confidentiality &
Attorney's Fees

Safekeeping Property
Rule 1.15

Who duties are owed to
 current clients
 former clients
 Prospective clients
 organizational clients

CONFIDENTIAL

Confidentiality of Information
Rule 1.6

Fees
Rule 1.5

Professional Duty
Based on Fiduciary
Relationship

Work Product
Immunity

Attorney-Client
Privilege

Chapter 5:
Confidentiality and Attorney's Fees

A. INTRODUCTION

The Model Rules of Professional Conduct act as a check on the attorney and paint an image of what is fair and reasonable in the representation of a client. Theoretically, one way that the Model Rules can impose a check on a lawyer's services is by ensuring that attorney's fees are reasonable. Model Rule 1.5(a) provides factors for determining a "reasonable fee," such as the time and labor involved, where the attorney is located, the nature and length of the professional relationship. Rule 1.5 also provides guidelines for contingent and fixed fees, indicating circumstances when that type of fee arrangement would not be appropriate. Furthermore, Rule 1.15 guides a lawyer in circumstances where disputed property forms the basis of the case.

Of all the Model Rules, one of the most encompassing, comprehensive, yet frequently misconstrued rules is Rule 1.6, which governs the confidentiality of information. The lawyer has a strict duty to her client to prevent disclosure of information relating to his representation. Rule 1.6, however, provides specific instances where exceptions to the confidentiality rule may be appropriate.

This chapter will discuss these rules as applied to difficult cases where attorneys had to weigh the significance of the Model Rules of Professional Conduct against a societal or moral need for disclosure. The famous *Belge* case raises the issue of the significance of confidentiality under Rule 1.6 within the criminal justice system and the way it is perceived by the general public. The *Godlewski* case serves as a reminder to safeguard and be aware of surroundings in attorney-client interactions and it also emphasizes the importance of preserving the attorney-client privilege.

How will the interests of society be weighed against attorney-client privilege and confidentiality? In what circumstances may a lawyer break confidentiality for the benefit of herself, or the public? How are attorney's fees set? This chapter will address these questions and more.

B. RULES

In preparation, read carefully the following sections of the Model Rules of Professional Conduct along with any relevant comments listed below.

- Rule 1.5: Fees
  - Comments [1], [2], [4], [6], & [7]
- Rule 1.15: Safekeeping Property
  - Comments [1] & [3]
- Rule 1.6: Confidentiality of Information
  - Comments [1-8], [13], [20]

C. CASES AND ADDITIONAL READINGS

A. v. B.
Supreme Court of New Jersey (1999)
726 A.2d 924

This appeal presents the issue whether a law firm may disclose confidential information of one co-client to another co-client. Specifically, in this paternity action, the mother's former law firm, which contemporaneously represented the father and his wife in planning their estates, seeks to disclose to the wife the existence of the father's illegitimate child.

A law firm, Hill Wallack (described variously as "the law firm" or "the firm"), jointly represented the husband and wife in drafting wills in which they devised their respective estates to each other. The devises created the possibility that the other spouse's issue, whether legitimate or illegitimate, ultimately would acquire the decedent's property.

Unbeknown to Hill Wallack and the wife, the husband recently had fathered an illegitimate child. Before the execution of the wills, the child's mother retained Hill Wallack to institute this paternity action against the husband. Because of a clerical error, the firm's computer check did not reveal the conflict of interest inherent in its representation of the mother against the husband. On learning of the conflict, the firm withdrew from representation of the mother in the paternity action. Now, the firm wishes to disclose to the wife the fact that the husband has an illegitimate child. To prevent Hill Wallack from making that disclosure, the husband joined the firm as a third-party defendant in the paternity action.

In the Family Part, the husband, represented by new counsel, Fox, Rothschild, O'Brien & Frankel ("Fox Rothschild"), requested restraints against Hill Wallack to prevent the firm from disclosing to his wife the existence of the child. The Family Part denied the requested restraints. The Appellate Division reversed and remanded "for the entry of an order imposing preliminary restraints and for further consideration."

Hill Wallack then filed motions in this Court seeking leave to appeal, to present oral argument, and to accelerate the appeal. Pursuant to *Rule* 2:8-3(a),[1] we grant the motion for leave to appeal, accelerate the appeal, reverse the judgment of the Appellate Division and remand the matter to the Family Part. Hill Wallack's motion for oral argument is denied.

I.

Although the record is both informal and attenuated, the parties agree substantially on the relevant facts. Because the Family Part has sealed the record, we refer to the parties without identifying them by their proper names. So viewed, the record supports the following factual statement.

In October 1997, the husband and wife retained Hill Wallack, a firm of approximately sixty lawyers, to assist them with planning their estates. On the commencement of the joint representation, the husband and wife each signed a letter captioned "Waiver of Conflict of Interest." In explaining the possible conflicts of interest, the letter recited that the effect of a testamentary transfer by one spouse to the other would permit the transferee to dispose of the property as he or she desired. The firm's letter also explained that information provided by one spouse could become available to the other. Although the letter did not contain an express waiver of the confidentiality of any such information, each spouse consented to and waived any conflicts arising from the firm's joint representation.

Unfortunately, the clerk who opened the firm's estate planning file misspelled the clients' surname. The misspelled name was entered in the computer program that the firm uses to discover possible conflicts of

---

[1] N.J. CT. R. 8:2-3. The rule provides:

Motion for Summary Disposition

(a) Supreme Court. On an appeal taken to the Supreme Court as of right from a judgment of the Appellate Division, any party may move at any time following the service of the notice of appeal for a summary disposition of the appeal. Such motion shall be determined on the motion papers and on the briefs and record filed with the Appellate Division and may result in an affirmance, reversal or modification. The pendency of such motion shall toll the time for the filing of briefs and appendices on the appeal. The Supreme Court may summarily dispose of any appeal on its own motion at any time, and on such prior notice, if any, to the parties as the Supreme Court directs.

interest. The firm then prepared reciprocal wills and related documents with the names of the husband and wife correctly spelled.

In January 1998, before the husband and wife executed the estate planning documents, the mother coincidentally retained Hill Wallack to pursue a paternity claim against the husband. This time, when making its computer search for conflicts of interest, Hill Wallack spelled the husband's name correctly. Accordingly, the computer search did not reveal the existence of the firm's joint representation of the husband and wife. As a result, the estate planning department did not know that the family law department had instituted a paternity action for the mother. Similarly, the family law department did not know that the estate planning department was preparing estate plans for the husband and wife.

A lawyer from the firm's family law department wrote to the husband about the mother's paternity claim. The husband neither objected to the firm's representation of the mother nor alerted the firm to the conflict of interest. Instead, he retained Fox Rothschild to represent him in the paternity action. After initially denying paternity, he agreed to voluntary DNA testing, which revealed that he is the father. Negotiations over child support failed, and the mother instituted the present action.

After the mother filed the paternity action, the husband and wife executed their wills at the Hill Wallack office. The parties agree that in their wills, the husband and wife leave their respective residuary estates to each other. If the other spouse does not survive, the contingent beneficiaries are the testator's issue. The wife's will leaves her residuary estate to her husband, creating the possibility that her property ultimately may pass to his issue. Under *N.J.S.A.* 3B:1-2; 3-48, the term "issue" includes both legitimate and illegitimate children. When the wife executed her will, therefore, she did not know that the husband's illegitimate child ultimately may inherit her property.

The conflict of interest surfaced when Fox Rothschild, in response to Hill Wallack's request for disclosure of the husband's assets, informed the firm that it already possessed the requested information. Hill Wallack promptly informed the mother that it unknowingly was representing both the husband and the wife in an unrelated matter.

Hill Wallack immediately withdrew from representing the mother in the paternity action. It also instructed the estate planning department not to disclose any information about the husband's assets to the member of the firm who had been representing the mother. The firm then wrote to the husband stating that it believed it had an ethical obligation to disclose to the wife the existence, but not the identity, of his illegitimate child. Additionally, the firm stated that it was obligated to inform the wife "that her current estate plan may devise a portion of her assets through her spouse to that child." The firm suggested that the husband so inform his wife and stated that if he did not do so, it would. Because of the restraints

[handwritten margin note:] • Firm believed ethical obligation

imposed by the Appellate Division, however, the firm has not disclosed the information to the wife.

II.

This appeal concerns the conflict between two fundamental obligations of lawyers: the duty of confidentiality, *Rules of Professional Conduct (RPC)* 1.6(a), and the duty to inform clients of material facts, *RPC* 1.4(b). The conflict arises from a law firm's joint representation of two clients whose interests initially were, but no longer are, compatible.

Crucial to the attorney-client relationship is the attorney's obligation not to reveal confidential information learned in the course of representation. Thus, *RPC* 1.6(a) states that "[a] lawyer shall not reveal information relating to representation of a client unless the client consents after consultation, except for disclosures that are impliedly authorized in order to carry out the representation." Generally, "the principle of attorney-client confidentiality imposes a sacred trust on the attorney not to disclose the client's confidential communication." *State v. Land*, 73 N.J. 24, 30, 372 A.2d 297 (1997).

A lawyer's obligation to communicate to one client all information needed to make an informed decision qualifies the firm's duty to maintain the confidentiality of a co-client's information. *RPC* 1.4(b), which reflects a lawyer's duty to keep clients informed, requires that "[a] lawyer shall explain a matter to the extent reasonably necessary to permit the client to make informed decisions regarding the representation." *See also Gautam v. De Luca*, 215 N.J. Super. 388, 397, 521 A.2d 1343 (App.Div.1987) (stating that attorney has continuing duty "to inform his client promptly of any information important to him"); *Passanante v. Yormark*, 138 N.J. Super. 233, 238, 350 A.2d 497 (App.Div.1975) ("[An attorney's] duty includes the obligation of informing his client promptly of any known information important to him."). In limited situations, moreover, an attorney is permitted or required to disclose confidential information. Hill Wallack argues that *RPC* 1.6 mandates, or at least permits, the firm to disclose to the wife the existence of the husband's illegitimate child. *RPC* 1.6(b) requires that a lawyer disclose "information relating to representation of a client" to the proper authorities if the lawyer "reasonably believes" that such disclosure is necessary to prevent the client "from committing a criminal, illegal or fraudulent act that the lawyer reasonably believes is likely to result in death or substantial bodily harm or substantial injury to the financial interest or property of another." *RPC* 1.6(b)(1). Despite Hill Wallack's claim that *RPC* 1.6(b) applies, the facts do not justify mandatory disclosure. The possible inheritance of the wife's estate by the husband's illegitimate child is too remote to constitute "substantial injury to the financial interest or property of another" within the meaning of *RPC* 1.6(b).

By comparison, in limited circumstances *RPC* 1.6(c) permits a lawyer to disclose a confidential communication. *RPC* 1.6(c) permits, but does not require, a lawyer to reveal confidential information to the extent the lawyer reasonably believes necessary "to rectify the consequences of a client's criminal, illegal or fraudulent act in furtherance of which the lawyer's services had been used." *RPC* 1.6(c)(1). Although *RPC* 1.6(c) does not define a "fraudulent act," the term takes on meaning from our construction of the word "fraud," found in the analogous "crime or fraud" exception to the attorney-client privilege. *See N.J.R.E.* 504(2)(a) (excepting from attorney-client privilege "a communication in the course of legal service sought or obtained in the aid of the commission of a crime or fraud"); Kevin H. Michels, *New Jersey Attorney Ethics* § 15:3-3 at 280 (1998) ("While the RPCs no longer incorporate the attorney-client privilege into the definition of confidential information, prior constructions of the fraud exception may be relevant in interpreting the exceptions to confidentiality contained in *RPC* 1.6(b) and (c). . . .") (internal citation omitted). When construing the "crime or fraud" exception to the attorney-client privilege, "our courts have generally given the term 'fraud' an expansive reading." *Fellerman v. Bradley*, 99 N.J. 493, 503-04, 493 A.2d 1239 (1985).

We likewise construe broadly the term "fraudulent act" within the meaning of *RPC* 1.6(c). So construed, the husband's deliberate omission of the existence of his illegitimate child constitutes a fraud on his wife. When discussing their respective estates with the firm, the husband and wife reasonably could expect that each would disclose information material to the distribution of their estates, including the existence of children who are contingent residuary beneficiaries. The husband breached that duty. Under the reciprocal wills, the existence of the husband's illegitimate child could affect the distribution of the wife's estate, if she predeceased him. Additionally, the husband's child support payments and other financial responsibilities owed to the illegitimate child could deplete that part of his estate that otherwise would pass to his wife.

From another perspective, it would be "fundamentally unfair" for the husband to reap the "joint planning advantages of access to information and certainty of outcome," while denying those same advantages to his wife. Teresa S. Collett, *Disclosure, Discretion, or Deception: The Estate Planner's Ethical Dilemma from a Unilateral Confidence*, 28 Real Prop. Prob. Tr. J. 683, 743 (1994). In effect, the husband has used the law firm's services to defraud his wife in the preparation of her estate.

***

Under *RPC* 1.6, the facts support disclosure to the wife. The law firm did not learn of the husband's illegitimate child in a confidential communication from him. Indeed, he concealed that information from both his wife and the firm. The law firm learned about the husband's child through its representation of the mother in her paternity action against the husband. Accordingly, the husband's expectation of nondisclosure of the information may be less than if he had communicated the information to the firm in confidence.

Consider how firm acquired info

In addition, the husband and wife signed letters captioned "Waiver of Conflict of Interest." These letters acknowledge that information provided by one client could become available to the other. The letters, however, stop short of explicitly authorizing the firm to disclose one spouse's confidential information to the other. Even in the absence of any such explicit authorization, the spirit of the letters supports the firm's decision to disclose to the wife the existence of the husband's illegitimate child.

Neither our research nor that of counsel has revealed a dispositive judicial decision from this or any other jurisdiction on the issue of disclosure of confidential information about one client to a co-client. Persuasive secondary authority, however, supports the conclusion that the firm may disclose to the wife the existence of the husband's child.

The forthcoming *Restatement (Third) of The Law Governing Lawyers § 112* comment *l* (Proposed Final Draft No. 1, 1996) ("the *Restatement*") suggests, for example, that if the attorney and the co-clients have reached a prior, explicit agreement concerning the sharing of confidential information, that agreement controls whether the attorney should disclose the confidential information of one co-client to another. *Ibid.* ("Co-clients . . . may explicitly agree to share information" and "can also explicitly agree that the lawyer is not to share certain information . . . with one or more other co-clients. A lawyer must honor such agreements."); *see also Report of the ABA Special Study Committee on Professional Responsibility: Comments and Recommendations on the Lawyer's Duties in Representing Husband and Wife*, 28 Real Prop. Prob. Tr. J. 765, 787 (1994) ("Although legally and ethically there is no need for a prior discussion and agreement with the couple about the mode of representation, discussion and agreement are the better practice. The agreement may cover . . . the duty to keep or disclose confidences."); American College of Trust and Estate Counsel, *ACTEC Commentaries on the Model Rules of Professional Conduct* 65-66 (2d ed. 1995) ("When the lawyer is first consulted by the multiple potential clients the lawyer should review with them the terms upon which the lawyer will undertake the representation, including the extent to which information will be shared among them.").

As the preceding authorities suggest, an attorney, on commencing joint representation of co-clients, should agree explicitly with the clients on the sharing of confidential information. In such a "disclosure agreement," the co-clients can agree that any confidential information concerning one co-client, whether obtained from a co-client himself or herself or from another source, will be shared with the other co-client. Similarly, the co-clients can agree that unilateral confidences or other confidential information will be kept confidential by the attorney. Such a prior agreement will clarify the expectations of the clients and the lawyer and diminish the need for future litigation.

In the absence of an agreement to share confidential information with co-clients, the *Restatement* reposes the resolution of the lawyer's competing duties within the lawyer's discretion:

> [T]he lawyer, after consideration of all relevant circumstances, has the . . . discretion to inform the affected co-client of the specific communication if, in the lawyer's reasonable judgment, the immediacy and magnitude of the risk to the affected co-client outweigh the interest of the communicating client in continued secrecy. [*Restatement (Third) of The Law Governing Lawyers, supra*, § 112 comment *l*.]

·lawyer has discretion

Additionally, the *Restatement* advises that the lawyer, when withdrawing from representation of the co-clients, may inform the affected co-client that the attorney has learned of information adversely affecting that client's interests that the communicating co-client refuses to permit the lawyer to disclose. *Ibid.*

party

In the context of estate planning, the *Restatement* also suggests that a lawyer's disclosure of confidential information communicated by one spouse is appropriate only if the other spouse's failure to learn of the information would be materially detrimental to that other spouse or frustrate the spouse's intended testamentary arrangement. *Id.* § 112 comment *l*, illustrations 2, 3. The *Restatement* provides two analogous illustrations in which a lawyer has been jointly retained by a husband and wife to prepare reciprocal wills. The first illustration states:

·materially detrimental ?

Lawyer has been retained by Husband and Wife to prepare wills pursuant to an arrangement under which each spouse agrees to leave most of their property to the other. Shortly after the wills are executed, Husband (unknown to Wife) asks Lawyer to prepare an inter vivos trust for an illegitimate child whose existence Husband has kept secret from Wife for many years and about whom Husband had not previously informed Lawyer. Husband states that Wife would be distraught at learning of Husband's infidelity and of Husband's years of silence and that disclosure of the information could destroy their marriage. Husband directs Lawyer not to inform Wife. The inter vivos trust that Husband proposes to create would not materially affect Wife's own estate plan or her expected receipt of property under Husband's will, because Husband proposes to use property designated in Husband's will for a personally favored charity. In view of the lack of material effect on Wife, Lawyer may assist Husband to establish and fund the inter vivos trust and refrain from disclosing Husband's information to Wife. [*Id.* § 112 comment *l,* illustration 2.]

In authorizing non-disclosure, the *Restatement* explains that an attorney should refrain from disclosing the existence of the illegitimate child to the wife because the trust "would not materially affect Wife's own estate plan or her expected receipt of property under Husband's will." *Ibid.*

The other illustration states:

Same facts as [the prior Illustration], except that Husband's proposed inter vivos trust would significantly deplete Husband's estate, to Wife's material detriment and in frustration of the Spouses' intended testamentary arrangements. If Husband will neither inform Wife nor permit Lawyer to do so, Lawyer must withdraw from representing both Husband and Wife. In the light of all relevant circumstances, Lawyer may exercise discretion whether to inform Wife either that circumstances, which Lawyer has been asked not to reveal, indicate that she should revoke her recent will or to inform Wife of some or all the details of the information that Husband has recently provided so that Wife may protect her interests. Alternatively, Lawyer may inform Wife only that Lawyer is withdrawing because Husband will not permit disclosure of information that Lawyer has learned from Husband.

[*Id.* § 112 comment *l,* illustration 3.]

Because the money placed in the trust would be deducted from the portion of the husband's estate left to his wife, the *Restatement* concludes that the lawyer may exercise discretion to inform the wife of the husband's plans. *Ibid.*

An earlier draft of the *Restatement* described the attorney's obligation to disclose the confidential information to the co-client as mandatory. *Id.* (Council Draft No. 11, 1995); *cf.* Collett, *supra,* at 743 (arguing that nature of joint representation of husband and wife supports mandatory disclosure rule). When reviewing the draft, however, the governing body of the American Law Institute, the Council, modified the obligation to leave disclosure within the attorney's discretion.

Similarly, the American College of Trust and Estate Counsel (ACTEC) also favors a discretionary rule. It recommends that the "lawyer should have a reasonable degree of discretion in determining how to respond to any particular case." American College of Trust and Estate Counsel, *supra,* at 68. The ACTEC suggests that the lawyer first attempt to convince the client to inform the co-client. *Ibid.* When urging the client to disclose the information, the lawyer should remind the client of the implicit understanding that all information will be shared by both clients. The lawyer also should explain to the client the potential legal consequences of non-disclosure, including invalidation of the wills. *Ibid.* Furthermore, the lawyer may mention that failure to communicate the information could subject the lawyer to a malpractice claim or disciplinary action. *Ibid.*

The ACTEC reasons that if unsuccessful in persuading the client to disclose the information, the lawyer should consider several factors in deciding whether to reveal the confidential information to the co-client, including: (1) duties of impartiality and loyalty to the clients; (2) any express or implied agreement among the lawyer and the joint clients that information communicated by either client to the lawyer regarding the subject of the representation would be shared with the other client; (3) the reasonable expectations of the clients; and (4) the nature of the confidence and the harm that may result if the confidence is, or is not, disclosed. *Id.* at 68–69.

The Section of Real Property, Probate and Trust Law of the American Bar Association, in a report prepared by its Special Study Committee on Professional Responsibility, reached a similar conclusion:

> Faced with any adverse confidence, the lawyer must act as a fiduciary toward joint clients. The lawyer must balance the potential for material harm to the confiding spouse caused by disclosure against the potential for material harm to the other spouse caused by a failure to disclose.

[Report of the Special Study Committee on Professional Responsibility: Comments and Recommendations on the Lawyer's Duties in Representing Husband and Wife, supra, 28 Real Prop. Prob. Tr. J. at 787.]

The report stresses that the resolution of the balancing test should center on the expectations of the clients. *Id.* at 784. In general, "the available ruling authority . . . points toward the conclusion that a lawyer is not required to disclose an adverse confidence to the other spouse." *Id.* at 788. At the same time, the report acknowledges, as did the *Restatement,* that the available ruling authority is "scant and offers little analytical guidance." *Id.* at 788 n. 27.

The Professional Ethics Committees of New York and Florida, however, have concluded that disclosure to a co-client is prohibited. New York State Bar Ass'n Comm. on Professional Ethics, Op. 555 (1984); Florida State Bar Ass'n Comm. on Professional Ethics, Op. 95–4 (1997).

The New York opinion addressed the following situation:

> A and B formed a partnership and employed Lawyer L to represent them in connection with the partnership affairs. Subsequently, B, in a conversation with Lawyer L, advised Lawyer L that he was actively breaching the partnership agreement. B preceded this statement to Lawyer L with the statement that he proposed to tell Lawyer L something "in confidence." Lawyer L did not respond to that statement and did not understand that B intended to make a statement that would

[handwritten marginalia: Factors L should consider when deciding whether to reveal]

be of importance to A but that was to be kept confidential from A. Lawyer L had not, prior thereto, advised A or B that he could not receive from one communications regarding the subject of the joint representation that would be confidential from the other. B has subsequently declined to tell A what he has told Lawyer L.

[New York State Bar Ass'n Comm. on Professional Ethics, Op. 555, *supra.*]

In that situation, the New York Ethics Committee concluded that the lawyer may not disclose to the co-client the communicating client's statement. The Committee based its conclusion on the absence of prior consent by the clients to the sharing of all confidential communications and the fact that the client "specifically in advance designated his communication as confidential, and the lawyer did not demur." *Ibid.*

The Florida Ethics Committee addressed a similar situation:

Lawyer has represented Husband and Wife for many years in a range of personal matters, including estate planning. Husband and Wife have substantial individual assets, and they also own substantial jointly-held property. Recently, Lawyer prepared new updated wills that Husband and Wife signed. Like their previous wills, their new wills primarily benefit the survivor of them for his or her life, with beneficial disposition at the death of the survivor being made equally to their children.

***

Several months after the execution of the new wills, Husband confers separately with Lawyer. Husband reveals to Lawyer that he has just executed a codicil (prepared by another law firm) that makes substantial beneficial disposition to a woman with whom Husband has been having an extra-marital relationship.[Florida State Bar Ass'n Comm. on Professional Ethics, Op. 95–4, *supra.*]

Reasoning that the lawyer's duty of confidentiality takes precedence over the duty to communicate all relevant information to a client, the Florida Ethics Committee concluded that the lawyer did not have discretion to reveal the information. In support of that conclusion, the Florida committee reasoned that joint clients do not necessarily expect that everything relating to the joint representation communicated by one co-client will be shared with the other co-client.

In several material respects, however, the present appeal differs from the hypothetical cases considered by the New York and Florida committees. Most significantly, the New York and Florida disciplinary rules, unlike *RPC* 1.6, do not except disclosure needed "to rectify the consequences of a client's . . . fraudulent act in the furtherance of which the lawyer's services had been used." *RPC* 1.6(c). *But see New York Code of Professional Responsibility* DR 4–101; *Florida Rules of Professional*

Conduct 4–1.6. Second, Hill Wallack learned of the husband's paternity from a third party, not from the husband himself. Thus, the husband did not communicate anything to the law firm with the expectation that the communication would be kept confidential. Finally, the husband and wife, unlike the co-clients considered by the New York and Florida Committees, signed an agreement suggesting their intent to share all information with each other.

• learned of info thru 3P

Because Hill Wallack wishes to make the disclosure, we need not reach the issue whether the lawyer's obligation to disclose is discretionary or mandatory. In conclusion, Hill Wallack may inform the wife of the existence of the husband's illegitimate child.

may inform

Finally, authorizing the disclosure of the existence, but not the identity, of the child will not contravene *N.J.S.A.* 9:17–42, which provides:

> All papers and records and any information pertaining to an action or proceeding held under [the New Jersey Parentage Act] which may reveal the identity of any party in an action, other than the final judgment or the birth certificate, whether part of the permanent record of the court or of a file with the State registrar of vital statistics or elsewhere, are confidential and are subject to inspection only upon consent of the court and all parties to the action who are still living, or in exceptional cases only upon an order of the court for compelling reason clearly and convincingly shown.

The law firm learned of the husband's paternity of the child through the mother's disclosure before the institution of the paternity suit. It does not seek to disclose the identity of the mother or the child. Given the wife's need for the information and the law firm's right to disclose it, the disclosure of the child's existence to the wife constitutes an exceptional case with "compelling reason clearly and convincingly shown."

• clear & convincing

The judgment of the Appellate Division is reversed and the matter is remanded to the Family Part.

Questions and Comments

1. In *A v. B*, the court had to determine whether it was appropriate for a law firm to disclose one client's confidential information to another co-client. Do you agree with the court's decision? What are your thoughts on joint representations in light of this case? *See* Model Rule 1.6.

2. In the case, the law for wills and estate planning in New Jersey provided that the illegitimate child ultimately may inherit property from the husband upon his death. As a result, Hill Wallack believed it had an ethical obligation to disclose the existence, but not the identity of the husband's illegitimate child. Considering that the wife retained the firm as part of joint representation with her husband, why not disclose the identity

• existence ≠ identity

of the child? Would the firm's disclosure of the child's identity serve their client's interest? Would potential harm come from not knowing the child's identity?

3. What reasons did the court give for disclosing the child's existence? Do you agree with the court's decision to do so?

PEOPLE V. BELGE
Onandaga County Court, New York State (1975)
372 N.Y.S.2d 798

In the summer of 1973 Robert F. Garrow, Jr., stood charged in Hamilton County with the crime of murder. The defendant was assigned two attorneys, Frank H. Armani and Francis R. Belge. A defense of insanity had been interposed by counsel for Mr. Garrow. During the course of the discussions between Garrow and his two counsel, three other murders were admitted by Garrow, one being in Onondaga County. On or about September of 1973 Mr. Belge conducted his own investigation based upon what his client had told him and with the assistance of a friend the location of the body of Alicia Hauck was found in Oakwood Cemetery in Syracuse. Mr. Belge personally inspected the body and was satisfied, presumably, that this was the Alicia Hauck that his client had told him that he murdered.

This discovery was not disclosed to the authorities, but became public during the trial of Mr. Garrow in June of 1974, when to affirmatively establish the defense of insanity, these three other murders were brought before the jury by the defense in the Hamilton County trial. Public indignation reached the fever pitch, statements were made by the District Attorney of Onondaga County relative to the situation and he caused the Grand Jury of Onondaga County, then sitting, to conduct a thorough investigation. As a result of this investigation Frank Armani was no-billed by the Grand Jury but Indictment No. 75-55 was returned as against Francis R. Belge, Esq., accusing him of having violated subdivision 1 of section 4200 of the Public Health Law, which, in essence, requires that a decent burial be accorded the dead, and section 4143 of the Public Health Law, which, in essence, requires anyone knowing of the death of a person without medical attendance, to report the same to the proper authorities. Defense counsel moves for a dismissal of the indictment on the grounds that a confidential, privileged communication existed between him and Mr. Garrow, which should excuse the attorney from making full disclosure to the authorities.

The National Association of Criminal Defense Lawyers, as *amicus curiae (Times Pub. Co. v Williams*, 222 So 2d 470, 475 [Fla]), succinctly [sic] state the issue in the following language: If this indictment stands,

"The attorney-client privilege will be effectively destroyed. No defendant will be able to freely discuss the facts of his case with his attorney. No attorney will be able to listen to those facts without being faced with the Hobson's choice of violating the law or violating his professional code of Ethics."

Initially in England the practice of law was not recognized as a profession, and certainly some people are skeptics today. However, the practice of learned and capable men appearing before the court on behalf of a friend or an acquaintance became more and more demanding. Consequently, the King granted a privilege to certain of these men to engage in such practice. There had to be rules governing their duties. These came to be known as "Canons". The King has, in this country, been substituted by a democracy, but the "Canons" are with us today, having been honed and refined over the years to meet the changes of time. Most are constantly being studied and revamped by the American Bar Association and by the bar associations of the various States. While they are, for the most part, general by definition, they can be brought to bear in a particular situation. Among those is the following, cited in *United States v Funk* (84 F Supp 967, 968): "Confidential communications between an attorney and his client are privileged from disclosure . . . as a rule of necessity in the administration of justice."

In the most recent issue of the New York State Bar Journal (June, 1975) there is an article by Jack B. Weinstein, entitled "Educating Ethical Lawyers". In a subcaption to this article is the following language which is pertinent: "The most difficult ethical dilemmas result from the frequent conflicts between the obligation to one's client and those to the legal system and to society. It is in this area that legal education has its greatest responsibility, and can have its greatest effects." In the course of his article Mr. Weinstein states that there are three major types of pressure facing a practicing lawyer. He uses the following language to describe these: "First, there are those that originate in the attorney's search for his own well-being. Second, pressures arise from the attorney's obligation to his client. Third, the lawyer has certain obligations to the courts, the legal system, and society in general."

Our system of criminal justice is an adversary system and the interests of the State are not absolute, or even paramount. "The dignity of the individual is respected to the point that even when the citizen is known by the state to have committed a heinous offense, the individual is nevertheless accorded such rights as counsel, trial by jury, due process, and the privilege against self-incrimination."

A trial is in part a search for truth, but it is only partly a search for truth. The mantle of innocence is flung over the defendant to such an extent that he is safeguarded by rules of evidence which frequently keep out absolute truth, much to the chagrin of juries. Nevertheless, this has been a part of our system since our laws were taken from the laws of England and over these many years has been found to best protect a balance between the rights of the individual and the rights of society.

The concept of the right to counsel has again been with us for a long time, but since the decision of *Gideon v Wainwright* (372 U.S. 335), it has been extended more and more so that at the present time a defendant is entitled to have counsel at a parole hearing or a probation violation hearing.

The effectiveness of counsel is only as great as the confidentiality of its client-attorney relationship. If the lawyer cannot get all the facts about the case, he can only give his client half of a defense. This, of necessity, involves the client telling his attorney everything remotely connected with the crime.

Apparently, in the instant case, after analyzing all the evidence, and after hearing of the bizarre episodes in the life of their client, they decided that the only possibility of salvation was in a defense of insanity. For the client to disclose not only everything about this particular crime but also everything about other crimes which might have a bearing upon his defense, requires the strictest confidence in, and on the part of, the attorney.

When the facts of the other homicides became public, as a result of the defendant's testimony to substantiate his claim of insanity, "Members of the public were shocked at the apparent callousness of these lawyers, whose conduct was seen as typifying the unhealthy lack of concern of most lawyers with the public interest and with simple decency." A hue and cry went up from the press and other news media suggesting that the attorneys should be found guilty of such crimes as obstruction of justice or becoming an accomplice after the fact. From a layman's standpoint, this certainly was a logical conclusion. However, the Constitution of the United States of America attempts to preserve the dignity of the individual and to do that guarantees him the services of an attorney who will bring to the Bar and to the Bench every conceivable protection from the inroads of the State against such rights as are vested in the Constitution for one accused of crime. Among those substantial constitutional rights is that a defendant does not have to incriminate himself. His attorneys were bound to uphold that concept and maintain what has been called a sacred trust of confidentiality.

The following language from the brief of the *amicus curiae* further points up the statements just made: "The client's Fifth Amendment rights cannot be violated by his attorney. There is no viable distinction between the personal papers and criminal evidence in the hands or mind of the client. Because the discovery of the body of Alicia Hauck would have presented 'a significant link in a chain of evidence tending to establish his guilt' [*Leary v United States*, 395 U.S. 6 (1969)], Garrow was constitutionally exempt from any statutory requirement to disclose the location of the body. And Attorney Belge, as Garrow's attorney, was not only equally exempt, but under a positive stricture precluding such disclosure. Garrow, although constitutionally privileged against a requirement of compulsory disclosure, was free to make such a revelation if he chose to do so. Attorney Belge was affirmatively required to withhold disclosure. The criminal defendant's self-incrimination rights become completely nugatory if compulsory disclosure can be exacted through his attorney."

In the recent and landmark case of *United States v Nixon* (418 U.S. 683, 713) the court stated: "the constitutional need for production of relevant evidence in a criminal proceeding is specific and neutral to the fair adjudication of a particular criminal case in the administration of justice. Without access to specific facts a criminal prosecution may be totally frustrated." In the case at bar we must weigh the importance of the general privilege of confidentiality in the performance of the defendant's duties as an attorney, against the inroads of such a privilege on the fair administration of criminal justice as well as the heart tearing that went on in the victim's family by reason of their uncertainty as to the whereabouts of Alicia Hauck. In this type situation the court must balance the rights of the individual against the rights of society as a whole. There is no question but Attorney Belge's failure to bring to the attention of the authorities the whereabouts of Alicia Hauck when he first verified it, prevented bringing Garrow to the immediate bar of justice for this particular murder. This was in a sense, obstruction of justice. This duty, I am sure, loomed large in the mind of Attorney Belge. However, against this was the Fifth Amendment right of his client, Garrow, not to incriminate himself. If the Grand Jury had returned an indictment charging Mr. Belge with obstruction of justice under a proper statute, the work of this court would have been much more difficult than it is.

There must always be a conflict between the obstruction of the administration of criminal justice and the preservation of the right against self-incrimination which permeates the mind of the attorney as the alter ego of his client. But that is not the situation before this court. We have the Fifth Amendment right, derived from the Constitution, on the one hand, as against the trivia of a pseudo-criminal statute on the other, which has seldom been brought into play. Clearly the latter is completely out of focus when placed alongside the client-attorney privilege. An examination of the Grand Jury testimony sheds little light on their reasoning. The testimony of Mr. Armani added nothing new to the facts as already presented to the Grand Jury. He and Mr. Belge were cocounsel. Both were answerable to the Canons of professional ethics. The Grand Jury chose to indict one and not the other. It appears as if that body were grasping at straws.

It is the decision of this court that Francis R. Belge conducted himself as an officer of the court with all the zeal at his command to protect the constitutional rights of his client. Both on the grounds of a privileged communication and in the interests of justice the indictment is dismissed.

Questions and Comments

1. To what extent does Model Rule 1.6 promote the underlying foundations of justice provided by the Constitution? How does justice for Mr. Garrow differ, if at all, from justice for society as a whole?

2. How can an attorney adequately represent his client alongside the interests of justice if crucial information is considered privileged? What does this implicate about the battle between a lawyer's legal obligations and what some would label as her "moral obligations?"

3. Do you agree with the way Rule 1.6 is drafted? If not, how would you revise it?

PEOPLE V. GODLEWSKI
Court of Appeals of California (1993)
17 Cal. App. 4th 940

[handwritten: AG hired Gene Flack to kill Dad]

Statement of Facts

Three defendants appeal following their convictions for murder. As none of the defendants directly raises a sufficiency of the evidence claim, we will briefly summarize, in accord with the traditional rule of appellate review (*People v. Johnson* (1980) 26 Cal.3d 557, 562 [162 Cal.Rptr. 431, 606 P.2d 738, 16 A.L.R.4th 1255]), the operative events of this murder-for-hire case. Additional facts will be set forth as necessary to evaluate the specific assignments of error.

Raymond E. Godlewski, desiring to kill his father, hired Gene Flack to commit the crime. Flack enlisted Michael Brown's assistance. At approximately 12:30 a.m. on July 4, 1989, Brown drove Flack to the victim's home in Sylmar. Flack knocked on the door. When the victim answered, Flack murdered him with a single shotgun blast to the head. Brown drove Flack from the scene.

On July 5, 1989, Flack told Paul Caines that he had committed the murder. Caines notified the police. The police interviewed Flack and Brown but released them. Several days later, the police arrested Godlewski and Brown. Flack fled to Louisiana but was soon apprehended.

The three men were jointly charged and tried. However, one jury was impanelled for Brown and Flack while another jury was impanelled for

Godlewski. At certain points, each jury was excluded during portions of the People's case although both juries heard all of the defense evidence.

Godlewski testified and admitted hiring Flack to kill his father. He asserted that he had done so because of a lifetime of physical and emotional abuse suffered at his father's hands. Additionally, he claimed he was fearful of his father because of threats he had made shortly before his death. The jury apparently credited Godlewski's claim to a certain extent because, although charged with first degree murder with the special circumstance allegation of murder for financial gain, he was convicted only of second degree murder.

Flack testified and denied having committed the murder. He admitted only that he had purchased a shotgun for Godlewski. Flack claimed that it was Godlewski who actually shot the victim. The jury disbelieved Flack and found him guilty of first degree murder and found true the special circumstance allegation of murder for financial gain.

Brown did not testify and presented no defense. Essentially, he argued that the People's circumstantial evidence case against him did not establish guilt beyond a reasonable doubt. The jury disagreed and found him guilty of first degree murder. (The special circumstance allegation against Brown had been stricken before trial at the request of the People.)

The Trial Court Properly Excluded Statements Godlewski Made to His Lawyer

Flack contends that prejudicial error occurred because the trial court ruled inadmissible, based upon the attorney-client privilege, statements made by Godlewski to his lawyer. Flack characterizes the statements as an admission by Godlewski that he (Godlewski), not Flack, actually committed the murder.

The issue arose during trial. Flack proposed to call as a witness Steve White, a county jail inmate, who allegedly overheard a conversation between Godlewski and his lawyer in the "lockup" on the day of Godlewski's arraignment in the superior court. Flack's offer of proof consisted of a written statement prepared by Flack's investigator, who had spoken with White. White apparently signed the statement under penalty of perjury. Flack did not offer the statement into evidence. Instead, he read it to the court as follows:

> The statement by the witness was that he heard the attorney say "You would have been better off saying that you did it instead of blaming it on these guys."
>
> "Then Ray [Godlewski] said, 'You are right. That's what I'm going to tell them, that I did it, not these guys."
>
> "The attorney then said, 'You got yourself in deeper trouble and are going to have to straighten it out.'"

"Ray [Godlewski] said he talked to Gene [Flack's] grandmother this morning and she said not to have someone else go down for something they didn't do."

Godlewski asserted the attorney-client privilege. Flack responded that the privilege had been waived because the conversation had taken place in the presence of a third person (White). The court found no waiver and sustained the assertion of the privilege.

Several days later, Flack renewed his motion to permit White to testify. Arguing that the evidence was so significant to his case that its exclusion would deny him a right to a fair trial, he asked the court to engage in a balancing process in deciding whether or not to uphold the claim of privilege. To explain the importance of White's proposed testimony, Flack pointed to the following testimony given by Flack's grandmother (Emma Baugh) and mother (Elizabeth McLemore).

Baugh had testified that during a phone conversation with Flack placed from the county jail following the defendants' arrests, Flack had another man come to the phone. The individual identified himself as "Ray, Jr." He admitted that he had personally killed the victim, and promised to exonerate Flack and Brown. Baugh conceded she did not recognize the voice, and Godlewski, in his subsequent testimony, denied Baugh's allegations about the conversation.

Likewise, McLemore testified that during a phone conversation with Flack, Flack brought a man he identified as "Ray" to the phone. McLemore did not recognize the voice. However, "Ray's" "confession" to McLemore was different from the one allegedly given to Baugh in that "Ray" told her that he had *accidentally* killed his father.

Flack urged that White's testimony was necessary to corroborate the phone conversations to which Baugh and McLemore had testified. Flack also renewed his earlier argument that Godlewski had waived the privilege by conversing with counsel in the "lockup." Flack averred that law enforcement personnel and criminal defense attorneys had told him that there was a policy that if a lawyer asked to speak to a client in private, the request would be accommodated. Flack offered to call these individuals as witnesses if the court so desired. Godlewski did not quarrel with the existence of the policy but noted that practically, there is neither the time nor the opportunity to arrange for such private interviews.

Last, Flack proposed that Godlewski's rights could be accommodated by permitting White to testify only in front of the Flack–Brown jury. With that procedure, the Godlewski jury would never learn of the statement. Godlewski had earlier rejected this "offer."

The court again denied Flack's request. It found that the attorney-client privilege was an integral part of the federal constitutional right to counsel and that the privilege should be liberally construed. It rejected the option of disclosing the statement only to the Flack–Brown jury. However, the court did grant Flack's request to preclude the People from arguing to the jury that there was no corroboration for the testimony of either Baugh or McLemore.

(1a) Flack now contends that the trial court erred in barring White's testimony. We disagree, for we conclude that only the most extraordinary circumstance would justify disclosure of privileged communications between lawyer and client and that Flack failed to make that showing.

(2) The attorney-client privilege, albeit a statutory one, is the oldest of the confidential communications privileges. (*Sullivan v. Superior Court* (1972) 29 Cal.App.3d 64, 71 [105 Cal.Rptr. 241].) Its purpose is to safeguard the confidential relationship between a client and counsel so as to promote full and open disclosure of facts and tactics surrounding the case. (*People v. Flores* (1977) 71 Cal.App.3d 559 [139 Cal.Rptr. 546].) These benefits justify the risk that an unjust decision may sometime result because the privilege suppresses relevant evidence. (*People v. Canfield* (1974) 12 Cal.3d 699, 705 [117 Cal.Rptr. 81, 527 P.2d 633].) In the context of condemning governmental conduct which had invaded the attorney-client relationship, our Supreme Court held that the attorney-client privilege helps to implement the accused's constitutional right to effective representation because "if an accused is to derive the full benefits of his right to counsel, he must have the assurance of confidentiality and privacy of communication with his attorney." (*Barber v. Municipal Court* (1979) 24 Cal.3d 742, 751 [157 Cal.Rptr. 658, 598 P.2d 818]; see also *Neku v. U.S.* (D.C. 1993) 620 A.2d 259, 262 ["In the criminal context the privilege acquires Sixth Amendment protection. [Citation.]"].)

Given this policy framework, it is not surprising that the California courts have not yet embraced Flack's position. In *People v. Flores, supra,* 71 Cal.App.3d 559, an accomplice, testifying pursuant to a grant of immunity, gave the "most damning" (*id.* at p. 565) evidence against the defendant. The defense sought to cross-examine the accomplice about discussions he had with his attorney prior to the grant of immunity. The trial court barred the questioning after the witness invoked the attorney-client privilege. On appeal, the defendant "in his argument against the use of the attorney-client privilege, contend[ed] that fundamental principles of social justice demand that help be extended by the courts in such circumstance to protect a defendant from a possible conviction predicated upon the biased and self-serving testimony of a witness." (*Id.* at pp. 564–565.)

The Court of Appeal rejected the request to breach the privilege. "The privilege of confidential communication between client and attorney should not only be liberally construed, but must be regarded as sacred. Courts should not whittle away at the privilege upon slight or equivocal circumstances. The grant of immunity and [the accomplice's] testimony admitting his complicity in the crime are not facts of such compelling force to require a waiver of the confidential nature of the attorney-client communication; its confidentiality must be kept inviolate. [Citations.]" (71 Cal.App.3d at p. 565.)

This division adopted a similar analysis in *Littlefield v. Superior Court* (1982) 136 Cal.App.3d 477 [186 Cal.Rptr. 368] (hg. den.). That writ proceeding arose out of the "Hillside Strangler" prosecution against Angelo Buono. The People's primary witness was Kenneth Bianchi. The People had originally jointly charged Bianchi with Buono but Bianchi agreed to plead guilty in exchange for testifying against Buono. Buono asserted that Bianchi's inculpating testimony was falsely given to escape the risk of capital punishment and thus sought to cross-examine Bianchi about his conversations with his counsel which led to the plea bargain. Buono's theory was that Bianchi's counsel had disclosed facts to Bianchi about the murders which enabled Bianchi to fabricate his testimony against Buono. We held, in part: "Assuming that the evidence would show that the public defender had done so, in counseling Bianchi about the wisdom of the plea bargain (a fact that Buono's counsel can only surmise), we see nothing to permit a violation of the traditional attorney-client privilege." (*Id.* at p. 481.)

Littlefield was followed in *People v. Johnson* (1989) 47 Cal.3d 1194, 1228 [255 Cal.Rptr. 569, 767 P.2d 1047], where the California Supreme Court rejected a defendant's claim that he had been denied due process by the trial court's ruling that the attorney-client privilege precluded most of the questions posed to an accomplice who testified as part of a plea bargain.

• no DP violation

(1b) Thus, it is patent that the attorney-client privilege is not one to be easily discarded merely because a defendant asserts that invocation of the privilege results in the denial of his right to a fair trial. In an effort to avoid the force of these authorities, Flack relies upon cases which have adopted a balancing approach to decide whether or not the attorney-client privilege should yield to the accused's right to confront and cross-examine.

• balancing

In *United States ex rel. Blackwell v. Franzen* (7th Cir. 1982) 688 F.2d 496, the People's only occurrence witness was the defendant's accomplice, who had entered into a plea bargain with the prosecutor. Defense cross-examination of the accomplice explored the terms of the plea bargain in an attempt to show a motive to fabricate. On redirect, the People rehabilitated the accomplice through a statement he had given to the police inculpating the defendant before the prosecutor had made any promises to him. On recross-examination, the defense sought to examine the accomplice about a statement he had made to his attorney in which he allegedly claimed that the prior consistent statement had been the fruit of police coercion. The trial court sustained the objection that the statement to counsel was protected by the attorney-client privilege. On appeal, the state court rejected the defense claim of error. In a subsequent federal habeas corpus proceeding, the district court found that the limitation placed on the defense cross-examination of the accomplice violated the constitutional right to confront and cross-examine. The Court of Appeals reversed that portion of the district court's holding. Noting the general principle that the right to confront and cross-examine is not an absolute right "and may, in appropriate cases, bow to accommodate other legitimate interests in the criminal trial process" (*id.* at p. 500, citing *Chambers v. Mississippi* (1973) 410 U.S. 284, 295 [35 L.Ed.2d 297, 309, 93 S.Ct. 1038]), it formulated the pertinent inquiry as follows: "The court must ultimately decide whether the probative value of the alleged privileged communication was such that the defendant's right to effective cross-examination was substantially diminished." (688 F.2d at p. 501.) Because defense counsel was otherwise given wide latitude in exploring the issue of the accomplice's credibility, the Court of Appeals concluded that the invocation of the attorney-client privilege had not prejudiced the defendant's right to cross-examine the state's principal witness.

The District of Columbia Court of Appeals applied *Blackwell's* approach in *Neku v. U.S., supra,* 620 A.2d 259. There, after observing the defendant obtain cocaine from Carter, an undercover officer purchased cocaine from the defendant. Both defendant and Carter were arrested. Before trial, Carter pled guilty to obtain sentencing benefits. Carter and the undercover officer testified against the defendant at his trial. The defendant sought to call Carter's former attorney to testify to prior inconsistent statements Carter had made to counsel which would allegedly impeach Carter's inculpatory trial testimony. The trial court sustained the objection that the statements were protected by the attorney-client privilege.

Relying upon *Blackwell,* the appellate court upheld the trial court's ruling. It reasoned that the value of the privileged communication "must be clear and substantial" to outweigh the interests served by the privilege. (620 A.2d at p. 263.) Essential to that determination are both the intrinsic probative value of the information conveyed by the privileged communication and the alternative means open to the accused to otherwise make the same point. (*Ibid.*) The *Neku* court concluded, after a careful review of the record, that the probative value of the proffered impeachment was inadequate to outweigh the interests protected by the attorney-client privilege, given the other methods available to impeach Carter. (*Id.* at p. 264.)

We do not believe that either *Blackwell* or *Neku* supports Flack's contention that the trial court erred in not permitting White's testimony about Godlewski's comments to counsel. Both cases are clearly distinguishable, in that each involved an attempt to breach the attorney-client privilege held by an accomplice who had already pled guilty; at bench, Flack seeks to penetrate the confidential attorney-client relationship of a codefendant who is being jointly tried. There is a great potential for mischief inherent in a case such as this where codefendants are jointly tried but each attempts to shift responsibility to the other. Moreover, as the *Neku* court itself noted, there is a valid concern that if the privilege is easily breached by a defendant, "the price may be to open up to view entire discussions between attorney and criminal defendant as the prosecutor in turn fairly seeks" to use privileged communications. (*Neku v. U.S.*, *supra*, 620 A.2d at p. 262.)

(3) In any event, neither case holds that the defendant has a per se right to breach the attorney-client privilege in order to present a defense. The most which can be distilled from the two cases is that a criminal defendant *may*, under certain circumstances, have the right to use privileged communications. To make that determination, a court must employ a balancing process to decide if a breach of the privilege is necessary to implement the accused's constitutional rights.

(1c) In both *Neku* and *Blackwell*, the trial and appellate courts found that the balance tilted in favor of sustaining the privilege. In fact, Flack has not cited any case in which a court has concluded that the balance weighed in favor of overriding the attorney-client privilege and disclosing the information at trial. Thus, the only question in this case is whether employment of a balancing process required overriding the privilege so as to permit White's testimony. We think not.

In regard to that prong of the determination which necessitates evaluating the "intrinsic probative weight" (*Neku v. U.S.*, *supra*, 620 A.2d at p. 263) of the proffered testimony, Flack greatly overstates his case when he claims that in the statements Godlewski "admitted guilt and exonerated his codefendants." Godlewski only stated, in response to a statement by counsel that he "would have been better off saying" that he had done it instead of blaming it on Flack and Brown, "That's what I'm going to tell them, that I did it, not these guys." This conversation merely suggests that as a matter of trial tactics, Godlewski was going to assert he had done the killing. The conversation contains no affirmative representation by Godlewski that, in fact, he actually did do the killing.

In regard to that prong of the determination which calls for evaluating "the availability of other means by which the defendant can pursue" the same point (*Neku v. U.S.*, *supra*, 620 A.2d at p. 263), the record discloses that Flack did, in fact, present other evidence to support his claim that Godlewski had admitted having actually committed the murder. Two witnesses (Baugh and McLemore) testified that "Ray" admitted that he had killed the victim. Flack's argument that White's testimony was necessary to corroborate their testimony overlooks two significant points. One is that the trial court prevented the prosecutor from taking unfair advantage of its ruling sustaining the privilege by ruling that he could not argue that there was no corroboration for the testimony of Baugh and

McLemore. The second, and more significant, is that Flack, in the course of his trial testimony, twice recounted a conversation with Godlewski in which the latter confessed to him that he had accidentally shot his father.

Given Flack's testimony that Godlewski said that he had *accidentally* shot the victim, an incredible claim in light of all of the other evidence in this case, we conclude that, on balance, Flack has not demonstrated a compelling need for the use of the statements. A fortiori, the trial court did not err.

Questions and Comments

1. After reading this case and understanding the essence of attorney-client privilege, do you think the privilege extends to communications between a client and her attorney if they are being accidently overheard by others? Would you need to know more? Are there any exceptions to the attorney-client privilege?

2. What measures, if any, should the attorney have taken to ensure the privileged communication was protected in various settings throughout his representation?

3. Given the facts, under what circumstances, if any, could the attorney have disclosed any communication from his client? *See* Model Rule 1.6. Why do you think the Model Rules have made the exceptions so narrow? What does this say about the importance of maintaining confidentiality?

D. DISCUSSION QUESTIONS

1. Rule 1.15 governs a scenario in which a lawyer keeps a piece of property owned by the client. What are the key aspects of the rule? One of the biggest mistakes a lawyer can make is commingling her own funds and her client's funds, even if accidentally. What are some reasonable steps a lawyer can take in order to ensure that commingling funds does not occur? Consider the importance of keeping records, staying organized, and staying up-to-date.

2. Rule 1.5 states that a contingent fee cannot be charged or collected in a domestic relations matter or for a defendant in a criminal case. What are the practical reasons for having these limitations to a contingent fee? Why would these types of situations make a contingent fee inappropriate?

3. As noted by the readings and the cases, Rule 1.6 and the protections it provides might seem controversial to someone who is not a lawyer. How would you explain the importance of Rule 1.6 and the protection it gives clients to a lay person? Consider the exceptions to the rule and the cases provided in this chapter.

CHAPTER 6:
Reality Check :

Waiving or Losing Confidentiality
&
Applicable Exceptions

Chapter 6:
Reality Check—Waiving Confidentiality and Applicable Exceptions

A. INTRODUCTION

Lawyers have both an ethical and moral obligation to advocate zealously on their client's behalf. The obligation, however, lies much deeper than zealous trial work. Under Model Rule 1.6, lawyers are bound by confidentiality in that they cannot reveal information *relating* to the client's representation, though, certain exceptions to confidentiality *may* apply. A lawyer *may* disclose information related to the representation of her client only as reasonably necessary to prevent harm, crime, or injury, to comply with Model Rules, or to defend herself against allegations from the course of her representation. These limited instances in which a lawyer may disclose information indicate just how deep Rule 1.6's protection runs.

This chapter will bring you a case and an article in which confidentiality is strained between a lawyer and her client. It is important to remember that a lawyer's duty is first and foremost to her client. The *Diamond v. Stratton* case presents an issue of confidentiality in regards to a possible scheme of fraud. The article entitled *When Innocence Is Confidential* discusses the Alton Logan case in which two attorneys withheld their client's guilty confession due to Rule 1.6, while Alton Logan remained incarcerated for a crime he did not commit. The article will help students understand how application of Rule 1.6 to real-life scenarios can raise issues of morality and societal values.

New concerns about confidentiality are discussed in the final article of the chapter, *Legal Ethics Lessons for a Digital World*. This article discusses the increasing number of lawyers on the Internet and the new concern for breaching confidentiality through new media, such as social media sites or personal blogs. While reading this article, consider the recent increase in lawyers using the Internet for communication purposes. Consider how the Internet and social media, although great in many aspects, might pose a new concern for protecting client confidentiality. Should the American Bar Association consider extending the rule of confidentiality by adding additional safeguards to postings on the Internet? If so, what should they be?

Where is the line drawn between serving a client as an ethical lawyer, and relaying information that could protect or benefit members of society? How can a lawyer, while keeping his client's confidences, do what is best to ensure a fair, working judicial system? Do the representation and a lawyer's duties to her client ever end? This chapter will assess these dilemmas through different circumstances testing the boundaries of confidentiality and it will also address various challenges and the issue of morality lawyers may face under these circumstances.

B. RULES

This chapter continues delving further into Model Rule 1.6, focusing in on the importance of the attorney-client privilege and confidentiality. In preparation, review the following section of the Model Rules of Professional Conduct along with any relevant comments listed below.

- Rule 1.6: Confidentiality of Information
  - Comments [1-8], [13], [20]

C. CASES AND ADDITIONAL READINGS

DIAMOND V. STRATTON
United States District Court (S.D.N.Y. 1982)
95 F.R.D. 503

Sand, District Judge:
This case arises out of a dispute over whether the death of Leo A. Diamond (the "insured") is covered by a travel insurance policy, issued by certain underwriters at Lloyd's, London, of which defendant is the lead underwriter. Plaintiffs' first of two causes of action asserts policy coverage, alleging that injuries resulting from a December, 1979 bus accident were the direct and independent cause of the insured's death in May, 1980. Plaintiffs' second cause of action states:

12. In refusing to pay the said principal sum, defendant and its agents have stated to plaintiffs that the proximate cause of the demise of LEO A. DIAMOND was the conduct of plaintiffs in removing life support systems from LEO A. DIAMOND, and was not the said bus accident.

13. The making by the defendant of the said statement and the willful refusal to pay the amount due has inflicted intentionally and recklessly upon plaintiffs extreme emotional suffering, for which plaintiffs seek damages, individually, of $100,000.

14. The making of the said statement and the willful refusal to pay the amount due is so outrageous and dishonest, and done in part because it is to defendant's direct economic benefit to delay payment due to high rates of interest, as to subject defendant to punitive damages in the amount of $1 million.

It appears that on April 14, 1981, Hogan & Hartson, counsel for the defendant, wrote to then counsel for the plaintiffs the letter annexed hereto as (Exhibit A) This is the basis of the second cause of action and it is clear that the "agents" referred to in para. 12 of the above-quoted complaint are Hogan & Hartson.

Defendant has moved to dismiss the second cause of action and plaintiffs have asked the Court to defer ruling on that motion until they have had the opportunity to examine certain documents in defendant's claim file, described in para. 7 of the affidavit of Harold E. Marshack, III, submitted on behalf of the defendant in opposition to such discovery. Plaintiffs have moved to compel production of these documents, which defendant resists on the grounds of attorney-client privilege and the work product rule.

At oral argument on these motions, the Court ruled that consideration of plaintiffs' motion to compel production should precede that of defendant's motion to dismiss and suggested, so as to obviate conjecture as to what the withheld documents might contain, that they be inspected *in camera,* a suggestion acceded to by the parties. This *in camera* inspection has taken place and the Court, having given substantial weight to the significant, generally compelling considerations underlying the attorney-client privilege and work product rule, is nevertheless of the view that the nature and sufficiency as a matter of pleading of plaintiff's second cause of action present adequate ground for denying to defendant the protections it asserts herein.

- agreeing w/ P

Inasmuch as the Court's jurisdiction in this case is founded on 28 U.S.C. § 1332, questions arising herein concerning privilege are governed, pursuant to *Fed.R.Evid. 501*, by New York law. The applicable statute is N.Y. CPLR § 4503(a) (McKinney Supp. 1981). That the documents in issue fall within the literal terms of this statute is not controverted.

However, in New York, as in virtually all jurisdictions, there exist several recognized instances in which the privilege is deemed inapplicable. *See, e.g.,* 5 Weinstein, Korn & Miller, N.Y.Civ.Prac. paras. 4503.07-08; 8 Wright & Miller, Fed.Prac. & Proc. para. 2017. One such instance is where the communication sought to be disclosed was made in furtherance of what the client knew or reasonably should have known to be a crime or fraud. *See In re Associated Homeowners & Bus. Org.,* 87 Misc. 2d 67, 385 N.Y.S.2d 449, 450 (Sup.Ct. 1976); 2 Weinstein's Evidence, para. 503(d)(1)[01], at 503-70; Note, The Future Crime or Tort Exception to Communications Privilege, 77 Harv.L.Rev. 730, 730-33 (1964).

Numerous opinions have, at least in dictum, formulated this exception to the privilege in broader terms. For example, in *People v. Belge,* 59 A.D.2d 307, 399 N.Y.S.2d 539, 540 (4th Dep't 1977), the court quoted with approval Judge Wyzanski's formulation of this exception in *United States v. United Shoe Mach. Corp.,* 89 F. Supp. 357, 358-59 (D.Mass. 1950), which holds unprotected by the privilege any communication that "relates to a fact of which the attorney was informed . . . . for the purposes of committing a crime or *tort*" (emphasis supplied). *See also* Uniform Rule of Evidence 26(a) (1953).

We are convinced that the consideration underlying the firmly established denial of the privilege for communications in furtherance of crime or fraud, *viz.,* that the privilege's policy of promoting the administration of justice would be undermined if the privilege could be used as a cloak or shield, 2 Weinstein's Evidence para. 503(d) (1) [01], at 503-70, is equally compelling with regard to communications in furtherance of the intentional tort of which plaintiffs herein complain. To deny the protection of the privilege to communications in aid of fraud while granting it to communications in aid of another intentional tort would draw a too "crude boundary," as characterized by Wigmore, who also questions "how the law can protect a deliberate plan to defy the law and oust another person of his rights, whatever the precise nature of those rights may be." 8 Wigmore, Evidence § 2298, at 577 (McNaughton rev. 1961). Having examined the documents in issue, we find as to those statements to which the attorney-client privilege is applicable that they bear directly on the question whether there was the intentional infliction of emotional distress that plaintiffs allege. Accordingly, plaintiffs should be allowed the opportunity to examine these documents.

Defendant's second objection is that the documents sought are protected from discovery by the work product rule of Fed.R.Civ.Proc. 26(b)(3). While we concur with defendant's characterization of some of this matter as work product, we are persuaded that plaintiffs have nevertheless shown a "substantial need" for the discovery of this material, pursuant to the Rule. *See O'Boyle v. Life Ins. Co. of N. Am.,* 299 F. Supp. 704, 706 (N.D. Fla. 1969); *Kennedy v. Senyo,* 52 F.R.D. 34, 36 (W.D. Pa. 1971); *cf. Prudential Ins. Co. of America v. Marine Nat'l Exch. Bank,* 52 F.R.D. 367 (E.D. Wis. 1971); *see generally* 4 Moore's Fed.Prac. para. 26.64, at 26-419 to 421

We recognize that [...] ery into a defendant insurer's claim file m [...] n unfounded fishing expedition. At this stag [...] re satisfied as to both the sufficiency as a r [...] ffs' second cause of action, *see Halio v. L* [...] .S.2d 759 (2d Dep't 1961) (defendant's l [...] basis for intentional infliction of emotion: [...] *cial Finance Co.,* 39 A.D.2d 11, 330 N.Y [...] 1972) (existence of legitimate motive for [...] at cause of action for intentional infliction o [...] significant bearing the sought-after documen [...]

Inasmuch as the [...] rected at the April 14 letter, the documents [...] to whether defendant's counsel in sending : [...] or recklessly or after careful investigation [...] ive and knowledge of defendant and counsel at that time. Unlike the usual controversy involving the attorney-client privilege and/or work product rule, in which statements made by the client or attorney are only corroborative or inconsistent with the client's subsequently assumed position, here the statements sought to be discovered are themselves crucial to resolving the central issues raised by plaintiffs' second cause of action.

In light of the foregoing, defendant is directed to produce to plaintiffs' counsel, within five (5) days of this date, the documents described in para. 7 of the affidavit of Harold E. Marshack, III.

We emphasize that at this stage of the proceedings we deal only with the allegations of the second cause of action as they appear on the face of the complaint and the discoverability of the documents in question. Nothing contained herein should be construed as a reflection of the Court's views on whether, after the discovery has been completed, the second cause of action can survive defendant's deferred motions.

SO ORDERED.

Handwritten note: Diamond v. Stratton re: fraud
- Π wants documents which Δ resists on A/c priv.
- Π 's allowed to look at documents & Ct ordered Δ's to produce

Exhibit A

April 14, 1981

Austin F. Canfield, Jr., Esquire
Gorman & Canfield
4701 Sangamore Road
Washington, D.C. 20016

RE: Leo A. Diamond, Deceased
Airline Passengers Association, Inc.
Member No. 9669
Personal Accident Insurance Policy
No. 535001700

Dear Mr. Canfield:

We have completed our preliminary review of documents furnished us by Dr. Morowitz, Dr. Brownlee, and the Medical Records Custodian of Georgetown University Hospital. These records suggest that in late March 1980 Mr. Diamond's family advised the medical staff at Georgetown University Hospital that it wished the staff to "stop all life support measures" on the patient. As you know, Mr. Diamond died approximately six weeks later, on May 6, 1980.

This circumstance, if true, raises profound issues—not the least of which are the predominant or proximate cause of Mr. Diamond's death and the insurer's obligations under the above-referenced policy. It is quite apparent that resolving these issues will require additional investigation into both the pertinent facts and the applicable law.

We write now, before undertaking the necessary additional investigation, so as to bring the facts revealed by the medical records to your attention. In addition, we would appreciate your advice as to whether, in light of the medical record, the beneficiaries wish to forward any additional information or withdraw their claim under the policy.

We note again that our continuing review of this matter and all communications are conducted under a full reservation of Underwriter's rights under the policy. If you have any questions concerning the foregoing, please do not hesitate to contact us.

Sincerely,
HOGAN & HARTSON

Questions and Comments

1. Consider and articulate the distinction between the confidentiality standard under Rule 1.6 and the attorney-client privilege. Which confidentiality requirement is broader/narrower? In *Diamond v. Stratton*, the court applied an exception in order to allow plaintiffs access to protected information. What exception to the attorney-client privilege did the court apply? Why was relaying the information critical to the case? Do you think the plaintiffs could have proven the case without the aid of the documents?

2. The court discusses "in camera" inspection of the documents in this case. What does it actually mean and when do the courts utilize such inspections? Do you think in camera inspection makes it easier for the court to view documents that are protected by evidentiary rules and the Model Rules?

3. The court agreed with the defendant that under the work-product doctrine, some contents of the letter were privileged and protected. The court, however, did order disclosure after having reviewed the documents in camera. Why did the court allow the plaintiffs to view the letter despite the finding that its part was protected by the work-product doctrine?

WHEN INNOCENCE IS CONFIDENTIAL: A NEW AND ESSENTIAL EXCEPTION TO ATTORNEY-CLIENT CONFIDENTIALITY
Santa Clara Law Review, Vol. 56, No. 1, A4, April 2, 2016
By Adam Belsey

Introduction

"That it is better 100 guilty Persons should escape than that one innocent Person should suffer, is a maxim that has been long and generally approved." Benjamin Franklin, 1785. That maxim, in one form or another, has been repeated throughout history and has permeated the legal system. It is a part of Supreme Court precedent and taught not just in law schools, but in grade schools as well. Worldwide, this truism has been accepted by many different cultures.

The legal system in the United States is based upon the foundation of the Constitution. Within that Constitution are certain rights that conform to the founding fathers' ideal. The Fourth Amendment provides the right to be secure in our homes, free from unlawful search and seizure without probable cause. The Fifth Amendment provides the right to protection against self-incrimination and requires due process of law before a person may be denied life, liberty or property. The Sixth Amendment provides that a person charged with a crime has the right to the effective assistance of counsel and to a compulsory process for obtaining favorable evidence in his case.

However, what should the legal system do when the rights of one person are pitted against the rights of another? How can we reconcile allowing one person to exercise their rights when the exercise of those rights pose a threat to the life of another? What would you think if I told you that there is currently a loophole within the legal system that not only allows a known guilty party to remain free, but also allows an innocent person to suffer for that crime while officers of the court are aware of the truth? As shocking and outlandish as this may sound, this loophole scenario has occurred numerous times, resulting in innocent people spending a large portion of their lives in prison for a crime they did not commit. This kind of result completely eviscerates the purpose behind the justice system. The purpose of the criminal legal system is to provide justice to those who are wronged, not to inflict punishment on those individuals the system knows are innocent. When a person spends time in prison for a crime that he or she did not commit, while the true perpetrator has confessed, there is a real problem that must be fixed.

Loophole where innocent suffers while guilty goes free

***

I. Example Cases

A. Alton Logan Case

On January 11, 1982, two men committed a robbery at a McDonald's in Chicago, Illinois. During the course of that robbery a security guard, Lloyd Wickliffe, was killed by a shotgun blast and another security guard, Alvin Thompson, was wounded. Both guard's' handguns were taken, though no money was stolen. On February 5, 1982, one of the perpetrators, Edgar Hope, was arrested after fatally shooting a police officer; he was still carrying the gun he had taken from Thompson at the McDonald's robbery. There was no way Alton Logan could have known that this incident would not only change his life, but steal a great portion of it from him due to the loophole in the legal system's ethical rules.

On February 7, 1982, Alton Logan was arrested and charged, along with Hope, for robbery and murder. This arrest was based on a tip to the police and the erroneous testimony of three eyewitnesses who identified Logan as a participant in the McDonald's robbery and murder. Alton Logan and Edgar Hope would later be convicted of the McDonald's robbery. Hope was sentenced to death, while Logan was sentenced to life in prison.

On February 9, 1982, only two days after Alton Logan's arrest in the McDonald's case, two Chicago police officers were shot to death. Brothers Andrew Wilson and Jackie Wilson were arrested and charged with the murders. While investigating this case, police recovered not only the weapons used to kill the police officers but also a cache of other weapons, including the murder weapon used in the McDonald's case. The guns were found hidden at a location where Andrew Wilson was known to stay. Police and prosecutors never pursued the connection between the killing of the police officers and the McDonald's murder.

Two Cook County assistant public defenders, Dale Coventry and Jamie Kunz, were appointed to represent Andrew Wilson in the officer murders. A few weeks later, Coventry and Kunz were approached by Marc Miller, Edgar Hope's defense attorney, with information indicating that Alton Logan had not committed the McDonald's murder. Kunz reported that, "Hope said that [Logan] had nothing to do with the McDonald's case, and that it was Andrew Wilson who was with him and Andrew Wilson who shotgunned the security guard." According to Kunz's recollection, when he and Coventry confronted Wilson about this claim "Wilson said, 'Yeah' or 'Uh-huh,' nodded, grinned, and said, 'That was me.'" Coventry also recalled that Wilson "kind of chuckled over the fact that someone else was charged with something he did."

Coventry and Kunz were bound by legal ethics rules not to disclose any of the conversation between them and Andrew Wilson. Without Wilson's express permission, their conversation was confidential, and Coventry and Kunz's metaphorical hands were tied. On March 17, 1982, in the hope that they may one day be able to reveal their conversation with Andrew Wilson, the two assistant public defenders drew up an affidavit stating, "I have obtained information through privileged sources that a man named Alton Logan who was charged with the fatal shooting of Lloyd Wickliffe at on or about 11 Jan. 82 is in fact not responsible for that shooting that in fact another person was responsible." Coventry and Kunz both signed the affidavit, as well as a witness and notary public. The affidavit was then sealed in a metal box, held by Coventry, until after Andrew Wilson's death twenty-five years later on November 19, 2007. Kunz stated that they prepared the document "so that if we were ever able to speak up, no one could say we were just making this up now."

Harold Winston, a Cook County Assistant Public Defender, was representing Alton Logan at the time of Andrew Wilson's death. He was aware of the rumor that for years, "Coventry and Kunz had information about Andrew Wilson's involvement in the McDonald's case." After Wilson's death, he contacted Kunz. Kunz then contacted Coventry, and he located the metal box and unsealed the envelope that he had been faithfully keeping for over twenty-five years. Coventry and Kunz were then summoned to court on January 11, 2008, "where Criminal Court Judge James Schreier ruled that they could reveal the conversation [they had with Andrew] Wilson and the contents of the affidavit."

On April 18, 2008, after twenty-six years in prison, Alton Logan's conviction was set aside. Logan was released on bail, pending a new trial. On September 4, 2008, the Illinois Attorney General's office dismissed the charges against Logan stating it was unable to prove Logan's guilt. Judge Schreier supported the decision, stating, "From all that I have heard, Mr. Logan, you did not commit this murder." Alton Logan responded, "I've been telling everybody for the last 26 years, 'I didn't do this,' and finally they did the right thing. . . . I'm happy that I can finally get on with my life, try to do some of the things I want to do." Later, Logan reported to 60 Minutes, "I never stopped giving up hope. I've always believed that one day is gone—somebody's gonna come forth and tell the truth. But I didn't know when."

Coventry and Kunz were faced with a strange dilemma though unfortunately one that is not uncommon in the legal system. In their interview with 60 Minutes, correspondent Bob Simon remarked that they "chose to allow [Alton Logan] to rot away in jail." Coventry replied, "It seems that way. But had we come forward right away, aside from violating our own client's privilege, and putting him in jeopardy, would the information that we had have been valued? Would it have proved anything?" Coventry and Kunz believe it would never have been allowed in court. As they felt there was no way out, they at least did what they believed to be their best option: write the affidavit and get Andrew Wilson's permission to reveal what he told them after his death.

Logan's case represents two major problems within the legal system. The first is the issue of confidentiality, and the loophole which allows an innocent man to remain imprisoned for twenty-six years while the true perpetrator remains unpunished for their crimes. The second issue is, had they come forward with the confession earlier, the system may have turned away such exculpatory evidence, effectively putting the constitutional rights of a confessed guilty party above the constitutional rights of an innocent man sitting in jail for a crime he did not commit. Perhaps this sounds completely absurd and improbable, but the next few sample cases will demonstrate the concerns raised by Coventry and Kunz in the Logan case.

B. Lee Wayne Hunt Case

Lee Wayne Hunt and Jerry Cashwell were both separately convicted in 1986 of killing Roland and Lisa Matthews. The Matthews had been shot execution style and had their throats slit in their home near Fayetteville, North Carolina. Lee Wayne Hunt was convicted based in large part on FBI testimony regarding bullet analysis, testimony later discredited by the FBI. In 2005, the FBI reported that composite bullet lead analysis was found to be scientifically invalid. While conceding that the FBI's testimony was unreliable, prosecutors still argued that Hunt's conviction should stand due to two witnesses implicating him in the murders. Both of those witnesses, one a prison informant, were provided plea deals at the time in exchange for their testimony. The circumstantial evidence matching bullets to Hunt stood unchallenged until 2002.

In 2002, after serving more than a decade in prison for the killings of Roland and Lisa Matthews, Jerry Cashwell committed suicide. Prosecutors had long maintained that Hunt participated in the killings, and Cashwell did nothing to refute them. However, after Cashwell's death, Staples Hughes, the public defender who represented Cashwell at trial, came forward with information that Cashwell confessed to him in private that he had single handedly killed the Matthews after an argument over the television being too loud. According to Hughes, "Lee Wayne Hunt had nothing to do with it." Hughes decided to testify regarding Cashwell's confession after his client's death stating that, "it seemed to me at that point ethically permissible and morally imperative that I spill the beans." Unfortunately, unlike the Alton Logan case, Hughes never received permission from Cashwell to reveal his secrets after death.

The Cumberland County Superior Court in Fayetteville did not agree with Hughes. At the 2007 hearing for Hunt's request for a new trial, Judge Jack A. Thompson told Hughes to stop. Judge Thompson warned Hughes, "If you testify . . . I will be compelled to report you to the state bar. Do you understand that?" Despite the dire warning, Hughes decided to continue. Hughes told Judge Thompson that he had "never, ever, ever before violated a client's confidence . . . [b]ut Jerry's dead. My disclosure can't hurt him and I have to weigh that disclosure against the continuing harm" to Lee Wayne Hunt. Judge Thompson refused to consider the evidence, writing in his opinion that Hughes committed professional misconduct. Staples Hughes was reported to the bar for violating attorney-client privilege by revealing what his client had told him.

The North Carolina Court of Appeals upheld Judge Thompson's ruling. The North Carolina Supreme Court refused to consider new evidence in the case. Today, Lee Wayne Hunt, now fifty-five years old, still sits in prison after serving twenty-eight years and counting. Richard Rosen, Hunt's attorney, stated, "I think as a whole, the judicial system of North Carolina should be ashamed of their treatment of this case form (sic) top to bottom." The state Supreme Court did not offer an explanation for its refusal to review the case. In 2008 Hunt's attorneys expressed their intention to appeal the case in federal court. In a letter written by Lee Wayne on September 2014, he stated "that he is possibly getting a new trial in federal court."

Once again, we have the situation of a lawyer withholding evidence exonerating an innocent man and a judicial system blocking his efforts to disclose the evidence after his client's death. The legal system has placed barriers for unfortunate people like Alton Logan and Lee Wayne Hunt to have exonerating evidence placed just out of reach. "Both the United States Supreme Court and the North Carolina Supreme Court have said the lawyer-client privilege survives death, though they recognized that narrow exceptions might be possible." Chief Justice William H. Rehnquist, writing for the majority in a 1998 Supreme Court decision said, "'[c]lients may be concerned about reputation, civil liability or possible harm to friends of' family if their secrets were disclosed after they died."

In Lee Wayne Hunt's case, the battle continues. The New York Times asked legal ethics professor Monroe Freedman, for his opinion on the case. Professor Freedman said that, "[i]f there is no threat of civil action against the client's estate and there are no survivors who continue to believe in the client's innocence . . . there is no confidentiality obligation to begin with." Hughes agreed, "[w]hat reputational interest did Jerry have? . . . He had pleaded guilty to killing two people. He didn't have an estate. His estate was a pair of shower shoes and two paperback books."

Lee Wayne Hunt had to wait, like Alton Logan, until the confessed killer died to gain access to the confidential information held by lawyers adhering to the rules of legal ethics. Now, he also faces the arduous task of convincing a court to consider the exonerating evidence and dismiss the case against him. The legal system prevents certain evidence from being admitted in a criminal court to ensure that a person found guilty was given a fair trial.

***

II. The Current Legal Environment Surrounding Attorney-Client Confidentiality

The argument has often been made, that a person's constitutional right to present witness testimony should outweigh a deceased client's right to confidentiality.

***

While attorney-client privilege and confidentiality of information are distinct doctrines, together they function as the gatekeeper of client secrets. The Supreme Court has asserted that a trial is a "search for truth." However, maintaining client secrets flies in the face of truth when those secrets are kept from the court. The American Bar Association's Model Rules of Professional Conduct (Model Rules) require devotion to the client despite the consequences of maintaining those secrets. Not once in the Model Rules, upon which most state ethical codes are based, will a direct reference to the discovery and production of the truth be found. Aside from the few exceptions currently allowed, strict attorney loyalty is required of all lawyers. This has been a long accepted standard in the legal profession dating back as far as 1820 when Lord Brougham famously described a lawyer's role:

> To save [the] client by all means and expedients, and at all hazards and costs to other persons, and, amongst them, to himself, is his first and only duty; and in performing this duty he must not regard the alarm, the torments, the destruction which he may bring upon others. Separating the duty of a patriot from that of an advocate, he must go on reckless of the consequences, though it should be his unhappy fate to involve his country in confusion.

Though certain rules do require that a lawyer not mislead, act deceptively, or commit fraud, there is no rule instructing a lawyer to proffer the truth. "Devotion to the client, not truth, is the lawyer's ultimate duty." The Model Rules, for example, instructs a lawyer to question the credibility of a witness the lawyer knows to be truthful. The judicial system charges a lawyer with the task of being a "zealous advocate for the client, putting that person's interest ahead of all others." Although attorney-client confidentiality is touted as one of the most highly valued precepts in the law, the Model Rules do recognize exceptions to confidentiality in certain situations.

A. The Model Rules of Professional Conduct

Most state ethics rules governing attorney conduct are based on the Model Rules. A large majority of the states have adopted some of the language and the numbering system suggested by the Model Rules. Every lawyer, while not subject to the Model Rules itself, is subject to discipline for a breach of the rules of professional conduct adopted by their state. In order to ensure that lawyers are well informed on the Model Rules, law students in all but three U.S. jurisdictions (Maryland, Wisconsin, and Puerto Rico) are required to take the MPRE before they may be admitted to the bar in their state. The Model Rules are a collection of proposed rules that provide guidelines for the states to draft their own professional conduct rules.

B. Confidentiality of Information

The Model Rules codify confidentiality of information in Rule 1.6. Rule 1.6 provides that, "A lawyer shall not reveal information relating to the representation of a client unless the client gives informed consent. . . ." This covers a very extensive range of information that a lawyer must keep confidential. The purpose in providing such an expansive protection is so that every client may receive competent representation as allotted by the constitution. Competent representation requires that a lawyer be "fully informed of all the facts of the matter he is handling." The widely held belief is that clients will not provide a lawyer with full disclosure without that promise of confidentiality.

Benefits aside, confidentiality is at odds with the truth. The Fifth Amendment provides protection against self-incrimination. An advocate, aware of his client's guilt, must not reveal that fact to the court. As every person has a right to competent representation, which requires full disclosure to a person's lawyer, as well as a right not to incriminate one's self, there must be a way to maintain both in a criminal case. Model Rule 1.6 is that answer, and it is meant to be upheld in all but the few cases where an exception applies. Adherence to this rule means that evidence of a person's guilt will be hidden from court proceedings, sometimes allowing the guilty to go free. The courts have accepted this as "the price that society must pay for the availability of justice to every citizen, which is the value that the privilege is designed to secure." They have explained that the "social good derived from the proper performance of the functions of lawyers acting for their clients . . . outweighs the harm that may come from the suppression of the evidence."

rationale

C. Attorney-Client Privilege

The United States Supreme Court recognized that the attorney-client privilege is one of the oldest recognized privileges of the different confidential communications. The basis for this privilege is premised on the theory that encouraging clients to make "full and frank" disclosures provides their attorneys the ability to offer candid legal advice and effective representation. The United States Supreme Court has stated that the, "public benefit in encouraging clients to fully communicate . . . outweighs the harm caused by the loss of relevant information."

While the attorney-client privilege is not expressly codified in the Model Rules, Rule 1.6 provides similar protection. The attorney-client privilege is derived from common law and the Federal Rules of Evidence. Each state may adopt their own version of the attorney-client privilege and, just as the Model Rules provide guidance, Proposed Federal Rule of Evidence 503 (Rule 503), also can assist in the creation of state rules governing attorney-client privilege. Under Rule 503, "[a] client has a privilege to refuse to disclose and to prevent any other person from disclosing confidential communications made for the purpose of facilitating the rendition of professional legal services to the client."

Thus, ethically, the combination of Model Rule 1.6 requiring a lawyer not to reveal "information relating to the representation of a client" and Rule 503 preventing disclosure of any "confidential communications made for the purpose of facilitating the rendition of professional legal services," requires an attorney to keep secret almost anything he may learn from his client. The combination of these two doctrines fortifies the rights every individual has to competent representation without self-incrimination. Although attorney-client confidentiality is generally upheld, there are certain situations in which the ethical guidelines have deemed exceptions acceptable. The Model Rules provide seven exceptions when a lawyer may be allowed to reveal confidential information. Relevant to this discussion is Model Rule 1.6(b)(1) providing a lawyer the ability to break confidentiality in order "to prevent reasonably certain death or substantial bodily harm."

III. Identification of the Legal Problem

In the cases described above, the legal system not only allowed, but also staunchly defended the right of a confessed guilty party over the rights of individuals falsely accused. A legal system that would knowingly allow an innocent person to remain in jail or face execution, while the true perpetrator remains protected by client confidentiality is a broken legal system. These cases, especially those of Alton Logan and Lee Wayne Hunt garnered quite a bit of media attention. CBS News' 60 Minutes aired specials on both cases. The heightened attention brought this issue to the forefront in academic and journalistic circles. Much of the discussion has centered around the question of, "how our society can allow lawyers to keep secrets about a man's innocence for decades because of some seemingly attenuated notion of confidentiality owed to a client imprisoned for murder, even, in some cases, after that client dies." One wonders "how we can praise defense lawyers who wait half a lifetime until their client dies before revealing that a long-imprisoned man is innocent, while criticizing and even punishing them if they say anything while the client is still alive."

***

C. Modifying Rule 1.6 to Allow Revelation to Prevent Wrongful Execution or Incarceration of Another

Modifying Model Rule 1.6 to specifically allow revelation in the case of wrongful incarceration would eliminate the guesswork for a lawyer faced with a scenario similar to the example cases. Simply allowing revelation of confidential information in order to prevent or rectify a wrongful incarceration would provide a much broader scope of exemptions to Model Rule 1.6. Adoption of such a rule would require an institutional choice to place the rights of those wrongfully incarcerated above the rights of the confessed lawbreaker. Considering the inverse view can lead to grave injustices against the innocent, as exemplified above, it should not be a difficult leap to make.

Two states have adopted a specific exception to prevent the wrongful execution or incarceration of another. Massachusetts and Alaska have adopted similar text in their versions of Model Rule 1.6 that specifically allow a lawyer to reveal confidential information in order to prevent the "wrongful execution or incarceration of another." Both states still provide that the lawyer exercise discretion deciding whether to disclose, it does not require disclosure.

Massachusetts Rule 1.6(b)(1) provides that a lawyer may reveal confidential information "to prevent the commission of a criminal or fraudulent act that the lawyer reasonably believes is likely to result in death or substantial bodily harm, or in substantial injury to the financial interests or property of another, or to prevent the wrongful execution or incarceration of another." Massachusetts comment [6A] further provides that Rule 1.6(b)(1) "also permits a lawyer to reveal confidential information in the specific situation where such information discloses that an innocent person has been convicted of a crime and has been sentenced to imprisonment or execution." Thus, a lawyer is permitted to reveal confidential information only after a known innocent person has been sentenced to imprisonment. A conviction without a prison sentence still requires a lawyer to maintain his clients secret. Currently, there are no legal opinions or cases that apply this particular exception in Massachusetts.

Alaska Rule 1.6(b)(1)(C) provides that, "A lawyer may reveal a client's confidence or secret to the extent the lawyer reasonably believes necessary to prevent reasonably certain . . . wrongful execution or incarceration of another." The Alaska Comment notes that, "In paragraph (b)(1)(C), the court included an additional limited exception to the normal rule requiring lawyers to preserve the confidences and secrets of their clients. This provision is modeled on the similar Massachusetts rule: its core purpose is to permit a lawyer to reveal confidential information in the specific situation in which that information discloses that an innocent person has been convicted of a crime and has been sentenced to imprisonment or execution." Analogous to the Massachusetts exception, a lawyer in Alaska may, at their discretion, reveal confidential information after an innocent person has been incarcerated.

While the addition of specific rules is a step in the right direction, they still fall short of protecting the rights of all the parties involved. These rules certainly hold the possibility that a lawyer could choose to assist an innocent person wrongfully imprisoned but it does not require it. The addition of a wrongful incarceration exception solves the dilemma of a lawyer who is unsure whether or not they may reveal confidential information, but it still leaves unsolved two of the major issues: 1) revealing confidential information of a living client violates their Fifth Amendment right not to incriminate themselves, possibly subjecting them to prosecution; and 2) this statute still only *allows* a lawyer to reveal the confidential information, it does not require it.

***

V. A Mandatory Exception for Wrongful Incarceration Should Be Adopted

The current exceptions to Model Rule 1.6 afford attorney's very broad discretion. The fact that, as of this writing, I was unable to find a single reported case of an attorney coming forward based on the Massachusetts or Alaska wrongful incarceration statutes supports the theory that an optional rule may not be effective. A mandatory rule would at least guarantee that the person wrongfully incarcerated would have a means of obtaining the truth.

In a wrongful incarceration scenario, where an attorney reveals confidential information of his client, we still have the problem of the clients Fifth Amendment privilege. The Fifth Amendment prevents *"the use*, in a criminal prosecution, of a defendant's testimony elicited by compulsion."* (emphasis added) The Supreme Court in *Fisher v. United States* held that an attorney cannot be compelled to break the attorney-client privilege, as it would be a violation of the clients Fifth Amendment right. *Fisher* ascertained that any information that would be protected under the Fifth Amendment for the individual must also be protected by their lawyer.

In a wrongful incarceration situation however, it is not the compulsion to elicit information that triggers a Fifth Amendment violation, it is triggered if used against that person. In order to resolve this problem of violating the confessed criminal's Fifth Amendment right not to incriminate themselves, use of immunity for the confessing client must be part of the solution.

Use of immunity prevents the prosecution from using the confidential information elicited by compulsion against the criminal defendant. In the case of a wrongful incarceration situation, the elicited confidential information would be used to free the innocent, but it would be unavailable in a criminal prosecution against the client. Without use of immunity, any attorney who reveals confidential information that is used against a client in a criminal prosecution is a violation of the client's constitutional rights.

Use of immunity in these cases would not necessarily constitute a get out of jail free card for self-confessed criminals. An attorney under these circumstances would only reveal confidential information to the extent necessary to ascertain the innocence of a person wrongfully incarcerated. While any information revealed by the attorney would be protected from use, it would not prevent the prosecution from continuing to investigate the unsolved crime and prosecuting the client based on independent evidence.

Use of immunity would protect a guilty client's constitutional rights at the expense of the evidence presented to prove the innocence of a person wrongfully incarcerated. Its use may be looked upon with disdain by victims and their families, knowing that the actual criminal cannot be held responsible for the crime in some situations. Even more difficult to accept is the knowledge that the self-confessed criminals who benefit from this rule may be free from prosecution and have the ability to continue committing similar crimes. The Supreme Court has said that the "social good derived from the proper performance of the function of lawyers acting for their clients . . . outweighs the harm that may come from the suppression of evidence." This reasoning should also apply to the social good of righting the injustice of wrongful incarceration.

A mandatory wrongful incarceration exception to the attorney-client privilege provides a solution to all the issues presented. While there are certainly serious drawbacks to this type of an exception, those drawbacks will likely still exist without an exception and an innocent person will be incarcerated for a crime he did not commit. The guilty party whose confessed crime remains confidential will still be free to commit similar crimes. While the victims and their family may feel better believing the responsible party is being held responsible, their comfort in a false belief does not justify the unjust suffering of an innocent person.

The following proposed modification to Model Rule 1.6215 should be adopted:

> Rule 1.6 Confidentiality of Information
>
> (a) A lawyer shall not reveal information relating to the representation of a client unless the client gives informed consent, the disclosure is impliedly authorized in order to carry out the representation or the disclosure is permitted or required by paragraph (b).
>
> (b) A lawyer may reveal, and **must reveal in subsection (8)**, information relating to the representation of a client to the extent the lawyer reasonably believes necessary:
>
> (Exceptions 1 through 7 excluded)
>
> > **(8) to rectify the wrongful execution or incarceration of another; a person whose information is revealed in this manner is granted use immunity for the information provided.**

This proposed modification should include a comment similar to Massachusetts's comment [6A] permitting "a lawyer to reveal confidential information in the specific situation where such information discloses that an innocent person has been convicted of a crime and has been sentenced to imprisonment or execution." The requirement that the innocent person has already been convicted and sentenced is absolutely necessary. Without a wrongful conviction requirement, there would be many self-confessed criminals attempting to take advantage of use immunity when revelation may not be necessary. The innocent person may still be found innocent by a court of law. The revelation of confidential information and subsequent granting of use immunity should only be used after an innocent person has been convicted and sentenced and the guilty party has essentially gotten away with their crime.

Granting use immunity also provides a solution to the client-trust issue. A client is more apt to trust a lawyer who discloses that he may be required to reveal confidential information, even against his will, and that any information disclosed will not be used to harm the client. In these cases, the attorney may even be seen as having more integrity obeying the rules while preventing harm to his client. With use of immunity required under the Fifth Amendment, the likelihood that this new exception would chill communication between clients and their attorneys would be minimal and any damage to the client lawyer trust relationship would be far outweighed by the injustice done to an innocent person wrongfully incarcerated.

Conclusion

Wrongful incarceration is a grievously unfortunate flaw in the legal system. In most cases, when an innocent person is wrongfully convicted, the truth is only ever known by the guilty parties and the unfortunate person wrongfully convicted. In those rare cases where a lawyer, who is an officer of the court, knows the truth, failure to right this wrong is an unacceptable breakdown within the justice system.

***

Endnotes omitted (See Adam Belsey, When Innocence is Confidential: A New and Essential Exception to Attorney-Client Confidentiality, Volume 56, Issue 1 (2016) for full article version). Reprinted with permission from the 2016 edition of the "Santa Clara Law Review"© 2016 Santa Clara Law Review. All rights reserved.

Questions and Comments

1. After reading the article and considering the cases presented, do you think the specific exception to Rule 1.6 to prevent wrongful convictions should be adopted by every state? If so, why do you think only two states have adopted such an exception? Consider the recent increase in wrongful convictions.

2. As the author points out, the current exceptions to Model Rule 1.6 gives the attorney very broad discretion. Why do you think the rule drafters have left the rule exceptions in such a broad form? In your view, does broad discretion for the attorney have any positive components? If not, how would you change the applicable language? Please be specific.

3. Think about the Alton Logan case, the conflict the attorneys representing Wilson faced, and the decision that they made to keep Wilson's confession confidential. Would you have made the same decision? Keep in mind that these attorneys, like all attorneys, are bound by the Model Rules (or, more specifically, their state equivalent). If Wilson's attorneys decided to go ahead and reveal the information, how should they have gone about it and, in your opinion, would it have made a difference for Alton Logan?

LEGAL ETHICS LESSONS FOR A DIGITAL WORLD
The Recorder (Online), September 24, 2014
By Suzanne Y. Badawi, Randy Evans, and Shari Klevens

Undeniably, the practice of law has gone digital. This extends beyond calendar systems, email and document drafting and filing. It now includes the world wide web and its many methods of communication through social media.

Most attorneys and law firms have some kind of presence on the Internet. This may include a website, blog, LinkedIn profile, Facebook page or Twitter feed. Most likely, it includes a combination of some or all of those. Perform an online search for an attorney or firm and you will not come up empty-handed. In 2010, the American Bar Association's Legal Technology Survey Report found that 56 percent of attorneys responding to the survey were part of an online community or social network.

Everybody's Doing It

Over the past few years this number has grown. The younger the attorney, the more likely he or she is to have an Internet presence. A recent LexisNexis survey shows 86 percent of attorneys aged 25 to 35 participate in online social networks. For attorneys over the age of 46, the number is less, 66 percent, but still significant. As social media continues to grow as a generation's primary medium for communication—and decision making—undoubtedly all industries will continue to increase their Internet presence. This necessarily includes the legal field.

A recent survey by Vizibility and LexisNexis shows small firms appear to be leading the way. Ninety-one percent of small firms and 86 percent of large firms use social media as part of their marketing strategy. Both small and large firms that responded to the survey measure the success of their social media initiatives, at least in part, by the amount of new business generated.

An online presence is undeniably an effective marketing technique for attorneys and law firms. However, it is not without risk. Internet posts often are much more carefree and less edited than face-to-face conversation or more traditional forms of communication.

Such uninhibited communication is bound to conflict with the structured and defined boundaries of legal conduct as defined by each state's ethics rules. With this obvious and inherent conflict, many states are applying their ethical rules governing attorneys and social media. Thus, the dilemma is becoming less muddled as states begin to tackle the various ethical issues arising from Internet use and misuse. And the consequences are significant.

Avoid Blurting

An attorney is not free to say whatever he or she likes on an Internet blog. Their cyber-statements are subject to ethical rules regarding confidentiality and honesty. For example, an attorney cannot vent about a judge without regard for the truth of those statements. An attorney in Florida learned this the hard way, receiving a public reprimand and $1,200 fine for calling a judge an evil unfair witch who was seemingly mentally ill on an Internet blog while complaining about the judge's trial schedule. The Florida Bar explained that because the attorney's statements were made with reckless disregard for their truth, they constituted unethical behavior. The Supreme Court of Florida concluded the attorney's statements were not protected speech under the First Amendment, confirming the State Bar's reprimand.

Keeping Client Secrets

In addition, an attorney must maintain client confidences when posting on the Internet. Model Rule of Professional Conduct 1.6(a) prohibits attorneys from revealing confidential client information, except for very limited situations. Specifically, it mandates: A lawyer shall not reveal information relating to the representation of a client unless the client gives informed consent, the disclosure is impliedly authorized in order to carry out the representation or the disclosure is permitted by paragraph (b).

Paragraph (b) limits such disclosure to seven discrete situations, including the prevention of death, bodily harm, crime or fraud and the compliance with a law or court order. Many states have adopted Model Rule of Professional Conduct 1.6 or similar language.

California's Rules of Professional Conduct, Rule 3-100, state that [a] member shall not reveal information protected from disclosure by

Business and Professions Code section 6068, subdivision (e)(1) without the informed consent of the client. . . Paragraph (A) relates to a member's obligations under Business and Professions Code section 6068, subdivision (e)(1), which provides it is a duty of a member: To maintain inviolate the confidence, and at every peril to himself or herself to preserve the secrets, of his or her client.

The consequences for failing to follow the confidentiality rule when posting on the Internet can be severe. Several states have suspended an attorney's license for utilizing the Internet in a manner that violates this rule. The Supreme Court of Georgia reprimanded an attorney for posting personal and confidential client information on a blog in response to a client's negative reviews. Both Illinois and Wisconsin state bars have suspended an attorney's license for 60 days for publishing a blog that contained confidential information about clients and derogatory statements about judges. The blog included enough information to identify both the clients and judges. Even more severe, the State Bar of Oregon imposed a 90-day suspension on an attorney who disclosed personal and medical information of a client through an email list, in addition to indicating the client was seeking a new attorney.

Off-Duty Posting

The risk of an Internet post violating ethical rules exists even when a licensed attorney is not actively practicing law. As a result, the communication does not have to be about an attorney's client or case. Instead, it is enough that the attorney posts something that disparages the judicial system in general.

This is best demonstrated in the context of jury duty. While a juror is subject to civil contempt charges, and attorney who misuses the Internet by posting about his or her experience as a juror is subject to professional discipline.

The State Bar of California has disciplined an attorney, who was not practicing at the time, for authoring blog postings about the details of a case for which he was a juror. That attorney specifically identified the crimes at issue in the case. He also posted the first name of the defendant and the name of the judge. But he did not stop there. He went on to describe the judge in a less than favorable manner. Because the attorney failed to maintain respect due to the courts, he received two years of probation, a 45-day suspension and had to take the MPRE within one year.

As attorneys and law firms continue to grow their Internet and social media presence, state bars across the country increasingly will be called upon to apply their ethical rules to various forms of Internet publications. It is important that attorneys be mindful of their ethical obligations when participating in social media. A failure to do so may carry severe consequences—consequences that can be easily avoided by simply complying with ethical rules in all communications, including social media.

Questions and Comments

1. Based on the article, *Legal Ethics Lessons for a Digital World* and your own experiences with social media and new technology uses, why and how do you think more issues of confidentiality may arise? Do you agree that social media and the Internet make it easier to breach the protections of confidentiality?

2. Where should the line be drawn as to what a lawyer can say on her social media accounts? Should a lawyer be allowed to say things about her cases as long as it does not reveal any confidential information? Or, should a lawyer not make any reference to her cases at all, even if it does not necessarily breach the rules of confidentiality?

3. Do you think the punishment for breaching Rule 1.6 should be more or less severe, or the same, when a lawyer breaches confidentiality on a social media site as compared to in-person? Does it make a difference that most social media pages are available to "friends only" and thus only a limited number of people?

D. DISCUSSION QUESTIONS

1. Model Rule 1.6 (with its exceptions) represents a fundamental and yet controversial idea of an advocate's zealous representation of her client and the absolute trust the client can place in his lawyer. Do you think this aspect of our adversarial legal system offers more benefits than detriment to the society as a whole?

2. If you were a drafter of the Model Rules, what changes would you make, if any, to prevent situations such as in the well-known Alton Logan and other cases? What difficulties do you see in possibly making any changes to Rule 1.6?

3. Laypersons will argue confidentiality under Rule 1.6 is viewed to be "more important than justice" (for example in the form of an innocent man sentenced to life in prison). How will you respond to such a position?

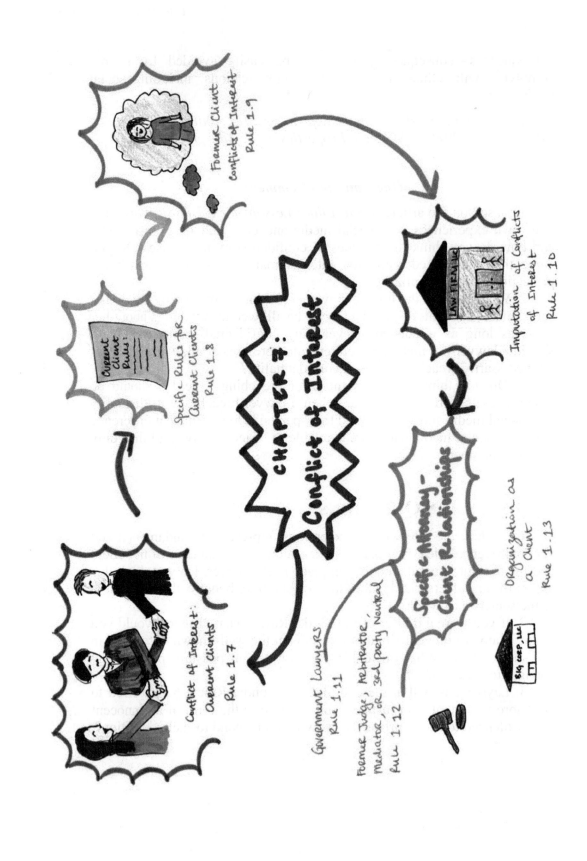

CHAPTER 7:
Conflict of Interest

Former Client
Conflicts of Interest
Rule 1.9

Imputation of Conflicts
of Interest
Rule 1.10

Specific Rules FOR
Current Clients
Rule 1.8

Conflict of Interest:
Current Clients
Rule 1.7

Specific Attorney-
Client Relationships

Government Lawyers
Rule 1.11

Former Judge, Arbitrator,
Mediator, oR 3rd party Neutral
Rule 1.12

ORganization as
a Client
Rule 1.13

LAW FIRM LLC

Big coRp, LLC

Chapter 7:
Conflict of Interest

A. INTRODUCTION

The legal community, although vast, is also considered a close-knit community of partners and colleagues. The Model Rules of Professional Conduct focuses on conflicts of interest in regards to legal representation to ensure justice is given through a fair and impartial proceeding. Under Model Rules 1.7 and 1.8, a lawyer who is providing representation to her client, must continue the duty of confidentiality with that client and may not enter into representation with another client that is *directly adverse* to or has *a significant risk* that *materially limits* proper representation to the initial client. Duties to clients extend even after representation and are governed by Rule 1.9 to protect against *materially adverse* situations in a *substantially related* matter. Rule 1.10 governs specific rules pertaining to past government lawyers, former judges, arbitrators, or third-party neutrals. Finally, Rules 1.11, 1.12, and 1.13 are specific rules that apply to unique attorney-client relationships.

These standards apply across a vast assortment of settings including governmental work, mediation settings, law firms, and more. The cases and articles that follow show how proper management of actual, as well as potential, conflicts of interest create the foundation for fair and just representation. The cases demonstrate examples of conflicts of interest between organizations, law clerks, and the government, and provide scenarios that can be used as a teaching mechanism to demonstrate the best way to avoid possible future ethical violations and malpractice claims.

This chapter will discuss the specific conflicts of interest that apply to given situations, as well as the different avenues and ways they may come up for members of the legal profession. The included article reviews how a lawyer may serve as a director of an organization without violating any ethical duties to current clients. The legal duty to a client extends far beyond just mere representation. This chapter will also demonstrate the importance of continued confidentiality and loyalty to a client.

B. RULES

In preparation, read carefully the following sections of the Model Rules of Professional Conduct along with any relevant comments listed below.

- Rule 1.7: Conflict of Interest: Current Clients
    - Comments [2-7], [10-12], [20] & [35]
- Rule 1.8: Conflict of Interest: Current Clients: Specific Rules
    - Comments [1], [6], [9-12] & [16]
- Rule 1.9: Duties to Former Clients
    - Comments [2-4]
- Rule 1.10: Imputation of Conflicts of Interest: General Rule
    - Comments [1 & 2]

Rules Guiding Specific Attorney-Client Relationships:
- Rule 1.11: Special Conflicts of Interest for Former and Current Government Officers and Employees
    - Comments [3 & 4]
- Rule 1.12: Former Judge, Arbitrator, Mediator or Other Third-Party Neutral
    - Comments [2 & 3]
- Rule 1.13: Organization as a Client
    - Comments [1-5], & [10]

C. CASES AND ADDITIONAL READINGS

SO YOU'VE SPOTTED A POTENTIAL CONFLICT OF INTEREST. WHAT NEXT?
The Recorder (Online), June 10, 2016
Randy Evans and Shary Klevens

As more attorneys run conflicts before opening a new matter and take advantage of available technology, attorneys and law firms are getting better at identifying potential conflicts of interest that could impact a matter. But identifying that there could be a conflict is only the first step. Many attorneys ask themselves, "What next?"

After attorneys identify a conflict, attorneys need to determine whether it is necessary to obtain the client's written consent to the representation after "full disclosure" and identify what this looks like in practice. After all, a conflict of interest that has not been resolved in accordance with the applicable ethical rules is still a conflict.

What Is "Full Disclosure"?

The purpose of the full disclosure requirement is to enable a client to make an informed decision regarding whether to agree or object to a representation. For a former client, this decision involves accepting the risk that their former attorney may have learned information in the prior representation that is relevant to the representation of a new client. For current clients who will share an attorney, the risk is that the attorney will not be able to take certain positions or pursue certain arguments if the attorney represents both parties rather than just one.

In order for the disclosure to be effective, therefore, it must contain enough detail to enable the consenting clients to fully understand and appreciate the risks of granting consent. It is not enough for an attorney to simply advise a client that there is a potential conflict of interest and ask for consent without providing more specific information.

Likewise, it usually is not sufficient just to ask for a client's waiver of the conflict or consent to the representation. An effective disclosure typically requires more. In the context of conflicts of interest, Rule 3-310 of the California Rules of Professional Conduct defines disclosure as "informing the client or former client of the relevant circumstances and of the actual and reasonably foreseeable adverse consequences to the client or former client."

There is no template that attorneys can use as a form for full disclosure when seeking a client's consent to a representation. Instead, the type and content of a disclosure required for effective consent varies depending on the facts and circumstances of each representation. For example, the scope and content of full disclosure will often depend on the sophistication of the client, the nature of the representation, prior representations of the client and the length of the attorney-client relationship.

What Do You Need for a Client's Waiver?

In general terms, the professional rules call for an attorney to disclose whatever information a reasonable person would expect and need to consider before waiving an important right, and then to confirm that consent in writing. That written consent is often referred to as a "waiver." In specific terms, there are topics that some attorneys typically include when seeking a client's consent or waiver.

First, in reviewing conflicts, many attorneys identify the proposed representation and what consent is sought from the client. "General" waivers typically call for a different kind of disclosure than a "limited" waiver for a specific representation. Therefore, tailoring the requisite full disclosure often involves making clear exactly which kind of waiver the attorney seeks.

In the multiple representation context, this often means advising the client that the attorney is requesting permission to jointly represent the client along with others. In the successive representations context, this generally means advising a former client that the attorney is requesting permission to represent a new client in a matter involving the former client.

Second, most attorneys faced with a conflict then identify the risks for the client. There should be no mincing of words when disclosing the potential risks to a client. Subtlety, implication, and suggestion do little when an attorney is attempting later to prove that a client consented to a representation after full disclosure. The most effective disclosures clearly and plainly articulate the risks so that a court can later determine that a client understood and accepted the risks by providing consent to the representation.

The point is to ensure that the consenting clients understand the limitations that arise from a joint representation as opposed to the representation of a single client. In the multiple representation context, this means identifying the kinds of things that an attorney cannot and will not do because the representation involves more than one client. For example, the attorney will not explore or pursue claims by one client against another client. In addition, information communicated by one client may be disclosed to the other clients.

In the successive representation context, this means explaining the risks that the attorney may have learned confidential information that may be used on behalf of a new client. Importantly, the standard is not whether an attorney did, in fact, learn confidential information in the prior representation that can be used against a former client. Instead, to trigger an attorney's obligation to obtain a former client's consent, the new representation be "substantially related" to the former representation. The existence of confidential information is presumed.

Third, attorneys may consider whether to advise their clients of the right to independent counsel in deciding whether to agree to the multiple or successive representation. Generally, attorneys seeking client consent do not advise their clients on whether to give consent. Instead, attorneys limit their role to fully disclosing the risks without advising the clients about whether to give consent.

Fourth, for those matters where a conflict has not yet arisen but could arise between the members of the shared representation, attorneys may confirm what will happen if an actual conflict develops that precludes the continued representation. Clients may agree, for example, that the attorney may continue to represent one of the clients if an actual conflict develops. Or the clients may insist that an attorney simply withdraw from the entire representation if an actual conflict develops. Regardless, it is usually better in the long run, although not required, for clients in this situation to agree to the "what ifs" before the representation begins.

Must a Client's Consent Be in Writing?

Under California Rules of Professional Conduct, the answer is "yes." Rule 3-310 requires informed "written" consent to representation following "written" disclosure.

As a risk management tool, establishing effective consent is most effective when in the form of a detailed piece of writing, typically a letter. To comply with professional rules, these letters are usually jointly addressed to all of the clients for a multiple representation, or to the former client for successive representations, and include a discussion of all the material risks of the representation.

Invariably, once problems arise, clients' memories may be foggy about the extent of the disclosure, their understanding of the risks, and whether they, in fact, consented to the representation. Requiring that clients consent in writing to a multiple or successive representation not only falls in line with what is legally required, but also provides a layer of protection for attorneys faced with this issue.

Many attorneys have found it helpful to simply include a signature line on the full disclosure letter and have the client return an executed copy. This simple step can serve to protect both the client, by making sure that they, in fact, receive full disclosure in writing, and the attorney.

Reprinted with permission from the June 2016 edition of the "Recorder"© 2016 ALM Media Properties, LLC. All rights reserved.

Questions and Comments

1. This article provides helpful tips informing lawyers how to handle conflicts of interest. Although the article makes it seem like a simple fix, there are multiple things to consider when dealing with a conflict of interest. What other tips or advice would you give a lawyer to help her handle a possible or actual conflict of interest?

2. The article provides an adequate description of "full disclosure." Why is it critical to provide so much detail in the disclosure? In other words, why is a simple statement saying that there is a conflict of interest insufficient under the circumstances?

3. Consider how many Model Rules are targeted at conflict of interest scenarios – current clients, former clients, judges and arbitrators, current government officers, etc. Why do you think so much space is allocated to the topic of conflicts with all the applicable scenarios articulated in separate rules?

DYNTEL CORP. V. EBNER
United States Court of Appeals for the Fourth Circuit (1997)
120 F.3d 488

Wilkinson, Chief Judge:

DynCorp sued attorney Susan Ebner, alleging that she had breached her ethical "duty of loyalty" to its subsidiary DynTel. The district court dismissed this claim with prejudice, finding that DynCorp had failed to state a claim and had brought suit in the wrong forum. DynCorp's challenge of these findings on appeal is meritless. As the district court correctly held, any ethical charges should have been resolved in the District of Columbia, where the contracts litigation underlying the ethics debate was taking place. Furthermore, we are convinced that DynCorp waged spurious ethical warfare in Virginia in an effort to apply leverage in the underlying District of Columbia disputes. Accordingly, we affirm the judgment of the district court and remand this case for the entry of appropriate sanctions against DynCorp and its counsel.

I.

On October 31, 1994, Cincinnati Bell sold its wholly-owned subsidiary, CBIS Federal Inc., to DynCorp. CBIS provided services under contract to the federal government. Upon the sale to DynCorp, CBIS was renamed DynTel. In connection with the sale, Cincinnati Bell agreed to indemnify DynCorp for certain legal proceedings against CBIS and to defend CBIS in those matters.

In October 1995, a dispute arose between DynTel and the government regarding a defect in CBIS's performance prior to its sale to DynCorp. As a result, the government began withholding payments from DynTel. DynCorp contended that Cincinnati Bell was obligated to indemnify DynCorp for this loss—a claim which Cincinnati Bell denied. However, while reserving its rights as to DynCorp's indemnification claim, Cincinnati Bell brought an action on behalf of CBIS and DynTel in the Court of Federal Claims challenging the government's position.

Shortly thereafter, DynCorp, in response to Cincinnati Bell's continuing denial of its duty to indemnify, sought to compel arbitration before the American Arbitration Association. The dispute between the parties came before the United States District Court for the District of Columbia, which entered an order compelling arbitration.

The current dispute arises from the involvement of Cincinnati Bell attorney Susan Ebner in the various legal disputes between it and DynCorp. Ebner has been employed by Cincinnati Bell since August 31, 1992 as in-house counsel. Cincinnati Bell pays Ebner's salary and benefits, and also provides office space, secretarial support, and business expenses. In return, Ebner provides ~~exclusive, full-time legal services to Cincinnati Bell.~~

Before the sale of CBIS to DynCorp, Ebner was involved in various CBIS legal matters. For example, Ebner participated as counsel for CBIS in a number of lawsuits, including federal contract litigation involving bid protests before the General Services Administration Board of Contract Appeals. However, CBIS never employed or paid Ebner, nor gave her any employment benefits.

Shortly after DynCorp bought CBIS, DynCorp informed Ebner that it would not offer her a job. In order to avoid any confusion as to whom she represented, Ebner relocated her office from the Cincinnati Bell offices which adjoined those of the newly renamed DynTel. She also informed DynCorp's legal department that she would be unavailable to give legal advice to DynTel or DynTel's employees. Ebner has never been retained by DynCorp or DynTel, and Ebner has never identified herself as counsel for DynCorp or DynTel, nor has she authorized anyone else to so identify her.

Ebner represented Cincinnati Bell in the United States District Court for the District of Columbia in the proceedings that led to arbitration, and DynCorp made no objection to her participation. However, after the order for arbitration was granted, DynCorp contacted Ebner to demand that she recuse herself from the arbitration, threatening a lawsuit and a report to the D.C. Bar if she refused. In response, Ebner voluntarily submitted the issue to the D.C. Bar Legal Ethics Committee on May 3, 1996. The Chair of the Committee stated:

> [I]t does not appear that a lawyer-client relationship exists or ever existed between Attorney X [Ebner] and company C [DynCorp]. It appears that Company A [Cincinnati Bell] has been the sole employer of Attorney X, and therefore the only party with whom Attorney X has a lawyer-client relationship.

In a further attempt to resolve this dispute, Ebner and Cincinnati Bell suggested that the conflict-of-interest dispute be submitted to the arbitration panel as the first issue in the arbitration. The panel indicated that it was willing to hear the dispute if both sides agreed to submit it, but DynCorp rejected this proposal. DynCorp also rejected having the issue decided by a neutral third party such as a law professor specializing in legal ethics.

On June 28, 1996, DynCorp brought this action in the United States District Court for the Eastern District of Virginia. While DynCorp's complaint failed even to specify a distinct cause of action for professional malpractice, it sought an order enjoining Ebner from "violation of her duty of loyalty to DynTel and DynCorp" and requiring Ebner "to comply with her duty of loyalty to DynTel in connection with DynTel's litigation with the Government and her serving as counsel in such litigation." The complaint also sought unspecified damages.

On August 14, 1996, the district court, after a conference with both parties, issued an order requiring DynCorp to show cause why its complaint should not be dismissed for failure to state a claim. After a hearing, the court dismissed DynCorp's complaint with prejudice for failure to state a claim and failure to seek relief in the proper forum. DynCorp now appeals.

II.

As an initial matter, DynCorp disputes the district court's conclusion that this litigation was brought in the wrong forum. It argues that since the underlying disputes were brought in different tribunals, it was most convenient to have the issue of Ebner's alleged conflict of interest settled in one separate case. Furthermore, DynCorp contends that no forum other than the Eastern District of Virginia could have provided it with a damages remedy.

***

The order in which jurisdiction was obtained in other tribunals also supports the conclusion that DynCorp should not have brought suit in the Eastern District of Virginia. Both the action before the Court of Federal Claims and DynCorp's demand for arbitration before the American Arbitration Association were filed nearly six months before this complaint. In addition, we note that DynCorp never lodged any protest to Ebner's representation of Cincinnati Bell until the parties were ordered to arbitrate. The timing of DynCorp's protest strongly suggests that this suit was filed in an attempt to leverage Cincinnati Bell in the underlying contractual disputes. The fact that DynCorp fought any effort to resolve this dispute in a proper forum only bolsters this conclusion.

III.

***

We agree with the district court that DynCorp's suit lacked any legally sound or factually supportable basis.

The district court concluded that DynCorp's claim that Ebner violated a "duty of loyalty" to DynCorp failed to state a claim upon which relief could be granted. DynCorp disputes this conclusion, arguing that under Virginia law it is clear that a lawyer owes his or her client a fiduciary duty. DynCorp's assertion is correct, as far as it goes. What DynCorp fails to recognize, however, is that breach of such a duty is but one element of a properly pleaded case for professional malpractice, which under Virginia law requires "[1] an attorney-client relationship, [2] breach of the standard of care, and [3] damages proximately caused by negligence." *Carstensen v. Chrisland Corp.*, 247 Va. 433, 442 S.E.2d 660, 668 (Va. 1994). Indeed, the Virginia Supreme Court has clearly stated that "[a] mere allegation of negligence or breach of a duty [is] insufficient to support an action for legal malpractice." *Gregory v. Hawkins*, 251 Va. 471, 468 S.E.2d 891, 893 (Va. 1996).

DynCorp's complaint does not even use the word "malpractice," and it makes no attempt to properly plead the elements of such a claim. DynCorp argues, however, that despite the fact that its complaint nowhere refers to any malpractice claim, it intended to plead such a theory. Even if we were to accept this assertion, DynCorp's claim was still properly dismissed with prejudice. DynCorp's assertion of malpractice fails because of one basic flaw—absolutely nothing indicates that Ebner ever entered into an attorney-client relationship with either DynCorp or DynTel. Such a relationship is fundamental to a malpractice action. *Carstensen*, 442 S.E.2d at 668.

The primary evidence that no attorney-client relationship existed in this instance is DynCorp's own decision not to retain Ebner as counsel to DynTel after CBIS was sold. Certainly neither DynCorp nor DynTel ever paid Ebner for any services rendered, and, indeed, Ebner testified that when she went to meet with DynCorp personnel after the sale of CBIS, she was required to sign in as a visitor, wear a visitor's badge, and be escorted at all times by a DynCorp employee. This hardly exemplifies a belief by DynCorp that Ebner was its or DynTel's attorney.

Despite the foregoing circumstances, DynCorp maintains that Ebner was DynTel's attorney. As a basis for finding an attorney-client relationship, DynCorp first relies upon the fact that Ebner did legal work for CBIS before its sale to DynCorp. This gets DynCorp nowhere. Ebner's legal work for CBIS prior to its sale cannot establish an ongoing attorney-client relationship with DynCorp after the sale. *See International Electronics Corp. v. Flanzer*, 527 F.2d 1288, 1292 (2d Cir. 1975). Here, as in *Flanzer*, there is no allegation that Ebner has attempted to use any confidences she gained while working for CBIS to the advantage of a third party. *Id.* Indeed, the only party she does represent, Cincinnati Bell, is the same entity which she represented when she did legal work for CBIS, which was then Cincinnati Bell's wholly owned subsidiary. Under these circumstances, Ebner's pre-sale relationship with CBIS is not a ground for disqualification or a malpractice claim.

Second, DynCorp argues that Ebner is DynTel's attorney because she was listed as "of counsel" on certain filings brought on behalf of DynTel and CBIS before the Federal Court of Claims after the sale of CBIS. DynCorp, however, conveniently ignores the fact that Ebner's participation before the Federal Court of Claims was merely to protect the interest of Cincinnati Bell as the potential indemnitor in that action.

Indeed, Cincinnati Bell had retained independent counsel to represent DynTel's interests in that litigation. The papers filed in that case make this relationship clear, referring to Ebner as representing only Cincinnati Bell. It is further clear from correspondence in the record that DynCorp fully understood the nature of Ebner's role in the litigation. Letters from DynCorp's legal department to Ebner use the terms "you" and "Cincinnati Bell" interchangeably, reflecting DynCorp's perception that Ebner was Cincinnati Bell's representative. In fact, those letters are addressed to "Susan Warshaw Ebner, Esq., Special Counsel, Cincinnati Bell, Inc."

Lastly, and most tellingly, up until the arbitration order was issued, Ebner took positions adverse to DynCorp on behalf of Cincinnati Bell without any objection. For example, Cincinnati Bell was required to put DynCorp on notice of conduct Cincinnati Bell regarded as violating the sale agreement. DynCorp raised no objection when Ebner acted on behalf of Cincinnati Bell to give DynCorp such notice. In addition, DynCorp did not object when Ebner represented Cincinnati Bell in the proceedings to compel arbitration. In light of its past acceptance of Ebner's representation of Cincinnati Bell, DynCorp's current contention that Ebner was DynTel's attorney all along strains credulity to the breaking point.

IV.

Finally, we address Ebner's motion for sanctions under Fed. R. App. P. 38. Ebner asserts that DynCorp brought this suit for purely predatory purposes. Our review of DynCorp's actions compels us to agree.

DynCorp first objected to Ebner's work for Cincinnati Bell when the parties were ordered to arbitrate their dispute regarding Cincinnati Bell's contractual indemnification obligations to DynCorp. At that point, DynCorp's silence on the issue was quickly replaced by a stream of threats. Despite this sudden objection, however, DynCorp was totally resistant to a convenient and efficient resolution of the dispute, rejecting several reasonable alternatives offered by Ebner. Indeed, despite the fact that DynCorp threatened to report Ebner to the D.C. Bar, it was unwilling to credit the opinion of the Chair of the D.C. Bar Legal Ethics Committee that Ebner's representation of Cincinnati Bell was entirely ethical. Rather, it insisted on pressing this lawsuit in a forum completely unrelated to the disputes underlying this case. In addition, it is clear that there was absolutely no legal or factual foundation for DynCorp's assertion that Ebner ever acted as DynTel's attorney. Given the lack of any objective basis for DynCorp's complaint and the timing of its opposition to Ebner's representation of Cincinnati Bell, we must agree with Ebner that DynCorp's staging of an ethical attack was "a thinly disguised attempt by DynCorp to gain a tactical advantage in a contractual dispute with Cincinnati Bell."

No attorney should be subject to the sort of predatory tactics demonstrated by DynCorp and its counsel in this case. The zealous representation of one's own client need not entail devouring opposing counsel in collateral malpractice litigation. Ebner has been the victim of such an attack, and we refuse to allow suits such as this one to become a routine risk of legal practice. Courts exist to adjudicate legitimate claims, not to provide a forum for vexatious tactics whose only denouement can be professional self-destruction.

V.

For the foregoing reasons, we affirm the judgment of the district court. We grant appellee's motion for sanctions under Fed. R. App. P. 38, and we remand this case to the district court with directions to assess the amount of attorney's fees and costs incurred in connection with this appeal. On remand, the district court may, in its discretion, entertain a motion for sanctions under Fed. R. Civ. P. 11 or related provisions.

Questions and Comments

1. The facts of *DynTel Corp. v. Ebner* indicate a miscommunication and lack of understanding between parties. How could Ebner have better handled the transition to DynTel differently, if at all? Do you think better communication could have mitigated this dispute?

2. What was the court's reasoning for ruling that no attorney-client relationship existed between Ebner and DynCorp, as well as Ebner and DynTel? Do you think Ebner took the steps necessary to ensure that she made it clear no attorney-client relationship existed? In a practical sense, what are some effective ways lawyers can communicate the absence of existence of the attorney-client relationship between themselves and a potential client?

3. Under Model Rules, a potential conflict can be waived. Explain what is required for such waiver.

FIRST INTERSTATE BANK OF ARIZ., N.A. V. MURPHY, WEIR & BUTLER

United States Court of Appeals for the Ninth Circuit (2002)
210 F.3d 983

Rymer, Circuit Judge:
The issue before us is whether a law firm owes a duty to its client to disclose that it hired the law clerk of a judge before whom it was appearing in a pending matter.

Murphy, Weir & Butler (Murphy) represented First Interstate Bank of Arizona and Talley Realty Finance Company (FIB/Talley) who were secured creditors in the Chapter 11 bankruptcy proceeding of Scottsdale Pinnacle Associates (SPA). The Honorable Leslie Tchaikovsky was the presiding bankruptcy judge. Although unknown to the Murphy partner assigned to this matter, the firm hired Judge Tchaikovsky's law clerk for employment at the end of the clerkship. As it turned out, the "Chinese wall" was not impermeable as it should have been, for the law clerk continued to have some contact with the case. Judge Tchaikovsky ruled in favor of FIB/Talley, but later recused herself upon SPA's motion after SPA found out about the clerk's relationship with Murphy. A new trial before a different judge resulted in a decision with which FIB/Talley was not as happy. As a result, it sued Murphy for malpractice.

The district court held it was not foreseeable that hiring the law clerk without disclosure would ultimately result in Judge Tchaikovsky's recusal, because judges and law clerks are required to preserve the court's impartiality and the appearance of impartiality. For this reason, Murphy had no duty to disclose that the firm had hired the Judge's clerk. We agree. Given the presumption of judicial impartiality, it was not reasonably foreseeable that the law clerk would continue to work on Murphy's matters contrary to the Code of Conduct for Law Clerks; that the Judge would fail to screen off the law clerk completely in violation of the Code of Judicial Conduct; and that the conduct of both the Judge and the law clerk would amount to an appearance of impropriety such as to require recusal. As judges and law clerks are in the best position to prevent impropriety, we decline to impose a duty of disclosure on law firms.

Accordingly, we affirm on FIB/Talley's appeal. Murphy also sought indemnification of expenses incurred in defending this lawsuit, but the district court denied its request. We affirm this decision as well.

In early 1993, FIB/Talley engaged Murphy as local counsel in the Chapter 11 bankruptcy of SPA. FIB/Talley, as holder of the first deed of trust on SPA's only asset, opposed confirmation of SPA's reorganization plan and sought relief from the automatic stay in order to foreclose on the property. On August 12, 1994, Judge Tchaikovsky entered final orders denying SPA's reorganization plan; granting the motion of FIB/Talley for relief from the automatic stay and to determine the value of their net secured claim, which she did at $ 4.75 million; and denying SPA's motion to amend the findings and for a new trial.

Meanwhile, on November 19, 1993, Murphy offered employment to the Judge's only law clerk, to begin at the end of the clerkship in September 1994. The clerk accepted shortly thereafter. A Murphy partner told Judge Tchaikovsky of the firm's interest in hiring the clerk, and the clerk was reminded during the interview with the Murphy hiring committee that she could not work on any Murphy matters if she were to accept employment with the firm. Judge Tchaikovsky instructed the clerk to do no more substantive work on any case in which Murphy represented a party in interest, but the clerk handled a few telephone calls pertaining to procedural matters, observed some courtroom proceedings, marked up a memorandum relating to an earlier plan of reorganization, and was told by the Judge of her intended decision on the final plan.

SPA found out about the clerk's employment in late August and moved on September 20, 1994 to recuse Judge Tchaikovsky and to vacate her orders. Judge Tchaikovsky certified the relevant facts on October 31, 1994, and acknowledged that she had violated 28 U.S.C. § 455(a) by failing to insulate the clerk completely from the SPA proceeding. She recused herself and the matter was reassigned to Bankruptcy Judge Randall Newsome. After holding an evidentiary hearing, Judge Newsome determined that the conduct of Judge Tchaikovsky and the law clerk amounted to an appearance of impropriety, and ordered a new trial. Subsequently, Judge Newsome valued the SPA property at $ 6 million, resulting in a net secured claim for FIB/Talley of $ 5.4 million. He confirmed SPA's plan of reorganization on September 11, 1995.

FIB/Talley brought this action for negligence, breach of fiduciary duty, and breach of contract on February 2, 1996. The district court declined to dismiss on statute of limitations grounds as it believed there was a factual dispute about when Murphy actually stopped representing FIB/Talley, but granted summary judgment on the merits. Murphy then moved for indemnification of attorney's fees and costs in the amount of $441,372, but the district court denied the motion.

Both parties have timely appealed.

II

FIB/Talley argues that Murphy owed a duty to it to ensure that the firm's hiring of the Judge's law clerk did not jeopardize its own litigation of the bankruptcy case. In FIB/Talley's view, the risk of harm was clearly foreseeable because failing to notify the client, the client's lead attorneys, opposing counsel, or the Judge would open the door to a later recusal motion and a possible vacatur of Judge Tchaikovsky's final orders. It notes that because recusal must be brought up as soon as there is a basis to challenge a judge's impartiality, SPA would have been precluded from raising the issue after Judge Tchaikovsky issued her final orders if Murphy had disclosed the hiring when it happened. Alternately, it points out, FIB/Talley's lead counsel could have replaced Murphy as local counsel.

The general principles that apply are well settled. Attorneys have a duty to "keep a client reasonably informed about significant developments relating . . . to the representation . . . ." California Rules of Professional Conduct 3-500. Although the attorney owes a basic obligation to provide sound advice in furtherance of a client's best interests, "such obligation does not include a duty to advise on all possible alternatives no matter how remote or tenuous." *Davis v. Damrell*, 119 Cal. App. 3d 883, 889, 174 Cal. Rptr. 257 (1981). A "legal malpractice [claim] is compounded of the same basic elements as other kinds of actionable negligence: duty, breach of duty, causation, and damage." *Nichols v. Keller*, 15 Cal. App. 4th 1672, 1682 (1993). FIB/Talley's negligence and breach of fiduciary duty claims likewise turn on whether Murphy owed them a duty and, if so, whether the breach of that duty caused the harm suffered." The question of the existence of a legal duty of care in a given factual situation presents a question of law which is to be determined by the courts alone. Entry of summary judgment in favor of the defendant in a professional negligence action is proper where the plaintiff is unable to show the defendant owed such a duty of care." *Id.* at 1682 (citing *Nymark v. Heart Fed. Savings & Loan Ass'n*, 231 Cal. App. 3d 1089, 1095, 283 Cal. Rptr. 53 (1991)). Whether there is a duty, in turn, depends largely on the foreseeability of the harm alleged: "Foreseeability of harm, though not determinative, has become the chief factor in duty analysis." 15 Cal. App. 4th at 1686. And the foreseeability component of duty analysis is a legal issue:

Foreseeability is a question of fact in many contexts. However, in defining the boundaries of duty, foreseeability is a question of law for the court. The question of foreseeability in a "duty" context is a limited one for the court and is readily contrasted with the fact-specific foreseeability questions bearing on negligence (breach of duty) and causation posed to the jury or trier of fact. *Id.*

Applying these principles, it is clear that the harm FIB/Talley posits—a new trial necessitated by the Judge's recusal—was neither foreseeable to Murphy nor preventable by it. Judicial impartiality is presumed. *See United States v. Herrera-Figueroa*, 918 F.2d 1430, 1436 n.8 (9th Cir. 1990); *In the Matter of Demjanjuk*, 584 F. Supp. 1321, 1324-25 (N.D. Ohio 1984); *United States v. Zagari*, 419 F. Supp. 494, 501 (N.D. Cal. 1976). Section 455(a), the Code of Judicial Conduct, and the Code of Conduct for Law Clerks all place the burden of maintaining impartiality and the appearance of impartiality on the judge and the law clerk.

Section 455(a) requires a judge to disqualify herself in any proceeding in which her impartiality might reasonably be questioned. 28 U.S.C. § 455(a). This mandate is identical to the duty set out in the Code of Judicial Conduct Canon 3(E)(1). And pursuant to Canon 3(C)(2), a judge "shall require staff, court officials and others subject to the judge's direction and control to observe the standards of fidelity and diligence that apply to the judge and to refrain from manifesting bias or prejudice in the performance of their official duties."

Canon 2 of the Code of Conduct for Law Clerks requires a law clerk to avoid impropriety and the appearance of impropriety; it states:

A law clerk should not engage in any activities that would put into question the propriety of the law clerk's conduct in carrying out the duties of the office. A law clerk should not allow family, social, or other relationships to influence official conduct or judgment. A law clerk should not lend the prestige of the office to advance the private interests of others; nor should the law clerk convey or permit others to convey the impression that they are in a special position to influence the law clerk.

Id. Canon 5(C)(1) directly speaks to the issue of prospective employment and instructs:

A law clerk should refrain from financial and business dealings that tend to detract from the dignity of the office, interfere with the proper performance of official duties, exploit the law clerk's position, or involve the law clerk in frequent transactions with individuals likely to come in contact with the law clerk or the court in which the law clerk serves. During the clerkship, a law clerk may seek and obtain employment to commence after the completion of the clerkship; if any law firm, lawyer, or entity with whom a law clerk has been employed or is seeking or has obtained future employment appears in any matter pending before the appointing judge, the law clerk should promptly bring this fact to the attention of the appointing judge, and the extent of the law clerk's performance of duties in connection with such matter should be determined by the appointing judge.

Id. It is expected that when a "clerk has accepted a position with an attorney or with a firm, that clerk should cease further involvement in those cases in which the future employer has an interest." Alvin B. Rubin & Laura B. Bartell, *Law Clerk Handbook* 23 (1989). It is up to the judge to make sure this happens. "Judges themselves are in the best position to forestall future difficulties with a few simple instructions and quick action where necessary." Kevin D. Swan, Comment, *Protecting the Appearance of Judicial Impartiality in the Face of Law Clerk Employment Negotiations*, 62 Wash. L. Rev. 813, 840 (1987).

Of course judges are not infallible. *See, e.g., Liljeberg v. Health Services Acquisition Corp.*, 486 U.S. 847, 862, 100 L. Ed. 2d 855, 108 S. Ct. 2194 (1988) (judge failed to inform the parties of association with institution that could be affected by outcome of litigation); *Hall v. Small Business Administration*, 695 F.2d 175 (5th Cir. 1983) (magistrate judge allowed law clerk who was a former member of the plaintiff class and had accepted employment with the class's counsel to work on the case); *Miller Industries, Inc. v. Caterpillar Tractor Co.*, 516 F. Supp. 84 (S.D. Ala. 1980) (district judge allowed law clerk who had accepted employment with defendant's counsel to continue to work on case). But despite this, judges (and their law clerks) are presumed to be impartial and to discharge their ethical duties faithfully so as to avoid the appearance of impropriety. Lawyers are entitled to assume that judges (and law clerks) will perform their duty. Further, there are well established and well known procedures for ensuring both the reality and appearance of impartiality. For this reason, it is not foreseeable that hiring a law clerk will result in recusal.

Relying on *Miller* and *Hall*, FIB/Talley points out that if Murphy had told SPA about hiring Judge Tchaikovsky's clerk, SPA might have agreed to waive any objection to Murphy continuing to represent FIB/Talley as local counsel, or set up a waiver in the absence of timely objection to the court, in either case averting the Judge's recusal and vacatur of her orders. Neither *Miller* nor *Hall* was concerned with the issue of foreseeability. Both involved the timeliness of a party's motion to disqualify a judge whose law clerk continued to work on a case in which his future employer was counsel. In each, the losing side did not learn of the basis for disqualification until after judgment had been entered. Their belated motion to disqualify was opposed on the ground of untimeliness and waiver, but the argument was rejected, the judge was disqualified, and the judgment was vacated. In *Miller* and *Hall*, as here, it is obvious in retrospect that the problems could have been averted if the law firm had refrained from offering employment so long as the clerk was working for the judge, or if the firm had told the other side. But hindsight is not the test for foreseeability.

More importantly, FIB/Talley submits no authority indicating that a law firm should refrain from recruiting judicial clerks—indeed, the Canons indicate otherwise—or must tell opposing counsel, its own clients or the court if it offers employment to a law clerk or its offer is accepted. Murphy had no basis for believing that the Judge's impartiality was reasonably subject to question. Both Judge Tchaikovsky and her law clerk knew about the clerk's prospective employment with Murphy. Typically, (and consistent with the duty to avoid the appearance of impartiality), in these circumstances a judge would either tell the clerk not to do *any* work on the matter, or disclose the clerk's disqualification on the record and proceed only if the disqualification were waived. Here, the Judge did not seek waivers, but rather told the clerk not to do *substantive* work on the SPA litigation. Regrettably, this did not go far enough to forestall recusal. But the fact that the wall was permeable in *this* case does not make it foreseeable that judges and law clerks will not fully honor their ethical duties in *all* cases. In sum, it is entirely reasonable for law firms to rely on the presumption that judges and law clerks will maintain their impartiality by adequately following appropriate procedures when the law clerk has obtained an offer or a position of future employment.

This leaves the burden where it should be as a matter of policy and practicality. The law clerk is the one person who is always sure to know of a conflict. Even in the computer age there is no reason to assume that counsel of record is aware of everyone whom his firm has hired and where each prospective employee is presently working. We therefore cannot agree with FIB/Talley that Murphy should bear the blame for Judge Tchaikovsky's recusal.

Nor does FIB/Talley articulate any compelling need for a new duty of the sort it proposes. On the one hand it would overcompensate for the occasional judicial lapse; but on the other hand, it would underachieve the objective for no amount of disclosure can guarantee the appearance of impartiality if the judge and clerk fall short of what duty turns out to demand. At the end of the day neither counsel nor clients can control what happens inside a judge's chambers. Accordingly, we agree with the district court that Murphy owed no duty to inform FIB/Talley, lead counsel, SPA, or Judge Tchaikovsky that Judge Tchaikovsky's law clerk had accepted an offer of future employment with the firm. In the absence of duty, none of the claims survives.

***

AFFIRMED.

Questions and Comments

1. In the above case, the court held that the law firm had no duty to disclose that it hired the judge's law clerk. Why did the court rule that way? Do you agree with the court's holding?

2. Rule 1.12(b) of the Model Rules of Professional Conduct states that a law clerk to a judge is permitted to negotiate for employment with a lawyer involved in a matter that the clerk is personally involved with. The caveat is that the law clerk *must notify the judge* that she is negotiating for employment with the lawyer or party *before* she begins such negotiation. If the law clerk begins working for a firm and she is confronted with a matter she participated in substantially as a law clerk, Rule 1.12(a) states that she may not represent anyone in connection with the matter unless all parties to the proceeding give informed consent in writing. Note that although law clerks are allowed to negotiate employment rather liberally while working as a law clerk, the rules provide safeguards to ensure no conflict of interest takes place. Does this explanation change your response to the question above?

3. According to the decision, it is law clerks that have the burden of informing the law firm of any conflicts that may arise based on their past employment as a law clerk. The decision emphasizes that law firms do not have to refrain from recruiting law clerks. Why do you think the rules place the burden on the law clerk to notify firms of conflict issues? Do you agree that the firm should rely on the word of a law clerk or do you think

the law firm should have an additional duty and play a bigger role in safeguarding against conflicts of interest as well?

THE LAWYER SERVING AS A DIRECTOR OF A CLIENT/ORGANIZATION
Wisconsin State Bar, February 27, 1998
By Timothy J. Pierce

This outline provides references for lawyers who wish to serve as directors of client organizations. Because of the complicated nature of this situation, space and time do not permit an in-depth discussion, but what I have attempted to do is to flag what I believe to be the most important sources of guidance and briefly describe those sources. It is hoped that this may provide a starting point for further research.

Wisconsin's Rules of Professional Conduct for Attorneys (the "Rules") do not directly address the situation wherein a lawyer is asked to serve as a director of and organization that the lawyer represents as a client (or conversely, when a lawyer who serves as a director of an organization is asked to also provide legal services to the organization). The Comment, however, to SCR 20:1.7 (Conflicts of interest: Current Clients) provides as follows in paragraph [35]:

> A lawyer for a corporation or other organization who is also a member of its board of directors should determine whether the responsibilities of the two roles may conflict. The lawyer may be called on to advise the corporation in matters involving actions of the directors. Consideration should be given to the frequency with which such situations may arise, the potential intensity of the conflict, the effect of the lawyer's resignation from the board and the possibility of the corporation's obtaining legal advice from another lawyer in such situations. If there is material risk that the dual role will compromise the lawyer's independence of professional judgment, the lawyer should not serve as a director or should cease to act as the corporation's lawyer when conflicts of interest arise. The lawyer should advise the other members of the board that in some circumstances matters discussed at board meetings while the lawyer is present in the capacity of director might not be protected by the attorney–client privilege and that conflict of interest considerations might require the lawyer's recusal as a director or might require the lawyer and the lawyer's firm to decline representation of the corporation in a matter.

The Rules thus implicitly recognize that lawyers can and do serve in such dual capacities, but that such service carries potential hazards for the lawyer. This comment reflects a consensus developed through ethics opinions, the most important being *ABA Formal Opinion 98-410,* which is discussed further herein. It is noteworthy that the sole mention of lawyers serving as directors of client organizations is made in the Comment to the main Rule governing conflicts of interest for lawyers (SCR 20:1.7). Conflicts are the primary hazard for lawyers acting in any dual capacity, and such problems arise for lawyers who choose to serve as directors for client organizations.

In the *Restatement (Third) of the Law Governing Lawyers* (the "Restatement"), the situation in which a lawyer serves as a director of a client organization is addressed in §135 and its accompanying comment, which provide as follows:

§ 135. A Lawyer with a Fiduciary or Other Legal Obligation to a Nonclient

Unless the affected client consents to the representation under the limitations and conditions provided in § 122, a lawyer may not represent a client in any matter with respect to which the lawyer has a fiduciary or other legal obligation to another if there is a substantial risk that the lawyer's representation of the client would be materially and adversely affected by the lawyer's obligation.

d. A lawyer as corporate director or officer. A lawyer's duties as counsel can conflict with the lawyer's duties arising from the lawyer's service as a director or officer of a corporate client. Simultaneous service as corporate lawyer and corporate director or officer is not forbidden by this Section. The requirement that a lawyer for an organization serve the interests of the entity (see § 96(1)(a)) is generally consistent with the duties of a director or officer. However, when the obligations or personal interests as director are materially adverse to those of the lawyer as corporate counsel, the lawyer may not continue to serve as corporate counsel without the informed consent of the corporate client. The lawyer may not participate as director or officer in the decision to grant consent (see § 122, Comment c(ii)).

Illustration:

3. Lawyer serves on the board of directors of Company and is also employed by Company as corporate secretary and inside legal counsel. Company proposes to give bonuses to its five highest-paid officers, including Lawyer. Authority to pay such bonuses presents a close legal question. The directors have requested Lawyer to render an opinion as counsel concerning the legality of the payments. Lawyer's status as recipient of the bonus and role as a director to whom the opinion will be addressed create a substantial risk that Lawyer's opinion for Company will be materially and adversely affected. The conflict would not be cured by having the opinion prepared by a partner of Lawyer, because conflicts under this Section are imputed to affiliated lawyers.

Both Lawyer's personal conflict and the imputed conflict are subject to effective consent by agents of Company authorized to do so (see § 122).

A second type of conflict that can be occasioned by a lawyer's service as director or officer of an organization occurs when a client asks the lawyer for representation in a matter adverse to the organization. Because of the lawyer's duties to the organization, a conflict of interest is present, requiring the consent of the clients under the limitations and conditions provided in § 122.

Illustration:

> 4. Lawyer has been asked to file a medical-malpractice action against Doctor and Hospital on behalf of Client. Hospital is operated by University, on whose Board of Trustees Lawyer serves. While Lawyer would not personally be liable for the judgment if Client prevails (compare § 125, Comment c), the close relationship between Lawyer and University requires that Lawyer not undertake the representation unless Client's consent is obtained pursuant to § 122.

e. A lawyer as director of a legal-services organization. Service of a private-practice lawyer on the board of directors of a legal-services organization can usefully support the delivery of legal services to persons unable to pay for them. However, the agency's clients might from time to time have interests opposed to those of the lawyer's clients. Such service does not constitute an inherent conflict of interest with the lawyer's private clients, but the lawyer must be alert to the possibility of a conflict with respect to particular decisions. In general, if there is a risk that the lawyer-director's performance of functions as a director with respect to a particular decision would materially and adversely affect the lawyer's representation of private clients, the lawyer may not participate in that decision without the informed consent of affected clients.

Illustration:

> 5. A significant part of Lawyer's practice consists of enforcing the claims of banks against borrowers. Lawyer is also on the board of directors of the local Legal Services Agency (LSA). LSA is considering a proposal that it bring an action to challenge the use of certain clauses in consumer sales contracts that facilitate collection of bank claims. Such litigation would materially and adversely affect the interests of Lawyer's bank clients. Accordingly, Lawyer may not participate in the LSA board's consideration of the proposal.

As in the Comment to SCR 20:1.7, the emphasis in the Restatement is on alerting the lawyer to potential conflicts between the dual roles.

Perhaps the most important resource for lawyers considering assuming these dual roles is *ABA Formal Opinion 98-410.* This opinion was issued as a result of extensive study by the ABA of this issue in the 1990s, and focuses on three primary areas of concern for lawyers serving in these dual roles:

I.   **The lawyer must carefully advise the client regarding the dual roles.**

II.   **The lawyer-director must exercise reasonable care to protect the organizations attorney-client privilege**

III.   **The lawyer-director must confront and resolve ethical issues that arise during the dual roles.**

In order to address these areas of concern, the opinion recommends that the lawyer-director follow these guidelines:

1. Reasonably assure that management and the board of directors understand (i) the different responsibilities of legal counsel and director; (ii) that when acting as legal counsel, the lawyer represents only the corporate entity and not its individual officers and directors; and (iii) that at times conflicts of interest may arise under the rules governing lawyers' conduct that may cause the lawyer to recuse herself as a director or to recommend engaging other independent counsel to represent the corporation in the matter, or to serve as co-counsel with the lawyer or her firm.

2. Reasonably assure that management and the board of directors understand that, depending upon the applicable law, the attorney-client evidentiary privilege may not extend to matters discussed at board meetings when the lawyer-director is not acting in her corporate counsel role and when other lawyers representing the corporation are not present in order to provide legal advice on the matters.

3. Recuse herself as a director from the board and committee deliberations when the relationship of the corporation with the lawyer or her firm is under consideration, such as issues of engagement, performance, payment or discharge.

4. Maintain in practice the independent professional judgment required of a competent lawyer, recommending against a course of action that is illegal or likely to harm the corporation even when favored by management or other directors.

5. Perform diligently the duties of counsel once a decision is made by the board or management, even if, as a director, the lawyer disagrees with the decision, unless the representation would assist in fraudulent or criminal conduct, self-dealing or otherwise would violate the Model Rules.

6. Decline any representation as counsel when the lawyer's interest as a director conflicts with her responsibilities of competent and diligent representation, for example, when the lawyer is so concerned over her personal liability as a director resulting from the course approved by management or the board that her representation of the corporation in the matter would be materially and adversely affected.

The ABA's opinion also identifies several important legal and risk issues for evaluation by a lawyer and client who is considering a lawyer's service on the client's board:

- Provisions of substantive law concerning agents, fiduciaries, and corporate governance.
- Stock exchange regulations and rules of the Securities and Exchange Commission.
- Possible exclusion of the lawyer-director from the corporation's officer and director insurance coverage.
- Possible exclusion of the lawyer-director from the lawyer's own professional liability coverage.
- Possible loss of indemnification under the statutes of some statutes in minority shareholder and derivative actions.
- Possible exposure of the lawyer's firm to vicarious liability.
- Increased likelihood of disqualification from representing the corporation. in litigation or other matters

Any lawyer considering assuming the dual roles of both lawyer and director should carefully consider these risks and their possible effects both on the individual lawyer and the lawyer's firm.

Reprinted with permission from the February 1998 edition of the "State Bar of Wisconsin" © 2016 State Bar of Wisconsin. All rights reserved.

Questions and Comments

1. What specifically does the author suggest a lawyer should do to protect herself from unethical dual representation? Can you think of any additional safeguards a lawyer may take to avoid any possible problems?

2. Model Rule 1.7(b) sets forth conditions that must be met before a lawyer may continue to represent a client in an instance of a concurrent conflict of interest. Comment 23 to Rule 1.7, however, states that a lawyer generally should not represent multiple co-defendants in a criminal case. Why do you think representing multiple co-defendants in a criminal case is strictly prohibited, but the rule leaves open the possibility of representing multiple parties in a civil case? What makes criminal cases more challenging for dual representation?

3. When is it mandatory for a lawyer to withdraw herself from representation? Why do the rules provide such limited instances in which a lawyer *must* withdraw from representation? Can you think of any other reason why a lawyer must withdraw from representation not already provided for in the rules?

STATE V. JONES[1]
Supreme Court of Connecticut (1980)
442 A.2d 939

The defendant appeals from the denial of his motion to disqualify every prosecutor affiliated with the office of the state's attorney for the judicial district of New Haven on grounds of failure to preserve the confidences and secrets of a former client and conflict of interest. The motion was granted in part by the Superior Court, *Kinney, J.,* and from that decision the defendant appeals.

The court's finding sets forth the following facts. The defendant Reginald Jones, a minor at seventeen years of age, is charged with the offense of murder. His father Sammie L. Jones, hereinafter referred to as Mr. Jones, has been appointed guardian ad litem in this prosecution. The defendant has filed notice that he may rely upon a defense of mental disease or defect in this case. Richard P. Sperandeo is the chief assistant state's attorney for the judicial district of New Haven. His responsibilities include the prosecution of crime and representation of the interests of the state. Sperandeo's responsibilities are, on occasion, supervisory when he assigns cases to other attorneys in the office and consults with those attorneys, but he is not so involved in all cases. Sperandeo is also a partner in the law firm of Sperandeo, Weinstein and Donegan, whose two other partners are Josef A. Weinstein and Harold C. Donegan. Sperandeo shares equally with his two partners the responsibilities of his law firm and the representation of all the firm's clients.

The law firm of Sperandeo, Weinstein and Donegan represented the defendant Reginald Jones in a civil action which arose out of an automobile accident in September, 1966, when the defendant was five years old. Reginald Jones suffered facial injuries and a possible concussion in that accident. Sperandeo and Donegan worked on the case and helped reach a settlement in 1970. Although the law firm maintained a file containing medical reports and other material on its representation of Reginald Jones in this action, Sperandeo has not represented the defendant

---

[1] *See* State v. Powell, 442 A.2d 939, 944 (Conn. 1982) (Peters, J., concurring) (explaining that "our procedural resolution of these cases in no way signals a retreat from the substantive standards of *State v. Jones*").

in any capacity nor has he looked at the file since the case was settled in 1970. Upon the request of the defendant's present attorney and with the authorization of Mr. Jones, Donegan provided the defendant's attorney with all the medical reports concerning the 1966 automobile accident. The defendant's attorney had requested the entire file, but Donegan refused to give it to him because he did not think the defendant's attorney was entitled to it.

In December, 1978, Mr. Jones consulted Donegan about a claim for property damage to his automobile. Donegan talked with Mr. Jones in his office and took information from him, but did nothing more than that. All that Donegan has in his office file regarding this matter is two sheets of paper, one containing notes from his conversation with Mr. Jones, the other indicating the name of the insurance adjuster handling the claim. The property damage claim did not involve the defendant Reginald Jones in any way. Nevertheless, upon the filing of the defendant's motion to disqualify the prosecutors, Donegan terminated his representation of Mr. Jones.

The information charging the defendant with murder was filed on December 15, 1978. The defendant's motion to disqualify prosecutors was filed on December 26, 1978. As of January 4, 1979, the law firm of Sperandeo, Weinstein and Donegan has not represented the defendant or his father in any pending business. Although Sperandeo has access to the defendant's criminal file in the state's attorney's office, he has not looked at this file nor has he had anything to do with the prosecution of the defendant. He has not discussed the case with any of the state's attorneys. Sperandeo is not prosecuting Reginald Jones.

The court concluded that the defendant failed to establish any substantial relationship between the injuries sustained by him in 1966 and possible defenses to this prosecution. The court concluded that the defendant failed to establish that Sperandeo had acquired confidential information from him as a result of his prior representation, or information which if disclosed would prejudice the defendant in the criminal prosecution. The court also concluded that legal disqualification of Sperandeo was not required, but ordered him not to participate in any way, directly or indirectly, in the prosecution of the case and not to discuss the case with any personnel of the state's attorney's office or other law enforcement authorities. With regard to participation in the case by other prosecutors affiliated with the office of the New Haven state's attorney, the court concluded that there was no actual conflict of interest, nor the appearance thereof, nor any impropriety which would preclude prosecution of the defendant by the remaining prosecutors at that office. The defendant's motion to disqualify them was denied.

The defendant assigns error to each of these conclusions, except to the extent that they forbid Sperandeo's participation in the case. The defendant continues to seek legal disqualification of Sperandeo, as well as every other prosecutor affiliated with the New Haven state's attorney's office. The defendant also assigns error to that portion of the finding which overrules his claims of law. These claims of law along with the briefs of the parties argue the standards of professional conduct articulated by other jurisdictions because the issues presented have not been addressed by this court.

***

Canon 4 of the Code of Professional Responsibility provides that "A Lawyer Should Preserve the Confidences and Secrets of a Client." Canon 9 provides that "A Lawyer Should Avoid Even the Appearance of Professional Impropriety." Practice Book, 1978, pp. 23, 50. An attorney should be disqualified pursuant to Canon 4 if he has accepted employment adverse to the interests of a former client on a matter substantially related to the prior litigation. *Allegaert* v. *Perot,* 565 F.2d 246, 250 (2d Cir. 1977); *Schloetter* v. *Railoc of Indiana, Inc.,* supra, 710; *American Can Co.* v. *Citrus Feed Co.,* 436 F.2d 1125, 1130 (5th Cir. 1971); *City of Cleveland* v. *Cleveland Electric Illuminating Co.,* 440 F. Sup. 193, 205 (N.D. Ohio 1977). The substantial relationship test has been honed in its practical application to grant disqualification only upon a showing that the relationship between the issues in the prior and present cases is "patently clear" or when the issues are "identical" or "essentially the same." *Government of India* v. *Cook Industries, Inc.,* 569 F.2d 737, 739-40 (2d Cir. 1978). Before the substantial relationship test is applied, however, the moving party must prove that he had in the past enjoyed an attorney-client relationship with the attorney sought to be disqualified in order to show that the attorney was in a position in which he could have received information which his prior client might reasonably have assumed would be withheld from his present client, in this instance the state. *Allegaert* v. *Perot,* supra; *American Can Co.* v. *Citrus Feed Co.,* supra, 1129; *Cord* v. *Smith,* 338 F.2d 516, 523 (9th Cir. 1964). Once the existence of a prior attorney-client relationship is established and a substantial relationship between the matters in issue is found, the court need not inquire whether the attorney in fact received confidential information, because the receipt of such information is presumed. *Government of India* v. *Cook Industries, Inc.,* supra, 740; *Allegaert* v. *Perot,* supra, 250; *Emle Industries, Inc.* v. *Patentex, Inc.,* 478 F.2d 562, 571 (2d Cir. 1973); *Canadian Gulf Lines, Inc.* v. *Triton International Carriers, Ltd.,* 434 F. Sup. 691, 693 (D. Conn. 1976); *T. C. Theatre Corporation* v. *Warner Bros. Pictures, Inc.,* 113 F. Sup. 265, 269 (S.D. N.Y. 1953). The court cannot inquire into whether the lawyer did *in fact* receive confidential information during his previous employment which might be used to his former client's disadvantage, because a rule requiring the moving party to prove actual disclosures would destroy the very same confidences which Canon 4 protects.

The defendant alleges two violations of Canons 4 and 9 which involve Sperandeo. The first is Sperandeo's prior representation of the defendant in a civil action which was settled approximately nine years before the prosecution of this case had begun. In that case, Sperandeo represented the defendant both as an individual attorney and as a member of the firm Sperandeo, Weinstein and Donegan. The second alleged violation is the former representation of the defendant's father, Mr. Jones, in a potential civil action by Sperandeo's partner Donegan and the law firm of Sperandeo, Weinstein and Donegan. Donegan and the law firm have voluntarily terminated their representation of Mr. Jones.

Donegan's former representation of Mr. Jones in December, 1978, establishes the existence of a prior professional relationship between Mr. Jones and Donegan, which extends to the law firm of Sperandeo, Weinstein and Donegan and to Sperandeo. *American Can Co.* v. *Citrus Feed Co.,* supra, 1129. The defendant, however, has failed to establish the second element of the disqualification test. The record does not show a substantial relationship between the criminal prosecution of Reginald Jones and the property damage claim contemplated by Mr. Jones. The court found that Mr. Jones' claim for property damage to his automobile did not involve Reginald Jones in any way. This finding is not attacked by the defendant. Donegan's prior representation of Mr. Jones does not require disqualification of Sperandeo.

Sperandeo's prior representation of the defendant in the civil action arising out of the automobile accident in 1966 establishes the existence of a prior attorney-client relationship, a relationship in which Sperandeo could have received medical information concerning the defendant which the defendant might reasonably assume would be withheld from the state in his criminal prosecution. In view of the notice given by the defendant that he may rely on a defense of mental disease or defect and the injuries to his head caused by the automobile accident, there is a substantial relationship between this criminal prosecution for murder and the prior civil litigation. Sperandeo's receipt of confidential information is therefore presumed, and his employment as chief assistant state's attorney for the judicial district of New Haven requires his disqualification pursuant to Canon 4. To the extent that the trial court's order denied the defendant's request to disqualify Sperandeo, it is in error.

The defendant contends that disqualification of Sperandeo necessitates disqualification of every prosecutor affiliated with the office of the state's attorney for the judicial district of New Haven. This claim is based solely on Canon 9 because there is no evidence or even a claim that any other attorney in the state's attorney's office has had a prior professional relationship with Reginald Jones. The admonition of Canon 9 that a lawyer should avoid even the appearance of impropriety would not be, without more, enough to disqualify Sperandeo, let alone every prosecutor in the New Haven state's attorney's office. *International Electronics Corporation* v. *Flanzer,* 527 F.2d 1288, 1295 (2d Cir. 1975); *Society for Good Will to Retarded Children, Inc.* v. *Carey,* 466 F. Sup. 722, 724 (E.D. N.Y. 1979); *City of Cleveland* v. *Cleveland Electric Illuminating Co.,* supra, 205-206. The Connecticut Bar Association has cautioned against the promiscuous use of Canon 9 as a "convenient tool for disqualification when the facts simply do not fit within the rubric of other specific ethical and disciplinary rules." *International Electronics Corporation* v. *Flanzer,* supra, 1295. Although Canon 9 may be applied together with Canon 4 to disqualify counsel; *Schloetter* v. *Railoc of Indiana, Inc.,* supra, 709; *Canadian Gulf Lines, Inc.* v. *Triton International Carriers, Ltd.,* supra, 695; the appearance of impropriety alone is "simply too slender a reed on which to rest a disqualification order except in the rarest of cases." *Board of Education of the City of New York* v. *Nyquist,* 590 F.2d 1241, 1247 (2d Cir. 1979).

The cases cited by the defendant in support of his claim that the entire New Haven office must be disqualified are distinguishable. In *Canadian Gulf Lines, Inc.* v. *Triton International Carriers, Ltd.,* supra, the third party garnishee's motion to disqualify the law firm representing the plaintiff was granted where one partner in the firm had incorporated the corporation in August, 1974, and the other partner proceeded to garnish its assets, alleged to be due and owing to the defendant, in September, 1975. The disqualification motions were based on the theory that the law firm had obtained or could have obtained confidential communications regarding the debt owed the defendant by the garnishee before deciding to represent the plaintiff. Id., 692. In *Government of India* v. *Cook Industries, Inc.,* supra, an associate who has been assigned to represent the defendant as a corporate client for three years at one law firm left that firm to become associated with another firm where he was assigned within the month to represent the plaintiff in a substantially related action against the defendant. Id., 738–39. The court disqualified the associate and the entire firm which had hired him from the case. Id., 740. In *NCK Organization Ltd.* v. *Bregman,* 542 F.2d 128 (2d Cir. 1976), the plaintiff's motion to disqualify the defendant's attorney and his law firm was granted because the attorney was formerly employed as house counsel for the plaintiff corporation and its wholly owned subsidiary and as vice-president of the subsidiary. The Court of Appeals upheld disqualification of the law firm because the defendant's attorney, as counsel for the plaintiff, had participated in drafting a contract for the corporation, but when his employment was terminated counseled both the defendant and the law firm in the litigation of the contract dispute against the corporation. Id., 131. In *Fund of Funds, Ltd.* v. *Arthur Andersen & Co.,* 567 F.2d 225 (2d

Cir. 1977), the defendant's law firm accepted a retainer from the plaintiff with knowledge that the defendant might be implicated in a securities action brought by the plaintiff. Despite its attempt to create a "Chinese wall" around the matter, the court found that the firm's attempt to segregate all material implicating the defendant and route it to outside counsel it had hired to represent the plaintiff required the firm to apply the knowledge it had gained through its confidential communications with the defendant. Id., 235–36. The court upheld the order granting the defendant's motion to disqualify outside counsel hired to represent the plaintiff. Id., 236. In each of these cases it appeared that the law firm had procured some advantage in the current litigation by virtue of its access to prior confidential communications between the lawyer and his former client in violation of Canon 4. This necessitated disqualification of the entire firm. *Canadian Gulf Lines, Inc.* v. *Triton International Carriers, Ltd.,* supra, 695; *NCK Organization Ltd.* v. *Bregman,* supra, 135. These cases are distinguishable from the case at bar because the court's finding in this case reveals no real or apparent advantage to the state's attorney's office by virtue of Sperandeo's prior confidential communications with the defendant. Sperandeo has had nothing to do with the prosecution of this case. He has not discussed the case with any of the assistant state's attorneys. He has not even looked at the defendant's criminal file. The defendant does not challenge these findings. Furthermore, it is unrealistic to assume that any prosecutor in the New Haven office has had or will have opportunity to read the private files of Sperandeo, Weinstein and Donegan on the 1966 civil action involving Reginald Jones. All the medical reports concerning Reginald Jones which were gathered by the firm have already been given to the defendant's attorney.

"[E]thical problems cannot be resolved in a vacuum." *Emle Industries, Inc.* v. *Patentex, Inc.,* supra, 565. A careful consideration of the facts as set out in the finding is required. These facts are not attacked. "Nor can judges exclude from their minds realities of which fair decisions would call for judicial notice." *Silver Chrysler Plymouth, Inc.* v. *Chrysler Motor Corporation,* 518 F.2d 751, 753 (2d Cir. 1975). This court will not presume unethical conduct by Sperandeo or by the assistant state's attorneys affiliated with the New Haven office where none has been found. The primary duty of a prosecutor is to seek justice, not merely to convict. Code of Professional Responsibility, EC 7-13; Practice Book, 1978, p. 37. Although rigid application of the law firm disqualification rule might afford an easy solution, the rule has been subject to severe criticism. *NCK Organization Ltd.* v. *Bregman,* supra, 135-36 (Mansfield, J., concurring); *Unchanging Rules in Changing Times: The Canons of Ethics and Intra-firm Conflicts of Interest,* 73 Yale L.J. 1058 (1964); American Bar Assn., Committee on Ethics and Professional Responsibility, Formal Opinion 342, November 24, 1975. It can be argued that withdrawal of the entire law firm, here the entire state's attorney's office, when the slightest chance of betrayal of confidential communications exists might better preserve the integrity of the judicial system. But a rule this broad would result in many unnecessary withdrawals, limit mobility in the legal profession, and restrict the state in the assignment of counsel where no breach of confidentiality has in fact occurred. See *Attorney's Conflict of Interests: Representation of Interests Adverse to that of Former Client*, 55 B.U. L. Rev. 61, 64 (1975). In view of the unchallenged findings of fact in this case, it cannot be said that the court abused its discretion in denying the motion to disqualify all the prosecutors.

There is error in part, the judgment is set aside and the case is remanded to enter an order disqualifying only Sperandeo from participating in the prosecution of this case.

Dissent

Cotter, C.J.

I disagree in the result and would suggest that the state's attorney invoke the jurisdictional provision in General Statutes § 51-281 to permit another state's attorney to proceed with the prosecution of this matter. It is evident that another state's attorney would be available to conduct the prosecution and there would be no reason to invoke the alternative course provided in § 51-277. The resolution of this matter involves a policy judgment and another state's attorney should continue with the prosecution without any suggestion, intimation or insinuation of impropriety.

I would reaffirm the oft iterated principles enunciated in *Low* v. *Madison*, 135 Conn. 1, 5-10, 60 A.2d 774, and apply the standards articulated therein to the situation where a public official acts in a prosecutorial capacity in which the functional interests or relationship may affect the office and create an appearance of possible conflict.

Although there has been no showing to the present of conduct evincing improper motives, bad faith, clear abuse of power or plain disregard of duty, since the potentiality of an aura or an appearance of divided loyalty which would create a disqualifying factor under the strict and scrupulous standards of *Low* is certainly possible, the more appropriate course to take would be to act under General Statutes § 51-281. Such a course would avoid any possible charge of impropriety under *Low*. I do not indulge in an assumption that public officials have acted dishonorably, but I would follow required standards involving a philosophy of conduct in which patent fairness and impartiality are fundamental. *Daly* v. *Town Plan & Zoning Commission,* 150 Conn. 495, 499, 191 A.2d 250.

Anything which tends to weaken public confidence is against public policy. *Kovalik* v. *Planning & Zoning Commission,* 155 Conn. 497, 498-99, 234 A.2d 838. The policy we have adopted heretofore is directed against the evil inherent in the creation of a situation which weakens public confidence. *Schwartz* v. *Hamden,* 168 Conn. 8, 18, 357 A.2d 488. No room should be given for suspicion or cavil; therefore, I am constrained to dissent.

Questions and Comments

1. What was the basis of the defendant's argument that Mr. Sperandeo should be disqualified? Was his disqualification imputed to the rest of the prosecutorial team?

2. How long does the duty of confidentiality and responsibilities regarding conflicts of interests to former clients last? What factors play into the lawyer's duties even after representation has ended? *See* Model Rule 1.9 that discusses a lawyer's duties to former clients.

3. Read the dissenting opinion and argument. Does the majority opinion weaken public confidence in the criminal system? Why or why not?

D. DISCUSSION QUESTIONS

1. Think of some examples to illustrate "directly adverse" representation and resulting conflicts of interest. Can such conflicts ever be waived?

2. What steps should an attorney take if she comes across unethical violations on the part of the organization she is representing? *See* Model Rule 1.13, which discusses the special rules for organizations as clients and the rules that specifically apply to in-house counsel. Note how the rule places the discretion on the lawyer before proceeding to the highest authority in the organization in terms of possibly revealing confidential information. Why do you think the rule allows the lawyer to have so much discretion in representing an organization?

3. A mediator is an unbiased third party, hired to help both sides of a dispute reach a civilized agreement benefiting both parties. Why are mediators not allowed to represent a client involved in the case she mediated once the mediation is over? Do you think the role of neutrality should extend past the date of mediation or do you think a mediator should be able to represent a client after her role of remaining neutral ends? Explain your answer.

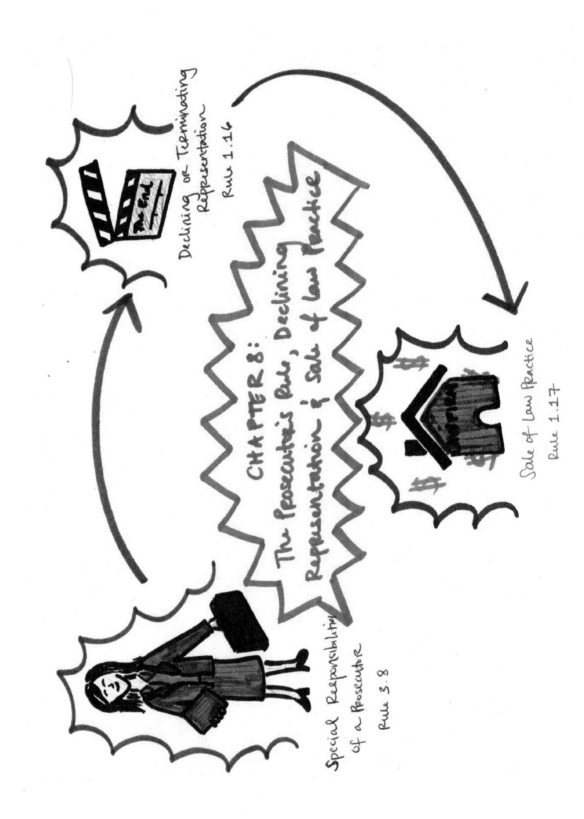

Declining or Terminating
Representation
Rule 1.16

CHAPTER 8:
The Prosecutor's Role, Declining
Representation & Sale of Law Practice

Sale of Law Practice
Rule 1.17

Special Responsibility
of a Prosecutor
Rule 3.8

Chapter 8:
The Prosecutor's Rule, Declining Representation, and Sale of Law Practice

A. INTRODUCTION

As the number of trials in America decreases due to alternative dispute resolution and mediation/arbitration practices, the world of criminal law remains trial heavy. Prosecutors have many governmental resources they can turn to for investigations involving their defendants. This is one aspect of what makes a defense attorney's work difficult— obtaining evidence that reveals the innocence of her client or, at a minimum, mitigates the offense. Because the world of criminal law deals with lives, the role of both prosecutors and defense attorneys is daunting. Over the years, cases revealed that innocent defendants were, at times, going to jail because their attorneys lacked information that would have been critical to their case. As a result of the Supreme Court decision in *Brady v. Maryland*, 373 U.S. 83 (1963), the Model Rules of Professional Conduct enacted Model Rule 3.8, also known as the "Prosecutor's Rule," which required prosecutors to hand over exculpatory evidence to the defense attorney.

This chapter includes articles and a case which give the legal history of the Prosecutor's Rule and why it is important in criminal trials. This rule encourages prosecutors to adhere to the professional ethics rules in criminal trials to prevent any violations, which could potentially ruin an innocent person's life. The case and articles in this chapter convey real life situations that show the implications of what could happen if this rule is not properly followed.

What are some drawbacks to the Prosecutor's Rule? When may a lawyer withdraw from counsel? Is an attorney required to take a case that her supervisor demands she take although no probable cause exists? How is the Prosecutor's Rule a vindication of justice? This chapter will answer these questions through examination of the case and articles presented.

B. RULES

In preparation, read carefully the following sections of the Model Rules of Professional Conduct along with any relevant comments listed below.

- Rule 3.8: Special Responsibilities of a Prosecutor
  - Comments: [1], [7-8]
- Rule 1.16: Declining or Terminating Representation
  - Comments: [1-4], [7]
- Rule 1.17: Sale of Law Practice
  - Comments: [4-5]

C. CASES AND ADDITIONAL READINGS

DISCOVERY AUDITS: MODEL RULE 3.8(d) AND THE PROSECUTOR'S DUTY TO DISCLOSE
119 The Yale Law Journal 1339 (2010)
By Christina Parajon

As a society, we have entrusted our prosecutors with discretion. Discussions of prosecutorial discretion often surround charging decisions, plea bargaining, and the general ability to "control the terms of [a defendant's] confinement." However, a prosecutor also exercises discretion in determining what information to share with his adversary.

In the discovery context, prosecutors have a two-fold ethical duty. They must not abuse their discretion by deciding whether to withhold or disclose evidence in ways that are generally "unfair or unwise." In addition, both the Supreme Court, in *Brady v. Maryland*, and Model Rule of Professional Conduct 3.8(d) have imposed positive limits on the prosecutor's disclosure discretion. The prosecutor's ethical exercise of discretion is also complicated by his duty, on the one hand, to "zealously assert [] the client's position under the rules of the adversary system," and on the other, to seek justice. The ethical complexities involved suggest that prosecutors require clear guidance regarding their professional responsibilities. A well-functioning criminal justice system also demands adequate structures to monitor compliance with the guidelines provided.

However, commentators and policymakers alike have recognized that the current system is inadequate to these tasks. After the Ted Stevens case was dismissed for discovery-related misconduct, the Department of Justice (DOJ) implemented a working group to review the Department's discovery policies and practices. Two recently issued DOJ memoranda, one providing "Guidance for Prosecutors Regarding Criminal Discovery" and another "Requir[ing] ....Office Discovery Policies in Criminal Matters," are the fruits of this effort. The contents of these memos are a testament to the DOJ's commitment to (and willingness to expend resources on) structural and policy changes to federal discovery practices. The challenge now is to continue this effort to draw brighter lines regarding the criteria, timing, and procedures for disclosing material to the defense, and to design more reliable structures for policing the boundaries of permissible discovery discretion.

***

I . Current Methods of Regulating Prosecutors' Disclosure

A. *The Brady Rule*

In a landmark criminal discovery case, *Brady v. Maryland*, the Supreme Court held that due process requires prosecutors to disclose exculpatory material and information to the defense. Accordingly, the prosecution's suppression of "favorable" evidence "where the evidence is material to either guilt or to punishment" requires reversal of a conviction on the grounds that the trial was fundamentally unfair.

Over time, a body of *Brady* jurisprudence developed that defined the doctrine's reach. Significantly, the Court devised a "materiality" standard in *United States v. Bagley*. Under the materiality standard, suppression of putatively favorable information will not give rise to a constitutional violation unless that piece of information or evidence "could reasonably be taken to put the whole case in such a different light as to undermine confidence in the verdict." This means that individual suppressions are not considered piecemeal—rather, the withheld evidence is considered in context, against all other evidence adduced in the case. While the materiality touchstone might provide a good metric for assessing due process violations, as an ethical standard, it sets a low bar. To this effect, critics have pointed out that "under the Supreme Court's current disclosure rules, the prosecutor's decision to suppress favorable evidence would be a perfectly rational, albeit unethical, act."

B. *Model Rule of Professional Conduct 3.8(d)*

The Model Rules of Professional Conduct, in theory and intent, compensate for *Brady*'s shortfalls. In particular, Rule 3.8(d) states that:

> The prosecutor in a criminal case shall . . . make timely disclosure to the defense of all evidence or information known to the prosecutor that tends to negate the guilt of the accused or mitigates the offense, and, in connection with sentencing, disclose to the defense and to the tribunal all unprivileged mitigating information known to the prosecutor . . . .

In a July 2009 formal opinion, the American Bar Association (ABA) tried to dispel the misconception "that the rule requires no more from a prosecutor than compliance with the constitutional and other legal obligations of disclosure."

To the contrary, the Rule's requirements exceed those of the Constitution in several key respects. First, disclosure of favorable information and evidence is required irrespective of its materiality, that is, "without regard to the anticipated impact of the evidence or information on a trial's outcome." The Rule intends for the defense, not the prosecution, to "decide on [the] utility" of the information, "thereby requir[ing] prosecutors to steer clear of the constitutional line, erring on the side of caution." Second, the Rule imposes a procedural responsibility on managers in prosecution offices to implement internal systems for ensuring compliance. This also arguably exceeds constitutional expectations, considering that the Supreme Court held in *Van de Kamp v. Goldstein* that prosecutorial supervisors enjoy immunity from suits complaining of failures to create internal data systems to ensure all *Giglio* material is discovered.

Notwithstanding the clarification, the Model Rule remains value on several scores. Indeed, the ABA has bemoaned that neither courts nor local disciplinary authorities have adequately considered the "separate obligations" regarding discovery that the Model Rule imposes. For one, interpretive guidance on what is considered "favorable" is scant. Moreover, there is no settled understanding of the level of care required to satisfy the Rule's instruction to disclose favorable evidence "known to the prosecutor." The Rule, on its face, does not require prosecutors to ferret out favorable information; they simply cannot "ignore the obvious." This stance suggests that the Rule requires no affirmative duty. Yet in some jurisdictions, courts have gestured toward a stricter test, under which knowledge is constructive and judged by an objective standard.

This vagueness inhibits the implementation of the Model Rule, a process that is demonstrably incomplete. Research indicates that local disciplinary authorities are generally reluctant to find and sanction 3.8(d) violations. Moreover, even where a disciplinary authority does find a violation, some courts appear equally unwilling to censure on 3.8(d) grounds, or to depart from a *Brady*-type analysis. This all suggests that reliance on the bar and the courts to effectuate the Model Rule may be misplaced. These institutions have not wholly resolved the broader question of what does, in fact, constitute "model" disclosure practices. A well-designed audit system, however, could further this end.

***

III. A Hybrid Tailored to the Prosecution-Discovery Context

An audit design tailored to the particular need to flesh out Rule 3.8(d) borrows elements from each of the models detailed above and adapts them to the prosecution-discovery context. In so doing, the audit structure accounts for the unique external/internal feature of the prosecution system. That is, entertaining the ways in which the Department of Justice is "external" to the "internal" workings of each U.S. Attorney's Office allows us to conceive of a more tailored audit system—one that admits consideration of independent review, on the one hand, and office autonomy, on the other. Such a system furthers the overarching goal of ethical quality assurance, yet appreciates the press of resource constraints. Then, when one considers how the two components might work in tandem, the possible synergies of a two-tiered audit system come into sharper relief.

A. Audits and External Review

The quality-related concerns presented in the benefits adjudication setting resemble those in the prosecution-disclosure context. In the benefits context, of the numerous classes of claims adjudicated, only a small number are ever reconsidered on appeal. Similarly, in the discovery context, only a small number of decisions *not* to disclose a piece of information are brought to light or otherwise challenged. Accordingly, in the discovery context, as in the benefits context, appeals (or disciplinary complaints) pose neither "an effective check on the fairness and accuracy" of discovery decisions nor a "supervisory check on [the] initial decision."

Given these similarities, the solution Professor Mashaw identifies for benefits adjudication programs, "[q]uality [a]ssurance . . . as a [m]anagement [t]echnique," is equally compelling in the prosecution-discovery context. Indeed, as Mashaw points out, performance and quality monitoring is ordinarily recognized as "such an obvious necessity" that in any other private enterprise "the failure to employ some method of quality control would be considered desperately poor, if not irresponsible, management."

A quality assurance program could bridge the substantive and structural gaps identified in the prosecution-discovery context. The DOJ Office of Professional Responsibility (OPR), as an auditor independent from and external to each office, is well-situated to spearhead such a program. In operation, OPR would select a random sample of recently completed cases to assign error types, and generally "evaluate the information supporting the decision, its origins and reliability, contradictory information, and the broader context in which the decision took place."

Initially, the auditor's evaluative capacity will be limited by the murkiness of the 3.8(d) criteria itself, which brings us back full circle to the audit policy's raison d'être. Still, this is not a reason to forgo the effort. As Mariano-Florentino Cuéllar notes, "Ideally the statutes or constitutional provisions implicated in the discretionary decision would provide *some* standard for the auditor to use, even when the standard is . . . vague . . . ." Here, as a starting point, OPR could prepare its auditors to evaluate case files by having them study *Brady* decisions (to gain a sense of the distinctions between the two violations) and what little 3.8(d) disciplinary opinion and case law exists. Where holes remain, OPR lawyers should have the authority, as auditors, to "articulate a reasonable standard," drawing on their "insights [into] . . . constitutional interpretation, policy considerations," or the drafting history and local analogs of Rule 3.8(d).

The product of the external audits would be substantive analysis, which would generate a body of gradually evolving guidelines that should guide prosecutors' decision-making in various situations. The January 4, 2010 memorandum on criminal discovery matters is a solid starting point: that guidance document laid out, in broad strokes, some threshold requirements related to gathering, reviewing, types, and timing of discovery. Continuing this nascent effort, OPR, like other regulatory agencies, would issue periodic guidance documents that synthesize the auditors' analyses and would share best practices between various prosecutorial offices. The interpretive guidance would, in turn, provide prosecution managers and supervisors with a source of concrete criteria for assessing the quality of the line prosecutors' discovery practices and a means of holding them internally accountable for compliance with the Rule.

B. Audits and Internal Compliance

The Model Rule intends for individual prosecution offices to establish internal compliance measures. The idea generally draws support from literature on the "internal law of administration," which emphasizes its importance in ensuring bureaucratic accountability. It was also impressed in the July 2009 ABA Opinion, and in the January 2010 DOJ Directive, which affirmatively "require[d] each office to establish a discovery policy with which prosecutors in that office must comply."

As a first approximation, the DOJ's prescription for a more robust internal law, combined with the cost savings possible through a management-based approach, counsels for a system in which prosecutors check one another. In the parlance of the management-based model, prosecutors should be incentivized "to conduct their own evaluations, find their own control solutions, and document all the steps they take." From this premise, several different design variations are possible. In larger offices, one can envision a system in which each prosecutor is paired with a secondary "discovery prosecutor" for every case. The secondary prosecutor would periodically review the case's progression, specifically monitoring the evidence and discovery status. In smaller offices, a more cost-effective approach might be to designate one or two supervisory prosecutors, such as the criminal chief and the appellate chief, to review cases where particularly thorny discovery issues arise.

Pursuant to the recent DOJ initiatives, each office has now designated a "discovery coordinator" to serve as a resource for discovery-related questions. But even beyond the basic requirement to designate a coordinator, an office could further develop this position in conjunction with its adoption of an audit-style compliance policy. The discovery coordinator could become a leading figure in the office—a "discovery chief"—analogous to the criminal and appellate chief positions, which would underscore the importance of, and increase focus on, the discovery decision-making process. A more prominent discovery chief could additionally assume an active role in the management of certain cases' discovery, either for randomly selected cases (in true audit form) or upon request. Again, as in the external arena, the discovery chief's ability to evaluate authoritatively the myriad discovery issues that arise will be tied, to some extent, to the development of more specific guidance. And this depends on the evolution of the external audit and quality assurance system. Over time, however, there is reason to believe the process will form valuable "feedback loops" among prosecutors in the office.

The distinct characteristics of the prosecution context recommend flexibility between the external and internal components of the system. Stated simply, USAOs that voluntarily implement audit-style compliance mechanisms should be less often the subjects of OPR audits. Individual USAOs would trade off the ostensibly more rigid OPR audits for adoption of internal audit programs. However, offices should still be required to provide OPR with standard types of qualitative information; OPR's data set remains complete, even without an attendant external audit. Such a proviso would thus allow OPR to further the system's overarching quality assurance goal—to analyze errors and furnish interpretive guidance—while remaining solicitous of internal supervisors' judgment and the autonomy necessary for a well-functioning, high-morale prosecution office.

Finally, it bears mention that an audit system, the aims of which are guidance and compliance rather than sanction and censure, avoids some of the underlying reasons why disciplinary authorities may be reluctant to sanction 3.8(d) violations. The emphasis on institutional learning excises any adversarial qualities of the system and increases the likelihood of holistic improvement in discovery practices.

Conclusion

This Comment makes the case for audits of prosecutors' discretionary discovery decisions. The system detailed above advances the DOJ's discovery initiative and provides a ready-made template for USAOs interested in improving or innovating internal compliance systems. More generally, audits will dredge up data on how prosecutors exercise their discovery discretion—revealing the good and the bad—so that prosecutors can learn, improve their characters and techniques, and attain those "qualities of a good prosecutor" that Justice Robert Jackson once considered so "elusive and . . . impossible to define."

Endnotes omitted (See Christina Parajon, Discovery Audits: Model Rule 3.8(d) and the Prosecutor's Duty To Disclose, 119 The Yale Law Journal1339 (2010) for full article version). Reprinted with permission from the 2010 edition of the "Yale Law Journal" © 2016 The Yale Law Journal. All rights reserved.

Questions and Comments

1. According to Rule 3.8, a prosecutor must turn over any evidence to the defendant that tends to negate the guilt of the accused. What must a prosecutor consider when determining whether a certain piece of evidence will tend to negate the guilt of the accused? Considering that our system is adversarial, why do you think this rule is specifically listed for prosecutors? Do you agree that such a rule is needed? Think about the consequences of a wrongful conviction in criminal law as compared to civil law.

2. The opinion provides a historical timeline of the Prosecutor's Rule. The rule has increasingly placed a higher burden on prosecutors to turn over exculpatory evidence. Why was the rule enacted? What implications, if any, does it have on modern-day society?

3. Rule 3.8 is explicitly directed at criminal prosecutors. Note that there is no rule specifically for criminal defense attorneys. Based on what you know about criminal law, why do you think the duty is on the prosecutor, and not the defense counsel, to turn over mitigating information? Why does the burden not extend to criminal defense attorneys to turn over evidence that shows the guilt of the defendant?

[handwritten margin notes, top left:] D + Doctor agreed that DNA analysis report would not include all results of the tests + limited to only positive reports

[handwritten margin notes, top right:] made approx 100 statements to the media that he knew or reasonably should have known had a pre-judicial likelihood on the crim. proceeding

THE NORTH CAROLINA STATE BAR V. NIFONG

Amended Findings of Fact, Conclusions of Law and Order of Discipline. Before the Disciplinary Hearing Commission of the North Carolina State Bar 06 DHC 35 (July 24, 2007)

[handwritten:] potentially exculpatory evidence not provided to defense

***

The Hearing Committee on its own motion pursuant to Rule of Civil Procedure 60(a) enters the following Amended Findings of Fact, Conclusions of Law and Order of Discipline in order to correct a factual mistake in Findings of Fact Paragraph 43 of its original Order in this cause, and to add an additional Conclusion of Law (b):

[handwritten margin notes, right:] failure to comply w/ mandated discovery requirements + him making misreps. + false statements of material fact to the court

A hearing in this matter was conducted on June 12 through June 16, 2007, before a Hearing Committee… Plaintiff, the North Carolina State Bar, was represented by Katherine E. Jean, Douglas J. Brocker, and Carmen K. Hoyme. Defendant, Michael B. Nifong, was represented by attorneys David B. Freedman and Dudley A. Witt. Based upon the admissions contained in the pleadings and upon the evidence presented at the hearing, this Hearing Committee makes, by clear, cogent and convincing evidence, the following FINDINGS OF FACT:

1. Plaintiff, the North Carolina State Bar, is a body duly organized under the laws of North Carolina and is the proper party to bring this proceeding.

2. Defendant, Michael B. Nifong, (hereinafter "Nifong"), was admitted to the North Carolina State Bar on August 19, 1978, and is, and was at all times referred to herein, an attorney at law licensed to practice in North Carolina, subject to the laws of the State of North Carolina, the Rules and Regulations of the North Carolina State Bar and the Revised Rules of Professional Conduct.

3. During all times relevant to this complaint, Nifong actively engaged in the practice of law in the State of North Carolina as District Attorney for the Fourteenth Prosecutorial District in Durham County, North Carolina.

4. Nifong was appointed District Attorney in 2005. In late March 2006, Nifong was engaged in a highly-contested political campaign to retain his office.

5. In the early morning hours of March 14, 2006, an exotic dancer named Crystal Mangum reported that she had been raped by three men during a party at 610 North Buchanan Boulevard in Durham. Ms. Mangum asserted that she had been vaginally, rectally, and orally penetrated with no condom used during the assault and with at least some of the alleged perpetrators ejaculating.

6. Various pieces of evidence were collected for later DNA testing, including evidence commonly referred to as a "rape kit," which contained

cheek scrapings, oral, vaginal, and rectal swabs, a pubic hair combing, and a pair of Ms. Mangum's underwear.

7. The Durham Police Department (DPD) initiated an investigation in what would come to be known as "the Duke Lacrosse case" and executed a search warrant on the house at 610 North Buchanan Boulevard on March 16, 2006. The investigation revealed that the residents of 610 North Buchanan were captains of the Duke University lacrosse team, and that a majority of the other attendees at the March 13, 2006, party were members of the team.

8. On March 16, 2006, the three residents of 610 North Buchanan voluntarily assisted DPD in executing a search warrant at their residence. During the search, numerous pieces of evidence were seized for later testing. The three residents also provided voluntary statements and voluntarily submitted DNA samples for comparison testing purposes. One of the three residents was David Evans, who was later indicted for the alleged attack on Ms. Mangum.

9. On March 22, 2006, Nifong's office assisted a DPD investigator in obtaining a Nontestimonial Identification Order (NTO) to compel the suspects in the case to be photographed and to provide DNA samples.

10. On March 23, 2006, DNA samples from all 46 Caucasian members of the Duke University 2006 Men's Lacrosse Team were obtained pursuant to the NTO.

11. When Nifong learned of the case on March 24, 2006, he immediately recognized that the case would garner significant media attention and decided to handle the case himself, rather than having it handled by the assistant district attorney in his office who would ordinarily handle such cases.

12. On March 24, 2006, Nifong informed DPD that he was assuming primary responsibility for prosecuting any criminal charges resulting from the investigation and directed the DPD to go through him for direction as to the conduct of the factual investigation of those matters.

13. On March 27, 2006, the rape kit items and DNA samples from the lacrosse players were delivered to the State Bureau of Investigation (SBI) lab for testing and examination, including DNA testing.

14. On March 27, 2006, Nifong was briefed by Sergeant Gottlieb and Investigator Himan of the DPD about the status of the investigation to date. Gottlieb and Himan discussed with Nifong a number of weaknesses in the case, including that Ms. Mangum had made inconsistent statements to the police and had changed her story several times, that the other dancer who was present at the party during the alleged attack disputed Ms. Mangum's story of an alleged assault, that Ms. Mangum had already viewed two photo arrays and had not identified any alleged attackers, and that the three team captains had voluntarily cooperated with police and had denied that the alleged attack occurred.

15. During or within a few days of the initial briefing by Gottlieb and Himan, Nifong acknowledged to Gottlieb and Himan that the Duke Lacrosse case would be a very hard case to win in court and said "you know, we're f*****."

16. Beginning on March 27, within hours after he received the initial briefing from Gottlieb and Himan, Nifong made public comments and statements to representatives of the news media about the Duke Lacrosse case and participated in interviews with various newspapers and television stations and other representatives of news media.

17. Between March 27 and March 31, Nifong stated to a reporter for WRAL TV news that lacrosse team members denied the rape accusations, that team members admitted that there was underage drinking at the party, and that otherwise team members were not cooperating with authorities.

18. Between March 27 and March 31, 2006, Nifong stated to a reporter for ABC 11 TV News that he might also consider charging other players for not coming forward with information, stating "[m]y guess is that some of this stonewall of silence that we have seen may tend to crumble once charges start to come out."

19. Between March 27 and March 31, 2006, Nifong stated to a reporter for the New York Times, "There are three people who went into the bathroom with the young lady, and whether the other people there knew what was going on at the time, they do now and have not come forward. I'm disappointed that no one has been enough of a man to come forward. And if they would have spoken up at the time, this may never have happened."

20. Between March 27 and March 31, 2006, Nifong stated to a reporter for NBC 17 News that the lacrosse team members were standing together and refusing to talk with investigators and that he might bring aiding-and-abetting charges against some of the players who were not cooperating with the investigation.

21, Between March 27 and March 31, 2006, Nifong stated to a reporter for the Durham Herald Sun newspaper that lacrosse players still refused to speak with investigators.

22. Between March 27 and March 31, 2006, Nifong made the following statements to Rene Syler of CBS News: "The lacrosse team, clearly, has not been fully cooperative" in the investigation; "The university, I believe, has done pretty much everything that they can under the circumstances. They, obviously, don't have a lot of control over whether or not the lacrosse team members actually speak to the police. I think that their silence is as a result of advice with counsel"; "If it's not the way it's been reported, then why are they so unwilling to tell us what, in their words, did take place that night?"; that he believed a crime occurred; that "the guilty will stand trial"; and "There's no doubt a sexual assault took place."

23. Between March 27 and March 31, 2006, Nifong made the following statements to a reporter for NBC 17 TV News: "The information that I have does lead me to conclude that a rape did occur"; "I'm making a statement to the Durham community and, as a citizen of Durham, I am making a statement for the Durham community. This is not the kind of activity we condone, and it must be dealt with quickly and harshly"; "The circumstances of the rape indicated a deep racial motivation for some of the things that were done. It makes a crime that is by its nature one of the most offensive and invasive even more so"; and "This is not a case of people drinking and it getting out of hand from that. This is something much, much beyond that."

24. Between March 27 and March 31, 2006, Nifong stated to a reporter for ESPN, "And one would wonder why one needs an attorney if one was not charged and had not done anything wrong."

25. Between March 27 and March 31, 2006, Nifong stated to a reporter for CBS News that "the investigation at that time was certainly consistent with a sexual assault having taken place, as was the victim's demeanor at the time of the examination."

26. Between March 27 and March 31, 2006, Nifong made the following statements to a reporter for MSNBC: "There is evidence of trauma in the victim's vaginal area that was noted when she was examined by a nurse at the hospital"; "her general demeanor was suggested-suggestive of the fact that she had been through a traumatic situation"; "I am convinced there was a rape, yes, sir"; and "The circumstances of the case are not suggestive of the alternate explanation that has been suggested by some of the members of the situation."

27. Between March 27 and March 31, 2006, Nifong stated to a reporter for the Raleigh News and Observer newspaper, "I am satisfied that she was sexually assaulted at this residence."

28. Between March 27 and March 31, 2006, Nifong stated to a reporter for the USA Today newspaper, "Somebody's wrong about that sexual assault. Either I'm wrong, or they're not telling the truth about it."

29. Between March 27 and March 31, 2006, Nifong made the following statements to a reporter for ABC 11 TV News: "I don't think you can classify anything about what went on as a prank that got out of hand or drinking that took place by people who are underage"; "In this case, where you have the act of rape -essentially a gang rape- is bad enough in and of itself, but when it's made with racial epithets against the victim, I mean, it's just absolutely unconscionable"; and "The contempt that was shown for the victim, based on her race, was totally abhorrent. It adds another layer of reprehensibleness, to a crime that is already reprehensible."

30. Between March 27 and March 31, 2006, Nifong stated to a reporter for ABC News, "It is a case that talks about what this community stands for."

31. Between March 27 and March 31, 2006, Nifong stated to a reporter for the New York Times, "The thing that most of us found so abhorrent, and the reason I decided to take it over myself, was the combination gang-like rape activity accompanied by the racial slurs and general racial hostility."

32. Between March 27 and March 31, 2006, Nifong stated to a reporter for CBS News, "The racial slurs involved are relevant to show the mindset . . . involved in this particular attack" and "obviously, it made what is already an extremely reprehensible act even more reprehensible."

33. Between March 27 and March 31, 2006, Nifong stated to a reporter for WRAL TV News, "What happened here was one of the worst things that's happened since I have become district attorney" and "[w]hen I look[ed] at what happened, I was appalled. I think that most people in this community are appalled."

34. On or after March 27, 2006, Nifong stated to a reporter for the Charlotte Observer newspaper, "I would not be surprised if condoms were used. Probably an exotic dancer would not be your first choice for unprotected sex."

35. On or about March 29, 2006, Nifong stated during an interview with a reporter for CNN that "[i]t just seems like a shame that they are not willing to violate this seeming sacred sense of loyalty to team for loyalty to community."

36. On March 30, 2006, the SBI notified Nifong that the SBI had examined the items from the rape kit and was unable to find any semen, blood, or saliva on any of those items.

37. On March 31, 2006, Nifong stated to a reporter for MSNBC, "Somebody had an arm around her like this, which she then had to struggle with in order to be able to breathe . . . She was struggling just to be able to breathe" and "[i]f a condom were used, then we might expect that there would not be any DNA evidence recovered from say a vaginal swab."

38. In March or April, 2006, Nifong stated to a representative of the news media that a rape examination of Ms. Mangum done at Duke Medical Center the morning of the alleged attack revealed evidence of bruising consistent with a brutal sexual assault, "with the most likely place it happened at the lacrosse team party."

39. In April 2006, Nifong stated to a reporter for Newsweek Magazine that the police took Ms. Mangum to a hospital where a nurse concluded that she had suffered injuries consistent with a sexual assault.

40. In April 2006, Nifong stated to a reporter for the Raleigh News and Observer newspaper, "I would like to think that somebody [not

involved in the attack] has the human decency to call up and say, 'What am I doing covering up for a bunch of hooligans?'"

41. In April 2006, Nifong stated to a reporter, "They don't want to admit to the enormity of what they have done."

42. In an April 2006 conversation with a representative of the Raleigh News and Observer newspaper, Nifong compared the alleged rape to the quadruple homicide at Alpine Road Townhouse and multiple cross burnings that outraged the city of Durham in 2005 and stated "I'm not going to let Durham's view in the minds of the world to be a bunch of lacrosse players from Duke raping a black girl in Durham."

43. On April 4, 2006, DPD conducted a photographic identification procedure in which photographs of 46 members of the Duke Lacrosse team were shown to Ms. Mangum. Ms. Mangum was told at the beginning of the procedure that DPD had reason to believe all 46 of the men depicted in the photographs she would view were present at the party at which she contended the attack had occurred. The procedure followed in this photographic identification procedure was conceived and/or approved by Nifong. During the photographic identification procedure, Ms. Mangum identified Collin Finnerty and Reade Seligman as her attackers with "100% certainty" and identified David Evans as one of her attackers with "90% certainty." Ms. Mangum had previously viewed photographic identification procedures which included photographs of Reade Seligman and David Evans and not identified either of them in the prior procedures.

44. On April 5, 2006, Nifong's office sought and obtained an Order permitting transfer of the rape kit items from the SBI to a private company called DNA Security, Inc. ("DSI") for more sensitive DNA testing than the SBI could perform. The reference DNA specimens obtained from the lacrosse players pursuant to the NTO were also transferred to DSI for testing, as were reference specimens from several other individuals with whom Ms. Mangum acknowledged having consensual sexual relations, including her boyfriend.

45. As justification for its Order permitting transfer of the evidence to DSI, the Court noted that the additional testing Nifong's office sought in its petition was "believed to be material and relevant to this investigation, and that any male cells found among the victim's swabs from the rape kit can be evidence of an assault and may lead to the identification of the perpetrator."

46. Between April 7 and April 10, 2006, DSI performed testing and analysis of DNA found on the rape kit items. Between April 7 and April 10, DSI found DNA from up to four different males on several items of evidence from the rape kit and found that the male DNA on the rape kit items was inconsistent with the profiles of the lacrosse team members.

47. During a meeting on April 10, 2006 among Nifong, two DPD officers and Dr. Brian Meehan, lab director for DSI, Dr. Meehan discussed with Nifong the results of the analyses performed by DSI to that point and explained that DSI had found DNA from up to four different males on several items of evidence from the rape kit and that the DNA on the rape kit items was inconsistent with the profiles of all lacrosse team members.

48. The evidence and information referred to above in paragraphs 46 and 47 was evidence or information which tended to negate the guilt of the lacrosse team members identified as suspects in the NTO.

49. After the April 10, 2006 meeting with Dr. Meehan, Nifong stated to a reporter for ABC 11 TV News that DNA testing other than that performed by the SBI had not yet come back and that there was other evidence, including the accuser being able to identify at least one of the alleged attackers.

50. While discussing DNA testing at a public forum at North Carolina Central University on April 11, 2006, in the presence of representatives of the news media, Nifong stated that if there was no DNA found "[i]t doesn't mean nothing happened. It just means nothing was left behind."

51. On April 17, 2006, Nifong sought and obtained indictments against Collin Finnerty and Reade Seligman for first-degree rape, first-degree sex offense, and kidnapping. (The indicted members of the Duke lacrosse team are referred to collectively herein as "the Duke Defendants").

52. Before April 17, 2006, Nifong refused offers from counsel for David Evans, who was eventually indicted, to consider evidence and information that they contended either provided an alibi or otherwise demonstrated that their client did not commit any crime.

53. On April 19, 2006, two days after being indicted, Duke Defendant Reade Seligman through counsel served Nifong with a request or motion for discovery material, including, inter alia, witness statements, the results of any tests, all DNA analysis, and any exculpatory information.

54. By April 20, 2006, DSI had performed additional DNA testing and analysis and found DNA from multiple males on at least one additional piece of evidence from the rape kit.

55. By April 20, 2006, from its testing and analysis, DSI had determined that all the lacrosse players, including the two who had already been indicted, were scientifically excluded as possible contributors of the DNA from multiple males found on several evidence items from the rape kit.

56. On April 21, 2006, Nifong again met with Dr. Meehan and the two DPD officers to discuss all of the results of the DNA testing and analyses performed by DSI to date. During this meeting, Dr. Meehan told Nifong that: (a) DNA from multiple males had been found on several items from the rape kit, and (b) all of the lacrosse players, including the

two players against whom Nifong had already sought and obtained indictments, were excluded as possible contributors of this DNA because none of their DNA profiles matched or were consistent with any of the DNA found on the rape kit items.

57. The evidence and information referred to above in paragraphs 54 through 56 was evidence or information which tended to negate the guilt of the Duke Defendants.

58. At the April 21 meeting, Dr. Meehan told Nifong that DSI's testing had revealed DNA on two fingernail specimens that were incomplete but were consistent with the DNA profiles of two un-indicted lacrosse players, including DNA on a fingernail found in David Evans' garbage can which incomplete but which was consistent with David Evans' DNA profile, and DNA from the vaginal swab that was consistent with the DNA profile of Ms. Mangum's boyfriend.

59. During the April 21, 2006 meeting, Nifong notified Dr. Meehan that he would require a written report to be produced concerning DSI's testing that reflected the matches found between DNA on evidence items and known reference specimens. Nifong told Dr. Meehan he would let Dr. Meehan know when he needed the report.

60. Sometime between April 21 and May 12, Nifong notified Dr. Meehan that he would need for him to prepare the written report for an upcoming court proceeding. As requested by Nifong, Dr. Meehan prepared a report that reflected the matches found by DSI between DNA found on evidence items and known reference specimens. This written report did not reflect that DSI had found DNA on rape kit items from multiple males who had not provided reference specimens for comparison ("multiple unidentified males") and did not reflect that all 46 members of the lacrosse team had been scientifically excluded as possible contributors of the male DNA on the rape kit items.

61. In May, 2006, Nifong made the following statements to a reporter for WRAL TV News: "My guess is that there are many questions that many people are asking that they would not be asking if they saw the results"; "They're not things that the defense releases unless they unquestionably support their positions"; and "So, the fact that they're making statements about what the reports are saying, and not actually showing the reports, should in and of itself raise some red flags."

62. On or before April 18, 2006, Nifong stated to a reporter for Newsweek Magazine that the victim's "impaired state was not necessarily voluntary . . . [I]f I had a witness who saw her right before this and she was not intoxicated, and then I had a witness who said that she was given a drink at the party and after taking a few sips of that drink acted in a particular way, that could be evidence of something other than intoxication, or at least other than voluntary intoxication?"

63. On May 12, 2006, Nifong again met with Dr. Meehan and two DPD officers and discussed the results of DSI's testing to date. During that meeting, consistent with Nifong's prior request, Dr. Meehan provided Nifong a 10-page written report which set forth the results of DNA tests on only the three evidence specimens that contained DNA consistent with DNA profiles from several known reference specimens. The three items in DSI's written report concerned DNA profiles on two fingernail specimens that were incomplete but were consistent with the DNA profiles of two unindicted lacrosse players, including DNA on a fingernail found in David Evans' garbage can which was incomplete but was consistent with David Evans' DNA profile, and DNA from the vaginal swab that was consistent with the DNA profile of Ms. Mangum's boyfriend. DSI's written report did not disclose the existence of any of the multiple unidentified male DNA found on the rape kit items, although it did list the evidence items on which the unidentified DNA had been discovered.

64. Nifong personally received DSI's written report from Dr. Meehan on May 12, 2006, and later that day provided it to counsel for the two Duke Defendants who had been indicted and for David Evans, among others.

65. When he received DSI's written report and provided it to counsel for the Duke Defendants, Nifong was fully aware of the test results that were omitted from the written report, including the test results revealing the existence of DNA from multiple unidentified males on rape kit items.

66. Three days later, on May 15, 2006, Nifong sought and obtained an indictment against David Evans for first-degree rape, first-degree sex offense, and kidnapping.

67. On May 17, Duke Defendant Collin Finnerty served discovery requests on Nifong, which specifically asked that any expert witness "prepare, and furnish to the defendant, a report of the results of any (not only the ones about which the expert expects to testify) examinations or tests conducted by the expert."

68. On May 18, 2006, Nifong provided various discovery materials to all three Duke Defendants, including another copy of DSI's written report, in connection with a hearing in the case on that same day. The discovery materials Nifong provided on May 18 did not include any underlying data or information concerning DSI's testing and analysis. The materials Nifong provided also did not include any documentation or information indicating the presence of DNA from multiple unidentified males on the rape kit items. Nifong also did not provide in the discovery materials any written or recorded memorialization of the substance of Dr. Meehan's oral statements made during his meetings with Nifong in April and May 2006 concerning the results of all DSI's tests and examinations, including the

existence of DNA from multiple unidentified males on the rape kit items ("memorializations of Dr. Meehan's oral statements").

69. DSI's tests and examinations revealing the existence of DNA from multiple unidentified males on rape kit items and Dr. Meehan's oral statements regarding the existence of that DNA were evidence that tended to negate the guilt of the accused; Collin Finnerty, Reade Seligman and David Evans.

70. Accompanying the discovery materials, Nifong served and filed with the Court written responses to the Duke Defendants' discovery requests. In these responses, Nifong stated: "The State is not aware of any additional material or information which may be exculpatory in nature with respect to the Defendant." In his written discovery responses, Nifong also identified Dr. Meehan and R.W. Scales, another person at DSI, as expert witnesses reasonably expected to testify at the trial of the underlying criminal cases pursuant to N.C. Gen. Stat. § 15A-903(a)(2). Nifong also gave notice in the written discovery responses of the State's intent to introduce scientific data accompanied by expert testimony. Nifong represented in the written discovery responses that all of the reports of those experts had been provided to the Duke Defendants.

71. At the time he made these representations to the Court and to the Duke Defendants in his written discovery responses, Nifong was aware of the existence of DNA from multiple unidentified males on the rape kits items, was aware that DSI's written report did not reveal the existence of this evidence, and was aware that he had not provided the Duke Defendants with memorializations of Dr. Meehan's oral statements regarding the existence of this evidence.

72. The representations contained in Nifong's May 18 written discovery responses were intentional misrepresentations and intentional false statements of material fact to opposing counsel and to the Court.

73. At the May 18, 2006 hearing, the Honorable Ronald Stephens, Superior Court Judge presiding, asked Nifong if he had provided the Duke Defendants all discovery materials.

74. In response to Judge Stephens' inquiry, Nifong stated: "I've turned over everything I have."

75. Nifong's response to Judge Stephens' question was a misrepresentation and a false statement of material fact.

76. On June 19, 2006, Nifong issued a press release to representatives of the news media stating, "None of the 'facts' I know at this time, indeed, none of the evidence I have seen from any source, has changed the opinion that I expressed initially."

77. On June 19, 2006, counsel for the Duke Defendants requested various materials from Nifong, including a report or written statement of the meeting between Nifong and Dr. Meehan to discuss the DNA test

results. This request was addressed at a hearing before Judge Stephens on June 22, 2006.

78. In response to the Duke Defendants' June 19 discovery request and in response to Judge Stephens' direct inquiry, Nifong stated in open court that, other than what was contained in DSI's written report, all of his communications with Dr. Meehan were privileged "work product." Nifong represented to Judge Stephens, "That's pretty much correct, your Honor. We received the reports, which [defense counsel] has received, and we talked about how we would likely use that, and that's what we did."

79. At the time Nifong made these representations to Judge Stephens on June 22, Nifong knew that he had discussed with Dr. Meehan on three occasions the existence of DNA from multiple unidentified males on the rape kits items, which evidence was not disclosed in DSI's written report, and knew that Dr. Meehan's statements to him revealing the existence of DNA from multiple unidentified males on the rape kits items were not privileged work product.

80. Nifong's representations to Judge Stephens at the June 22 hearing were intentional misrepresentations and intentional false statements of material fact to the Court and to opposing counsel.

81. During the June 22 hearing, Judge Stephens entered an Order directing Nifong to provide Collin Finnerty and later all the Duke Defendants with, among other things, "results of tests and examinations, or any other matter or evidence obtained during the investigation of the offenses alleged to have been committed by the defendant" and statements of any witnesses taken during the investigation, with oral statements to be reduced to written or recorded form.

82. Nifong did not provide the Duke Defendants with "results of tests and examinations, or any other matter or evidence obtained during the investigation of the offenses alleged to have been committed by the defendant" and did not provide the Duke Defendants with statements of any witnesses taken during the investigation, with oral statements reduced to written or recorded form.

83. Nifong did not comply with Judge Stephens' June 22 Order.

84. On August 31, 2006, the Duke Defendants collectively filed a Joint Omnibus Motion to Compel Discovery seeking, among other things, the complete file and all underlying data regarding DSI's work and the substance of any discoverable comments made by Dr. Meehan during his meetings with Nifong and two DPD officers on April 10, April 21, and May 12, 2006. The Joint Omnibus Motion was addressed by the Honorable Osmond W. Smith III, Superior Court Judge presiding, at a hearing on September 22, 2006.

85. At the September 22 hearing, counsel for the Duke Defendants specifically stated in open court that the Duke Defendants were seeking

the results of any tests finding any additional DNA on Ms. Mangum even if it did not match any of the Duke Defendants or other individuals for whom the State had provided reference DNA specimens for comparison.

86. In response to a direct question from Judge Smith, Nifong represented that DSI's written report encompassed all tests performed by DSI and everything discussed at his meetings with Dr. Meehan in April and May 2006. The following exchange occurred immediately thereafter on the Duke Defendants' request for memorializations of Dr. Meehan's oral statements:

> Judge Smith: "So you represent there are no other statements from Dr. Meehan?"
> Mr. Nifong: "No other statements. No other statements made to me."

87. At the time Nifong made these representations to Judge Smith, he was aware that Dr. Meehan had told him in their meetings about the existence of DNA from multiple unidentified males on the rape kit items, was aware that he had not provided the Duke Defendants with a written or recorded memorialization of Dr. Meehan's statements, and was aware that the existence of that DNA was not revealed in DSI's written report.

88. Nifong's statements and responses to Judge Smith at the September 22 hearing were intentional misrepresentations and intentional false statements of material fact to the Court and to opposing counsel.

89. On September 22, Judge Smith ordered Nifong to provide the Duke Defendants the complete files and underlying data from both the SBI and DSI by October 20, 2006.

90. On October 19, 2006 counsel for David Evans faxed to Nifong a proposed order reflecting Judge Smith's September 22 ruling. The proposed order stated, in paragraph 4, "Regarding the defendants' request for a report of statements made by Dr. Brian Meehan of DNA Security, Inc., during two separate meetings among Dr. Meehan, District Attorney Mike Nifong, Sgt. Mark Gottlieb, and Inv. Benjamin Himan in April 2006 . . . Mr. Nifong represented that those meetings involved the State's request for YSTR testing, Dr. Meehan's report of the results of those tests, and a discussion of how the State intended to use those results in the course of the trial of these matters. Mr. Nifong indicated that he did not discuss the facts of the case with Dr. Meehan and that Dr. Meehan said nothing during those meetings beyond what was encompassed in the final report of DNA Security, dated May 12, 2006. The Court accepted Mr. Nifong's representation about those meetings and held that there were no additional discoverable statements by Dr. Meehan for the State to produce."

91. On October 24, 2006, Nifong responded by letter to defense counsel's October 19, 2006 letter and proposed order. In his response, Nifong identified two changes he believed were appropriate to two

portions of the proposed order, made no mention of any changes he believed were appropriate to paragraph 4, and said "the proposed order seems satisfactory" and "it seems to reflect with acceptable accuracy the rulings of Judge Smith on September 22."

92. On October 27, 2006, Nifong provided 1,844 pages of underlying documents and materials from DSI to the Duke Defendants pursuant to the Court's September 22, 2006 Order but did not provide the Duke Defendants a complete written report from DSI setting forth the results of all of its tests and examinations, including the existence of DNA from multiple unidentified males on the rape kit items, and did not provide the Duke Defendants with any written or recorded memorializations of Dr. Meehan's oral statements.

93. After reviewing the underlying data provided to them on October 27 for between 60 and 100 hours, counsel for the Duke Defendants determined that DSI's written report did not include the results of all DNA tests performed by DSI and determined that DSI had found DNA from multiple unidentified males on the rape kit items and that such results were not included in DSI's written report.

94. On December 13, 2006, the Duke Defendants filed a Motion to Compel Discovery: Expert DNA Analysis, detailing their discovery of the existence of DNA from multiple unidentified males on the rape kit items and explaining that this evidence had not been included DSI's written report. The motion did not allege any attempt or agreement to conceal the potentially exculpatory DNA evidence or test results. The Motion to Compel Discovery: Expert DNA Analysis was addressed by the Honorable Osmond W. Smith III, Superior Court Judge presiding, at a hearing on December 15, 2006.

95. At the December 15 hearing, both in chambers and again in open court, Nifong stated or implied to Judge Smith that he was unaware of the existence of DNA from multiple unidentified males on the rape kit items until he received the December 13 motion and/or was unaware that the results of any DNA testing performed by DSI had been excluded from DSI's written report. Nifong stated to Judge Smith in open court: "The first I heard of this particular situation was when I was served with these reports—this motion on Wednesday of this week."

96. Nifong's representations that he was unaware of the existence of DNA from multiple unidentified males on the rape kit items and/or that he was unaware of the exclusion of such evidence from DSI's written report, were intentional misrepresentations and intentional false statements of material fact to the Court and to opposing counsel.

97. During the December 15 hearing, Dr. Meehan testified under oath to the following statements:

a. he discussed with Nifong at the April 10, April 21, May 12 meetings the results of all tests conducted by DSI to date, including the potentially exculpatory DNA test results;

b. he and Nifong discussed and agreed that "we would only disclose or show on our report those reference specimens that matched evidence items";

c. DSI's report did not set forth the results of all tests and examinations DSI conducted in the case but was limited to only some results;

d. the limited report was the result of "an intentional limitation" arrived at between him and Nifong "not to report on the results of all examinations and tests" that DSI performed;

e. the failure to provide all test and examination results purportedly was based on privacy concerns; and

f. he would have prepared a report setting forth the results of all DSI's tests and examinations if he had been requested to do so by Nifong or other representatives of the State of North Carolina at any time after May 12.

98. Immediately after the December 15 hearing, Nifong stated to a representative of the news media: "And we were trying to, just as Dr. Meehan said, trying to avoid dragging any names through the mud but at the same time his report made it clear that all the information was available if they wanted it and they have every word of it."

99. On January 12, 2007, Nifong recused himself from the prosecution of the Duke Defendants.

100. On January 13, 2007, the Attorney General of North Carolina took over the Duke Lacrosse case and began to review evidence and undertake further investigation.

101. After an intensive review of the evidence, the Attorney General concluded that Ms. Mangum's credibility was suspect, her various inconsistent allegations were incredible and were contradicted by other evidence in the case, and that credible and verifiable evidence demonstrated that the Duke Defendants could not have participated in an attack during the time it was alleged to have occurred.

102. Based on its finding that no credible evidence supported the allegation that the crimes occurred, the Attorney General declared Reade Seligman, Collin Finnerty, and David Evans innocent of all charges in the Duke Lacrosse case. The cases against the Duke Defendants were dismissed on April 11, 2007.

103. Nifong had in his possession, no later than April 10, 2006, an oral report from Dr. Meehan of the reports of test results showing the existence of DNA from multiple unidentified males on rape kit items.

104. From at least May 12, 2006 through January 12, 2007, Nifong never provided the Duke Defendants a complete report setting forth the results of all examinations and tests conducted by DSI and never provided the Duke Defendants with memorializations of Dr. Meehan's oral statements concerning the results of all examinations and tests conducted by DSI in written, recorded or any other form.

105. On or about December 20, 2006, Nifong received a letter of notice and substance of grievance from the Grievance Committee of the North Carolina State Bar alleging that: (a) he failed to provide the Duke Defendants with evidence regarding the existence of DNA from multiple unidentified males on the rape kit items; (b) he agreed with Dr. Meehan not to provide those results; and (c) he falsely represented to the Court that he was unaware of these results or their omission from DSI's report prior to receiving the Duke Defendants' December 13 motion to compel discovery.

106. Nifong initially responded to the Grievance Committee in a letter dated December 28, 2006, and supplemented his initial response, at the request of State Bar counsel, in a letter dated January 16, 2007.

107. In his responses to the Grievance Committee, Nifong: (a) acknowledged that he had discussed with Dr. Meehan during meetings in April and May 2006 the results of all DSI's testing, including the existence of DNA from multiple unidentified males on the rape kit items; (b) denied that he had agreed with Dr. Meehan to exclude the potentially exculpatory DNA test results from DSI's report; (c) stated that he viewed the evidence of DNA from multiple unidentified males on the rape kit items as "non-inculpatory" rather than as "specifically exculpatory"; and (d) represented that the discussion and agreement with Dr. Meehan to limit the information in DSI's report was based on privacy concerns about releasing the names and DNA profiles of the lacrosse players and others providing known reference specimens.

108. DSI's written report listed DNA profiles for Ms. Mangum, Ms. Mangum's boyfriend, and David Evans and Kevin Coleman, two lacrosse players who had not been indicted at the time the report was released, and listed the names of all 50 persons who had contributed reference DNA specimens for comparison.

109. Nifong further represented in his responses to the Grievance Committee that he did not realize that the existence of DNA from multiple unidentified males on the rape kit items was not included in DSI's report when he provided it to the Duke Defendants or thereafter, until he received defense counsel's December 13 motion to compel.

110. Nifong's representation to the Grievance Committee that he did not realize that the existence of DNA from multiple unidentified males on the rape kit items was not included in DSI's report from May 12 until he received the December 13 motion to compel was a false statement of

material fact made in connection with a disciplinary matter, and was made knowingly.

111. Nifong also represented in his responses to the Grievance Committee that, by stating to the Court at the beginning of the December 15 hearing that the motion was the "first [he] heard of this particular situation," he was referring not to the existence of DNA from multiple unidentified males on the rape kit items but to the Duke Defendants' purported allegation that he had made an intentional attempt to conceal such evidence from them.

112. Counsel for the Duke Defendants did not allege any intentional attempt by Nifong to conceal the DNA evidence from them in either their December 13 motion to compel or their remarks to the Court prior to Nifong's statement.

113. Nifong's responses to the Grievance Committee set forth in paragraph 111 concerning his representations to the Court at the December 15, 2006, hearing were false statements of material fact made in connection with a disciplinary matter, and were made knowingly.

114. Nifong was required by statute and by court order to disclose to the Duke Defendants that tests had been performed which revealed the existence of DNA from multiple unidentified males on the rape kit items.

115. Nifong knew or reasonably should have known that his statements to representatives of the news media set forth in paragraphs 17-35, 37-42, 49-50, 61-62, and 76 above would be disseminated by means of public communication.

116. Nifong knew or reasonably should have known that his statements to representatives of the news media set forth in paragraphs 17-35, 37-42, 49-50, 61-62, and 76 above had a substantial likelihood of prejudicing the criminal adjudicative proceeding.

117. Nifong knew or reasonably should have known that his statements to representatives of the news media set forth in paragraphs 17-35, 37-42, 49-50, 61-62, and 76 above had a substantial likelihood of heightening public condemnation of the accused.

Based upon the preceding FINDINGS OF FACT, the Hearing Committee makes the following

Conclusions of Law

(a) By making statements to representatives of the news media including but not limited to those set forth in paragraphs 17-35, 37-42, 49-50, 61-62, and 76, Nifong made extrajudicial statements he knew or reasonably should have known would be disseminated by means of public communication and would have a substantial likelihood of materially prejudicing an adjudicative proceeding in the matter, in violation of Rule 3.6(a), and made extrajudicial statements that had a substantial likelihood of heightening public condemnation of the accused, in violation of Rule 3.8(f) of the Revised Rules of Professional Conduct.

(b) By instructing Dr. Meehan to prepare a report containing positive matches, Nifong knowingly disobeyed an obligation under the rules of a tribunal in violation of Rule 3.4(c) of the Revised Rules of Professional Conduct.

(c) By not providing to the Duke Defendants prior to November 16, 2006, a complete report setting forth the results of all tests and examinations conducted by DSI, including the existence of DNA from multiple unidentified males on the rape kit items and including written or recorded memorializations of Dr. Meehan's oral statements, Nifong:

> i. did not make timely disclosure to the defense of all evidence or information known to him that tended to negate the guilt of the accused, in violation of former Rule 3.8(d) of the Revised Rules of Professional Conduct; and

> ii. failed to make a reasonably diligent effort to comply with a legally proper discovery request, in violation of former Rule 3.4(d) of the Revised Rules of Professional Conduct.

(d) By never providing the Duke Defendants on or after November 16, 2006, and prior to his recusal on January 12, 2007, a report setting forth the results of all tests or examinations conducted by DSI, including the existence of DNA from multiple unidentified males on the rape kit items and including written or recorded memorializations of Dr. Meehan's oral statements, Nifong:

> i. did not, after a reasonably diligent inquiry, make timely disclosure to the defense of all evidence or information required to be disclosed by applicable law, rules of procedure, or court opinions, including all evidence or information known to him that tended to negate the guilt of the accused, in violation of current Rule 3.8(d) of the Revised Rules of Professional Conduct; and

> ii. failed to disclose evidence or information that he knew, or reasonably should have known, was subject to disclosure under applicable law, rules of procedure or evidence, or court opinions, in violation of current Rule 3.4(d)(3) of the Revised Rules of Professional Conduct.

(e) By falsely representing to the Court and to counsel for the Duke Defendants that he had provided all discoverable material in his possession and that the substance of all Dr. Meehan's oral statements to him concerning the results of all examinations and tests conducted by DSI were included in DSI's written report, Nifong made false statements of material fact or law to a tribunal in violation of Rule 3.3(a)(1), made false statements of material fact to a third person in the course of representing a client in violation of Rule 4.1, and engaged in conduct involving dishonesty, fraud, deceit or misrepresentation in violation of Rule 8.4(c) of the Revised Rules of Professional Conduct.

(f) By representing or implying to the Court that he was not aware of the existence on rape kit items of DNA from multiple unidentified males who were not members of the lacrosse team and/or that he was not aware of the exclusion of that evidence from DSI's written report at the beginning of the December 15, 2006, hearing, Nifong made false statements of material fact or law to a tribunal in violation of Rule 3.3(a)(1) and engaged in conduct involving dishonesty, fraud, deceit or misrepresentation in violation of Rule 8.4(c) of the Revised Rules of Professional Conduct.

(g) By falsely representing to the Grievance Committee of the State Bar that: (i) he did not realize that the test results revealing the presence of DNA from multiple unidentified males on the rape kit items were not included in DSI's report when he provided it to the Duke Defendants or thereafter, and (ii) his statements to the Court at the beginning of the December 15 hearing referred not to the existence of DNA from multiple unidentified males on the rape kit items but to the Duke Defendants' purported allegation that he had engaged in an intentional attempt to conceal such evidence, Nifong made knowingly false statements of material fact in connection with a disciplinary matter in violation of Rule 8.1(a), and engaged in conduct involving dishonesty, fraud, deceit or misrepresentation in violation of Rule 8.4(c) of the Revised Rules of Professional Conduct.

(h).Each of the violations set forth above separately, and the pattern of conduct revealed when they are viewed together, constitutes conduct prejudicial to the administration of justice in violation of Rule 8.4(d) of the Revised Rules of Professional Conduct.

Based upon the foregoing findings of fact and conclusions of law, the Hearing Committee makes by clear, cogent, and convincing evidence, the following additional FINDINGS OF FACT REGARDING DISCIPLINE:

1. Nifong's misconduct is aggravated by the following factors:

    a. dishonest or selfish motive;
    b. a pattern of misconduct;
    c. multiple offenses;
    d. refusal to acknowledge wrongful nature of conduct in

connection with his handling of the DNA evidence;

    e.   vulnerability of the victims, Collin Finnerty, Reade Seligman and David Evans; and

    f.   substantial experience in the practice of law.

2. Nifong's misconduct is mitigated by the following factors:

    a.   absence of a prior disciplinary record; and

    b.   good reputation.

3. The aggravating factors outweigh the mitigating factors.

4. Nifong's misconduct resulted in significant actual harm to Reade Seligman, Collin Finnerty, and David Evans and their families. Defendant's conduct was, at least, a major contributing factor in the exceptionally intense national and local media coverage the Duke Lacrosse case received and in the public condemnation heaped upon the Duke Defendants. As a result of Nifong's misconduct, these young men experienced heightened public scorn and loss of privacy while facing very serious criminal charges of which the Attorney General of North Carolina ultimately concluded they were innocent.

5. Nifong's misconduct resulted in significant actual harm to the legal profession. Nifong's conduct has created a perception among the public within and outside North Carolina that lawyers in general and prosecutors in particular cannot be trusted and can be expected to lie to the court and to opposing counsel. Nifong's dishonesty to the court and to his opposing counsel, fellow attorneys, harmed the profession. Attorneys have a duty to communicate honestly with the court and with each other. When attorneys do not do so, they engender distrust among fellow lawyers and from the public, thereby harming the profession as a whole.

6. Nifong's misconduct resulted in prejudice to and significant actual harm to the justice system. Nifong has caused a perception among the public within and outside North Carolina that there is a systemic problem in the North Carolina justice system and that a criminal defendant can only get justice if he or she can afford to hire an expensive lawyer with unlimited resources to figure out what is being withheld by the prosecutor.

7. Nifong's false statements to the Grievance Committee of the North Carolina State Bar interfered with the State Bar's ability to regulate attorneys and therefore undermined the privilege of lawyers in this State to remain self-regulating.

8. This Hearing Committee has considered all alternatives and finds that no discipline other than disbarment will adequately protect the public, the judicial system and the profession, given the clear demonstration of dishonest conduct, multiple violations, the pattern of dishonesty

established by the evidence, and Nifong's failure to recognize or acknowledge the wrongfulness of his conduct with regard to withholding of the DNA evidence and making false representations to opposing counsel and to the Court. Furthermore, entry of an order imposing discipline less than disbarment would fail to acknowledge the seriousness of the offenses committed by Nifong and would send the wrong message to attorneys regarding the conduct expected of members of the Bar in this State.

Based upon the foregoing findings of fact, conclusions of law and additional findings of fact regarding discipline, the Hearing Committee hereby enters the following ORDER OF DISCIPLINE:

1. Michael B. Nifong is hereby DISBARRED from the practice of law.

2. Nifong shall surrender his law license and membership card to the Secretary of the State Bar no later than 30 days from service of this order upon him.

***

Questions and Comments

1. The material above obviously pertains to the well-known Duke Lacrosse case in which multiple college students were accused of committing sexual assault although they were all innocent. Mr. Nifong violated a number of ethical standards in the Model Rules of Professional Conduct. What parts of Rule 3.8 did he violate? Did he violate any of the other Model Rules besides Rule 3.8 specifically pertaining to prosecutors?

2. Mr. Nifong knew early on the defendants were innocent of the crimes they were charged with. At what point should Mr. Nifong have disclosed the exculpatory evidence to the defense attorneys? Consider the difference it would have made in the life of the wrongly accused defendants had Mr. Nifong come forward with this information at the point in time when he was supposed to do so.

3. Mr. Nifong disclosed a plethora of information, although untrue, to the media. What information was he permitted to disclose under the Model Rules? *See* Model Rule 3.6. Do you believe Mr. Nifong's use of the media ultimately made his penalty more extreme? Consider the fact that people who do not have legal knowledge use the media to form their opinion on criminal cases.

THE MICHAEL MORTON ACT: MINIMIZING PROSECUTORIAL MISCONDUCT

46 St. Mary's L.J. 407, 408 (2015)
By Cynthia E. Hujar Orr & Robert G. Rodery

I. Introduction

Imagine being accused, convicted, and sentenced to life in prison for murdering your family member; a murder that you did not commit. Twenty-five years slowly pass, and the world outside changes to the point of unfamiliarity while family and friends drift away. Imagine knowing that your child is growing to adulthood while your youth is withering away. Such a tragedy seems unfathomable, but Michael Morton suffered it after being wrongly convicted for the murder of his wife.

Morton was wrongfully convicted and imprisoned for nearly twenty-five years for the murder of his wife, Christine, because the prosecution withheld favorable evidence, or *Brady* material.[1] The withheld evidence included a bandana found behind Michael's house, stained by Christine's blood with the actual killer's hair dried in it; Michael's son's eyewitness account of the murder containing a description of the murderer and a statement that Michael was not home when it happened; and neighbors' eyewitness accounts of a man carrying a wooden club casing the area behind the Morton home. Worse yet, after Michael's release, police linked Christine Morton's actual killer to the murder of another wife and mother killed two years after Christine, using the same modus operandi.

In response to this tragedy, the Texas legislature enacted Senate Bill 1611 (SB 1611), the Michael Morton Act, which took effect on January 1, 2014 and radically changed the criminal discovery process in Texas. Prior to this Act, the discovery procedures disadvantaged defendants and provided limited information. Accordingly, the Act attempts to provide relevance-based discovery in a rational way. This Recent Development provides background on Michael Morton's case and describes the prosecutor's constitutional duty to disclose evidence favorable to the accused first, as set out in *Brady v. Maryland*, as well as provides an in-depth discussion of article 39.14 of the Texas Code of Criminal Procedure and its implications.

---

[1] Brady v. Maryland, 373 U.S. 83, 87 (1963) ("We now hold that the suppression by the prosecution of evidence favorable to an accused upon request violates due process where the evidence was material either to guilt or to punishment, irrespective of the good faith or bad faith of the prosecution.").

II. The Michael Morton Case

While his wife, Christine, lay asleep, Michael left for work to confront the normal "blur of customers and demands, co-workers, corny jokes, and busywork." But an eerie thought pulled at Michael when he did not hear from Christine. The eerie thought turned into panic when the babysitter told him Christine never dropped off Michael's son, Eric. Michael called his home, "feel[ing] sick when an unfamiliar male voice answered [his] home phone." On the other end of the line was Sheriff Jim Boutwell who would only tell Michael to come home as quickly as possible. Losing no time, Michael drove to his home and scrambled to his front door. After Michael identified himself, Sheriff Boutwell delivered the crippling news: "Chris is dead." Thus began Michael's nightmare.

Bill White and Bill Allison, Michael's lawyers, discussed the case as Christine's murder was making headlines. In town to support Michael, his mother left before the next horrifying event. Sheriff Boutwell knocked on Michael's door, delivering devastating words, "Michael Morton," he said flatly, "I'm here to arrest you." After a meager two-hour deliberation, a jury wrongfully convicted Michael Morton for Christine's murder. Michael spent the next twenty-five years incarcerated as his relationships, family, and life diminished. Years later, after much perseverance from John Raley, Nina Morrison, and Innocence Project co-founder Barry Scheck, Morton's counsel discovered prosecutorial misconduct. Withheld evidence showed that someone else committed the crime, and new DNA evidence identified the true killer. The Innocence Project reached out to the law firm of Goldstein, Goldstein, and Hilley to assist, and Gerry Goldstein and Cynthia Orr helped the team obtain Michael Morton's release on October 4, 2011.

III. *Brady v. Maryland* and Its Progeny

The extent to which a prosecutor is constitutionally required to disclose favorable evidence to the accused is outlined in *Brady v. Maryland* and its progeny. In *Brady*, the prosecution withheld evidence that, even though Brady was guilty of murder, his co-defendant admitted to actually killing the victim during their jointly undertaken robbery. On writ of certiorari, the issue was whether the prosecutors' suppression of favorable evidence violated Brady's right to due process. In Justice Douglas's majority opinion, the Court held "the suppression by the prosecution of *evidence favorable to an accused* upon request violates due process where the evidence is material either to guilt or to punishment, irrespective of the good faith or bad faith of the prosecution." Subsequent cases refined the *Brady* rule so that the accused need not request the favorable evidence.

The Brady Line of cases not only requires favorable evidence from prosecutors but also from their agents and "others acting on the government's behalf in the case, including the police." This group is labeled "the prosecution team." In *United States v. Bagley*, 473 U.S. 667 (1985), the Court confronted the standard of review of such errors on appeal. *Bagley* concerned impeachment evidence over payments made to secure the cooperation of several government witnesses. Regarding the standard necessary for reversal of a conviction, the Court held that if admission of withheld evidence presents a "reasonable probability" that the result might have been different, then it is sufficiently material to require a new trial. The *Bagley* Court therefore made it clear that *Brady* evidence includes impeachment evidence. In *Kyles v. Whitley*, 514 U.S. 419 (1995), the Court further explained that this is not a sufficiency of the evidence test. "A reviewing court must consider the suppressed evidence cumulatively, and if the review undermines the court's confidence in the verdict, the conviction must be overturned. In *Kyles*, the suppressed *Brady* evidence showed that one in four eyewitnesses described the perpetrator in a manner that did not match the defendant's description, that the state's undisclosed informant had reasons to point the finger of suspicion at the defendant, and that photos of license plates outside the apartment where the crime occurred did not include the defendant's license plate. Thus, *Kyles* emphasizes the broad nature of *Brady* evidence as being merely favorable evidence. What *Brady* does not do is impose any obligation on the prosecution to produce incriminating evidence. In this regard, the Texas Rules of Criminal Procedure govern discovery.

IV. The Repealed Discovery Rule

Texas has traditionally recognized only limited pretrial discovery rights. Before the Michael Morton Act, the state had no general duty to provide the defense pretrial access to the evidence in the prosecution team's possession or inform the defense as to the evidence available. The prior version of Texas Code of Criminal Procedure article 39.14(a) provided the defendant the ability to inspect discoverable items, if the defendant established sufficient good cause for the trial court to direct the state to produce a tangible item or to allow for inspection with the possibility of copying any discoverable records. Items that previously were not discoverable included written witness statements, written communications between the State and its agents, and work product. Such an onerous rule did little to stem incidents of misconduct. Data released by the Innocence Project, co-founded by Peter J. Neufeld and Barry C. Scheck in 1992, showed that in ninety-one criminal cases, "courts decided that prosecutors committed misconduct, ranging from hiding evidence to making improper arguments to the jury." The data only covered adjudicated exonerations, so logic dictates that the toll of wrongful convictions attributable to prosecutorial misconduct is likely much higher. Michael Morton's case was one of the primary catalysts for reform in Texas discovery rules.

V. The Michael Morton Act

The prior version of article 39.14 recognized the constitutional duty to produce favorable evidence under Brady despite limited criminal discovery. Also, prior to the relevance-based discovery scheme in revised article 39.14, prosecutors enjoyed a great deal of discretion in determining what constituted *Brady* material. Revised article 39.14 attempts to eliminate hindsight arguments over what was, or should have been, produced by the opposing party in a proceeding. The changes also require the state and the defendant to document and produce records of all information provided under the new rules. The change should prompt parties to memorialize essential communications, thereby protecting prosecutors from claims of misconduct.

Under the Michael Morton Act, codified in amended article 39.14, a person charged with a crime who desires discovery must *ask for it*. The state must permit the defendant access to the discovery or produce the requested information "as soon as practicable after receiving a timely request from the defendant." However, for the first time, the prosecution is under a statutory duty to *continually* disclose exculpatory evidence. According to the statute, this includes evidence that is exculpatory, mitigating, or of an impeaching nature. This creates an open file policy, obviating the need for the defense team to continue requesting discovery. The Supreme Court has made clear that where there is such an open file, the defense has the right to rely upon continuing disclosure of favorable evidence by the prosecution.

The Act carves out a few exceptions to discovery. Restrictions set out in section 264.408 of the Family Code and article 39.15 of the Code of Criminal Procedure concern crimes involving children. Section 264.408 provides that any request from the defendant "to copy, photograph, duplicate, or otherwise reproduce a video" shall be denied by the court. However, such recordings need to be readily available to the defense team (including the defendant) under article 39.15 of the Code of Criminal Procedure. Article 39.15 mandates that child pornographic material "must remain in the care, custody, or control of the court or the state," and the defendant may examine the video at a state-controlled facility. With the exception of this carve-out, the new discovery scheme is relevance-based. It requires all information from the prosecution, its agents, and contractors that is material to any matter in the case.

Article 39.14 additionally contains rules for documenting and recording discovery. Article 39.14(a) specifically requires that the State produce evidence "material to *any matter involved* in the action and that [is] in possession, custody, or control of the state or any person under contract with the state." Even with these changes, a continuity issue exists among the 254 Texas counties regarding the procedure for implementing the Act. For example, in Harris County, Texas, defense counsel may draft a document describing what they would like to receive from the state. The state can then provide copies of police reports, log entries from on the scene police reports, and witness statements. The last page of the state's file offers a fill-in-the-blank form for defense counsel to request what they want and to note the date the state discloses that information to the defense. The defense also signs off on this document, initialing to affirm they have received the documents in their conference with the state. As a matter of strategy, however, there may be some discovery that counsel may want to pursue on their own volition in order to maintain the confidentiality of their work product or theory for trial. Harris County also has a pre-printed waiver form for a defendant to waive discovery. However, such a waiver cannot be knowing or intelligent since what is given up is unknown and in the vast majority of circumstances advising a client to execute such a waiver may very well be ineffective. In Bexar and Tarrant County, discovery is achieved by electronic means. Whatever method is employed, it varies widely from county to county and may even differ among courts.

The plain language of article 39.14(a) also imposes no requirements on the form of the discovery to be produced. Items now discoverable span from "written or recorded statements of the defendant or a witness" to "witness statements of law enforcement officers." Furthermore, the statute does not specify the timing for production, only stating that it must occur "as soon as practicable" given the dynamic nature of discovery. Since saying "practicable" is another way of saying "feasible," this requirement is designed to eliminate any withholding of information. As exemplified in the Michael Morton case, such information may prove to be critical to a client's rights to a fair trial and a lawyer's obligation to provide adequate representation.

Article 39.14 further requires that the prosecution document the discovery supplied to the defense, and continue to offer discovery "promptly" even after initial disclosures.

> (k) If at any time before, during, or after trial the state discovers any additional document, item, or information required to be disclosed under subsection (h), the state shall *promptly* disclose

the existence of the document, item, or information to the defendant or the court.[2]

Subsection (k) therefore implies that the "as soon as practicable" time frame indicates immediate production when it is feasible. The prompt disclosure provision also encompasses exculpatory, impeaching, or mitigating evidence. While the Act does not define "promptly," it may be construed to mean within five days of a request.

***

Additionally, article 39.14 references the Texas Rules of Disciplinary Conduct. The Disciplinary Rules expressly provide in Rule 1.03 that counsel must fully communicate with the client to allow him or her to make fully informed decisions. Subsection (g) does not prevent communication with the client, it but does prevent counsel from essentially exposing information to the public outside of trial, except when necessary to make a good faith complaint against the victim or witness.

To preserve error, however, for a writ of habeas corpus, defense attorneys still must file a *Brady* motion.

The Michael Morton Act does much to remedy discovery misconduct outlined above by codifying the requirement that the prosecution must provide favorable evidence wherever it resides, going so far as to include favorable information contained in the prior statement of a witness or even in work product. In Michael Morton's case, the prosecution was able to hide the favorable eyewitness account-indicating that someone else had killed Christine Morton-by deciding not to call its case agent to the stand, in the authors' opinion, to avoid its obligation to turn over *Gaskin* material.[3] It also failed to provide favorable evidence to the trial court upon direct questioning.

VI. Conclusion

The Michael Morton Act is a progressive discovery act designed to prevent and combat prosecutorial misconduct that took the freedom of Michael Morton and others. Michael's testimony to the Texas Senate is reflective of his understanding of the crucial importance of the Act. "There's nothing you can do that will allow me to get back my [twenty-five] years-it's gone and there's really nothing I can do about it, nothing you can do about it . . . . What I am seeking and what I'm asking you to help me obtain is some transparency and most of all, some accountability . . . ." Ken Anderson was arrested after a court of inquiry made a finding

---

[2] Tex. Code Crim. Proc. Ann §39.14 (West 2014).

[3] *See Gaskin v. State*, 353 S.W.2d 467, 470 (Tex. Crim. App. 1961) (instructing the State to provide a witness's prior statement upon which their testimony is based after their testimony, or to provide it for the appellate record if it is not produced).

that he intentionally hid evidence to secure Morton's 1987 conviction for murder. He served less than ten days in jail for criminal contempt after his guilty plea. Michael Morton helped accomplish much more than obtain a slight amount of personal accountability; he ignited progressive discovery reform in Texas that will affect those accused in the future.

Endnotes omitted (See Cynthia E. Hujar Orr & Robert G. Rodery, The Michael Morton Act: Minimizing Prosecutorial Misconduct, 46 St. Mary's L.J. 407, 408 (2015) for full article version). Reprinted with permission from the 2015 edition of the "St. Mary's Law Journal" © 2016 St. Mary's Law Journal. All rights reserved.

Questions and Comments

1. Williamson County prosecutor Ken Anderson became a County district judge. During the post-conviction proceedings, the district attorney John Bradley resisted attempts to have the bloody bandana tested. A court of inquiry was initiated to determine if criminal charges should be filed against Anderson for tampering with evidence and contempt of court. In exchange for the State dropping charges of evidence tampering, Anderson agreed to give up his license to practice law, but faced a fine of $500 and six months in jail on the charge of criminal contempt. Ultimately, Anderson was convicted for contempt of court and was sentenced to ten days in county jail. He was fined $500 and ordered to perform 500 hours of community service. Additionally, in 2012, John Bradley lost his Williamson County District Attorney re-election bid in the republican primary. *See* Chuck Lindell, Ken *Anderson to Serve 10 Days in Jail*, STATESMAN (Nov. 8, 2013) *http://www.statesman.com/news/news/ken-anderson-to-serve-10-days-in-jail/nbmsH/.*

2. Constitutional standards require a prosecutor to disclose evidence and information that is likely to lead to an acquittal unless relieved of the obligation by court order. Paragraph (d) of Rule 3.8 requires prosecutorial disclosure of all such material known to the prosecutor that "tends to negate the guilt of the accused or mitigates the offense." Violating these standards prejudices a criminal defendant and generally results in a new trial. Is a new trial enough? Should a prosecutor be punished criminally, civilly, or disciplined by a state bar association? The Model Rules do not provide any guidance for punishing prosecutors who engage in misconduct. Do you think it is needed? Does the severity of prosecutorial misconduct affect your answer?

3. In 2003, the Center for Public Integrity conducted a study exposing the rarity of prosecutors being held accountable for misconduct. Steve Weinberg and Center for Public Integrity, *Breaking the Rules: Who Suffers When a Prosecutor Is Cited for Misconduct?* (2003). The study

highlights the reluctance of disciplinary boards to impose serious penalties in cases where misconduct is proven. Why? Who refers the prosecutor to a disciplinary board? Do criminal defense attorneys have incentives not to report misconduct? Under the Model Rules, do defense attorneys or judges violate their professional duties if prosecutorial misconduct remains unreported?

D. DISCUSSION QUESTIONS

1. Consider the requirement in Rule 3.8 that commands a prosecutor to turn over all mitigating evidence to the defense. Do you think a formal discovery process, similar to the one used in civil cases, would increase or decrease the likelihood that a prosecutor could withhold mitigating evidence?

2. Prosecutors have been called the most powerful officials in the criminal justice system, as it is their decisions that control the direction and sometimes even possible outcomes of criminal cases. Should Prosecutors be held to an even higher standard of ethical behavior than they are subject to currently? Prosecutors are rarely reprimanded for misconduct, even when the misconduct causes harm to its victims. In 2003, the Center for Public Integrity studied 11,000 cases of alleged prosecutorial misconduct since 1970 and found of these cases, only 44 prosecutors were brought before disciplinary boards for misconduct. Aditi Sherikar, *Prosecuting Prosecutors: A Need for Uniform Sanctions*, 25 Geo. J. Legal Ethics 1011, 1020 (2012).

3. You are a defense attorney in a criminal trial in which your client is being tried for homicide. Right after the start of the trial, your client confesses to you that he indeed committed the crime. What are your duties to your client? What should you do at this point? How would you approach this issue? *Compare* Model Rule 3.8 *with* Model Rule 1.16 *and* Model Rule 3.3, comment [10].

4. Model Rule 1.16 sets out the rule for terminating representation of a client. The rule provides conditions under which it is *mandatory* to withdraw from representation, as well as *permissible* to withdraw from representation. What situations call for mandatory withdrawal from representation? Do you think anything should be added to this list? If not, why is it proper for the rule to contain such a limited number of conditions in which a withdrawal is mandatory?

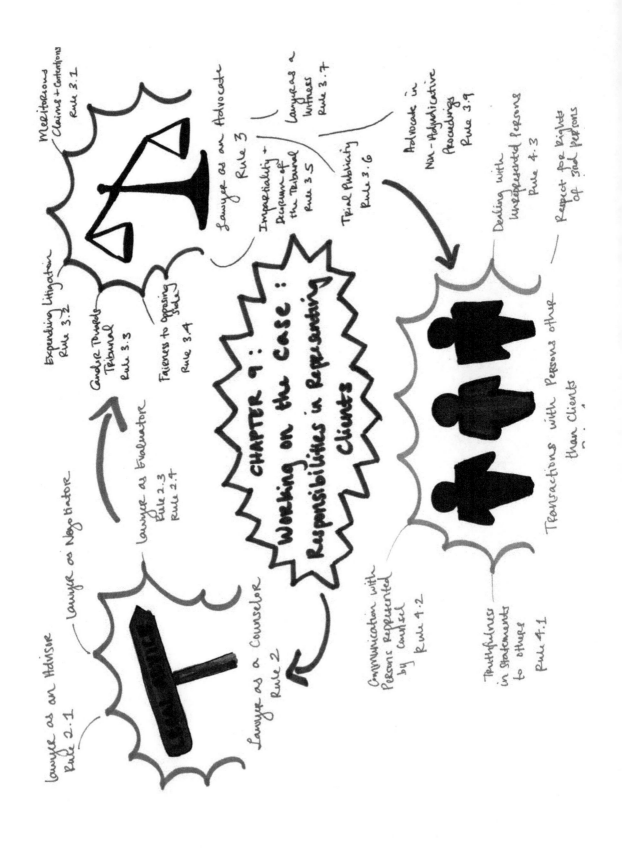

Lawyer as an Advisor
Rule 2.1

Lawyer as Negotiator

Lawyer as Evaluator
Rule 2.3
Rule 2.7

Lawyer as a Counselor
Rule 2

Meritorious
Claims + Contentions
Rule 3.1

Expediting Litigation
Rule 3.2

Candor Towards
Tribunal
Rule 3.3

Fairness to Opposing
Party
Rule 3.4

Lawyer as an Advocate
Rule 3

Impartiality +
Decorum of
the Tribunal
Rule 3.5

Lawyer as a
Witness
Rule 3.7

Trial Publicity
Rule 3.6

Advocate in
Non-Adjudicative
Proceedings
Rule 3.9

CHAPTER 9:
Working on the Case:
Responsibilities in Representing
Clients

Dealing with
Unrepresented Persons
Rule 4.3

Respect for Rights
of 3rd Persons

Communication with
Persons Represented
by Counsel
Rule 4.2

Truthfulness
in Statements
to others
Rule 4.1

Transactions with Persons other
than Clients

Chapter 9:
Working on the Case—Responsibilities in Representing Clients

A. INTRODUCTION

As mentioned in a previous chapter, a lawyer's duty to her client far exceeds mere representation. Lawyers are bound by the Model Rules of Professional Conduct to act in the fullest extent of professionalism to ensure effective and efficient representation of their client. To promote the values of justice, lawyers must be fair and candid through all of their actions, in and outside of the court. A lawyer is bound by rules such as Rule 2.1, which states a lawyer should exercise professional judgment and render candid advice. Rules 3.1 to 3.9 govern how a lawyer should act as an advocate for a client, including fairness to the opposing party and what not to say regarding the occurrence of trials when in the public light. It is also important for a lawyer to be truthful and respectful in her dealings with individuals who are not her clients.

This chapter will provide an overview of some of these rules in selected cases. The *In re Litz* case discusses how although a lawyer would want to make a statement as to the innocence of her client, there may be circumstances where that would violate the Model Rules. Moreover, *Phila. Indem. Ins. Co. v. Hamic* provides an example of such violation of rendering only truthful statements to pursue a claim. These cases provide examples of a lawyer's violation of the rules governing one's role as a counselor, advocate, or a lawyer speaking to a non-client.

To what extent, if at all, may a lawyer voice her opinion to the press? When, if ever, is it appropriate to talk to the opposing party without his lawyer's presence? When, if ever, will a lawyer be able to testify as a witness in court? The following rules will shed some light on these different roles of a lawyer and offer reasons for such distinctions.

B. RULES

In preparation, read carefully the following sections of the Model Rules of Professional Conduct along with any relevant comments listed below.

Counselor:
- Rule 2.1: Lawyer as an Advisor
  - Comment [4]
- Rule 2.3: Evaluation for Use by Third Parties
- Rule 2.4: Lawyer Serving as Third Party Neutral

Advocate:
- Rule 3.1: Meritorious Claims & Contentions
- Rule 3.2: Expediting Litigation
  - Comment [1]
- Rule 3.3: Candor Toward the Tribunal
  - Comments [1-6], [8-10] &[15]
- Rule 3.4: Fairness to Opposing Party and Counsel
- Rule 3.5: Impartiality and Decorum of the Tribunal
  - Comments [2-3]
- Rule 3.6: Trial Publicity
  - Comment [7]
- Rule 3.7: Lawyer as Witness
  - Comment [6]
- Rule 3.9: Advocate in Nonadjudicative Proceedings

Transactions with Persons Other Than Clients:
- Rule 4.1: Truthfulness in Statements to Others
  - Comments [1] & [3]
- Rule 4.2: Communication with Person Represented by Counsel
  - Comments [3-7]
- Rule 4.3: Dealing with Unrepresented Person
- Rule 4.4: Respect for Rights of Third Persons
  - Comments [2] & [3]

C. Cases and Additional Readings

In re Litz
Supreme Court of Indiana (1999)
721 N.E.2d 258

Per Curiam.

The respondent, Steven C. Litz, defended a woman accused of neglect of a dependent. While a retrial of that case proceeded, the respondent caused to be published in several newspapers a letter which stated his client had committed no crime, criticized the prosecutor's decision to retry the case, and mentioned that his client had passed a lie detector test. For that, we find today that the respondent violated Ind. Professional Conduct Rule 3.6(a), which forbids attorneys from making extrajudicial statements which they know or reasonably should know have a substantial likelihood of materially prejudicing an adjudicative proceeding.

This case is now before us for approval of a *Statement of Circumstances and Conditional Agreement for Discipline* reached by the parties in resolution of this matter pursuant to Ind. Admission and Discipline Rule 23 § 11(c). Our jurisdiction here is a result of the respondent's admission to this state's bar on October 12, 1984.

The parties agree that the respondent represented a client in criminal proceeding in Morgan County in which a jury found the client guilty of neglect of a dependent resulting in serious bodily injury. The respondent represented the client in the appeal of her conviction and succeeded in obtaining a reversal of the conviction from the Indiana Court of Appeals. The Court of Appeals remanded the case to the trial court, finding that the lower court erred in determining that evidence of "battered women's syndrome" was irrelevant and inadmissible in the first trial.

After remand on June 2, 1997, the trial court set the matter for a new jury trial on November 3, 1997. On June 25, 1997, a "Letter to the Editor" written and submitted by the respondent appeared in the Bloomington, Indiana *Herald-Times* and the Mooresville, Indiana *Times*. An identical letter from the respondent appeared in the June 26, 1997, edition of the *Indianapolis Star*. The respondent's letter stated this his client had spent the "last 18 months in jail for a crime she did not commit" and revealed that she had passed a lie detector test. The letter also decried the decision to retry his client, characterizing it as "abominable." On September 29, 1997, the respondent, on behalf of the client, filed a *Motion for Change of Venue* from Morgan County, citing "prejudicial pre-trial publicity." The court granted the motion.

Indiana Professional Conduct Rule 3.6(a) provides:

A lawyer shall not make an extrajudicial statement that a reasonable person would expect to be disseminated by means of public communication if the lawyer knows or reasonably should know that it will have a substantial likelihood of materially prejudicing an adjudicative proceeding.

Indiana Professional Conduct Rule 3.6(b) provides that certain types of extrajudicial [sic] statements referred to in subsection (a) are "rebuttably presumed" to have a substantial likelihood of materially prejudicing an adjudicative proceeding, including the results of any examination or test, any opinion as to the guilt or innocence of a defendant in a criminal case that could result in incarceration, or information that the lawyer knows or reasonably should know is likely to be inadmissible as evidence in a trial. Prof.Cond.R. 3.6(b)(3), (4), (5).

Preserving the right to a fair trial necessarily entails some curtailment of the information that may be disseminated about a party prior to trial, particularly where trial by jury is involved. *Comment* to Prof.Cond.R. 3.6. The respondent's letters to area newspapers created a substantial likelihood of material prejudice to the pending jury retrial of the respondent's own client. Some of the statements contained therein presumptively presented that risk: his description of evidence that could have been inadmissible at trial (i.e., the fact and result of the lie detector test), and his opinion that his client did not commit the crime for which she was charged. Further, the respondent's identification of the prosecution's decision to retry the case as "abominable," despite the fact that retrial of the case was well within the prosecutor's discretion, tended to contribute to a pre-trial atmosphere prejudicial to the prosecution's case. In sum, the respondent's letters created an environment where a fair trial was much less likely to occur. Additionally, the respondent effectively set the stage for his own subsequent motion for change of venue based on prejudicial pre-trial publicity. Accordingly, we find that the respondent's published commentary created a substantial likelihood of materially prejudicing retrial of his client's criminal case, and thus violated Prof. Cond. R 3.6(a).

The parties agree that the appropriate sanction for the misconduct is a public reprimand. Among the factors we consider in assessing the adequacy of that proposed sanction are aggravating and mitigating circumstances. *See, e.g., Matter of Christoff*, 690 N.E.2d 1135 (Ind. 1997); *Matter of Darling*, 685 N.E.2d 1066 (Ind. 1997); *Matter of Conway*, 658 N.E.2d 592 (Ind. 1995). In mitigation, the parties agree that the respondent has not previously been the subject of a disciplinary proceeding, that he cooperated with the Commission, and that he continued to represent the client through the resolution of her case. No factors in aggravation were cited.

We view the respondent's actions as a purposeful attempt to gain an unfair advantage in retrial of his client's case. Although the respondent had no real selfish motive (and instead apparently sought only to advocate zealously his client's cause), he nonetheless was bound to do so only within the bounds of our ethical rules. His public comments were inappropriate because they threatened or in fact impinged the prospect of a fair trial for his client. Whether extrajudicial statements of this sort warrant reprimand or suspension is fact sensitive. Here, we take into account the fact that the respondent's primary motivation appears to have been the welfare of his client. We are also cognizant while assessing the proposed sanction of our policy of encouraging agreed resolution of disciplinary cases. We find that, in this case, the agreed sanction of a public reprimand is appropriate.

Accordingly, the respondent, Steven C. Litz, is hereby reprimanded and admonished for the misconduct set forth above.

The Clerk of this Court is directed to provide notice of this order in accordance with Admis. Disc. R. 23(3)(d) and to provide the clerk of the United States Court of Appeals for the Seventh Circuit, the clerk of each of the United States District Courts in this state, and the clerks of the United States Bankruptcy Courts in this state with the last known address of respondent as reflected in the records of the Clerk.

Costs of this proceeding are assessed against the respondent.

Questions and Comments

1. The attorney discussed evidence and his own opinion regarding the client in the midst of the ongoing trial. Are attorneys ever allowed to comment on a case they are involved in? If so, under what circumstances is it permissible to do so and how much can one say? *See* Model Rule 3.6. What practical reasons are there for limiting an attorney's ability to publicly comment on her own case?

2. Why, specifically, were the attorney's public comments and opinions on the ongoing case inappropriate? The rules explicitly list instances in which an attorney can make comments about their own case. Could the attorney in *In re Litz* possibly make an argument that his comments were appropriate in light of that exact factual scenario?

3. The sanction imposed in *In re Litz* was a public reprimand. Do you think this is an adequate punishment for the attorney's conduct? Do you think the court appropriately considered the mitigating factors?

PHILA. INDEM. INS. CO. V. HAMIC
United States Middle District Florida (2012)
No. 8:12–cv–829–T–26EAJ, 2012 WL 3835088

Order

Before the Court is Plaintiff's Motion for Final Summary Judgment and Statement of Undisputed Facts (Dkts. 44 & 45), and Defendants' Response in Opposition and Statement of Supplemental Facts. (Dkts. 47 & 48). After careful consideration of the motion, the applicable law, and the entire file, the Court concludes the motion should be denied.

Background

Plaintiff Philadelphia Indemnity Insurance Company (Philadelphia) brings this action against Stephen H. Hamic (Hamic), Hamic, Jones, Hamic & Sturwold, P.A. (the Firm), William L. Nicholas, and Molly Wescomb seeking a declaration of rights as to both the duty to defend and the duty to indemnify Hamic and the Firm under the Firm's professional liability insurance policy. (Dkt. 1, para. 9). The complaint alleges that the underlying suit seeks damages for intentional torts only: conspiracy to commit malicious prosecution, malicious prosecution, conspiracy to commit abuse of process, abuse of process, and a violation of Florida's RICO statute. (Dkt. 1, para. 10). Philadelphia alleges in the complaint that these claims "are not by reason of a negligent act, error, or omission in the performance of services performed or advice given by Stephen Hamic to another, for a fee or otherwise, in the course of his practice as an accountant." (Dkt. 1, para. 10). Plaintiff requests in this motion for summary judgment that this Court find no duty to defend nor duty to indemnify either Hamic or the Firm.

The Professional Liability Policy

The policy provides coverage for professional liability for the Firm and Hamic "by reason of a negligent act, error or omission in the performance of professional services, . . ." "Professional services" is defined as any "services performed or advice given by any insured to others for a fee or otherwise in the conduct of the insured's practice as an accountant; . . ." Professional services includes libel, slander or invasion of privacy "if arising out of" the professional services just described. Professional services also includes "consulting in the course of the practice of accountancy" and "acting as a personal fiduciary."

Section E under the exclusions portion of the policy excludes "any claim or damages arising out of any dishonest, fraudulent, criminal, malicious or knowingly wrongful or reckless act, error or omission of any insured, provided that such determination results from either a legal adjudication, regulatory ruling or legal admission." The policy provides that exclusion E does "not invalidate this insurance as to any insured who did not act with knowledge or consent in the matter in which the exclusion applies."

Duty to Defend

The duty to defend is determined solely from the allegations of the complaint. *Wellcare of Fla., Inc. v. American Int'l Specialty Lines Ins. Co.*, 16 So.3d 904, 906 (Fla.Dist.Ct.App. 2009) (citing *Biltmore Constr. Co. v. Owners Ins. Co.*, 842 So.2d 947, 949 (Fla.Dist.Ct.App. 2003)). "If the underlying complaint alleges facts showing two or more grounds for liability, one being within the insurance coverage and the other not, the insurer is obligated to defend the entire suit." *Lime Tree Vill. Cmty. Club Ass'n Inc. v. State Farm Gen. Ins. Co.*, 980 F.2d 1402, 1405 (11th Cir. 1993) (quoting *Baron Oil Co. v. Nationwide Mut. Fire Ins. Co.*, 470 So.2d at 813-14 (Fla.Dist.Ct.App. 1985)). "[A]ny doubt about the duty to defend must be resolved in favor of the insured." *Estate of Tinervin v. Nationwide Mut. Ins. Co.*, 23 So.3d 1232, 1238 (Fla.Dist.Ct.App 2009) (quoting *Amerisure Ins. Co. v. Gold Coast Marine Distribs.*, Inc., 771 So.2d 579, 580-81 (Fla.Dist.Ct.App. 2000)); *Baron Oil*, 470 So.2d at 814.

Facts as Alleged in the Complaint

The underlying case travels on the Fourth Amended Complaint. The gist of the lawsuit concerns the arrest of Bill Nicholas and Molly Wescomb on May 28, 2009, after Steve and Mike Hamic approached the state attorney's office with information that Nicholas and Wescomb stole over $60,000 from Exit Realty. As alleged, Steve Hamic and the Firm provided accounting services for Exit Realty, a real estate brokerage firm that consisted of Bill and Susan Nicholas, Molly Wescomb, and Mike Hamic, from its inception in 2002 through early 2007. Hamic and the Firm prepared Exit Realty's state and federal tax returns, rendered business financial advice, and assisted in internal corporate bookkeeping. As part of these services, Hamic and the Firm "verified that Molly was a member and employee of Exit Realty and reflected her wages paid as an employee." According to the complaint, Molly Wescomb worked as an employee both while she was part owner in Exit Realty and after she transferred her ownership. She often worked from home via the internet and telephone.

After a dispute arose between Mike Hamic and Exit Realty concerning the value of Mike's interest in the company, Steve Hamic, on behalf of Mike Hamic, analyzed the books and records of Exit Realty and performed valuations of Mike Hamic's interest. Exit Realty eventually filed a lawsuit against Mike Hamic when it became obvious a resolution was unattainable and after, according to the complaint, Mike Hamic, not

Steve Hamic, made threats of filing complaints against Bill Nicholas. Two days after the filing of the action, both Hamics and the Firm "conspired" to commit malicious prosecution, extortion and abuse of process. The complaint alleges that Steve Hamic agreed to use his professional skills, resources, and access to Exit's Realty business records through the Firm to fabricate false criminal charges against Nicholas and Wescomb.

Steve Hamic then delivered a memorandum with confidential documents he had prepared for Exit Realty to the state attorney, contending that Nicholas and Wescomb had stolen money from Exit Realty by paying Wescomb a salary and benefits. At the first meeting with the state attorney's office, Mike Hamic, not Steve, gave a statement that in December 2007, after Steve Hamic and the Firm were no longer providing accounting services for Exit Realty, a bookkeeper brought to his attention that Wescomb was being paid as an employee when she was not working there. Mike Hamic further stated that after he confronted Nicholas, Wescomb continued to receive paychecks and coverage under the company's health insurance in the amount of over $60,000.

Steve and Mike Hamic continued to provide more documents to the state attorney's office and the state attorney's office then subpoenaed documents from a bank, a credit card company, and a health insurance company regarding Wescomb's payments and benefits. Steve Hamic prepared a forensic accounting analysis of those documents and provided more analyses at the request of the state attorney's office. The threatening communications enumerated in the complaint are alleged to have been made by Mike Hamic only. Steve Hamic concluded his analysis with the assertion that Nicholas and Wescomb had committed felony grand theft of $70,156.91 from Exit Realty through wages and health insurance benefits. The state attorney's office arrested Nicholas and Wescomb one month later. The complaint alleges that Mike, not Steve Hamic, continued to negotiate with Nicholas concerning the money owed. The state attorney nolle-prossed the criminal charges about two months after the May 2009 arrest.

With respect to the communications made by the Hamic brothers, the complaint alleges that Steve Hamic concealed from the state attorney's office the state and federal tax forms and returns, including the ones he had prepared as accountant for Exit Realty, which would show that Wescomb was an employee drawing legitimate wages and benefits. Both Hamic brothers "either knew these assertions were false when made or acted in reckless disregard of their truth or falsity." The complaint further alleges that the Hamic brothers acted with "legal malice in that they procured the criminal actions: (a) without probable cause; (b) knowing the allegations were false or in willful ignorance of their falsity; . . ."

Negligent Act, Error and Omission

The counts that encompass the relevant dispute regarding the duty to defend include the counts for malicious prosecution and civil conspiracy, as those counts, argue Hamic and the Firm, fall under the "negligent act, error or omission" clause in the policy and not under the exclusion clause concerning wrongful acts. The issue is whether the facts as alleged include any negligent conduct in the performance of professional services. Based on Florida law, the Court finds that the allegations of the complaint include such conduct, thereby triggering the duty to defend the entire underlying action.

The tort of malicious prosecution consists of six elements, one of the elements being malice. *Burns v. GCC Beverages, Inc.*, 502 So.2d 1217 (Fla. 1986); *Adams v. Whitfield*, 290 So.2d 49 (Fla. 1974). There are two types of malice: actual malice and legal malice. *Wilson v. O'Neal*, 118 So.2d 101, 105 (Fla. Dist. Ct. App. 1960). The parties agree that only legal malice is implicated in this case. Legal malice can be inferred from the lack of probable cause. *Alamo Rent–A–Car, Inc. v. Mancusi*, 632 So.2d 1352, 1355 (Fla. 1994). Malice, however, is not synonymous with want of probable cause. *White v. Miami Home Milk Producers Ass'n*, 143 Fla. 518, 197 So. 125, 126 (Fla. 1940). Legal malice may also be inferred from "gross negligence or great indifference to persons, property, or the rights of others." *Mancusi*, 632 So.2d at 1357.

Despite the clear Florida mandate that malice may be inferred from gross negligence, Philadelphia strenuously argues that legal malice "requires proof of an *intentional* act performed without justification or excuse" and therefore does not constitute negligent conduct covered by the policy. *See Olson v. Johnson*, 961 So.2d 356, 359 (Fla.Dist.Ct.App. 2007) (emphasis added). The quoted language from *Olson* is taken from a criminal case, *Reed v. State*, 837 So.2d 366, 368-69 (Fla. 2002), and *Olson*, later on in the opinion, cites *Mancusi* for the proposition that legal malice may be based on gross negligence. What is evident from reading the plethora of cases discussing intentional acts versus intentional torts versus nonnegligent acts, is the difficulty in differentiating the context within which each term is used. As Hamic and the Firm point out, gross negligence is alleged in the complaint by its assertion of legal malice and that Hamic acted in reckless disregard of the truth or falsity of the communications made to the state attorney.

Philadelphia relies heavily on *Wellcare* for the premise that Hamic's actions described in the complaint do not constitute the kind of mistakes inherent in the practice of accountancy. *Wellcare* is inapposite. There, an insurance agent hired by a third party administrator, Wellcare, sued Wellcare for breach of a marketing agreement based on Wellcare's "deliberate, intentional, systematic" desire to exclude unprofitable health care plans as a product. The actions of Wellcare had nothing to do with its rendering professional services as a third party administrator to its own insurance agent as a marketer of Wellcare products. Unlike *Wellcare*, there is no question that Hamic was performing professional services, or services customarily performed by an accountant, when he ran spread sheets, reviewed tax returns, analyzed financial documents, and performed forensic accounting. He performed accounting services for Exit initially, and relied on documents he prepared for it, to provide information to the state attorney's office regarding Wescomb being paid as an employee. He then performed forensic accounting services from his documents and from additional subpoenaed records for the state attorney. The policy's definition of professional services specifically includes those services rendered "to others for a fee or otherwise." Under the plain language of the policy, Nicholas, Wescomb, Mike Hamic and the state attorney's office are "others" and the fact that Hamic and the Firm did not receive money for Hamic's services is irrelevant.

While there is no blanket provision in the policy that excludes all intentional acts, section E does exclude "any dishonest, fraudulent, criminal, malicious or knowingly wrongful or unlawful act, error or omission" and such limitation in errors and omissions policies for professionals is common. 9A Lee R. Russ & Thomas F. Segalla, *Couch on Insurance* 3d §131.38 (Nov. 2011). There is authority to suggest that these specific exclusions would be unnecessary if the policy covered only negligent conduct in the first instance. *S.E.C. v. Credit Bancorp, Ltd.*, 147 F.Supp.2d 238, 264 (S.D.N.Y. 2001). Section E further conditions the exclusion on a legal adjudication of the wrongful act. At this juncture, no legal adjudication has occurred and therefore this clause comes into play only concerning the duty to indemnify.

"By Reason of" the Performance of Professional Services

The phrase "because of" has been held to mandate causation, as opposed to the broader term "arising out of," which merely indicates some causal connection short of proximate cause. *See Garcia v. Federal Ins. Co.*, 969 So.2d 288, 292 (Fla. 2007) (holding that "because of" is defined as "by reason of" which means caused by); *Taurus Holdings, Inc. v. U.S. Fid. & Guar. Co.*, 913 So.2d 528, 539-40 (Fla. 2005) (holding that "arising out of" requires "some causal connection, or relationship" but not proximate cause). The complaint alleges that Hamic was the legal cause of malicious prosecution. Hamic performed professional accounting services in the review and analysis of the financial documents obtained through subpoenas issued in connection with the investigation of Wescomb and Nicholas. Hamic had prepared the tax returns and corporate books for Exit Realty from 2004 through 2006, some of which he turned over to the state attorney's office. Thus, the charges brought against Nicholas and

Wescomb were "by reason of" the rendering of accounting services by Hamic. The complaint does allege that Hamic was mistaken or grossly negligent in his analysis that Wescomb was not an employee for purposes of receiving a salary and benefits.

***

It is therefore ORDERED AND ADJUDGED as follows:

Plaintiff's Motion for Final Summary Judgment (Dkt. 44) is DENIED.

***

Questions and Comments

1. Rule 4.1 requires a lawyer to make truthful statements to others. Specifically, what false assertions did the Hamic brothers make that resulted in a violation of Model Rule 4.1? What implications did these false statements have in the case?

2. Does it make a difference the assertions were made to the state attorney and not to an ordinary person? What consequences might telling false facts to a state attorney have? Should the fact that the state attorney has means to verify false statements whereas the average person may not have access to information in which he can verify what the attorney said, be taken into consideration?

3. Given the facts of the case, would an honest mistake negate a violation of Model Rule 4.1? How stringent is the "knowing" standard? Is there any merit in the argument that misleading or possibly misleading statements are not necessarily false statements? Can you think of a situation in which a lawyer may mistakenly make a false statement that would not be a violation of the rule?

IN RE JOHNSON

United States Bankruptcy Court for the Eastern District of Virginia, Richmond Division (2008)
No. 07-33312-KRH, Chapter 13

MEMORANDUM OPINION. Jessica Ashley Johnson (the "Debtor") was 18 years old when she filed this Chapter 13 bankruptcy case on September 12, 2007 (the "Petition Date"). She had just graduated from high school three months prior to the Petition Date. She was still a full time student. Jessica Ashley Johnson did not file bankruptcy to obtain relief from her creditors. She did not have sufficient time to incur significant debt. Rather, the Debtor's grandmother and the Debtor's father used this teenager as part of a scheme to hinder, delay and defraud their own creditors. They did this by transferring to the Debtor certain real property on the eve of a foreclosure sale and then by having her file for bankruptcy.

Included in the schedules annexed to the Debtor's bankruptcy petition were two parcels of real property located on 4th Avenue in the City of Richmond, VA, one at 2202 4th Avenue (the "2202 Property") and the other at 3309 4th Avenue (the "3309 Property," and together with the 2202 Property, the "Two Parcels of Real Property").

***

Peter P. Balas ("Balas") held a note secured by a deed of trust on the 3309 Property. The Debtor's bankruptcy petition was filed for the purpose of forestalling a foreclosure sale that was scheduled for September 13, 2007 on the 3309 Property. Balas filed a motion in this Court for in rem relief from the automatic stay (the "Motion") pursuant to § 362(d)(4) of the Bankruptcy Code.

***

At the Hearing the Court became aware of the involvement of Debtor's counsel, Andrew George Adams, III ("Adams"), in the scheme to hinder, delay and defraud Balas. Adams had represented Ms. Johnson and Mr. Johnson in three of the later serial bankruptcy filings that were part of the scheme to hinder, delay and defraud Balas. The Court also learned that Adams was counsel of record for Ms. Johnson in a fourth bankruptcy case that was pending before this Court (Case No. 07-32620-KRH).

After the Hearing, the Court issued an order for Mr. Adams to show cause why the filing of the Debtor's bankruptcy case "was not presented for an improper purpose as proscribed by Rule 9011(b) of the Federal Rules of Bankruptcy Procedure and if he cannot show such cause, why he should not be sanctioned for filing this bankruptcy case" (the "Order to Show Cause").

***

At the Sanctions Hearing, the office of the U.S. Trustee presented evidence (i) regarding the prior bankruptcy cases of Ms. Johnson and Mr. Johnson, (ii) regarding the transfers of the Two Parcels of Real Property to the Debtor, and (iii) regarding Adams's involvement in three of the prior bankruptcy cases of Ms. Johnson and Mr. Johnson and Ms. Johnson's pending bankruptcy case. Adams appeared on his own behalf.

***

Between the time of Judge Tice's ruling dismissing Ms. Johnson's case and the entry of the Court's order commemorating that ruling, Adams hurriedly filed yet another bankruptcy case for Ms. Johnson on October

15, 2005 (Case No. 05-42416-DOT). This case was filed in complete derogation of the Court's ruling three days earlier. The case was subsequently dismissed on October 27, 2005, again with prejudice.

***

Mr. Johnson brought his daughter to meet with Adams on September 7, 2007. Adams agreed that the best way to stop the scheduled foreclosure sale was for Mr. Johnson's daughter to file a chapter 13 bankruptcy petition quickly. Adams insisted at the Sanctions Hearing that he had conducted a review of the Debtor's financial situation. Adams admitted that he learned from this review that the Debtor had no bank account. He learned about the Debtor's age. He also learned that the Debtor was unemployed. Adams found out that the Debtor had no wage statements for the six months prior to filing, as the Debtor was a full-time student. The Debtor had never filed a tax return. Adams knew that the Debtor had just recently acquired both the 3309 Property and the 2202 Property from Ms. Johnson and Mr. Johnson by way of gift. Adams already was aware of the prior bankruptcy filings of Mr. Johnson and Ms. Johnson and was familiar with their financial affairs from his prior representation of them.

Adams became aware that the Debtor's primary assets, other than the Two Parcels of Real Property that had just been transferred into her name, were her schoolbooks, school supplies, clothes, electronics, and a computer. The Debtor had no other substantial assets and claimed no other property exempt under Schedule C. Adams did not bother to review the rent rolls for either of the properties for the six months prior to filing. That was because Adams was confident that the Debtor was not collecting the rents on the Two Parcels of Real Property. He assumed that Mr. Johnson was collecting those rents. Adams did not review the deeds of trust or the notes secured by those deeds of trust for either of the Two Parcels of Real Property. Adams feigned that he was ignorant of the fact that the Debtor was not personally liable on the two deed of trust notes. Adams admitted that the sole purpose for putting the Debtor into bankruptcy was to avoid foreclosure on the 3309 Property. Adams admitted that he never counseled the Debtor against filing for bankruptcy, nor did he ever suggest to her that filing a bankruptcy petition might be ill-advised.

The federal courts should hold attorneys that appear before them to the recognized standards of conduct in their jurisdiction. *In re Computer Dynamics, Inc.* 252 B.R. 50, 64 (Bankr. E.D. Va. 1997), aff'd, 181 F.3d 87, 1999 WL 350943 (4th Cir. 1999). Rule 2090-1(I) of the Local Rules of Bankruptcy Procedure provides that the ethical rules applicable to this Court are the Virginia Rules of Professional Conduct. Violations of the Virginia Rules of Professional Conduct may lead to the imposition of sanctions. *Computer Dynamics*, 252 B.R. at 64. The Court finds that Adams has violated certain of these rules. In so doing, he has failed to adhere to the minimum standard of acceptable conduct for a lawyer practicing before this Court.

Rule 1.4(b) of the Virginia Rules of Professional Conduct requires an attorney to "explain a matter to the extent reasonably necessary to permit the client to make informed decisions regarding the representation." Comment 3 specifies that normally an attorney need only provide information "appropriate for a client who is a comprehending and responsible adult. . . However, fully informing the client according to this standard may be impracticable, for example, where the client is a child or suffers from mental disability. *See* Rule 1.14." Rule 2.1 of the Virginia Rules of Professional Conduct requires an attorney to "exercise independent professional judgment and render candid advice" to clients. Comment 3 to that Rule states that even though a client may ask for "purely technical advice" if that client is "inexperienced in legal matters . . . the lawyer's responsibility as advisor may include indicating that more may be involved than strictly legal considerations." "As advisor, a lawyer provides a client with an informed understanding of the client's legal rights and obligations and explains their practical implications." *Virginia Rules of Prof'l Conduct*, Preamble P 1 (2001), Va. Sup. Ct. R. Pt. 6, §II. Comment 5 to Rule 2.1 notes that "when a lawyer knows that a client proposes a course of action that is likely to result in substantial adverse legal, moral or ethical consequences to the client or to others, duty to the client under Rule 1.4 may require that the lawyer act if the client's course of action is related to the representation."

The Debtor in this case was unsophisticated as to financial affairs. She had no bank account and no employment. She had never filed a tax return. She was barely out of high school. In spite of this, Adams failed to advise her against filing for bankruptcy despite the fact that she had no substantial debt. He could not have advised her that she was not personally liable on the deeds of trust, as Adams himself claims that he was unaware of that fact. He also allowed her to become a participant in a scheme to hinder, delay and defraud creditors of her father and her grandmother without advising her that there was a substantial likelihood that this would occur if she filed.

Rule 1.3(c) of the Virginia Rules of Professional Conduct prohibits an attorney from intentionally prejudicing or damaging "a client during the course of the professional relationship." Comment 1 to that rule emphasizes that "[a] lawyer should act with commitment and dedication to the interests of the client and with zeal in advocacy upon the client's behalf." By putting this Debtor into a bankruptcy that was timed to postpone an inevitable foreclosure sale, Adams caused catastrophic and irreversible damage to his client's credit record. Starting off in life, this teenager's credit report will now reflect this bankruptcy for years to come. 15 U.S.C. §1681(a)(1). The bankruptcy filing may prevent the Debtor from purchasing or renting a home. It may keep her from acquiring a vehicle. Knowing that the gambit to frustrate the foreclosure sale faced a likely challenge for in rem relief due to the recent amendments to the Bankruptcy Code Adams, nevertheless, subjected this unsophisticated Debtor to that risk. Then, when the expected motion was filed charging that his client was involved in a scheme to hinder, delay, and defraud creditors, Adams provided no defense to the very serious allegations on the Debtor's behalf.

Rule 1.7(a) of the Virginia Rules of Professional Conduct prohibits an attorney from representing a client if "there is significant risk that the representation of one or more clients will be materially limited by the lawyer's responsibilities to another client, a former client or a third person or by a personal interest of the lawyer." It is painfully obvious to this Court that in representing the Debtor, Adams was not acting in her best interests, but rather he was serving the interests of her father and her grandmother. No reasonable attorney could maintain that filing for bankruptcy was in the best interests of this teenager. The Debtor had no substantial debt. Yet, Adams chose to represent the Debtor when there was a significant risk that the actions he would take during the course of that representation would benefit clients Mr. and Ms. Johnson rather than the Debtor, his client in this case. Adams was representing the interests of Mr. and Ms. Johnson, not the Debtor, in violation of Rule 1.7(a) and 1.3(c) of the Virginia Rules of Professional Conduct.

Rule 9011(a) of the Federal Rules of Bankruptcy Procedure requires the attorney of record to sign the client's bankruptcy petition in the attorney's individual name. Through this signature, the attorney certifies that the signed document:

> 1, . . . is not being presented for any improper purpose, such as to harass or to cause unnecessary delay or needless increase in the cost of litigation;

> 2. the claims, defenses, and other legal contentions therein are warranted by existing law or by a nonfrivolous argument for the extension, modification, or reversal of existing law or the establishment of new law;

> 3. the allegations and other factual contentions have evidentiary support or, if specifically, so identified, are likely to have evidentiary support after a reasonable opportunity for further investigation or discovery; and

> 4. the denials of factual contentions are warranted on the evidence or, if specifically, so identified, are reasonably based on a lack of information or belief.

Fed. R. Bankr. P. 9011(b).

Adams may be held "liable for sanctionable conduct engaged in by counsel on the party's behalf if" he "knew or should have known that" the "conduct in the case was improper." Cal. Fed. Bank, *FSB v. Douglas* (*In re Douglas*), 141 B.R. 252, 256 (Bankr. N.D. Ga. 1992). Adams signed the Debtor's bankruptcy petition in this case. Signing a petition filed for the improper purpose of furthering a scheme to hinder, delay, and defraud a creditor is sanctionable misconduct. *In re Computer Dynamics, Inc.* 252 B.R. at 64 (holding that an attorney improperly signing pleadings filed with the court is sanctionable misconduct).

***

The Court finds that Adams was a willing and active participant in the scheme to hinder, delay and defraud Balas and holds that his signature on the Debtor's petition furthered that scheme. In determining that Adams's involvement in these matters was not superficial, the Court has relied upon the evidence surrounding the filing. Based upon an objective review of this evidence, the Court finds that these events did not transpire due to inadvertent oversight or from a failure to properly investigate. Adams took advantage of the Debtor's lack of sophistication. Adams was involved in four of the prior bankruptcies filed by Mr. Johnson and Ms. Johnson. He was familiar with the serial filing history. From his representation of Mr. and Ms. Johnson in their previous bankruptcy cases, Adams was familiar with the 2202 Property and 3309 Property. Although he did not admit as much at the Sanctions Hearing, through this past involvement with Mr. Johnson and Ms. Johnson, Adams had to become aware of their motives. He never met with the Debtor without her father being present. Adams knew that the bankruptcy filing was being orchestrated solely for the purpose of avoiding foreclosure of the 3309 Property. Like all of the previous bankruptcies that had been filed by Mr. Johnson and Ms. Johnson, the purpose for putting the Debtor into bankruptcy was not to reorganize her debts so that she could repay them. The Court so finds by looking at the Debtor's lack of income independent of the Two Parcels of Real Property and lack of substantial debt. Mr. Johnson admitted that he wanted to delay the foreclosure. Based upon Mr. Johnson's behavior in the past bankruptcy filings, it is clear that he wanted to continue to collect the rental income from the 3309 Property as long as possible. Adams was not only aware of this scheme to hinder, delay and defraud Balas, he helped to perpetuate it by allowing the Debtor to become part of that scheme. Based upon objective evidence of Adams's purposes in filing the bankruptcy, it is apparent that Adams became a willing and knowing participant in the scheme.

Adams put the Debtor, a teenage girl, into bankruptcy shortly after the 3309 Property had been transferred into her name for the sole purpose of delaying an impending foreclosure. No reasonable attorney would engage in such action. A reasonable attorney would not participate in a scheme to hinder, delay and defraud creditors. More importantly, a reasonable attorney would realize that this petition would not result in a successful reorganization. The Debtor had neither income nor debt. Adams allowed a teenager to be used by her father and her grandmother as the pawn in a desperate gambit to further delay the inevitable foreclosure of a piece of rental property. The Court holds that Adams filed the Debtor's bankruptcy petition for an improper purpose in violation of Bankruptcy Rule 9011.

***

Adams's behavior was willful, not negligent. He filed this petition to further a scheme in which he was an active, willing participant. Adams's behavior caused harm that was not unintended. Filing the bankruptcy petition caused Balas to incur attorney's fees by having to file and prosecute (i) a motion for relief from the automatic stay imposed by §362(a) and (ii) an objection to the Debtor's Chapter 13 plan. The petition delayed Balas from foreclosing on the 3309 Property by almost two months. Filing the petition has significantly impaired this teenage Debtor's credit history.

The Court may consider whether Adams's past behavior is part of a pattern of conduct in determining what sanctions are appropriate to deter future conduct. *Smyth v. City of Oakland (In re Ralbert Rallington Brooks-Hamilton)*, 329 B.R. 270, 284-85, 290 (B.A.P. 9th Cir. 2005). This Court has had to issue orders for Adams to show cause on several prior occasions. This Court recently has had to issue an order for Adams to show cause why he had not pursued the dismissal of a bankruptcy case that he filed "inadvertently" (Case No. 06-33278-KRH). The Court in another recent case issued an order for Adams to show cause why he had failed to comply timely with deadlines established by the Court (Case No. 07-31932-KRH). This second matter has been continued several times at the suggestion of the Office of the U.S. Trustee in order to allow Adams time to complete Continuing Legal Education courses offered by the Virginia State Bar and to undergo a small practice audit offered by the Virginia State Bar in the hope of improving Adams's practice. Based upon Adams's transgressions in this case, it is apparent that his practice and conduct are still not at the minimum level required to practice before this Court.

Applying the foregoing factors, this Court has determined that suspending Mr. Adams from filing bankruptcy cases in this Court for a period of not less than 120 days is an appropriate sanction. Suspension of an attorney from practice before a court is a harsh sanction, but it is one available for Rule 9011 violations. *Smyth*, 329 B.R. at 287, 290-91. Mr. Adams has a history of failing to adhere to the standards and principles that this Court expects attorneys to follow. Here he has abused his position as an officer of the Court by participating in a scheme to hinder, delay and defraud creditors.

"A lawyer should use the law's procedures only for legitimate purposes and not to harass or intimidate others." *Virginia Rules of Prof'l Conduct*, Preamble P 4 (2001), Va. Sup. Ct. R. Pt. 6, § II.

Adams manipulated the bankruptcy laws to improperly hinder the ability of Balas to enforce his legal rights. In so doing, Adams violated a fundamental principle behind the attorney-client relationship, the zealous representation of one's client. Instead of providing such representation, Adams needlessly ruined the credit record of his client. Adams pursued this course at the expense of one client in order to further the cause of another of his clients. In order to provide Adams with the additional resources to understand the attorney-client relationship, the Court has determined that (i) compelling Adams to complete not less than 17 hours of Continuing Legal Education under the supervision of and satisfactory to the Office of the United States Trustee and (ii) requiring Adams to undergo the small practice audit offered by the Virginia State Bar before he be allowed again to practice before this Court are appropriate additional sanctions.

Finally, the Court has determined that the disgorgement of the attorney's fees that Adams charged the Debtor is an appropriate sanction in this case.

***

Questions and Comments

1. Rule 1.4(b) requires an attorney to inform her client to make an informed decision. Comment 3 to that rule specifies it must be "appropriate for a client who is a comprehending and responsible adult." The Debtor was a recent high school graduate and only 18 years old. Does this make her a "responsible adult"? Provide an argument to support your position.

2. How did the Debtor's attorney act in this respect? Did he explain the important aspects of the case reasonably enough for the debtor to make an informed decision, per Rule 1.4(b)? What evidence provides proof that he did not fully explain the matter to the Debtor?

3. Rule 1.3(c) prohibits an attorney from intentionally prejudicing or damaging "a client during the course of the professional relationship." Additional comments emphasize a lawyer's duty as acting in the client's best interest and with zeal. By allowing the bankruptcy filing on the young client's financial record, the attorney was able to save her parents' real estate. Whose best interest was the attorney actually representing? Does there appear to be a different "client" in the attorney's mind?

MARINO V. USHER
United States District Court (E.D. Pa.2014)
Civ. No. 11-6811

MEMORANDUM. Throughout this copyright litigation, Plaintiff's Counsel, Francis Malofiy, has behaved in a flagrantly unprofessional and offensive manner. Seventeen of the twenty Defendants in this action have moved for the imposition of sanctions against Mr. Malofiy. I decline to impose sanctions for Malofiy's abusive, disruptive discovery conduct, serious though that is. Rather, I will impose sanctions because Malofiy: (1) inveigled an inculpatory affidavit from unrepresented Defendant William Guice; and (2) after falsely assuring Guice that he was only a witness, entered a default against him.

***

II. Factual Findings

A. Discovery Misconduct

Malofiy's behavior throughout discovery was outrageous. I will set out several examples.

The Parties were unable to schedule depositions because of Malofiy's refusal to consent to mutually agreeable dates and locations. (*See* Doc. Nos. 70-74.) When depositions finally took place, Malofiy did what he could to disrupt or obstruct them. At Malofiy's request, I directed all counsel to refrain from making repeated, lengthy objections. (*See* Avila Dep. at 57-58.) His request notwithstanding, Malofiy himself continually made lengthy speaking objections. In a single deposition, he made 65 speaking objections after I directed the Parties to refrain from the practice.

***

In making an objection that is, unfortunately, representative of his conduct, Malofiy went on:

> I want to object, if he's not going to define the words he's using in his questions, it's silly for you to answer, because you don't know how to answer them. So, naturally, what's going to happen is you're going to get an answer that's not even responsive to your question because your question hasn't even been defined, when it was asked to be defined by the witness. Now you gave him instructions in the beginning and made it very clear. You said this gentlemen, the witness, if he doesn't understand your question let me know. He's not a professional expert. It's his first case and his first deposition in his entire life of fifty—how many years sir? . . . Fifty three years, and if he asked you a question saying, you sir, can you define a word, and you can't define the words that you're using in a question, well that poses a serious problem.

Because the answer you're going to get, as you know, is not going to be an answer that's going to be responsive to your question. If this gentleman, following your instructions, asks you to define a word, or a question, I think it's imperative, and the burden is upon you, by providing him that instruction, to clarify your question or the word that you are using.

(Bricklin Dep. 40-42; *see also* Guice Dep. at 7-9, 13-14; Stewart Dep. at 79-80; Einhorn Dep. at 46, 64-65; Leak Dep. at 75-76; Calderone Dep. at 30-31, 57-59, 137-39, 165-66; Famulari Dep. at 172; Pardo Dep. at 162)).

More disturbing are Malofiy's sexist, abusive remarks. For instance, during one deposition, Malofiy stated the following to Defense Counsel:

MALOFIY: Don't be a girl about this . . .

DEFENSE COUNSEL: Mr. Malofiy, I would appreciate you not referring me to as a girl, which you have done repeatedly off the record and on the record.

(Stewart Dep. at 79-80).

The record teems with similarly abusive comments, or worse. (*See, e.g. also*, Guice Dep. June 4, 2013 ("Usher has 130 million. . . . I'm going to take every penny of it."); Marino Dep. 62-63 ("Don't be tricky . . . Do you want lies?"); *id.* at 148 ("You don't like the truth, it disturbs you. You've never seen the truth in a deposition."); *id.* at 150 ("You don't like the answer, too bad. The answer is the answer."); *id.* at 168-70 ("You can't handle the truth."); *id.* at 256-60

***

During one deposition, Malofiy became so aggressive that he prompted the following exchange with *pro se* Defendant Tommy van Dell:

MALOFIY: Are you done, Tom?

VAN DELL: I'm done. And for the record, I would like to say that I feel—this is subsequent to the LA depositions—that I *feel menaced and threatened by Mr. Malofiy and his continual outbursts and seemingly anger-driven conduct today and also during the Los Angeles deposition really concerned me.*

MALOFIY: What I am concerned about is, you rooked a man who wrote a song. You stole $200 million, you and the defendants, and he got nothing. And you're a cheat, and you cheated this man. You rooked him out of a song. And everyone made money, including you, and you put it in your pocket.
And now you're sitting here trying to play spin doctor. And if I'm a little upset, I am. And I'm going to represent my client. I'm

going to be a zealous advocate. And that's what I'm required to do. You took the money, you put it in your pocket, and you ran. And now you want to stick your head in the sand and pretend that no one knew that Mr. Marino wrote the song when you knew, and you told him that he was part of your publishing company. And that's the truth.

(Guice Dep. June 4, 2013 at 146-47) (emphasis supplied).

Malofiy's written submissions to the Court are as bad. He captioned one of his filings: "Response in Opposition Re Joint Motion for Sanctions by Moving Defendants *Who Are Cry Babies*." (Doc. No. 117) (emphasis supplied).

***

B. Conduct Pertaining to William Guice

***

Guice lacks sophistication in legal matters and knows virtually nothing about copyrights. (*Id.* at 110:4-8; Guice Dep., June 4, 2013 at 83-84, 163-64) Before this case, Guice had never been a party in a civil action. He was served with Plaintiff's Amended Complaint on February 14, 2012. (*Id.*at 16:1-4.) Guice did not know why his name was on the first page of the document. (*Id.* at 18:14-23.) Although he reviewed the pleading, he did not understand that Marino was suing him. (*Id.* at 18:8-13; 14:1-10.)

"[S]ometime around Valentine's Day, 2012," Guice (then living in Colorado) telephoned Malofiy, whose name and telephone number were on the pleading's first page. (*Id.* at 20:5-7; 18:8-13; 16:20-17:14; 57:25-58:9; 29:13-16.) Malofiy said that he represented Plaintiff and that Guice had no obligation to speak with him. Malofiy did not ask if Guice was represented by counsel, nor did he advise Guice to obtain counsel. (*Id.*20-21.) Malofiy did not inform Guice that Marino's interests were adverse to Guice's. (*Id.* at 21.) To the contrary, Malofiy untruthfully assured Guice: "don't worry about it, he [Plaintiff] is not coming after you, it's everyone else." (*Id.* at 32:2-8.) Malofiy thus dishonestly convinced Guice that Marino was pursuing claims against only Barton and moving Defendants. (*Id.* at 23-24.)

During this first conversation, Malofiy discussed with Guice the substance of Plaintiff's lawsuit, including the failure to give Plaintiff credit for writing and producing "Club Girl/Bad Girl." (*Id.* at 27-28.) Guice sought to help Plaintiff. Malofiy persuaded Guice to sign an affidavit memorializing their discussion. (*Id.*) When the two spoke a second time, Malofiy again elicited Guice's "side of the story." (Tr. Jan. 6. 2014 at 31:18-20; 38:13-19; Ex. R-2 at 1.) Once again, Malofiy did not advise Guice to secure counsel or inform him that Plaintiff and Guice had adverse interests. (*Id.*) After the second conversation ended, Malofiy drafted an affidavit for Guice's signature. (*Id.*)

Later that day, Malofiy called Guice; once again Malofiy did not advise Guice to secure counsel or inform him that Marino's interests were adverse to his. With Guice's permission, Malofiy tape recorded this third conversation. (Doc. No. 148 at Ex. D-2; Exs. R-1 and R-2.) Malofiy read Guice the draft affidavit, which included, *inter alia*, Guice's admission to the elements of Plaintiff's accounting, constructive trust, and breach of contract claims. (Doc. No. 79, at 14.) The affidavit also included: the statement that Guice was "a named defendant"; Guice's acknowledgment that he, Barton, and Marino created "Club Girl" together; and Guice's belief that Marino was entitled to producing and writing credit. (*Id.*) After Guice suggested minor changes to omit profanity, Malofiy persuaded Guice to acknowledge that he was "comfortable" with the affidavit. (Exs. R-1 and R-2.) Several hours later, Malofiy emailed Guice a revised draft. (Tr. at 34:4-15; Ex. D-2 at 1.) The subject line of the email reads "*Marino v. Usher*," (mentioning no other Defendants). Once again, Malofiy did not advise Guice to secure counsel before reviewing and signing the affidavit. (Ex. D-2 at 1; Tr. Jan. 6, 2014 at 37:1-25.)

The next afternoon, apparently concerned that he had not heard from Guice, Malofiy reminded Guice by email to return a signed copy of the affidavit, stating that Guice could modify the document, and that if he wanted to "review it with a lawyer, that's fine too." (Ex. D-2 at 1.) Without consulting an attorney, Guice signed the affidavit and returned it to Malofiy. (*Id.* at 43:5-16; 38:23-39:9.)

Relying on Malofiy's misrepresentations, Guice did not believe he was obligated to respond to the Amended Complaint and never did so. Without informing Guice, on June 14, 2012, Malofiy caused the Clerk of this Court to enter a default against Guice for his failure to answer the Amended Complaint. (*Id.* at 44:1-3; Doc. 31.)

In the spring of 2013, Malofiy called Guice to arrange for his videotaped deposition in Philadelphia. Once again, Malofiy did not advise Guice to retain counsel or that Marino's interests were averse to those of Guice. Malofiy paid for Guice's air travel from Colorado, accommodations, and expenses. (*Id.* at 46:7-15; 54:3.) Guice could not afford to hire a lawyer. Moreover, he did not believe he needed counsel because Malofiy had untruthfully told Guice that he was only a witness. (Guice Dep. June 4, 2013 at 144 ("I was told I was a—I was a witness. . . . ." Defense Counsel: "Did [Malofiy] make representations to you that proved to be untrue? . . . . Guice: "I would say—I would say yes.").)

Guice thus attended his May 2, 2013 deposition unrepresented. Malofiy led Guice through his affidavit, and had him swear to its truth. After Malofiy completed his examination, Defense Counsel's questioning of Guice revealed that Guice did not know: the meaning of "defendant";

that he was a party to the copyright litigation; that Plaintiff was seeking money damages from him personally; or that Malofiy had obtained a default against him. (*Id.* at 47:24-48:21; 92:18-21.)

***

Guice became "ang[ry]," "confused," and "infuriated" that Malofiy had taken advantage of and made a "fool" of him. (Tr. Jan 6, 2014 at 48:5-10; 48:16-21; 49:12-21; *see also* Guice Dep. June 4, 2013 at 147 ("I would say I was duped.").) The Philadelphia deposition session abruptly ended at Guice's request. (Tr. Jan 6, 2014 at 51:25-52:2; 55:21-24; 76:9-77:4.) His upset was evident. (Guice Dep. May 2, 2013 at 206-07 (Video Operator: "We're adjourning the deposition with witness Mr. William Guice." Guice: "Not a witness. A defendant now at this point. I guess I've always been a defendant.").)

***

III. Legal Standards

Moving Defendants seek sanctions against Malofiy. *See*, e.g., *Carter v. Albert Einstein Med. Ctr.*, 804 F.2d 805, 808 (3d Cir. 1986) (attorney is liable for sanctions where attorney, rather than client, is responsible for challenged conduct). Defendants base their Motion on 28 U.S.C. §1927 and the Court's inherent authority. *Gaiardo v. Ethyl Corp.*, 835 F.2d 479, 484 (3d Cir. 1987) (§1927 sanctions may only be imposed on attorney, not client). As the movants, Defendants must show by clear and convincing evidence that sanctions are warranted. *Rich Art Sign Co. v. Ring*, 122 F.R.D. 472, 474 (E.D. Pa. 1988); *see also Gregory P. Joseph, Sanctions: The Federal Law Of Litigation Abuse* §17(A)(5) (2008); Ali, 636 F.3d at 627.

A. Section 1927

"Any attorney or other person admitted to conduct cases in any court of the United States . . . who so multiplies the proceedings in any case unreasonably and vexatiously may be required by the court to satisfy personally the excess costs, expenses, and attorneys' fees reasonably incurred because of such conduct." 28 U.S.C. §1927. To impose sanctions under this statute, I must find that an attorney "has (1) multiplied proceedings; (2) in an unreasonable and vexatious manner; (3) thereby increasing the cost of the proceedings; and (4) doing so in bad faith or by intentional misconduct." *In re Schaefer Salt Recovery, Inc.*, 542 F.3d 90, 101 (3d Cir. 2008) (citing *In re Prudential Ins. Co. Am. Sales Practice Litig.*, 278 F.3d 175, 188 (3d Cir. 2002)). I may not impose sanctions for misunderstanding, bad judgment, or well-intentioned zeal. *Zuk v. E. Pennsylvania Psychiatric Inst.*, 103 F.3d 294, 297 (3d Cir. 1996) (willful bad faith or intentional misconduct is required). "An attorney's conduct must be egregious, stamped by bad faith that violates recognized standards in the conduct of litigation." *Grider v. Keystone Health Plan Central, Inc.,* 580 F.3d 119, 142 (3d Cir. 2009) (internal quotations omitted).

B. Inherent Authority

The Court may also impose sanctions pursuant to its inherent power to discipline attorneys who appear before it. *In re Prudential Ins. Co.,* 278 F.3d at 188-89. Such sanctions could be warranted in various circumstances, including "cases where a party has acted in bad faith, vexatiously, wantonly, or for oppressive reasons." *Id.* at 189 (quoting *Chambers v. NASCO, Inc.,* 501 U.S. 32, 45-46, 111 S. Ct. 2123, 115 L. Ed. 2d 27 (1991)). Sanctions may be imposed pursuant to this inherent power even if much of the misconduct at issue is also sanctionable under statute or rules of court. *Id.*

IV. Discussion

It is difficult to convey the poisonous atmosphere created by Malofiy's continual belligerence to opposing counsel. Recently proposed amendments to the Federal Rules of Civil Procedure emphasize the need—repeatedly recognized by the courts—for opposing counsel to cooperate with each other. *See, e.g.,* Committee Note to Preliminary Draft of Proposed Amendment to Fed. R. Civ. P. 1 ("Rule 1 is amended to emphasize that just as the court should construe and administer these rules to secure the just, speedy, and inexpensive determination of every action, so the parties share the responsibility to employ the rules in the same way. *Most lawyers and parties cooperate to achieve these ends.*"); *Grider,* 580 F.3d at 125 ("one expects. . . civility and professionalism" from experienced attorneys during discovery); *Huggins v. Coatesville Area Sch. Dist.,* No. 07-4917, 2009 U.S. Dist. LEXIS 84971, 2009 WL 2973044, at *4 (E.D. Pa. Sept. 16, 2009) ("Treating an adversary with advertent discourtesy, let alone with calumny or derision, rends the fabric of the law").

***

Cooperation between opposing counsel is entirely consistent with a lawyer's obligations to his or her client, and ensures the efficient and rational resolution of civil litigation. Indeed, without such cooperation, litigation would break down, as it almost did here. Malofiy's unprofessional behavior throughout discovery was the antithesis of cooperation. *See* Pa. R. Prof. Conduct 3.5(d) ("A lawyer shall not engage in conduct intended to disrupt a tribunal"); *id.* at Cmt. 5 ("The duty to refrain from disruptive conduct applies to any proceeding of a tribunal, including a deposition.").

Malofiy, who has been a member of the Pennsylvania bar since 2008, contends that I should excuse this behavior as a function of his inexperience and his need of a "mentor." (Tr. Jan. 6, 2014 at 3-4; Tr. Jan. 28, 2014 at 52-54, 63-67.) I reluctantly accept that Malofiy's conduct was, at least in part, a function of the grotesquely exaggerated zeal common to less experienced lawyers. Accordingly, although I condemn Malofiy's discovery behavior, I decline to impose sanctions on that basis.

Malofiy's treatment of unrepresented Defendant, Guice, however, is quite another matter. Defendants have shown by clear and convincing evidence that this conduct is egregious and sanctionable under both § 1927 and the Court's inherent authority.

A. Section 1927

Moving Defendants have presented clear and convincing evidence that Malofiy contravened all four prongs of the *In re Schaefer Salt* sanctions test. First, Malofiy misrepresented to Guice that Plaintiff had not sued him, but, rather, was suing "everyone else." (Tr. Jan. 6 2014 at 22 (Guice: "[I]t was told to me that it was against everyone but me." Defense Counsel: "That's what Attorney Malofiy told you?" Guice: "Yes.").) Guice learned only during his own deposition that Malofiy had not been truthful and that he had entered a default against Guice, thus causing Guice to end the Philadelphia deposition session prematurely. This necessitated two Court rulings extending the time for his deposition so Guice could try to obtain counsel. His deposition resumed some four weeks later in Colorado. Malofiy thus "multiplied proceedings" and "increase[ed]" their costs." §1927; *In re Schaefer Salt*, 542 F.2d at 102.

Courts have repeatedly sanctioned counsel under §1927 for causing similar delays. *See e.g., Hilburn v. Bayonne Parking Auth.*, 562 Fed. Appx. 82, 2014 U.S. App. LEXIS 6246, 2014 WL 1328146 (3d Cir. 2014) (upholding sanctions where counsel delayed deposition by filing frivolous opposition brief requiring continuance)

***

Moreover, Malofiy's behavior toward Guice was obviously "vexatious and unreasonable." *In re Schaefer Salt*, 542 F.2d at 102. Malofiy's conduct served no legitimate purpose. He lied to Guice that Marino was not proceeding against him, thus convincing Guice that he did not need to respond to Marino's Amended Complaint. Having thus dishonestly ensured Guice's failure to respond, Malofiy entered a default against Guice for that failure. It is difficult to imagine more vexatious or unreasonable behavior. *United States v. Ross*, 535 F.2d 346, 349 (6th Cir. 1976) (unreasonable and vexatious conduct is an "intentional departure from proper conduct").

Finally, Malofiy's discussions with Guice are the paradigm of bad faith and intentional misconduct. Although a lawyer's violation of the Rules of Professional Conduct cannot, alone, make out a violation of §1927, an intentional violation can confirm that the lawyer acted in bad faith. *Gomez v. Vernon*, 255 F.3d 1118, 1134 (9th Cir. 2001) (violation of "ethical and professional duty" constitutes bad faith and intentional misconduct under both § 1927 and court's inherent power). The Eastern District, like virtually all others, has adopted the rules of conduct of the state in which the Court is located. E.D. Pa. Civ. R. 83.6. Malofiy violated Pennsylvania Rule of Professional Conduct 4.3, which provides as follows:

> (a) In dealing on behalf of a client with a person who is not represented by counsel, a lawyer shall not state or imply that the lawyer is disinterested.
>
> (b) During the course of a lawyer's representation of a client, a lawyer shall not give advice to a person who is not represented by a lawyer, other than the advice to secure counsel, if the lawyer knows or reasonably should know the interests of such person are or have a reasonable possibility of being in conflict with the interests of the lawyer's client.
>
> (c) When the lawyer knows or reasonably should know that the unrepresented person misunderstands the lawyer's role in the matter, the lawyer should make reasonable efforts to correct the misunderstanding.

Pa. R. Prof. Conduct. 4.3. The Comment to the Rule provides that to avoid misunderstandings, an attorney may need to "explain that the client has interests opposed to those of the unrepresented person," especially if the person is confused. *Id.* at Cmt. 1.

Nearly every state has enacted some version of 4.3, recognizing that it is critical to protect unrepresented individuals from what occurred here. *Rule 4.3 Dealing with Unrepresented Person*, Ann. Mod. Rules Prof. Cond. 4.3 (explaining purpose of rule and variations adopted by different states);

***

Although Guice's confusion was manifest both as to the copyright litigation as well as his and Marino's status in the litigation, Malofiy did not ask Guice if he had a lawyer, did not advise Guice to get a lawyer, and did not explain to Guice that Marino's interests were adverse to Guice's. Malofiy's manipulation of Guice is exactly what Rule 4.3 was intended to prevent. Richman & Goodman, *Communicating with Unrepresented*

Parties, at 24 ("[T]he attorney's role as an advocate for his or her client must be made crystal clear to the unrepresented party."); *id.* at n.2 ("Courts . . . . have found violations of Rule 4.3 in cases where lawyers have prepared documents for the signature of an unrepresented party without explaining the potential adverse consequences of signing the documents.");

***

Even worse, Malofiy's dishonest assurances that Marino was not seeking damages from Guice caused Guice to make damaging—albeit unreliable—statements. This grossly unprofessional conduct meets §1927's bad faith and intentional misconduct standard. *Cf. Price v. Trans Union, L.L.C.,* 847 F. Supp. 2d 788, 797 (E.D. Pa. 2012) (no bad faith under § 1927 where attorney's conduct complied with Rule 4.3).

Malofiy bases the bulk of his arguments against sanctions on his challenge to Guice's credibility. (*See, e.g.*, Doc. No. 150, at 16-18, 22, 28-37.) I fully credit Guice's testimony, however. He was a compelling witness.

Malofiy also argues that Guice's statement in the affidavit that he was a defendant, combined with Malofiy's belated email advice ("if you want to review [the affidavit] with a lawyer, that's fine too") demonstrate that Malofiy complied with Rule 4.3. (Doc. No. 79, at 14; Doc. No. 150, at 17.) I do not agree. Malofiy did not provide Guice with the draft affidavit until after their second discussion. By then, Malofiy had repeatedly violated the Rule. In any event, as I have found, regardless of what Malofiy wrote in the draft affidavit, Guice did not understand the meaning of the word "defendant." Similarly, Malofiy made his email suggestion that Guice could review the affidavit with a lawyer after their third conversation. By this point, Malofiy had convinced Guice he was only a witness and did not need a lawyer. Accordingly, even assuming the suggestion fulfilled Malofiy's obligations under Rule 4.3 (and plainly it did not), it, too, was made only after Malofiy had repeatedly violated the Rule.

Finally, contrary to Malofiy's arguments, he needed neither more experience nor a "mentor" to know that he was obligated not to: (1) violate the Rules of Professional Conduct; and (2) lie to an unrepresented party about whether Malofiy's client was proceeding against him. These transgressions were intentional and outrageous.

In sum, moving Defendants have shown that Malofiy's conduct respecting Guice meets the four *Schaefer Salt* criteria: Malofiy multiplied discovery proceedings, thus increasing their cost. *In re Schaefer Salt*, 542 F.2d at 102. Malofiy's behavior certainly was "unreasonable and vexatious." *Keller*, 55 F.3d at 94. Finally, in light of his repeated, intentional violations of Rule 4.3, Malofiy acted in bad faith and with "intentional misconduct." *Gomez*, 255 F.3d at 1134; Loatman, 174 F.R.D. at 600; Price, 847 F. Supp. 2d at 797. In these circumstances, I am compelled to conclude that Malofiy's behavior is sanctionable under §1927.

B. Inherent Authority

Because, as I explain below, the remedies available under §1927 cannot fully correct the harm caused by Malofiy's egregious conduct, I will also impose sanctions pursuant to the Court's inherent authority. *Ferguson v. Valero Energy Corp.*, 454 F. App'x 109, 114 (3d Cir. 2011) ("Even though inherent-authority sanctions are generally disfavored where another provision—such as §1927—authorizes sanctions, . . .Prudential allows a district court to [impose sanctions pursuant to its inherent authority] when the conduct is egregious or where the statutory provision is not adequate to sanction the conduct. . . .").

Malofiy undoubtedly "acted in bad faith, vexatiously, wantonly, or for oppressive reasons." *Chambers*, 501 U.S. at 45-46. As I have explained, Malofiy violated Rule 4.3. Through his misrepresentations, Malofiy induced Guice to sign an inculpatory affidavit. Malofiy had Guice repeat those admissions under oath at his deposition. In thus taking improper advantage of an unsophisticated, impoverished, unrepresented party and violating a rule of Professional Conduct, Malofiy's conduct is sufficiently egregious to trigger the Court's inherent authority. *See, e.g., Erickson v. Newmar Corp.*, 87 F.3d 298, 303 (9th Cir. 1996) (intentional violation of RPC warranted sanctions under the court's inherent power) (citations omitted).

V. Sanctions

Having considered other available sanctions, I conclude that no lesser sanction than the exclusion of the improperly obtained evidence would be adequate.

VII. Conclusion

Defendants have shown clearly and convincingly that Attorney Francis Malofiy has acted disgracefully: lying to an unsophisticated, impoverished, unrepresented Defendant, thus convincing that Defendant to expose himself (probably baselessly) to substantial liability. Malofiy also needlessly increased discovery costs. Denying Plaintiff the "fruits" of Malofiy's misconduct and requiring Malofiy to pay these increased costs are the least sanctions I can impose.

In suggesting that Malofiy's misconduct was the result of inexperience, Malofiy's extremely experienced counsel acknowledged "[i]f I was doing something like this now, I certainly would warrant sanctions and possibly removal from practice." (Tr. Jan. 28, 2014 at 53.) Whether Malofiy should be removed from practice is a question properly answered in another forum.

Questions and Comments

1. The judge refers to Malofiy's behavior as conveying a "poisonous atmosphere" by his "continual belligerence to opposing counsel." Malofiy, however, refers to his conduct as zealously representing his client. How was his conduct outside the scope of zealousness that is referenced in the Model Rules? Do you agree with the judge? Why or why not?

2. Malofiy argues that his conduct should be excused because he is inexperienced and in "need of a 'mentor.'" Should less experienced lawyers be given leniency by the courts for their exaggerated zeal? Why or why not? What outcomes may arise if different standards are set based on experience?

3. The court found Malofiy's conduct to be "unreasonable and vexatious." He also acted in "bad faith with 'intentional misconduct,'" thus intentionally violating Rule 4.3. Do you agree with the court, or was Malofiy simply exploiting a weakness of the opposing party? Wasn't Malofiy just doing his job in advocating for his client? Who determines when the blurred lines get crossed?

D. DISCUSSION QUESTIONS

1. Rule 4.2 prevents a lawyer from speaking to the opposing party without his counsel present. Are there any exceptions to this rule? What if the opposing party contacts the attorney herself? What measures, if any, should the attorney take to prevent such a situation?

2. Rule 3.7 discusses the very limited circumstances in which a lawyer can be a witness at trial. What are they? Why do the rules limit the situations in which a lawyer can be a witness? Think about the potential for conflict and confidentiality issues that might arise if a lawyer has to be a witness in the same case she represents her client. How can a lawyer go about avoiding testimony in a case involving her client?

3. Rule 4.2 has exclusive standards for lawyers dealing with third parties. Considering a lawyer's duty is to her client, why do the Model Rules need to address interactions with others? Consider the extensive list of people lawyers have to communicate with while representing a client. Do you think dealings with parties other than a client could have an impact on the client's case?

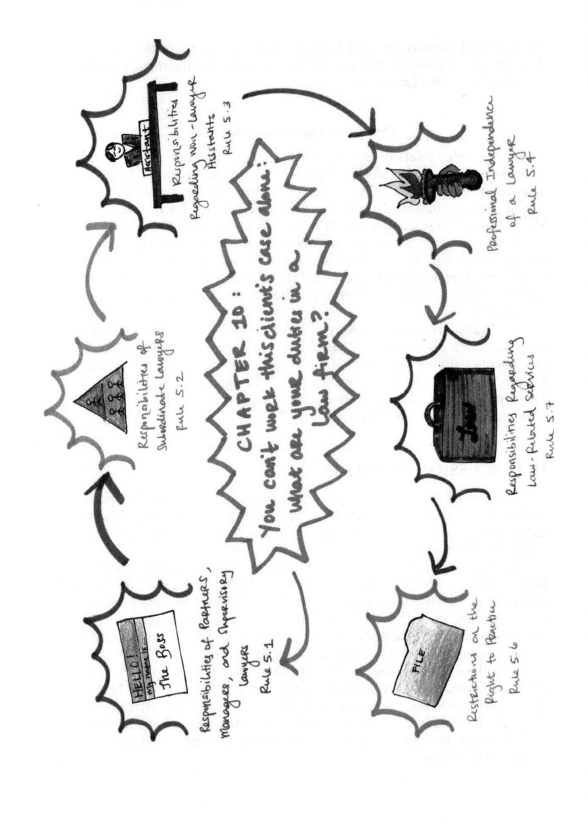

CHAPTER 10 :
You can't work this client's case alone:
what are your duties in a
Law firm?

Responsibilities of Partners,
Managees, and Supervisory
Lawyers
Rule 5.1

Responsibilities of
Subordinate Lawyers
Rule 5.2

Responsibilities
Regarding Non-Lawyer
Assistants
Rule 5.3

Professional Independence
of a Lawyer
Rule 5.4

Restrictions on the
Right to Practice
Rule 5.6

Responsibilities Regarding
Law-Related Services
Rule 5.7

HELLO!
My name is...
The Boss

Assistant

law

FILE

Chapter 10:
You Can't Work This Client's Case Alone; What Are Your Duties in a Law Firm?

A. INTRODUCTION

Many firms place a high emphasis on quantity, rather than quality, of work, which may lead to mishandling of client matters compromising associates, partners, and the firms themselves. Under Model Rules 5.1 through 5.3, a lawyer is ethically responsible for those working under her and any violation by a junior lawyer could, therefore, fall on the responsible senior lawyer. Rule 5.1 clearly makes a lawyer responsible for the ethical conduct of any other lawyer if she orders or, with knowledge of the specific conduct, ratifies the conduct involved. Rule 5.2 makes a lawyer ethically responsible for her own actions even if at the behest of her superior. Rule 5.3 holds a lawyer responsible for the ethical violations of non-lawyers working under her.

These standards apply to lawyers in any setting, including private firms, government attorneys, or in-house counsel and adherence to these rules could save attorneys and the entities they work for time and money for defending future allegations of misconduct. The cases and articles that follow show how an attorney acting as a supervisor may be found to have acted unethically based on the conduct of her subordinates. Additionally, this chapter discusses the ethical principles relating to an attorney's conduct or that of her subordinate relating to their actions online or via social media.

In addition to Rules 5.1 through 5.3, this chapter discusses the rules regarding restrictions on the right of lawyers to practice law. Under common law, both contractual and fiduciary duties exist and can be triggered when a partner is terminated, withdraws or retires from a law firm. Model Rule 5.6, however, does not allow a lawyer to participate in agreements that restrict the rights of other lawyers to practice after leaving a firm. This rule, however, has been met with some controversy, as firms want to be able to protect their client base and financial position by restricting the parting lawyer from competing against her former employer. The rule has several public policy considerations, which are discussed more fully in *Hoff v. Mayer* near the end of the chapter.

B. RULES

In preparation, read carefully the following sections of the Model Rules of Professional Conduct along with any relevant comments listed below.

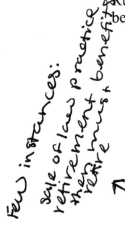

- Rule 5.1: Responsibilities of Partners, Managers, and Supervisory Lawyers
  - Comment [1], [2], [5], & [8]
- Rule 5.2: Responsibilities of Subordinate Lawyers
  - Comment [1]
- Rule 5.3: Responsibilities Regarding Non-Lawyer Assistants
  - Comment [2], [3], & [2]
- Rule 5.4: Professional Independence of a Lawyer
- Rule 5.6: Restrictions on Right to Practice
  - Comment [1]
- Rule 5.7: Responsibilities Regarding Law-Related Services
  - Comment [6] & [9]

C. CASES AND ADDITIONAL READINGS

LAWYER DISCIPLINARY BD. V. VENERI
Supreme Court of Appeals of West Virginia (1999)
524 S.E.2d 900

PUR CURIAM

This disciplinary proceeding is before this Court upon a review of the March 31, 1999, Recommended Disposition of the Hearing Panel Subcommittee of the Lawyer Disciplinary Board ("Board") concerning the respondent, Randall L. Veneri ("Veneri"), a member of the West Virginia State Bar. Veneri was charged with violating Rules 3.4(c) [1989] and 8.4(c) [1995] of the *Rules of Professional Conduct* for failing to file an asset disclosure form listing his client's two separate employee benefit plans during the course of his client's divorce. The Board recommends that the charges alleging violations of Rules 3.4(c) and 8.4(c) be dismissed. We accept the Board's findings and recommendations and dismiss those two charges.

Veneri was also charged with violating Rule 8.4(d) [1995] of the *Rules of Professional Conduct* by engaging in conduct prejudicial to the administration of justice when he failed to inform the family law master or opposing counsel that a proposed Qualified Domestic Relations Order ["QDRO"] had been altered while in Veneri's office. The Board found

[handwritten margin note: Few instances: sale of law practice; retirement; then must retire benefit]

that this charge was substantiated and that sanctions were warranted. The Board recommends that Veneri be suspended from the practice of law for 12 months, and that he be required to pay the costs of these proceedings. Upon a thorough review of the record, we agree that the charge of professional misconduct in violation of Rule 8.4(d) [1995] was established by clear and convincing evidence. However, under the circumstances of this case, we find that an admonishment and the payment of costs are more appropriate penalties for Veneri.

I.

In 1976, Michele Montgomery and Gary Montgomery were married; the Montgomerys separated in December of 1989. At the time of the couple's separation, Mr. Montgomery worked for Pocohantas Land Company, a wholly-owned subsidiary of Norfolk Southern Corporation. Mr. Montgomery was a participant in two benefit plans through his employment. The first, the Retirement Plan of Norfolk Southern, was a defined benefit plan maintained solely by employer contributions, and payable either at the payee's retirement or the earliest retirement date. The second benefit plan was a tax deferred savings plan consisting of employee contributions that were matched by Norfolk Southern. This second benefit plan was established under Section 401(k) of the Internal Revenue Code and referred to as a Thrift and Investment Plan ("TIP").

Mr. Montgomery retained the respondent, Veneri, to represent Mr. Montgomery in his divorce; Mrs. Montgomery also retained separate counsel. The attorneys entered into negotiations concerning the Montgomerys' marital property, including Mr. Montgomery's retirement benefits. Apparently, throughout the negotiations both parties and their counsel were under the mistaken impression that Mr. Montgomery had only one benefit plan.

On August 20, 1992, Mrs. Montgomery completed a Disclosure of Assets and Liabilities form as required by *W.Va.Code*, 48–2–33 [1993] wherein she indicated that she possessed no security, pension or profit-sharing plans other than an interest in a retirement plan belonging to Mr. Montgomery. On September 8, 1992, Veneri wrote a letter to Mrs. Montgomery's counsel and informing her counsel that Mr. Montgomery accepted the assets and liabilities listed by Mrs. Montgomery, and that Mr. Montgomery knew of no other asset or liability; consequently, Mr. Montgomery would not file a separate disclosure form.

At the final divorce hearing before a family law master the parties recited for the record the settlement agreement that they had reached concerning the parties' property. At the hearing, the parties demonstrated their belief that only one employee benefit plan existed. A recommended order was prepared by the family law master, and Mrs. Montgomery's

Judge wants additional QDRO

attorney was instructed to draft the Qualified Domestic Relations Order ["QDRO"], which would control the division of Mr. Montgomery's pension benefits.

The QDRO, as prepared by Mrs. Montgomery's attorney, provided for the division of the TIP benefit plan and was forwarded to respondent Veneri for his inspection. Veneri turned the document over to the tax specialist at his law firm, his son, Anthony Veneri. Mr. Montgomery was also provided a copy of the proposed QDRO. Anthony Veneri was contacted by Mr. Montgomery, who stated that the proposed QDRO was incorrect. According to Mr. Montgomery, the TIP plan was not to be divided. Anthony Veneri examined the order of the law master that provided for a division of "pension rights," but made no reference to a profit-sharing plan or TIP, and agreed with Mr. Montgomery. Without speaking to respondent Veneri about the matter, Anthony Veneri instructed his secretary to white-out the words "Thrift and Investment Plan" and type over them "Corporation Retirement Plan."

Anthony Veneri took the altered copy of the QDRO to respondent Veneri without alerting him to the change, obtained his signature, and returned the same to counsel for Mrs. Montgomery. The Board found that while it was common practice for a secretary at the Veneris' law offices to contact opposing counsel and inform them of a change in a proposed order, for some reason this was not done in this case. The altered QDRO was then forwarded to the family law master by Mrs. Montgomery's counsel for the law master's signature, and then Mrs. Montgomery's counsel sent a certified copy of the QDRO to Norfolk Southern Corporation.

Norfolk Southern Corporation returned the QDRO to Mrs. Montgomery's counsel, informing her that the proposed QDRO did not qualify because the benefit plan described was not properly defined. The letter further informed Mrs. Montgomery's attorney that there were in fact two separate benefit plans—not one.

Counsel for Mrs. Montgomery modified the QDRO, in accordance with the Norfolk Southern letter, to provide for the division of both plans. This modified QDRO was sent to Veneri. Mr. Montgomery refused to sign the modified QDRO. Subsequently Mrs. Montgomery filed a contempt petition alleging that Mr. Montgomery had refused to carry out the obligations required under the Agreed Order.

After a contempt hearing before the circuit court, the judge returned the case to the family law master for a determination of what was precisely meant by "pension rights," the language contained in the Agreed Order. It was the position of Mr. Montgomery that the TIP was to be awarded to him alone and that only the retirement plan was to be divided. From a review of the record it appears that there was still some confusion of exactly what type of benefit plans Mr. Montgomery had. The record does reflect that during negotiations the parties contemplated the division of "stocks;" nevertheless, Veneri argued before the family law master that the agreement was only for the regular retirement plan, and not the TIP—a stock plan.

No mention was made during the remanded proceedings before the family law master that the original QDRO had been altered at Veneri's law office. The family law master ruled that the TIP was marital property and that the TIP should be divided equally between the parties in addition to the retirement plan.

On December 16, 1993, the Circuit Court upheld the ruling of the family law master and the final order was entered. On June 12, 1995, Mrs. Montgomery filed an ethics complaint against Veneri. After an investigation by the Board, Veneri was charged with failing to file an asset disclosure form listing Mr. Montgomery's two retirement plans as required by *W.Va.Code*, 48–2–33 [1993] in violation of Rules 3.4(c) and 8.4(c) of the *Rules of Professional Conduct*. Veneri was also charged with altering language in the QDRO and then failing to inform the family law master or opposing counsel of the alteration in violation of Rules 8.4(c) and 8.4(d) of the *Rules of Professional Conduct*.

A hearing was conducted before the Hearing Panel Subcommittee of the Board. Following the hearing, the Subcommittee filed its report, making findings of fact and conclusions of law. The Subcommittee found there was insufficient evidence to prove that Veneri knowingly disobeyed a known obligation of a tribunal (Rule 3.4(c)) or that he knowingly engaged in conduct involving fraud, deceit, dishonesty or misrepresentation (Rule 8.4(c)) when he failed to disclose Mr. Montgomery's two employee benefit plans.

The Subcommittee further found that there was insufficient evidence to prove that Veneri deliberately set out to deceive Mrs. Montgomery or her counsel by altering the QDRO in violation of Rule 8.4(c). However, the Subcommittee did find that there was sufficient evidence to prove that Veneri's conduct in connection with the alteration of the QDRO and his failure to advise opposing counsel or the family law master of the alteration, constituted a violation of Rule 8.4(d).

Based upon the report of the Subcommittee, the Board recommended to this Court that Veneri's license be suspended for 12 months and that he be required to pay the costs of the proceedings. Following the filing of Veneri's objection to the recommendation, this case was submitted to this Court for review.

II.

At the outset we recognize that situations exist when an attorney may be held responsible for the actions of others. Rule 5.1 [1989] of the *Rules of Professional Conduct* outlines certain situations in which a partner or supervisory lawyer may be held responsible for the actions of another attorney or employee of the firm. Rule 5.1(c) of the *Rules of Professional Conduct* provides in pertinent part:

> (c) A lawyer shall be responsible for another lawyer's violation of the Rules of Professional Conduct if:
>
> (1) the lawyer orders or, with knowledge of the specific conduct, ratifies the conduct involved; or
>
> (2) the lawyer is a partner in the law firm in which the other lawyer practices, or has direct supervisory authority over the other lawyer, and knows of the conduct at a time when its consequences can be avoided or mitigated but fails to take reasonable remedial action.

Veneri is a partner in his law firm and was the supervising attorney over the tax specialist, Anthony Veneri, in the Montgomery divorce. Following its investigation, the Board determined that respondent Veneri had no actual knowledge of the specific conduct and did not ratify the conduct of Anthony Veneri prior to the hearing before the family law master. However, the Board did find that respondent Veneri was responsible nevertheless for Anthony Veneri's conduct because the respondent was both the supervising attorney and a partner. The Board determined that due to his position, Veneri was required under Rule 5.1(c)(2) to take remedial action so as not to prejudice the administration of justice.

There can be no question that the alteration of a proposed order without notice to opposing counsel is improper. Rule 4.1 [1989] of the *Rules of Professional Conduct* provides:

> In the course of representing a client a lawyer shall not knowingly:
>
> (a) make a false statement of material fact or law to a third person[.]

Veneri argued before the Board that the alteration of the QDRO was technically correct. Veneri's argument does not excuse his failing to notify opposing counsel of the alteration, failing to notify the law master of the alteration, or excuse his conduct when he argued that the parties had never agreed to divide Mr. Montgomery's stock plan.

We consequently find by clear and convincing evidence that Veneri violated Rule 8.4(d) by engaging in conduct prejudicial to the administration of justice.

***

While we are assisted by the Board's recommendation of discipline, we must examine each case individually and provide appropriate discipline. In our efforts to determine a proper sanction we must "consider not only what steps would appropriately punish the respondent attorney, but also whether the discipline imposed is adequate to serve as an effective deterrent to other members of the Bar[.]" Syllabus Point 3, in part, *Committee on Legal Ethics v. Walker*, 178 W.Va. 150, 358 S.E.2d 234 (1987). We have further stated that:

> "In disciplinary proceedings, this Court, rather than endeavoring to establish a uniform standard of disciplinary action, will consider the facts and circumstances [in each case], including mitigating facts and circumstances, in determining what disciplinary action, if any, is appropriate, and when the committee on legal ethics initiates proceedings before this Court, it has a duty to advise this Court of all pertinent facts with reference to the charges and the recommended disciplinary action." Syl. pt. 2, *Committee on Legal Ethics v. Mullins*, 159 W.Va. 647, 226 S.E.2d 427 (1976).

Syllabus Point 2, *Committee on Legal Ethics v. Higinbotham*, 176 W.Va. 186, 342 S.E.2d 152 (1986).

We are also assisted in our determination by Rule 3.16 of the *Rules of Lawyer Disciplinary Procedure* which provides:

> In imposing a sanction after a finding of lawyer misconduct, unless otherwise provided in these rules, the Court or Board shall consider the following factors: (1) whether the lawyer has violated a duty owed to a client, to the public, to the legal system, or to the profession; (2) whether the lawyer acted intentionally, knowingly, or negligently; (3) the amount of the actual or potential injury caused by the lawyer's misconduct; and (4) the existence of any aggravating or mitigating factors.

In addition to the above factors we have also held that "prior discipline is an aggravating factor in a pending disciplinary proceeding because it calls into question the fitness of the attorney to continue to practice a profession imbued with a public trust." Syllabus Point 5, *Committee on Legal Ethics v. Tatterson*, 177 W.Va. 356, 352 S.E.2d 107 (1986).

We recognize that this is not the first time Veneri has had to address disciplinary charges. However, an examination of the previous disciplinary matter and the one now before this Court reveals no similarities between the two separate incidents. The previous discipline matter concerned the administration of Veneri's mother's estate and Veneri's conduct with his sister. The matter now before us is quite dissimilar.

Applying the remaining factors set forth in Rule 3.16. of the *Rules of Lawyer Disciplinary Procedure*, we find the Board's recommended punishment to be harsh. According to the record, neither of the parties knew that there were two employee benefit plans and it would appear that the actions and omissions of Veneri did not prejudice the rights of Mrs. Montgomery. Consequently, we find the Board's recommendation of a year's suspension to be extreme.

Accordingly, we find that Veneri should be admonished and be required to pay the costs of these proceedings.

takes away 1yr suspension

Questions and Comments

1. The Board found Veneri violated Rule 5.1 for his role as a supervising attorney, but nevertheless the court found the Board's recommendation of a year's suspension to be extreme. The court concluded Veneri should be admonished and required him to pay the costs of the proceedings in lieu of suspension. Why did the court reverse the suspension and hold this way?

2. For a supervisory attorney to be held in violation of a rule from the conduct of a subordinate, does it matter whether the subordinate is a licensed attorney? Do you think the outcome of the case would have been different had Veneri's subordinate been an attorney?

3. If a supervisory attorney were held civilly liable for the conduct of a subordinate employee, could the supervisory attorney then sue the employee for contribution for the judgment against her based on the subordinate's negligence?[1]

ETHICS OF "FRIENDING" ADVERSE WITNESSES
New Jersey Law Journal (Online), Law Technology News,
September 1, 2009
By Mara E. Zazzali-Hogan & Jennifer Marino Thibodaux

Consider the following hypothetical scenario: An attorney searches for an adverse party in an Internet search engine and discovers that the party has a Facebook page. The attorney reviews the limited public information available on the party's Facebook page, but he realizes that if he asks to be online "friends" with the party he will be able to access much more detailed, private information about that party. This private information is only available to users the party accepts as "friends." The attorney suspects that the private information may contain relevant information about the party's credibility or the lawsuit. Taking advantage of the fact that many social networking users are less than discriminating

---

[1] *See* Kramer v. Nowak, 908 F. Supp. 1281, 1292 (E.D. Pa. 1995) (concluding that, "under generally applicable principles of agency, supervising attorneys may sue subordinate attorneys for their negligence in representing clients.").

when accepting "friend" requests, the attorney wonders whether he may ask a third party, such as his paralegal, to attempt to "friend" the party in order to obtain access to the party's private information. The party and the paralegal are not acquaintances, but the paralegal would use his actual name and other identifying information in an attempt to "friend" the party. Of course, to gain access without raising suspicion, the paralegal would not reveal his affiliation with the attorney or the motivation for becoming "friends." The question that arises out of this hypothetical is whether, from an ethical perspective, a cyberspace "friend" could become a foe.

In March, the Philadelphia Bar Association Professional Guidance Committee ("Committee") advised in Opinion 2009-02 that a similar scenario would violate the Pennsylvania Rules of Professional Conduct. In Opinion 2009-02, a nonparty witness was deposed; the witness testified that she had Facebook and MySpace accounts; the attorney believed that the witness would grant access to any user who asked for access to her accounts; the attorney wished to use a third person to seek access to her accounts; and, the third person intended to state "only truthful information, for example, his or her true name, but would not reveal that he or she is affiliated with the lawyer or the true purpose for which he or she is seeking access, namely, to provide the information posted on the pages to a lawyer for possible use antagonistic to the witness." While the committee recognized the existence of a "controversy regarding the ethical propriety of a lawyer engaging in certain kinds of investigative conduct that might be thought to be deceitful," the committee concluded that the proposed course of conduct would violate several PRPCs. (*See* New York Lawyers' Association Committee on Professional Ethics Formal Opinion No. 737*; In re Paulter*, 47 P.3d 1175 (Colo. 2002); *In re Gatti*, 8 P.3d 966, 974 (Ore. 2000); Oregon RPC 8.4).

First, the committee concluded that the proposed conduct would violate PRPC 5.3, "Responsibilities Regarding Nonlawyer Assistants," which states that "a lawyer shall be responsible for conduct of such person that would be a violation of the Rules of Professional Conduct if engaged in by a lawyer if the lawyer orders or, with the knowledge of the specific conduct, ratifies the conduct involved." The committee reasoned that the attorney "plainly is procuring the conduct, and, if it were undertaken, would be ratifying it with full knowledge of its propriety or lack thereof . . . Therefore, he is responsible for the conduct under the [PRPC] even if he is not himself engaging in the actual conduct that may violate a rule."

Second, the committee concluded that the proposed course of conduct would violate PRPC 8.4, "Misconduct," which provides that it is professional misconduct for a lawyer to "knowingly assist or induce another" to violate or attempt to violate the PRPC, or to "engage in conduct involving dishonesty, fraud, deceit or misrepresentation." The committee focused on the deceptive nature of the attorney's plan, which "omits [the] highly material fact" that the third party is seeking access to obtain information to share with a lawyer for possible use and impeachment in the lawsuit. The committee noted that purposeful concealment of this fact to induce the witness to allow the third person access was deceptive, and declined to "excus[e] the deceit" on the basis that the witness appeared to allow any user access. The committee also rejected the attorney's suggestion that the proposed course of conduct was not deceptive because it is similar to the "practice of videotaping the public conduct of a plaintiff in a personal injury case to show that he or she is capable of performing physical acts he claims his injury prevents." The committee reasoned that the videographer's conduct is permissible because he simply records the plaintiff as he presents himself to the public without asking the plaintiff for access to a private area to actually videotape the plaintiff.

4.1

Third, the committee explained that PRPC 4.1, "Truthfulness in Statements to Others," would also be violated if the attorney proceeded because the rule prohibits a lawyer from knowingly making a false statement of material fact or law to a third person in the course of representing a client. In other words, the committee determined that the "false statement" was the intentional omission of the fact that the paralegal works for the attorney and is "friending" the person to gain access to her private information for purposes of the lawsuit. The committee stated that the attorney's conduct constituted the making of a false statement of material fact to the witness in violation of PRPC 4.1. Because the false statement would be made through a third person's acts, the conduct would

8.4(a)

also violate PRPC 8.4a.

In sum, the committee found that the proposed conduct violated the rules of professional conduct due to its inherently deceptive nature.

***

A good rule of thumb for attorneys before poking around cyberspace is to consider whether an analogous noncyberspace situation would raise concerns. For example, viewing the public portion of a person's MySpace page or his post on a public message board is analogous to conducting surveillance on a subject. In both instances, there is no communication made with the person, nor is any misrepresentation made about the investigating individual's identity. The conduct would not invade a zone of privacy in either circumstance. Similarly, videotaping someone walking down the street, such as a plaintiff in a personal injury case, is akin to printing out information a person publicly posts online for all to see. The videotape or printout is a record of what that person has held out to the public.

The waters are muddied, however, when an attorney's concealment of the facts becomes a variable in the equation. The hypothetical we present is problematic because the paralegal attempting to "friend" the subject would not disclose his relationship with the attorney and true intentions. The paralegal's conduct is more invasive than simple surveillance but more importantly, it would occur under false pretenses. An analogy outside of the cyberspace context is if the paralegal knocked on the party's door; the party, without questioning the visitor's background or motives, allowed him to come inside; and, they engaged in a discussion that included information relevant to the lawsuit. While the party's voluntary act of allowing the paralegal to enter her home -- like the party's voluntary acceptance of an online invitation to become "friends" -- may mitigate invasion of privacy concerns and call into question the party's discretion, the element of deception still exists. Until a New Jersey court or ethics committee makes a clear pronouncement, all attorneys should exercise caution before becoming "friendly" with adverse witnesses or parties on social networking sites.

(See Mara E. Zazzali-Hogan and Jennifer Thiboadaux, Ethics of 'Friending' Adverse Witnesses, New Jersey Law Journal, Law Technology News, (2009) for full article version.) Reprinted with permission from the 2009 edition of the "New Jersey Law Journal, Law Technology News" © 2016 ALM Media Properties, LLC. All rights reserved.

Questions and Comments

1. In the *Philadelphia Bar Association Professional Guidance Committee Opinion* 2009-02, the lawyer believed the "witness tends to allow access [to her MySpace and Facebook profiles] to anyone who asks." If this statement were true, would there be any deception for which an attorney may be reprimanded? Does the witness's view of the online account have any bearing on the attorney's ethical responsibility and conduct?

2. Social networks are inherently public in nature. Could the information found on social media be legitimately viewed as protected from public use? Does is matter if a particular profile has "privacy settings"?

3. Do you think it is ever a good idea for a lawyer to befriend a witness or party in the case, who is not her client? Explain.

what if already "friends", have obligation to de-friend if conflict arises?

FRIENDING ADVERSE WITNESSES: WHEN DOES IT CROSS THE LINE INTO UNETHICAL CONDUCT[2]

The Lexis Hub, February 17, 2011
By Lisa McManus

You represent the defendant in a personal injury case in which the 20-year-old plaintiff claims that she can no longer enjoy the pleasures of life and is confined to her home. During the course of examining plaintiff's witness in deposition, the witness mentions communicating with the plaintiff on her Facebook account. You'd like to see her Facebook account to determine whether any evidence exists that the plaintiff is exaggerating her symptoms. Moreover, you'd like to investigate whether any information exists on the witness' page to impeach her testimony.

Can you send a friend request to the witness yourself, using a false name? Can you send a friend request to the witness yourself, using your name? Can you ask and employee or acquaintance to send a friend request to the witness so that you can see what is on her page?

Those well versed in social media know that Facebook and MySpace allow users to create personal "pages" on which they post information on any topic, sometimes including highly personal information. Users may dictate who accesses their pages by granting or denying permission to those who seek access to the account. A user can grant access to his or her page with almost no information about the person seeking access or can ask for detailed information about the person seeking access before deciding whether to allow access. Where does "friending" cross the line into unethical conduct?

Pretexting

Pretexting is the use of impersonation or fraud to trick another person into releasing personal information.

Model Rules

The Model Rules of Professional Conduct (Model Rules), . . . do not specifically address the use of social media by counsel to obtain discovery by pretextual means; however, several state bar ethics opinions suggest that the following sections are implicated with regard to contacts with adverse witnesses.

---

[2] This article is an excerpt of the written materials from Using Facebook and Other Social Networking Sites as Informal Discovery, a continuing legal education course presented by the ABA Young Lawyers Division at the 2011 ABA Mid-Year Meeting in Atlanta, Georgia. Reprinted from The Lexis Hub with permission. Copyright 2011 Matthew Bender & Company, Inc., a LexisNexis company. All rights reserved.

- Model Rule 4.1(a) forbids a lawyer from making false statements of material fact to a third person. Accordingly, failure to identify the true purpose of a contact with a third party constitutes a "false statement" could violate this Rule.

- Model Rule 4.4 prohibits attorneys from gaining evidence in a way that violates the rights of another:

  (a) In representing a client, a lawyer shall not use means that have no substantial purpose other than to embarrass, delay, or burden a third person, or use methods of obtaining evidence that violate the legal rights of such a person.

- Model Rule 8.4(c) bans conduct by a lawyer that involves dishonesty, fraud, deceit, or misrepresentation. Thus, unless there is an exception that permits misrepresentation for good purpose, this Rule may also prohibit friending an adverse witness.

The prohibitions against deceptive practices also apply a lawyer's employment of others to obtain information through social media accounts by less-than-transparent means.

- Model Rule 1.2 prohibits attorneys from advising their clients to engage in fraudulent behavior:

  (d) A lawyer shall not counsel a client to engage, or assist a client, in conduct that the lawyer knows is criminal or fraudulent, but a lawyer may discuss the legal consequences of any proposed course of conduct with a client and may counsel or assist a client to make a good faith effort to determine the validity, scope, meaning or application of the law.

- Model Rule 3.4 specifies that attorneys shall not perpetuate fraud:

  (b) A lawyer who represents a client in an adjudicative proceeding and who knows that a person intends to engage, is engaging or has engaged in criminal or fraudulent conduct related to the proceeding shall take reasonable remedial measures, including, if necessary, disclosure to the tribunal.

- Model Rule 8.4 bars attorneys from hiring agents to engage in unethical practices:

It is professional misconduct for a lawyer to:

  (a) violate or attempt to violate the Rules of Professional Conduct, knowingly assist or induce another to do so, or do so through the acts of another.

New York

New York City Bar Ethics Opinion 2010-2

The Association of the Bar of the City of New York Committee on Professional and Judicial Ethics issued its Formal Opinion 2010-2, Obtaining Evidence from Social Networking Websites, addressing the issue of friending. In addressing the question as to whether a lawyer, either directly or through an agent, may contact an unrepresented person through a social networking website and request permission to access her web page to obtain information for use in litigation, the Committee concluded that an attorney or her agent may use her real name and profile to send a "friend request" to obtain information from an unrepresented person's social networking website without also disclosing the reasons for making the request. While there are ethical boundaries to such "friending," in our view they are not crossed when an attorney or investigator uses only truthful information to obtain access to a website, subject to compliance with all other ethical requirements . . .

Rather than engage in "trickery," lawyers can—and should—seek information maintained on social networking sites, such as Facebook, by availing themselves of informal discovery, such as the truthful "friending" of unrepresented parties, or by using formal discovery devices such as subpoenas directed to non-parties in possession of information maintained on an individual's social networking page. Given the availability of these legitimate discovery methods, there is and can be no justification for permitting the use of deception to obtain the information from a witness on-line.

In coming to this conclusion, the Committee relied upon N.Y. Prof'l Conduct R. 4.1, 8.4(c) (2010), which the Committee opined are violated whenever an attorney "friends" an individual under false pretenses to obtain evidence from a social networking website. Based on Rules 5.3(b)(1) and 8.4(a), the Committee determined that the prohibition applies regardless of whether the lawyer employs an agent, such as an investigator, to engage in the deception.

Moreover, the Committee noted that N.Y. Prof'l Conduct R. 4.2 governed the situation where the witness is known to be represented by counsel, in which case the prior consent of the party's lawyer must be obtained or the conduct must be authorized by law. In New York, the term "party" is generally interpreted broadly to include "represented witnesses, potential witnesses and others with an interest or right at stake, although they are not nominal parties." N.Y. State 735 (2001). Compare N.Y. State 843 (2010), concerning whether a lawyer may view and access the Facebook or MySpace pages of a party other than his or her client in pending litigation in order to secure information about that party for use in the lawsuit, including impeachment material, if the lawyer does not "friend" the party and instead relies on public pages posted by the party that are accessible to all members in the network. While the Committee's opinion addressed accessing the public profile pages of a party, the Committee's reasoning indicates that the Committee would find the accessing of a witness' public profile to be acceptable if no subterfuge were involved.

Reprinted with permission from February 2011 edition of the "Lexis Hub" © 2011 Matthew Bender & Company, Inc., a LexisNexis company. All rights reserved.

Questions and Comments

1. What are the key differences in the *New York Judicial Ethics Formal Opinion* 2010-2 from the *Philadelphia Bar Association Professional Guidance Committee Opinion* 2009-02?

2. Rule 5.3 holds a lawyer responsible for the ethical violations of non-lawyers working under her. If an investigator "acts as [a] lawyer's 'alter ego,' the lawyer is ethically responsible for the investigator's conduct." In an instance when the client hires the investigator, would the attorney still be possibly responsible for the investigator's conduct?[3]

3. How would/should a young associate lawyer respond to a supervisor asking him to do something unethical? What would her optons be?

HOFF V. MAYER
Appellate Court of Illinois (2002)
772 N.E.2d 263

McBride, Justice.

On August 16, 2000, William Bruce Hoff, Jr. (Hoff), and Catherine Hoff, his wife, filed a complaint for declaratory judgment and other relief in the circuit court of Cook County against Mayer, Brown & Platt (MBP), a Chicago law firm. Thereafter, MBP filed a motion to dismiss plaintiff's complaint pursuant to section 2–615 of the Illinois Code of Civil Procedure (735 ILCS 5/2–615 (2000)). On June 12, 2001, the trial court granted defendant's motion. Hoff now appeals.

---

[3] *See Jones v. Scientific Colors, Inc.*, 201 F. Supp. 2d 820 (N.D. Ill. 2001) (finding no ethical violations when investigators were hired and directed by the clients rather than the attorneys and the investigator did not provide regular updates to the attorney).

Hoff argues on appeal: (1) that the retirement provision in MBP's restated plan is a restrictive covenant and is contrary to Illinois public policy; (2) that the provision is unreasonably broad; and (3) that under any circumstance, Hoff is entitled to a trial on the issues of whether he has materially competed with MBP and whether MBP can reasonably refuse to determine that any alleged damage caused by Hoff has ended.

According to the complaint, Hoff resigned as a partner with MBP on July 9, 1993. At the time of his resignation, Hoff was 60 years old and had been with MBP for 36 years. Hoff requested retirement income from MBP. MBP has refused to pay Hoff retirement income based on its "Restated Partnership Agreement, Retirement, Disability & Death Benefit Program" (Restated Plan or Plan). In his complaint, Hoff alleges that he should have been receiving in excess of $94,000 per year in retirement income, plus additional cost-of-living adjustments, pursuant to the Plan, since his resignation in 1993. From the record below, there is no dispute that Hoff left MBP to become a founding partner in another Chicago firm—Kasowitz, Hoff, Benson & Torres. Additionally, Hoff received all earned fee income, capital shares, financial benefits and other revenue to which he was entitled, based on his association with MBP and his years of service to the firm. He disputes only MBP's decision to deny him retirement benefits.

***

The dispute here centers around sections 3.1 and 3.2 of MBP's Restated Plan, and Rule 5.6 of the Illinois Rules of Professional Conduct (134 Ill.2d R. 5.6). MBP's Restated Plan states:

> "3.1 *In General.* If a member's membership in the firm is terminated by reason of his or her retirement on a retirement date (as described in subsection 3.2) on or after January 1, 1987, he or she will be provided with a retirement income in an amount determined in accordance with the provisions of subsection 3.3.

> 3.2 *Retirement Date.* The 'retirement date' for a member is the one of the following dates that applies in his or her case:

> (a) *Normal Retirement Date.* The "normal retirement date" for a member shall be the first day of the calendar month as of which he or she elects to retire or is retired by the firm, provided in either event that, as of such day, he or she shall have also either (i) attained at least 65 years of age or (ii) attained at least 62, but not yet attained 65, years of age and completed at least 20 years' associated with the firm.

(b) *Early Retirement Date.* The 'early retirement date' for a member shall be the first day of the calendar month as of which he or she elects to retire or is retired by the firm, provided in either event that, as of such day, he or she shall have also attained at least 60, but not yet 62, years of age and completed at least 20 years' associated with the firm."

For purposes of this program, a member shall not be deemed to have elected to retire prior to attaining age 65 unless he or she substantially ceases the active practice of law on a permanent basis or his or her post-retirement practice of law is determined by the firm to be consistent with his or her status as a retiree."

Rule 5.6(a) of the Illinois Rules of Professional Conduct, entitled "Restrictions on Right to Practice," provides: "A lawyer shall not participate in offering or making: (a) a partnership or employment agreement that restricts the rights of a lawyer to practice after termination of the relationship, except an agreement concerning benefits upon retirement ..." 134 Ill. 2d R. 5.6(a).

Hoff first claims that MBP's Restated Plan is basically a restrictive covenant and is contrary to Illinois public policy. Hoff argues that whether MBP's Plan comports with Rule 5.6(a) depends on whether the "benefits" under the Plan constitute "retirement Benefits" under Rule 5.6(a).

Hoff correctly points out in his brief that under Rule 5.6(a), a lawyer may not participate in an agreement that "restricts the rights of a lawyer to practice" after a relationship between the lawyer and firm has ended. 134 Ill. 2d R. 5.6(a). Illinois public policy has consistently discouraged law firm employment agreements that contain noncompetition clauses or restrictive covenants. *Stevens v. Rooks Pitts & Poust*, 289 Ill. App.3d 991, 998, 225 Ill. Dec. 48, 682 N.E.2d 1125 (1997). Historically, these provisions have been strictly scrutinized by the courts as they can result in restraints on trade. *Williams & Montgomery, Ltd. v. Stellato*, 195 Ill. App. 3d 544, 553, 142 Ill. Dec. 359, 552 N.E.2d 1100 (1990). "The rule is designed both to afford clients greater freedom in choosing counsel and to protect lawyers from onerous conditions that would unduly limit their mobility." *Dowd & Dowd, Ltd. v. Gleason*, 181 Ill. 2d 460, 481, 230 Ill. Dec. 229, 693 N.E.2d 358 (1998). Noncompetition clauses are especially discouraged in the legal profession where the lawyer is not selling or promoting a commodity but rather his or her personal service. Rule 5.6 was also designed to protect lawyers and clients from "illegitimate anti-competitive practices that will distort the market and ultimately drive up the price of legal services." 2 G. Hazard & W. Hodes, The Law of Lawyering §5.6:101, at 823 (1992 Supp.).

Rule 5.6(a), however, provides for an exception to the rule that noncompetition provisions are generally unenforceable. The rule states that an agreement concerning benefits upon retirement is exempt from the general rule. It has been noted that "[t]he purpose and meaning of the exception for 'benefits upon retirement' * * * is not crystal clear." 2 G. Hazard & W. Hodes, The Law of Lawyering § 5.6:201, at 824 (1992 Supp.). The Annotated Model Rules of Professional Conduct interprets the retirement benefits exception to mean that

> "when a lawyer is retiring or winding up his or her affairs with a firm, the lawyer's receipt of full retirement benefits entails an assumption that he or she is truly retiring from practice. This further suggests that the lawyer may be required to agree to 'stay retired' as a condition of the settlement." Annotated Model Rules of Professional Conduct 466–67 (4th ed.1999).

We find this interpretation instructive.

The parties have noted, and we agree, that no Illinois case directly addresses this issue. Hoff does, however, draw our attention to Illinois cases that he argues provide guidance. Hoff cites a United States District Court, Northern District, case for the proposition that a broad reading of the retirement benefits exception to Rule 5.6(a) is flawed. Prior to oral argument, Hoff cited *Cummins v. Bickel & Brewer*, No. 00 C 3703, 2002 WL 187492 (N.D. Ill. February 6, 2002), as additional authority. Before its summary judgment order of February 6, 2002, the district court filed a motion to dismiss order in *Cummins v. Bickel & Brewer*, No. 00 C 3703, 2001 WL 204797 (N.D. Ill. March 1, 2001). In that set of cases, Cummins, a former partner with the law firm of Bickel & Brewer, sued his former firm for refusing to pay him interest in the partnership upon his withdrawal from the firm. The *Cummins* court relied on *Dowd & Dowd, Ltd. Cummins*, slip op. at 4 (N.D. Ill. March 1, 2001). In *Dowd & Dowd, Ltd.*, the law firm sought relief from the Illinois Supreme Court, contending that the appellate court erred in refusing to uphold the noncompetition clause in its employment contracts. The noncompetition clause in that case stated that an employee of the law firm was prohibited from handling any client of the firm for two years following termination of employment with the firm. The court held that that provision was in direct violation of Rule 5.6 and held it to be unenforceable. *Dowd & Dowd, Ltd.*, 181 Ill.2d at 480, 230 Ill. Dec. 229, 693 N.E.2d 358. In *Cummins*, the district court stated that the facts in *Dowd & Dowd, Ltd.* were "almost identical" to the facts in *Cummins. Cummins*, slip op. at 4 (N.D. Ill. March 1, 2001). We find that the facts in *Dowd & Dowd, Ltd.*, together with the limited precedential value of *Cummins*, make these cases unpersuasive. Because the rules committee found it important to include a specific retirement benefits exception to the noncompetition provisions of law firm agreements, we are obligated to base our decision on the plain language of the rule as it applies to the facts of the matter before us.

Hoff also notes that in *Stevens*, the court found the law firm's employment agreement violative of public policy. The agreement limited compensation payable to any withdrawing partner if the partner competed with the firm in a certain geographical area. The firm unsuccessfully argued that their employment agreement did not violate Rule 5.6 because it merely provided a "modest measure of recoupment to [the firm] for the economic harm caused by the departure and subsequent competition of one of its partners." *Stevens*, 289 Ill. App. 3d at 995, 225 Ill. Dec. 48, 682 N.E.2d 1125. The firm did not argue and the *Stevens* court did not address the retirement benefits exception to Rule 5.6. Therefore, we do not find that the case provides guidance.

As MBP has pointed out in its brief, courts in other states have addressed the public policy considerations of Rule 5.6 and have upheld retirement benefits provisions in law firm employment contracts similar to the one at issue here. In *Neuman v. Akman*, 715 A.2d 127 (D.C. App. 1998), Neuman left his former law firm to engage in private practice and sued his former firm alleging that their partnership agreement violated Rule 5.6(a) of the District of Columbia Rules of Professional Conduct. The agreement provided that a partner leaving the firm would be eligible for capital contributions and a share of the net partnership profits but would be denied an "Additional Amount" linked to the future earnings of the firm if the partner retired and engaged in the private practice of law anywhere in the United States. The trial court held that the "Additional Amount" constituted a retirement benefit and, as such, fit within the exception under Rule 5.6(a). The appellate court affirmed and held that the "Additional Amount comes entirely from firm profits that post-date the withdrawal of the partner. ...It is only future firm revenues that Neuman will be deprived of, and only because he is at least potentially competing with the firm and effecting a depression of those revenues." *Neuman*, 715 A.2d at 136. As we find the facts in *Neuman* to be on point, we are persuaded by that court's reasoning and holding. From the record below, Hoff is requesting that MBP provide him with future firm revenues through his retirement benefits while he competes against MBP in the same city. Like *Neuman*, we find that Rule 5.6(a) was designed specifically to address and correct this situation.

The *Neuman* court notes that the leading case interpreting Rule 5.6(a) or its equivalent is *Cohen v. Lord, Day & Lord*, 75 N.Y.2d 95, 551 N.Y.S.2d 157, 550 N.E.2d 410 (1989). We, too, find this case helpful. In *Cohen*, the New York court held that a law firm partnership agreement which conditioned payment of earned but uncollected partnership revenues upon the withdrawing partner's obligation to refrain from competing with the firm was unenforceable. The court found the provision to be a significant monetary penalty and an impermissible restriction on the practice of law. The *Cohen* court distinguished financial disincentives and penalties from the retirement exception in the applicable rule. Specifically, the court found that retirement benefits are separate and distinct from the financial penalties at issue; otherwise the exception would swallow the rule. "[T]o treat departure compensation as a retirement benefit would invert the exception into the general rule, thus significantly undermining the prohibition against restraints on lawyers practicing law." *Cohen*, 75 N.Y.2d at 100, 551 N.Y.S.2d 157, 550 N.E.2d at 412. *Gray v. Martin*, 63 Or. App. 173, 663 P.2d 1285 (1983), cited by both parties here and the *Cohen* court, holds similarly. Like *Cummins*, the *Gray* court held that the law firm partnership agreement which required a forfeiture of financial benefits if the withdrawing attorney practiced law in competition with the firm was in violation of the noncompetition clause restrictions found in the professional conduct rules. The provision in the partnership agreement did not discriminate between retiring and withdrawing partners. The *Gray* court noted that, but for the distinction, "[e]very termination of a relationship between law partners would be a retirement, and agreements restricting the right to practice would always be allowed." *Gray*, 63 Or.App. at 179, 663 P.2d at 1290. The provision in the partnership agreement at issue here addresses retirement only. The distinction between this provision and one found in *Cohen, Gray* and *Cummins* is important.

MBP also draws our attention to *Donnelly v. Brown, Winick, Graves, Gross, Baskerville, Schoenebaum & Walker, P.L.C.*, 599 N.W.2d 677 (Iowa 1999). In *Donnelly*, the Iowa Supreme Court held that the benefits under the law firm's retirement plan could be conditioned on an attorney remaining out of the practice of law. Donnelly, a partner in Brown, Winick, left the firm after over 25 years of service to join a firm in the same city. Donnelly's length of time with Brown, Winick would have qualified him for retirement benefits under the firm's plan. The firm denied Donnelly retirement benefits arguing that, under the plan, in order to qualify for these benefits, Donnelly would have to "terminate his TTT practice of law within the State of Iowa." *Donnelly*, 599 N.W.2d at 679. Donnelly countered by arguing that that provision of the plan was a covenant not to compete and in violation of the Iowa Code of Professional Conduct. *Donnelly*, 599 N.W.2d at 679. Iowa's rule addressing this issue, virtually identical to our Rule 5.6, states that covenants not to compete are a violation of the rule except as a condition of payment of retirement benefits. Reviewing the firm's plan in that case, the court held that "retirement benefits" under the Iowa Code of Professional Conduct were required to be payments pursuant to a bona fide retirement plan. The court found that the firm's retirement plan—requiring 10 years of service and 60 years of age or 25 years of service—qualified as a retirement plan and benefits under the firm's plan could be conditioned on Donnelly remaining out of the practice of law in Iowa, pursuant to the exception to the rule.

Donnelly, 599 N.W.2d at 680. Like *Donnelly*, we find MBP's retirement plan to be a bona fide retirement plan. Additionally, we find MBP's provision comports with Rule 5.6(a), and any retirement benefits offered by MBP may be conditioned upon Hoff remaining out of the practice of law.

We recognize the concern that law firms may unfairly take advantage of the exception in Rule 5.6(a). Citing *Cohen* and *Gray*, the Annotated Model Rules of Professional Conduct opines: "in cases when a law firm attempts to categorize a lawyer's departure from the firm as a 'retirement' for purposes of restricting his or her subsequent right to practice law, the courts have rejected such retirement provisions." Annotated Model Rules of Professional Conduct 467 (4th ed.1999). Here, we do not find MBP's plan characterized Hoff's departure from the firm as a retirement for purposes of restricting his right to practice law. Rather, "retirement" has been defined under the plan for purposes of receiving future benefits. As noted in the Model Rules, law firms are restricted from using "retirement" for other such purposes. Annotated Model Rules of Professional Conduct 467 (4th ed.1999). Here, Hoff was 60 years old and had been with MBP for 36 years when he made the decision to resign from the firm and begin a new partnership, and MBP provided Hoff with all fees and benefits due and owing to him at the time of his resignation. MBP denied Hoff only future benefits under the firm's retirement provision. In interpreting the exception to Rule 5.6, the annotated rules explain that receipt of retirement benefits would "entail [ ] an assumption that [a lawyer] is truly retiring from practice * * * [and] that a lawyer may be required to agree to 'stay retired' as a condition of the settlement." Annotated Rules of Professional Conduct 466–67 (4th ed.1999).

The Connecticut Supreme Court addressed the issue of postemployment benefits in *Schoonmaker v. Cummings & Lockwood of Connecticut, P.C.*, 252 Conn. 416, 747 A.2d 1017 (2000). In that case, Schoonmaker, a former partner with the defendant law firm, argued that his former firm's decision to withhold compensation upon his departure from the firm and decision to compete was a violation of the public policy embedded in Rule 5.6. The court held that while it agreed that public policy favors a client's access to an attorney of choice:

> "It would be illogical to expect law firms to pay out large sums of cash to departing lawyers while fearing that their cash flow will be threatened by competing lawyers and the loss of potential clients. Implicit in the retirement benefits exception, therefore, is the notion that the public's interest in fostering liberal competition among practitioners must be balanced against a law firm's interest in maintaining a steady income flow for the purpose of providing former members with substantial remuneration upon retirement."

Schoonmaker, 252 Conn. At 440, 747 A.2d at 1031.

In the instant case, we find, reading and interpreting MBP's Restated Plan regarding retirement benefits in light of Rule 5.6(a), the proper balance between the public's interest in choice and a law firm's interest in maintaining income. Keeping in mind the public policy embodied in Rule 5.6, we cannot say that MBP violated this policy by denying Hoff retirement benefits. Hoff relinquished retirement benefits from MBP by resigning from the firm and continuing to practice law.

***

The trial court's granting of MBP's motion to dismiss is affirmed. Affirmed.

Questions and Comments

1. In *Hoff,* the court stated that an agreement to confer retirement benefits may require the attorney to actually cease practicing. Hoff was 60 and had worked at the firm for 36 years. Do you think the court took into consideration his age and years of service? Would the outcome likely be different if a lawyer receives retirement benefits under a government plan, and then retires from government work and goes into private practice? If so, how?

2. Do you think the financial disincentive provisions in law firm partnership agreements possibly indirectly do what the Model Rules do not allow a firm to do, i.e., restrict competition and one's right to practice law?

3. You and another lawyer are the founding partners of a law firm. In an ugly departure, the founding partner left your firm and decided to open a competing law firm just across the street. You now decide to adopt a partnership provision to withhold retirement benefits from any of the other partners who may leave under such circumstances and compete with your firm. Under the circumstances, may your law firm make the payment of retirement benefits contingent on the retirees' compliance with a non-compete agreement signed in advance of retirement?

BRIDGING THE GREAT DIVIDE: PARALEGALS AND REGULATION
The Legal Intelligencer, June 16, 2016
By Valerie A. Wilus

When the American Bar Association (ABA) began discussing a model for regulatory objectives to develop a framework for standards for the delivery of legal services by nonlawyers, the legal community stood up and took notice. In its written opposition to the ABA dated Oct. 27, 2015, the New Jersey State Bar Association believes "the commission should first address the underlying -questions of whether nonlawyers should be permitted to provide legal services" and reminds the readers that "in 2013, [the] ABA president ... called upon states to meet unmet legal needs by connecting those in need of legal services with the vast number underemployed and unemployed attorneys." The New Jersey State Bar Association goes on to state that this "resolution is in direct conflict with these prior initiatives and contrary to the core principle of our legal system that lawyers are singularly and uniquely qualified to provide legal counsel" and that the "commission should focus on solutions that live up to our justice system's promise of providing 'equal justice under the law.' The ABA is uniquely situated to protect the public and the justice system from unethical and illegal -infringement by nonlawyers into the justice system."

In its final report delivered at the midyear meeting in February 2014, the ABA Task Force on the Future of Legal Education encouraged courts, bar associations and other regulators to develop programs for limited legal services to be provided by nonlawyers and directed schools to develop educational programs to train nonlawyers to provide limited legal services. There are currently certain governmental agencies that allow nonlawyer practice, some with certain examinations or registrations: Department of Commerce, Department of Health and Human Services, Department of Labor and the Department of Transportation. Certain states also allow nonlawyer practice for certain agencies: Pennsylvania, 246 Pa. Code Rule 207—representation in magisterial district court proceedings (Rule 207 is intended to permit a nonlawyer representative to appear, but not to allow a nonlawyer to establish a business for the purpose of representing others and is allowed on a case-by-case basis) and Act 5 of 2005, Section 214 in the Unemployment Compensation Law—representation of employers by nonlawyers to advocate at hearings and file Unemployment Compensation appeals and briefs, as in Harkness v. Unemployment Compensation Board of Review, 867 A.2d 728 (Pa. Commw. Ct. 2005).

There are reasons that paralegals should become regulated and certified by passing a nationally recognized test or a newly created statewide test that would establish levels of knowledge, skill and competency. Some of those reasons would be that it would clarify roles, establish standards, there would be surety that paralegals are qualified, it would expand the utilization of paralegals, it would restrict the use of the title and there would be public benefits. There are various reasons why regulation for paralegals should be supported: attorneys need to be assured that the paralegals that assist in their practice are better educated and qualified to provide legal services; members of the public directly or indirectly rely on the work performed by paralegals; paralegals would know and understand their ethical duties and meet the minimum standards

[handwritten margin note: pros to regulating paralegals]

of paralegal competency; it would give attorneys and the public a benchmark to working with a paralegal; and would identify qualified candidates and allow attorneys to publicize the employment of a certified paralegal to the public and clients.

The ABA Standing Committee on Paralegals touches on these exact areas in its Oct. 29, 2015, comments Related to ABA Commission on the Future of Legal Services Report:

- "The utilization of paralegals allows for the expansion of the delivery of the legal services to all clients, lowers the costs of those services, but protects the public by ensuring that the nonlawyers are being adequately supervised by lawyers."
- "Attorneys employing paralegals and delegating certain substantive legal work to the paralegals allow for the extension of the legal services to a greater number of individuals and the delivery of legal services at a more affordable rate."
- "Properly trained and supervised -paralegals aid lawyers in the delivery of legal services, increasing efficiency in the delivery of legal services, while maintaining the high ethical requirements demanded of the legal profession."
- "The one constant has been that paralegals have been working under the direction and supervision of the attorney."

In order to showcase the point and need for paralegal regulation even further, in May, the Unemployment Compensation Board of Review (UCBR) argued in a brief before the Pennsylvania Supreme Court that while a law license was not necessary under its rules to represent individuals in unemployment appeals, suspended attorneys were in a special class that the public needed to be protected from. The UCBR further argued that it was required to uphold state disciplinary rules barring so-called formerly admitted attorneys from appearing on behalf of a client before any adjudicative body.

"To permit these suspended attorneys to appear before a referee in these proceedings is fundamentally wrong for two reasons," the brief said. "First, it -undermines the disciplinary orders of this court and makes the UCBR complicit in intentional violations of the disciplinary rule. Second, it fails to protect commonwealth citizens from persons this court determined to be unsuitable to provide such representation," as in Powell v. Unemployment Compensation Board of Review, Case Number 38 MAP 2016.

There are two national paralegal associations that currently offer certification exams, National Federation of Paralegal Associations (NFPA) and National Association of Legal Assistants (NALA). NFPA offers two exams, the Paralegal CORE Competency Exam for the CORE Registered Paralegal (CRP) credential and the Paralegal Advanced Competency

Exam for the PACE Registered Paralegal (RP) credential. NALA offers the Certified Paralegal/Certified Legal Assistant Exam for the Certified Paralegal (CP)/Certified Legal Assistant (CLA) credential. The National Association of Legal Secretaries also offers a Professional Paralegal Exam for the Professional Paralegal (PP) credential. Each exam has its own eligibility (education or experience) requirements to sit for the exam, fees, testing dates and locations, testing times, composition of the exam and renewal requirements, which include a certain amount of Continuing Legal Education (CLE) hours in legal substance and ethics. These examinations should be considered when reviewing any type of statewide regulation.

There are three main types of regulation: certification—a voluntary process that is granted to an individual who has met certain qualifications such as education, work experience or examination; license—restrictive license that always involves a test given by a competent authority; and registration—can be voluntary or mandatory for individuals that register with an authority, that mostly does not include special training or experience. Currently, the state of Washington, under Washington Supreme Court authorization, has developed the Limited License Legal Technician (LLLT) program for paralegals in that state in order to meet the needs of those unable to afford the services of an attorney. This program is currently only offered in the practice area of domestic relations. An LLLT is not a fully licensed attorney, cannot represent clients in court and has certain other limitations, such as: "cannot negotiate on behalf of a client and can only prepare legal documents that have been approved by the LLLT board." An LLLT must: "obtain an associate's degree or higher; complete 45 credit hours of core curriculum through an ABA approved legal program; complete applicable practice area course (family law) offered through the University of Washington School of Law; complete 3,000 hours of paralegal experience involving substantive legal work in any practice area under the supervision of a lawyer; take and pass the Legal Technician Exam; and fulfill other licensing requirements."

Why did the Washington Supreme Court create and authorize the licensing of LLLTs? "From a 2003 Civil Legal Needs Study, we know that more than 80 percent of people in Washington with low- or moderate-income experienced a legal need and went without help because they couldn't afford it or didn't know where to turn. This new level of legal service provider is intended to help meet the unmet civil legal needs in our state."

Currently 11 states have developed a Voluntary Paralegal Certification, either through their bar association or their local paralegal association and three have an exam in connection to their program. Four states have decided to adopt paralegal standards that have been approved by their local bar associations instead of tackling the regulation issues in their state. Delaware, New Jersey and Pennsylvania have developed a Voluntary Paralegal Certification program. In Pennsylvania, the Keystone Alliance of Paralegal Associations administers the program requiring paralegals to meet minimum educational and employment standards in order to qualify for and maintain the Pa.C.P. credential. Paralegals certified by the alliance receive the alliance's express authorization to use the credential "Pa.C.P.," which is the designation and registered state trademark for "Pennsylvania Certified Paralegal." The program identifies individuals whose education, training, and work experience have equipped them with the knowledge, skills and proficiencies to perform substantive legal work in a professional and ethical manner. These individuals are employed or retained by a lawyer, law office, corporation, governmental agency, or other entity to work under the direction of a lawyer or pursuant to state statute, administrative regulation, or court authority in a capacity that, in most instances, would be performed by a lawyer in the absence of a paralegal. The Pa.C.P. credential offers employers a benchmark for hiring and promoting paralegals.

In its February Resolution 105, the ABA adopted "Model Regulatory Objectives for the Provision of Legal Services:

- Protection of the public.
- Advancement of the administration of justice and the rule of law.
- Meaningful access to justice and information about the law, legal issues, and the civil and criminal justice systems.
- Transparency regarding the nature and scope of legal services to be provided, the credentials of those who provide them, and the availability of regulatory protections.
- Delivery of affordable and accessible legal services.
- Efficient, competent and ethical delivery of legal services.
- Protection of privileged and confidential information.
- Independence of professional judgment.
- Accessible civil remedies for negligence and breach of other duties owed, and disciplinary sanctions for misconduct.
- Diversity and inclusion among legal services providers and freedom from discrimination for those receiving legal services and in the justice system.

The resolution goes on to "urge that each state's highest court ... be guided by the ABA Model Regulatory Objectives for the provision of legal services when they assess the court's existing regulatory framework and any other regulations they may choose to develop concerning nontraditional legal service providers."

In April, the Philadelphia Bar Association sent a resolution to the Pennsylvania Supreme Court regarding "Emerging Models for Nonlawyer Assistance and Practice." In this resolution, they agree that the "legal marketplace at present is not organized in a way that can fully meet the legal needs of all Pennsylvanians" and mention the "rapid changes in technology [that] have created both opportunities and risks ... unregulated online legal providers ... limited employment opportunities and the rising cost of obtaining a legal education" and go on to acknowledge how "several states are exploring nontraditional, nonlawyer models to enhance access to justice while protecting the public." The resolution "requests the opportunity to participate and assist in any exploration or evaluation of such models that the Pennsylvania Supreme Court may choose to undertake."

Now is the time that Pennsylvania should take under consideration the role that a nonlawyer, such as a paralegal, can play in bridging the gap to those who need it most, through a regulatory scheme that includes education, experience and examination.

Reprinted with permission from the June 2016 edition of the "Legal Intelligencer" © 2016 ALM Media Properties, LLC. All rights reserved.

Questions and Comments

1. Consider the arguments made in this article for requiring regulation for paralegals and other non-lawyers providing legal services. Do you agree with these arguments? Do you think regulation of these individuals would sharpen the integrity of our profession? Would it possibly make lawyers' jobs easier or lower their exposure?

2. Some states have started to regulate paralegals and nonlawyers who provide legal services. Can you think of duties or activities performed by these individuals that should be regulated? Consider some of the typical job descriptions of a paralegal – communicate with clients, file paperwork, schedule appointments for the lawyer, etc.

3. What arguments could you make against regulating non-lawyers providing legal services? Do you think that lawyers and paralegals should be held to the same standard of care when working on a case?

D. Discussion Questions

1. Rule 5.1 sets out the responsibilities of partners, managers, and supervisory lawyers. This rule essentially requires a partner or managing lawyer of a law firm to assure that other lawyers adhere to the Rules of Professional Conduct. How specifically are these duties supposed to be fulfilled? When a debatable question of ethics arises, how might a supervisory attorney deal with the issue and still be in compliance with the Rules?

2. Under Rule 5.2(b), a lawyer will not be disciplined for her conduct as long as she is complying with a supervisory lawyer's reasonable resolution of an arguable question of professional duty. Scholars have opined that this rule gives a false comfort to subordinate and some states have rejected this rule altogether—California, Connecticut, and Virginia[4]. The argument is that the rule seems to rarely serve a purpose as "compliance with a reasonable resolution of an arguable question of professional duty will not typically lead to discipline of anyone in any jurisdiction, and compliance with an unreasonable resolution would lead to the discipline of both lawyers in any jurisdiction."[5] Do you agree?

3. Can you think of an instance where a lawyer may violate a rule of professional conduct for not using Facebook, LinkedIn, or other social media platforms? Does a lawyer meet the standard of "competent representation" if she ignores social media avenues to collect information?[6]

---

[4] Andrew M. Perlman, *The Silliest Rule of Professional Conduct: Model Rule 5.2(b)*, 19 PROF. LAW. 14, 14–17 (2009).

[5] *Id.*

[6] *See* Canedy v. Adams, 2009 WL 3711958, *34 (C.D. Cal. Nov. 4, 2009) (holding that a lawyer's failure to locate a sexual abuse victim's recantation on her social media profile could have constituted ineffective assistance of counsel).

Disqualifying Judges

Role of a Judge

CHAPTER 11:
The Role of Judges and the
License to Practice Law

Political
Involvement

Activities of
Judges

Practice Only with License

License
to
Practice
Law

Unauthorized Practice;
Multijurisdictional Practice
of Law
Rule 5.5

Chapter 11:
The Role of Judges and the License to Practice Law

A. INTRODUCTION

Judges play many roles in the American legal system. They interpret the law, control the courtroom process, rule on the admissibility of evidence, and sometimes serve as the fact finder. The most important role of a judge, however, is her role as an impartial decision maker. A judge's ability to provide an independent and fair evaluation of opposing arguments is essential to the preservation of the principles of our justice system. Just like lawyers, judges must abide by certain duties that govern their conduct. A model for these rules is found in the Model Code of Judicial Conduct and consists of four canons setting forth the ethical standards for judges and judicial candidates. These standards are the canon of independence, the canon of impartiality, the canon of conflicts, and the canon of politics.

Canon 1 focuses on the critical element of independence in upholding impartiality in the judiciary. Thus, this canon states that a judge should always promote impartiality and avoid impropriety or even the appearance of it. Canon 2 focuses on the duties of the judge and how all judges should perform their duties in an impartial and competent way and do so diligently. The second canon requires judges to not comment to the jury concerning the strength or weakness of the evidence, not show bias or prejudice on protected classes, and show competence and diligence in performing their duties. Further, this canon specifically provides instances in which a judge must disqualify herself in order to keep the judiciary impartial.

Canon 3 requires that a judge conduct extra-judicial activities in a way that will minimize conflict with her duties as a judge. This canon focuses on how a judge should avoid getting caught in conflict when determining whether to engage in various activities. In addition, the judges should strive to reduce the need for disqualification as much as possible. Most important, a judge's judicial duties should be preserved above all other extra-judicial activities. Finally, Canon 4 is the canon of politics. It states that judge shall refrain from engaging in inappropriate political activity and making certain statements in order to preserve the integrity of the judiciary.

This chapter's reading begins with a case analyzing a judge's ability to be fair and impartial and circumstances requiring a judge to recuse or be disqualified from hearing a particular matter. Additionally, this chapter includes cases discussing the rules requiring licensing to engage in the practice of law. Under the Rules of Professional Conduct, it is prohibited for an individual or organization to engage in the practice of law without being licensed to do so by a state bar. In the cases that follow, the court determines what conduct constitutes the "the practice of law" and whether an individual has a valid license required to engage in that conduct.

While reading these cases, compare and contrast the specific rules for judges in the Code of Judicial Conduct with the rules in the Model Rules of Professional Conduct. Although many of the rules appear to be similar, consider some of the more stringent rules for judges especially when it comes to showing bias, prejudice, and the need to disqualify themselves in certain situations. How do these rules help maintain a judicial system that is honest and unprejudiced? Are these canons so essential to upkeep the faith and trust in a balanced judicial system?

B. RULES

In preparation, read the following sections of The Model Code of Judicial Conduct. Additionally, read carefully the following section of the Model Rules of Professional Conduct along with any relevant comments listed below.

Code of Judicial Conduct:
- Rule 2.3 Bias, Prejudice, and Harassment
  - Comment [1], [2], [3], & [4]
- Rule 2.11 Disqualification
  - Comment [3], [4], [5], & [6]
- Rule 4.1 Political and Campaign Activates of Judicial Candidates in General
  - Comment [3], [4], [8], [10], & [15]
- Rule 4.2 Political and Campaign Activates of Judicial Candidates in Public Elections
  - Comment [1], [2], [3], [6] & [7]

Model Rules of Professional Conduct
- Rule 5.5 Unauthorized Practice; Multijurisdictional Practice of Law
  - Comment [1], [2], [3], & [4]

C. CASES AND ADDITIONAL READINGS

Appelloxk ct denied writ of mandurneis reavest

HOOK V. MCDADE

United States Court of Appeals for the Seventh Circuit (1996)
89 F.3d 350

Coffey, Circuit Judge

George C. Hook, an attorney, was indicted along with Carmen Viana, the owner of Wittek Industries, for stealing funds from the Wittek company's employee pension plan, in violation of 18 U.S.C. §664; wire fraud, in violation of 18 U.S.C. §1343; and money laundering, in violation of 18 U.S.C. §1956. Viana fled to Brazil and there is an outstanding warrant for her arrest, although according to the Assistant United States Attorney, extradition is unlikely. After the trial judge had denied a number of Hook's pretrial motions, Hook requested that the trial judge, the Hon. Joe B. McDade, recuse himself, pursuant to 28 U.S.C. §455. After the district court denied the motion, the defendant Hook petitioned this court for a writ of mandamus to order the recusal of the district court judge. We deny the petition.

I. Background

The factual grounds that give rise to Hook's claim of judicial bias in his criminal trial arose from a civil lawsuit (the *Cannon* litigation) filed in 1993 before Judge McDade. In that suit, Holly Cannon, a former secretary of Wittek Industries (an automobile parts manufacturer in Peoria, Illinois) sued her former employer, as well as its owner, Carmen Viana, and the Blue Cross Blue Shield Health Plan, claiming that she had been improperly denied health benefits under the Employee Retirement Income Security Act of 1974 (ERISA). Carmen Viana, over the objection of her insurance company, Kemper (who provided insurance coverage for employee suits regarding benefits), retained attorney George Hook to defend the action. The district court (Judge McDade) granted summary judgment for Wittek, Viana, and Blue Cross; the secretary appealed and Hook submitted a $10,000 legal bill to the insurance company.

The insurance company believed Hook's legal fees to be excessive, refused to pay the same, and in November 1994 Kemper Insurance retained the firm of Quinn, Johnston, Henderson, and Pretorius to review Hook's attorney's fees. One of the attorneys at the Quinn firm was Mary McDade, the wife of Judge McDade and she was assigned to review the legal charges. Upon the Quinn firm's recommendation, the insurance company paid only 75 percent of the bill and at this time Hook withdrew his representation for the appeal. According to Hook, Mary McDade, in

'judge's wife assigned to review legal charges'
. insurance paid only 75%.

[margin note: Wife withdrew but firm still represented]

the course of her review of Hook's legal bill, questioned whether Hook's termination of representation for Wittek and Viana during the time period when their appellate brief was due in the Seventh Circuit might be considered as and constitute legal malpractice.

In January 1995, prior to oral argument in *Cannon* before this court, Mary McDade withdrew as counsel for the defendants. Her firm, however, continued to represent Wittek and Viana on appeal.

In February 1995, an indictment was returned against George Hook and Carmen Viana, Wittek's owner, alleging that from about June to September 1992, Hook and Viana transferred and embezzled funds from a pension plan sponsored by Wittek for its employees, in violation of 18 U.S.C. §§ 664(theft from an employee benefit plan), 1343 (wire fraud), and 1956 (money laundering). Viana is believed to have fled to Brazil.

***

[margin note: appearance of bias]

[O]n July 7, 1995, Hook filed his motion requesting that Judge McDade recuse himself from Hook's case and vacate any orders previously issued, claiming that Judge McDade had been influenced by his wife's assessment of Hook's conduct in the *Cannon* litigation, and that there was an appearance of bias. On July 14, 1995, Judge McDade conducted a hearing on this motion and stated in part:

> [L]et me start off by saying I find the motion totally offensive and I consider it to impugn my integrity and [it is] unprofessional for a lawyer to knowingly make a false statement impugning the integrity of the judge ... you have not acted like an officer of the court in filing this motion.

[margin note: Hook's argument]

Judge McDade then questioned Hook under oath. Hook stated that he felt there was an inherent conflict of interest because of Mary McDade's (Judge McDade's wife) representation of Viana, Hook's co-defendant, during the initial stages of the appeal of Judge McDade's grant of summary judgment to Viana and Wittek on a former employee's health insurance claim in *Cannon*. Hook further cited the fact that Mary McDade had questioned in conversation whether Hook, who had represented Viana (and Wittek) during the *Cannon* proceedings, might have exercised bad judgment and committed malpractice in withdrawing as counsel when an appellate brief was due in the Seventh Circuit on behalf of his clients. Hook went on to state that he was "aghast by" Judge McDade's ruling on his motions. After hearing Hook's version, Judge McDade replied that Hook's motions were without merit. Hook also asserted on the record that he believed that Judge McDade gave his arguments "very short shrift" and further complained that the court had denied him the opportunity to file replies to the government's responses to his motions. Following this colloquy, Judge McDade denied Hook's motion to disqualify himself as the presiding judge and the accompanying motion to vacate his orders.

On July 31, 1995, on the date that his trial was to begin, Hook filed the instant petition for a writ of mandamus with this court, requesting that we order Judge McDade to disqualify himself from the case.

II. Discussion

Hook argues that section 455 of Chapter 28 of the United States Code mandates that Judge McDade disqualify himself from Hook's trial. That section provides in pertinent part:

> (a) Any justice, judge, or magistrate of the United States shall disqualify himself in any proceeding in which his impartiality might reasonably be questioned.
>
> (b) He shall also disqualify himself in the following circumstances:
>
> > (1) Where he has a personal bias or prejudice concerning a party, or personal knowledge of disputed evidentiary facts concerning the proceeding; . . .
> >
> > (4) He knows that he, individually or as a fiduciary, or his spouse or minor child residing in his household, has a financial interest in the subject matter in controversy or in a party to the proceeding, or any other interest that could be substantially affected by the outcome of the proceeding.

28 U.S.C. §455.

The district court judge refused to disqualify himself; Hook has petitioned this court to issue a writ of mandamus to order the judge disqualified. Our review of the petition is de novo. *Taylor v. O'Grady*, 888 F.2d 1189, 1201 (7th Cir.1989) (citing *Balistrieri*, 779 F.2d at 1201). We will consider each applicable provision of section 455 in turn.

A. Disqualification Under 28 U.S.C. §455(a)

28 U.S.C. § 455(a) requires a federal judge to "disqualify himself in any proceeding in which his impartiality might reasonably be questioned." We have stated:

> Section 455(a) asks whether a reasonable person perceives a significant risk that the judge will resolve the case on a basis other than the merits. This is an objective inquiry. *Liljeberg v. Health Services Acquisition Corp.*, 486 U.S. 847, 865, 108 S. Ct. 2194, 2205, 100 L. Ed.2d 855 (1988); *New York City Housing Develop. Co. v. Hart*, 796 F.2d 976 (7th Cir.1986); *Pepsico, Inc. v. McMillen*, 764 F.2d 458 (7th Cir.1985). An objective standard is essential when the question is how things appear to the well-informed, thoughtful observer rather than to a hypersensitive or unduly suspicious person. . . Trivial risks are endemic, and if they were enough to require disqualification we would

have a system of preemptory strikes and judge-shopping, which itself would imperil the perceived ability of the judicial system to decide cases without regard to persons. A thoughtful observer understands that putting disqualification in the hands of a party, whose real fear may be that the judge will apply rather than disregard the law, could introduce a bias into adjudication. Thus the search is for a risk substantially out of the ordinary.

In re Mason, 916 F.2d 384, 385-86 (7th Cir.1990).

search is for a risk substantially out of the ordinary [margin note]

Hook argues that Mary McDade, the Judge's wife, formerly represented Carmen Viana, a co-defendant in Hook's criminal trial, and that fact raises the appearance of bias.

As a threshold matter, certainly we agree that a judge's spouse or close relation cannot appear as counsel in any trial or proceedings before that Judge. Further, the Judicial Code of Conduct directs a Judge should be disqualified if the law firm in which his or her spouse is a partner appears before the Judge. *See* Canon 3C(1) of the Judicial Code of Conduct (1994); Advisory Opinion No. 58 (1993). However, we emphasize that neither Mary McDade nor the Quinn firm has ever appeared before Judge McDade in any proceeding relating to the civil suit or the criminal case. The Quinn firm entered the *Cannon* litigation for the sole purpose of reviewing Hook's legal fees submitted to Kemper (Wittek and Viana's insurance company) and represented Viana's interests on appeal in the civil case only after George Hook withdrew from the case. The Quinn firm became involved in the case *after* Judge McDade had ruled, and the insurance company did not challenge the court's decision, but merely sought review of the legal fees that Hook presented to the insurance company for payment.

Further, the *Cannon* case has no bearing on Hook's criminal trial. The issue in *Cannon* was whether an employee had worked sufficient consecutive days at Wittek to qualify for Blue Cross coverage under the terms of Wittek's health insurance plan. In contrast, Hook has been indicted (along with Carmen Viana, Wittek's owner) for illegally transferring funds from Wittek's pension plan. The issues raised in the *Cannon* case concerning an employee's qualification for health insurance benefits are not related to and do not influence the criminal allegations that Hook and Viana stole from the Wittek pension fund. Neither Mary McDade nor the Quinn firm is involved in the criminal trial of Hook and Viana. Finally, Carmen Viana has fled to Brazil, and as far as this record recites she seems unlikely to be a participant in either the criminal trial or any further civil proceedings in *Cannon*.

We fail to see how the involvement of Judge McDade's wife in an unrelated civil suit involving one of the same parties could lead to the appearance of an impartial criminal trial. From the facts in the record, we disagree with Hook that there is any bias that can reasonably be inferred

no bias that can reasonably be inferred [margin note]

impartial criminal trial [margin note]

★ the facts do not lead to the appearance of an [margin note]

from Mary McDade's involvement in the suit that would justify the disqualification of Judge McDade. *See Del Vecchio v. Illinois Dept. of Corrections, 31 F.3d 1363, 1375 (7th Cir.1994)* (en banc) (holding that recusal was not required in a murder trial on the ground that the judge had prosecuted the defendant for a different murder fourteen years earlier); *United States v. Barnes*, 909 F.2d 1059, 1072 (7th Cir.1990) (holding that bias alleged to have been caused by past cases (and the present case) in which the judge and litigant were involved was not grounds for the judge's disqualification).

B. Disqualification Under 28 U.S.C. §455(b)(1)

A federal judge must disqualify himself from a proceeding, "*[w]here he has a personal bias or prejudice concerning a party...*" 28 U.S.C. §455(b)(1). In determining whether a judge must disqualify himself under 28 U.S.C. §455(b)(1), "the question is whether a reasonable person would be convinced the judge was biased." *Lac du Flambeau Indians v. Stop Treaty Abuse-Wis.*, 991 F.2d 1249, 1255 (7th Cir.1993) (citing*Taylor*, 888 F.2d at 1201;*Balistrieri*, 779 F.2d at 1202)."The negative bias or prejudice from which the law of recusal protects a party must be grounded in some personal animus or malice that the judge harbors against him, of a kind that a fair-minded person could not entirely set aside when judging certain persons or causes." *Balistrieri*, 779 F.2d at 1201. Moreover, recusal is required only if actual bias or prejudice is "proved by compelling evidence." *Id.* at 1202. Bias against a litigant must, however, arise from an extrajudicial source:

[J]udicial remarks during the course of a trial that are critical or disapproving of, or even hostile to, counsel, the parties, or their cases, ordinarily do not support a bias or partiality challenge. They *may* do so if they reveal an opinion that derives from an extrajudicial source; and they *will* do so if they reveal such a high degree of favoritism or antagonism as to make fair judgment impossible.... *Not* establishing bias or partiality, however, are expressions of impatience, dissatisfaction, annoyance, and even anger, that are within the bounds of what imperfect men and women, even after having been confirmed as federal judges, sometimes display. A judge's ordinary efforts at courtroom administration-even a stern and short-tempered judge's efforts at courtroom administration-remain immune.

Liteky v. United States, 510 U.S. 540, 127 L. Ed. 2d 474, 114 S.Ct. 1147, 1157 (1994). *See also United States v. Griffin*, 84 F.3d 820, 831 (7th Cir.1996).

In the present case, Hook's claim of bias is rooted in Judge McDade's rulings and comment that he found the disqualification motion offensive.

Hook also cites the fact that Mary McDade questioned Hook's handling of the *Cannon* matter. According to Hook, Mary McDade's legal evaluation and suggestion of possible malpractice should be imputed to her husband, Judge McDade, and are therefore evidence of the judge's prejudice. Hook also argues that Judge McDade's pre-trial rulings, such as Hook's motion for a bill of particulars and motion to transfer the case from the Central to the Northern District of Illinois, demonstrate his prejudice against Hook.

As noted above, unless there are exceptional circumstances, judicial rulings are grounds for appeal, not disqualification. After scrutiny of the record, we find nothing in Judge McDade's rulings or comments that demonstrate an alleged extrajudicial personal prejudice against Hook. The judge stated that he considered Hook's motion for disqualification "offensive," and thought that it "impugn[ed]" his integrity. In addition, the judge, after reviewing Hook's motion for disqualification, directed Hook to testify about the alleged bias under oath because he believed that Hook had failed to act as an ethical member of the bar in filing the recusal motion. *See In re Kelly*, 808 F.2d 549, 552 (7th Cir.1986) (observing that "lawyers who make statements to courts under oath concerning the conduct of fellow lawyers and judges and other participants in the administration of justice [must] be scrupulous regarding the accuracy of those statements."). While Judge McDade's remarks are critical of Hook, the Judge was reacting, albeit strongly, to a disqualification motion brought on the eve of trial concerning himself vis a vis his wife's participation in an unrelated trial, a motion that claimed that the Judge ruled against Hook's pre-trial motions based on personal prejudice. We can reasonably infer that the Judge's reaction (and surprise at the motion) demonstrates that he had no idea that Mary McDade had any prior involvement with either Viana or Hook. From our review of the transcript we do not believe that the Judge's comments in reaction to Hook's accusation of impartiality reflect a bias or prejudice gained from outside the courtroom that would lead a reasonable observer to conclude that McDade is incapable of ruling fairly in a case involving Hook. *See Liteky*, 114 S.Ct. at 1157. Judge McDade's comments in the present case are clearly not of this nature and thus are not grounds for recusal. *See Federal Trade Comm'n v. Amy Travel Svc., Inc.*, 875 F.2d 564 (7th Cir.), *cert. denied*, 493 U.S. 954, 110 S.Ct. 366, 107 L.Ed.2d 352 (1989) (holding that friction between a judge and counsel was not grounds for disqualification); *In re Drexel Burnham*, 861 F.2d at 1316 (holding that sharp criticism of petitioner's counsel's behavior is not grounds to find personal bias).

C. Disqualification Under 28 U.S.C. § 455(b)(4)

A federal judge is required to disqualify himself from a case, if "[h]e knows that he ... or his spouse ... has a financial interest in the subject matter of the controversy or in a party to the proceeding, or any other interest that could be substantially affected by the outcome of the proceeding." 28 U.S.C. §455(b)(4). Financial interest is defined as "ownership of a legal or equitable interest, however small...." 28 U.S.C. §455(d)(4). However, "where an interest is not direct, but is remote, contingent, or speculative, it is not the kind of interest which reasonably brings into question a judge's impartiality." In re Drexel Burnham, 861 F.2d at 1313. Hook argues that here that the judge's wife has a financial interest in the outcome of this case because her firm represents the insurance company of Carmen Viana, the absent co-defendant of Hook.

The Quinn law firm, of which Mary McDade is a partner, as a result of its representation of Viana's insurance company, did represent the financial interests of Carmen Viana in an appeal of a civil suit concerning health insurance. We fail to understand how Hook can allege that Judge McDade has a financial interest in the outcome of a criminal trial of Hook and Viana, whose issues have no relation to those raised in the civil case. As a threshold matter, Carmen Viana has fled the country and seems unlikely to participate in either the criminal trial or civil proceedings in the *Cannon* litigation. Secondly, Hook's conviction (or non-conviction) would not seem to alter in any tangible fashion the business relationship between the Quinn firm and the insurance company. Hook has not demonstrated, and we are hard-pressed to envisage, any financial interest of Mary McDade's that is directly affected by the criminal trial of George Hook. We fail to understand under what circumstance Judge McDade might conceivably have a financial interest in the subject matter in controversy or in a party involved in Hook's case. *See In re Drexel Burnham*, 861 F.2d at 1316-17 (holding that district court judge has no financial interest warranting disqualification where his wife stood to gain $30 million in leveraged buyout of her family's business financed in part by an investment bank that is a co-defendant in an insider trading lawsuit brought by the Securities and Exchange Commission).

III. Conclusion

After review, we hold that the record is devoid of any facts that would tend to demonstrate bias or an appearance of bias on the part of Judge McDade. However, in light of Hook's personal accusation against Judge McDade of bias, the judge might want to consider whether the remote possibility of the *appearance* of bias might exist as a result of this attack on his integrity. We repeat that we neither infer nor suggest that Judge McDade should recuse himself for the record reveals absolutely no evidence of even an appearance of personal bias; the decision lies clearly with the judge.

Hook's petition for a writ of mandamus is
DENIED.

Questions and Comments

1. In *Hook*, the court determined the plaintiff failed to provide compelling evidence that would establish Judge McDade's personal bias based solely on his comments. Do you agree? Is it possible this determination may cause litigants to fear bringing valid recusal motions because they could anger judges while the odds of prevailing seem extremely low?

2. Under Canon 2.3 of the Model Code of Judicial Conduct, "A judge shall perform the duties of judicial office, including administrative duties, without bias or prejudice." Additionally, Comment 2 emphasizes a "judge must avoid conduct that may reasonably be perceived as prejudiced or biased." Whose perception should be the determining factor under these circumstances: is it the perception of the parties and/or their lawyers, lay persons or other judges?

3. The 7th Circuit Court of Appeals applied a *de novo* standard of review in *Hook*. Many circuit courts have used an *abuse of discretion* standard in evaluating whether a trial court judge should have recused herself from the proceeding. *See* Richard K. Neumann, Jr., *Conflicts of Interest in Bush v. Gore: Did Some Justices Vote Illegally?*, 16 GEO. J. LEGAL ETHICS 375, 389 (2003). Would an appellate court be in a better position than a trial court judge when determining the allegations of bias or prejudice in a litigant's recusal motion? Explain your position.

4. Canons 2.11(A)(2) & (3) set out specific instances when a judge must recuse herself based on her spouse's conduct or interest relating to or affected by the proceeding. After reading comment [4] to Rule 2.11, assume a judge's spouse was a partner in a law firm representing a party before that judge. Would the spouse's interests likely be substantially affected by the proceeding? How should the judge proceed under the circumstances?

IN RE NATIONAL LEGAL PROFESSIONAL ASSOCIATION
United States District Court (N.D.N.Y. 2010)
No. 1:08-MC-101 (NAM/DRH), 2010 WL 624045

Mordue, Chief Judge.

Introduction

Presently before the Court is United States Magistrate Judge David R. Homer's Report and Recommendation (Dkt. No. 21) concerning the activities of National Legal Professional Associates ("NLPA") in connection with the criminal prosecutions of Cash Whitmore and King S. Burden in *United States v. Whitmore,* Case No. 1:08-CR-385, in this district. Magistrate Judge Homer concludes that these activities did not constitute practicing law and recommends that no order be issued enjoining NLPA from the unauthorized practice of law in this district or compelling NLPA to refund any fees paid by the families of Whitmore and Burden. Not surprisingly, NLPA has interposed no objection. Upon review of the matter, the Court concludes that NLPA engaged in the unauthorized practice of law in connection with these two defendants.

Accordingly, the Court issues an order enjoining NLPA and all individuals associated therewith from engaging in the unauthorized practice of law in the Northern District of New York and directing the return of the fees paid by the families of Cash Whitmore and King S. Burden, defendants in *United States v. Whitmore,* Case No. 1:08-CR-385.

Background

Magistrate Judge Homer's Report and Recommendation sets forth the background of the matter. Very briefly, the matter stems from the requests for appointment of new counsel made by two defendants, Cash Whitmore and King S. Burden ("defendants"), both charged in the same criminal complaint with conspiracy to distribute cocaine base . . . Magistrate Judge Homer held hearings regarding the requests (*id.,* Dkt. Nos. 49, 50), and learned in both cases that the defendants' families had contracted to receive services from NLPA and that NLPA had mailed materials to defendants.

At the September 29, 2008 hearing regarding Cash Whitmore's request for appointment of new counsel in place of Timothy Austin, Esq., Assistant Federal Public Defender, the following colloquy took place between Whitmore and Magistrate Judge Homer:

THE DEFENDANT: Been doing my legal studies in the library and my mother also hired like a legal team, but they can't represent me though. Information I got from the law library and legal team just don't add up to what Mr. Austin (inaudible)...

THE COURT: When you say a legal team, are you talking about lawyers?

THE DEFENDANT: It's like a team of lawyers, but they can't represent you. Something called NLPA. National Legal Professional Associates.

THE COURT: Is this a service that your mother has paid for?

THE DEFENDANT: Yes. Right now (inaudible)

THE COURT: All-right. So have you received some advice through your mother from this legal team?

THE DEFENDANT: The legal team themself sent me package, legal stuff to read, and I believe they call the law library in jail, and I feel a few helpful things from books that I'm reading, packages that they sent me, and um...

THE COURT: Can you give me an example?

THE DEFENDANT: Might be—not off the top. I'm trying to think of (inaudible). Might be talking about on the rap sheet, how to beat your client's rap sheet. I really—I can't pinpoint things right now. (inaudible) Legal material with me though. How to beat your client rap sheet. And Mr. Austin, he might say something different, the papers might tell me something different right now, things of that nature.

***[Redacted]

THE COURT: And that this legal team is recommending that you go to trial and seek a verdict of not guilty, is that correct?

THE DEFENDANT: No. They not allowed to give you that type of advice; go to trial or take a plea; they not allowed to give that type of advice. If I ask them-if—I go to the law library and find information out, they'll send me further information about the law.

***

THE DEFENDANT: I feel there's a mistake on my-I feel a mistake on my rap sheet that say I have two felony when I should have one. Things

I'm reading from the law library and NLPA also saying things that I feel, Mr. Austin is saying that this is the reason why.

***

THE COURT: All right. Mr. Whitmore, Mr. Austin said that there might be some other reasons why you would seek new counsel. Was there anything you wanted to tell me?

THE DEFENDANT: [Redacted.] To my knowledge I don't understand why don't want to work with somebody to make their job a little easier.

[Redacted.] I didn't feel like he was working real in a timely fashion, I guess you could say. I ask him—

THE COURT: Well, what do you know about NLPA? This is the first I've ever heard of their existence.

THE DEFENDANT: There's a few people in Albany jail who have them. And they also send me a—I guess like a report of cases they won and people they help out, like things of that nature.

THE COURT: Do you know if they're lawyers?

THE DEFENDANT: They have their own senior lawyers but they use like a—I don't know how to pronounce it. They work as your lawyer but like they—I'm not sure Mr. Austin got in contact with them, but they was able to work aside of him. (inaudible) I know put aside working, finding out things, he ain't one to do that. So basically they work with me and my family. But they have also their own lawyers that I have to hire myself.

***

THE COURT: ... [Y]ou probably haven't talked to any of them, have you?

THE DEFENDANT: Yes.

THE COURT: You have talked to them?

THE DEFENDANT: Yeah.

At King S. Burden's November 7, 2008 hearing regarding whether he should be given new counsel to replace his assigned lawyer, James E. Long, Esq., the transcript includes the following:

302 | Connecting Ethics & Practice

THE COURT: What's the National Legal Professional whatever it is?

THE DEFENDANT: They just some people that my mom had paid to work with my lawyer. It's a group of lawyers and associates that sent me all kind of paperwork and stuff and just make sure my lawyer is doing his job.

THE COURT: What's the paperwork?

THE DEFENDANT: Different kind of packets and motions that I could put in and, um, basically regular legal documents that I could go to the law library and find out myself.

THE COURT: Do they—did they advise you as to what the contents of your Plea Agreement would look like?

THE DEFENDANT: No, your Honor.

THE COURT: Did they tell you what you should ask for?

THE DEFENDANT: No, your Honor. Said it's up to the Judge's discretion. It's under the Judge's discretion.

THE COURT: Did they give you legal advice?

THE DEFENDANT: Yes.

(Pause ...)

THE DEFENDANT: Nothing nothing really concerning my case just, um what kind of motion I could file or—basically I asked them a question, and then they send me that package from what I asked them cuz I can't call my lawyer so I can't call him and ask him. I called the National Legal Professional and they—I asked them a question that I would have asked my lawyer if I was able to contact him over the phone.

On November 12, 2008, the Court referred the matters to Magistrate Judge Homer for further proceedings as necessary regarding the possible unauthorized practice of law by NLPA (Dkt. No. 1). On November 17, 2008, Magistrate Judge Homer issued an Order to Show Cause (Dkt. No. 2) directing NLPA to show cause why an order should not be entered enjoining NLPA and any individuals associated therewith from engaging in the unauthorized practice of law in the Northern District of New York and directing the return of the fees paid by defendants' families.

***

Among the inherent powers incidental to all courts is the power to regulate and discipline attorneys who appear before it. *See* Chambers v. NASCO, Inc., 501 U.S. 32, 43 (1991). Such power extends to enjoining and sanctioning the unauthorized practice of law. *See* United States v. Johnson, 327 F.3d 554, 560 (7th Cir.2003). In the exercise of its inherent powers, this Court holds that NLPA engaged in the unauthorized practice of law in its relationship with Whitmore and Burden in *United States v. Whitmore,* Case No. 1:08-CR-385; rejects the Report and Recommendation as contrary to law; issues an injunction prohibiting NLPA from engaging in the unauthorized practice of law in the Northern District; and directs NLPA to refund the monies received for its services to Whitmore and Burden.

Facts

Cash Whitmore

July 7, 2008 Mailing

The affidavit of H. Wesley Robinson, Director of Client Services for NLPA, states:

> Defendant Cash Whitmore contacted NLPA by telephone on July 7, 2008. He advised that he was facing a federal conspiracy case and that he was interested in having any assistance that NLPA's attorneys could provide to his lawyer. He provided his family's contact information and asked that NLPA send him and his family information about the assistance which could be provided. Accordingly, NLPA sent to Mr. Whitmore and his mother a letter explaining the services that could be provided by NLPA.

The July 7, 2008 letter NLPA sent to Whitmore explained the two levels of service as follows:

> For the past two decades, NLPA's attorneys have provided consulting and research assistance to thousands of lawyers throughout the United States in preparing for the defense of a case at trial. NLPA does not replace your attorney but rather adds to the defense team to assist your counsel in your case. We have two different levels of assistance that we can provide to you:
>
> • Preliminary Pre-trial Consultation (PPT) 2500 upfront & then 4950
> • Full Pre-trial Services (FPT)
>
> Each of these levels of services is outlined in the enclosed information. The first level, which we call "Preliminary Pre-Trial Consultation" only costs $2,500.00. This is a nonrefundable fee. This Preliminary Pre-trial

Consultation involves NLPA helping to keep you and your family advised as to what is happening in your case and liaison with you and your family on many very important aspects of your defense. As your attorney is busy researching, drafting, and preparing your case, NLPA can serve a supporting role to enhance communication. Please review the enclosed information so you can get a clearer understanding as to the important assistance this level of service can provide to you and your family.

Once we are retained for the PPC, we will contact retained counsel. If you have appointed counsel, we must wait to receive communication from your attorney that he or she is willing to accept our attorney's assistance. We will explain to your counsel how NLPA's attorneys can assist the defense team as you prepare for trial. If your counsel agrees to include NLPA in the legal arm of your defense team, then your family can pay the remaining balance of our total $4,950.00 pre-trial research fee. We will then shift the focus of our assistance to the research and consulting that will directly impact your pre-trial process. This assistance, as outlined below, would include the drafting of pretrial motions that are case specific to your circumstance, legal research addressing defenses you may have, consulting with counsel as to the investigation of the defense, and the like.

Of course, if you already know that counsel is willing to have NLPA assist in your defense as a consultant, we can move quickly to this second stage based upon a $4,950.00 research fee.

Enclosed with the July 7, 2008 letter was a six-page "Newsletter" from NLPA dated Summer 2008, headed, "Pre-trial and the Need for a Strong Defense Team." The first paragraph stated:

Michael Jackson, Robert Blake, and O.J. Simpson aren't the only people who can benefit from the team approach in a criminal case. You can too and it costs less than you may think. National Legal Professional Associates (NLPA) is a technical legal research and consulting firm, owned by attorneys, and dedicated to the professional mission of providing consultation, research, and related work product to members of the Bar. Although our attorney research department stands ready to assist in all phases of pre-trial management, our expertise extends from pre-trial assistance, to sentencing, appeals and all types of post-conviction relief litigation. Our research is prepared by licensed attorneys.

In describing the PPS level of service, the Newsletter stated in part:

Examples of the services that NLPA can provide to you and your family, should you retain us for this level of assistance, are as follows:

a. We will provide you and your family with information concerning exactly what is happening in the case. This will include following up with the court to advise you of what pre-trial motions have been filed, responses filed by the government, and the status of the case in general. In this way, by having NLPA involved, we can assist you in getting a clearer understanding of exactly what is happening with the case. This will assist you in communicating with your attorney as to what you want him to do in defending your case.

b. We will assist you and your family in getting copies of court documents.

c. If available, we will provide to you with a copy of the Docket Sheet from the court. In this way, you will know exactly what the status of the case is according to the Clerk of Courts records. This will include advising you of approaching deadlines, motions filed by defense counsel or the prosecutor, and any court rulings that have been made on those motions.

***

i. We will provide you and your family with general information that will be extremely helpful to you in understanding the criminal process and how your case will be handled by your attorney and the court. This information can be of benefit to you in explaining to your lawyer what you expect of him and what you want him to do on your behalf in the defense of the charges pending against you.

***

The Newsletter next addressed the FPS level, stating: "[S]hould your attorney be willing to have our lawyers assist him in the actual research and preparation of pretrial motions as well as work with him on the strategy to pursue in your defense, NLPA is happy to provide this additional service."

***

Discussion

It is undisputed that NLPA is not authorized to practice law in the Northern District of New York. The issue before the Court is whether NLPA did practice law here in its interactions with Whitmore and Burden. The Court adopts Magistrate Judge Homer's summary of the applicable law. As Magistrate Judge Homer notes, "[t]he orderly functioning of our judicial system and the protection of our citizens require that legal advice should be offered only by those who possess the requisite qualifications and authorization for the practice of law." *Dacey v. New York Co. Lawyers' Ass'n*, 423 F.2d 188, 189 (2d Cir. 1969). Courts possess the inherent power to control admission to the bar and to discipline attorneys who appear before them. *See Chambers v. NASCO, Inc.*, 501 U.S. 32, 43, 111 S. Ct. 2123, 115 L. Ed. 2d 27 (1991). Such power extends to enjoining and sanctioning the unauthorized practice of law. *See United States v. Johnson*, 327F.3d 554, 560 (7th Cir. 2003). Rules for admission to the practice of law, rules regulating the conduct of the bar, and laws against the unauthorized practice of law were enacted "to protect the public from ignorance, inexperience and unscrupulousness." *People v. Alfani*, 227 N.Y. 334, 339, 125 N.E. 671, 38 N.Y. Cr. 117 (1919).

In considering what constitutes the practice of law, New York's high court observed:

> There are certain fundamental requirements and features which, according to our conception, in this state attend and surround the practice of law and rendition of truly legal services. These are the possession of sufficient knowledge and skill, the existence of a relationship of trust and confidence upon which the client may securely rely, and the power of courts to use summary proceeding, if necessary, to enforce on the part of the attorney observance of the obligations and duties growing out of this relationship.

People v. Title Guarantee & Trust Co., 227 N.Y. 366, 372, 125 N.E. 666, 38 N.Y. Cr. 128 (1919). It has long been the law in New York that the practice of law includes giving legal advice as well as appearing in court and holding oneself out to be a lawyer. *See El Gemayel v. Seaman*, 72 N.Y.2d 701, 706, 533 N.E.2d 245, 536 N.Y.S.2d 406 (1988); *Spivak v. Sachs*, 16 N.Y.2d 163, 166, 211 N.E.2d 329, 263 N.Y.S.2d 953(1965); *Alfani*, 227 N.Y. at 337-38; *see also Spanos v. Skouras Theatres Corp.*, 364 F.2d 161, 165 (2d Cir. 1966). More specifically, the practice of law includes "the rendering of legal advice and opinions directed to particular clients." *Matter of Rowe*, 80 N.Y.2d 336, 341-42, 604 N.E.2d 728, 590 N.Y.S.2d 179 (1992). In *Rowe*, New York's high court held that publishing an article in the "Journal of Urban Psychiatry" on the legal rights of psychiatric patients who refuse treatment did not constitute the practice of law. The court observed: "Respondent's article sought only to present the state of the law to any reader interested in the subject. Inasmuch as it neither rendered advice to a particular person nor was intended to respond to known needs and circumstances of a larger group, its publication did not constitute the practice of law." *Id.* at 342. Similarly, New York has held that authoring a book, "How to Avoid Probate," which was sold to the public at large, did not constitute the practice of law, on the ground that:

> There is no personal contact or relationship with a particular individual. Nor does there exist that relation of confidence and trust so necessary to the status of attorney and client. This is the essential of legal practice —the representation and the advising of a particular person in a particular situation.

Matter of New York County Lawyers Association v. Dacey, 28 A.D.2d 161, 283 N.Y.S.2d 984, 998 (1st Dep't 1967) (Stevens, J., dissenting), *aff'd on the dissenting opinion*, 21 N.Y.2d 694, 234 N.E.2d 459, 287 N.Y.S.2d 422 (1967); *accord State v. Winder*, 42 A.D.2d 1039, 348 N.Y.S.2d 270 (4th Dep't 1973) (layperson's sale of "Divorce Yourself Kit" was not practice of law, but giving "legal advice in the course of personal contacts concerning particular problems which might arise in the preparation and presentation of the purchaser's asserted matrimonial cause of action or pursuit of other legal remedies and assistance in the preparation of necessary documents" was practice of law); *see generally In re Gaftick*, 333 B.R. 177, 188 (Bankr. E.D.N.Y. 2005); *In re Herren*, 138 B.R. 989, 995-96 (Bankr. D.Wyoming 1992).

NLPA contends it did not practice law in Whitmore's and Burden's cases because it did not give "case-specific" advice. "Case-specific" is not a term used in applicable case law. Rather, the question, as articulated in *Rowe* and *Dacey*, is whether NLPA rendered legal advice directed to each defendant regarding his particular situation. As set forth below, the Court finds that it did.

The Evidence

First Mailings

In reviewing the evidence supporting its conclusion that NLPA engaged in the practice of law in its relations with defendants, the Court begins with the promotional materials sent by NLPA in its first mailings to Whitmore and Burden, on July 7, 2008 and July 14, 2008, respectively. These materials comprised a cover letter to each defendant and a number of enclosures, including a NLPA Newsletter dated Summer 2008 headed "Pre-trial and the Need for a Strong Defense Team" (Summer 2008 Newsletter") and an NLPA memorandum headed "Victory List." In these materials, NLPA held itself out as a company "owned and staffed by licensed attorneys" and having unique legal expertise that could greatly enhance a criminal defendant's defense. For example, in the Summer 2008 Newsletter, NLPA stated: "Through our involvement in literally thousands of cases, coupled with our national professional staff, NLPA has developed an unique and unmatched expertise in pretrial, trial, sentencing, appellate, and post-conviction matters." There are numerous similar examples. Also, the enclosed NLPA "Victory List" memorandum stated: "The following is a list of just some of the cases in which NLPA has provided research assistance to counsel as a member of the Defense Team. With the help of NLPA's experienced team of investigators, paralegals, and attorneys, the cases listed below all resulted in a victory for the defendant." (Emphasis in original.) Attached was a list of over 200 cases, mostly federal, with index numbers ranging from 1990 to the late 2000's.

Besides describing NLPA's unique legal expertise, these materials offered to enter into a relationship of trust and confidence with each defendant. In the first letter, NLPA proposed to "serve a supporting role to enhance communication" during the PPS stage and to keep each defendant and his family advised "as to what is happening in [his] case and liaison with [defendant and his family] on many very important aspects of [his] defense." The enclosed Summer 2008 Newsletter offered in the PPS stage to "follow [] up with the court to advise [defendants and their families] of what pre-trial motions have been filed, responses filed by the government, and the status of the case in general" and to assist defendants and their families "in getting a clearer understanding of exactly what is happening with the case."

***

Once NLPA received payments from defendants' families, it sent a second packet of materials to Whitmore on July 23, 2008, and to Burden on July 25, 2008. These mailings included practically identical letters from NLPA acknowledging receipt of partial PPS payments and introducing Konerman as case manager. The letters indicated that NLPA would perform original legal research for defendants during PPS. In particular, the second letter from NLPA to each defendant referred to PPS payments as "NLPA's research fee," and described the case manager as "your main contact at NLPA, acting as a connection **between you, as the client, and the NLPA's research staff.**" (Emphasis added.)

***

NLPA's promotional materials repeatedly emphasized that NLPA research was performed by attorneys. According to the second letter, then, during the PPS stage, NLPA's research staff—that is, its lawyers—would perform original legal research at each defendant's request addressing specific issues arising in his case.

Subsequent Mailings

Having entered into the PPS relationship and introduced Konerman in the second mailings, NLPA began providing PPS services. Konerman sent two packets of legal materials to each defendant: to Whitmore on July 31, 2008 and August 27, 2008, and to Burden on August 4, 2008 and August 12, 2008. In these mailings, Konerman sent each defendant copies of his docket sheet and mailed him articles and other materials pertinent to what NLPA knew about his particular situation and in response to his questions. 16 In addition, NLPA sent Whitmore an NLPA memorandum on September 11, 2008.

Most of the materials Konerman sent were either memoranda from NLPA or articles written by lawyers who had no apparent connection to

NLPA. Most either purported to explain the law applicable to a certain issue, such as pretrial release, or recommended specific defense tactics, such as placing certain language in a plea agreement. All addressed a particular topic in general or hypothetical terms. The articles dated as far back as 1993 and included several items on sentencing that predated *United States v. Booker*, 543 U.S. 220, 125 S. Ct. 738, 160 L. Ed. 2d 621 (2005).

The materials NLPA sent Whitmore included two letters from Konerman with extensive enclosures, apparently sent in response to Whitmore's questions. In the first letter, dated July 31, 2008, Konerman noted: "[Y]ou have communicated with our office that you cannot decide whether to enter a plea in your case or take your case to trial" and stated: "We wanted to take this opportunity to send you some information that may be of assistance to you concerning plea negotiations." Enclosed were articles on plea and sentencing issues, including articles by public defenders and an assistant United States attorney about federal plea agreements, and three undated NLPA memoranda with the following headings: "How to Avoid the Use of Dismissed Charges from an Indictment in Determining Your Client's Sentence"; "Techniques for Enforcing Stipulations in Plea Agreements at Sentencing -- Another NLPA Victory!"; and "Remedies Available to Defendants Who Have Waived Their Appellate or § 2255 Post Conviction Rights in a Plea Agreement." It does not appear that NLPA sent any of these items to Burden.

***

Finally, on September 11, 2008, NLPA sent Whitman an NLPA newsletter headed: "Great News for Crack Case Defendants and Their Families: New Sentencing Guidelines Go into Effect. BOP Projects 20,000 Defendants Eligible for Early Release!" discussing *Kimbrough v. United States* 552 U.S. 85, 128 S. Ct. 558, 169 L. Ed. 2d 481 (2007), thus advising Whitmore about the law.

***

Although Whitmore understood that NLPA could not "represent" him, he viewed its mailings as information sent by the "legal team" about the law applicable to his particular situation. Similarly, Burden described NLPA to Magistrate Judge Homer as "a group of lawyers and associates that sent me all kind of paperwork and stuff and just make sure my lawyer is doing his job." When asked if NLPA gave him legal advice, Burden answered "Yes," then, after a pause, stated: "Nothing nothing really concerning my case just, um what kind of motion I could file or -basically I asked them a question, and then they send me that package from what I asked.... I asked them a question that I would have asked my lawyer if I was able to contact him over the phone."

Analysis

Based on the above, the Court finds that NLPA engaged in the practice of law in its relationships with defendants. NLPA held itself out as an expert in criminal defense law, entered into a relationship of trust and confidence with each defendant, obtained information from him about his particular case, mailed him letters and legal materials purporting to contain reliable information about the law applicable to specific aspects of his particular situation or responding to his questions, and charged a substantial fee for doing so. The nature of the services provided by NLPA were those of a legal advisor upon whose information and recommendations each defendant could rely in his particular case. It is immaterial whether the materials were sent by a lawyer or by a case manager; in the circumstances, they bore the imprimatur of having been selected and approved by a lawyer or under a lawyer's supervision. It is also immaterial that (with the possible exception of Konerman's letters) the mailings comprised already-existing materials, not original research prepared for each defendant; NLPA in its role as legal advisor selected and sent different materials to each defendant for the purpose of providing him with reliable information about the law applying to aspects of his particular situation and, in some instances, recommending certain actions. As such, the mailings constituted "legal advice and opinions directed to particular clients[,]" and did not simply "present the state of the law to any reader interested in the subject." *Rowe*, 80 N.Y.2d at 341-42.

It is true that a layperson might have found the same articles on the internet and mailed them to defendants. It is unlikely, however, that defendants would have relied on the articles as containing legal advice about their particular cases—or that their families would have agreed to pay $2,500—were it not for NLPA's representations about its legal expertise and the nature of its services. Each defendant here reasonably viewed NLPA's mailings as advice from NLPA's lawyers about the law pertaining to his particular situation. Indeed, each relied on the advice to such an extent that he no longer trusted the advice given by his own lawyer. In considering the implications of NLPA's conduct, the Court notes that the materials frequently interfered in the relationship between defendants and defense counsel. For example, the materials included recommendations as to how defense counsel should handle certain legal matters; in fact, Burden viewed NLPA's role as "mak[ing] sure his lawyer was doing his job." NLPA went so far as to suggest that defense lawyers who refused to use NLPA's services should be replaced; the Summer 2008 Newsletter included in the initial mailings stated: "[I]f you want our assistance and ... your attorney declines to work with NLPA, you will need to engage an attorney who values NLPA's services." (Emphasis added.) As a result of NLPA's mailings, both defendants requested and obtained new counsel, although Magistrate Judge Homer stated in both cases that defendants already had excellent representation. The expense and delay involved in the substitution of counsel creates a burden on the orderly functioning of the judicial system, particularly regarding the courts' control of their calendars and the provision of assigned counsel and public defender services.

Even more importantly, NLPA's interference in the defense of defendants' cases raises serious issues regarding the protection of defendants' interests. In its guise as a provider of services that do not constitute the practice of law, NLPA has evaded supervision by the bar associations and courts and avoided the strictures imposed by the New York Rules of Professional Conduct. Of particular concern are the lack of supervision of fee arrangements, the absence of protection against conflicts of interest in simultaneous representation of multiple clients, and the inapplicability of the attorney-client privilege to information given to NLPA by defendants.

***

Conclusion

It is therefore

. . .

ORDERED that NLPA, its representatives, and all individuals associated therewith are hereby enjoined from engaging in the unauthorized practice of law in the Northern District of New York. . .

Questions and Comments

1. In determining whether non-lawyers are engaging in the unauthorized practice of law, a court must determine what activities constitute the "practice of law." Was the court's conclusion that NLPA engaged in the unauthorized practice of law based on the nature of its services, or was it due to the criminal defendant's reliance on NLPA's representations?

2. Explain the actual test/standard, if any, that was applied by the court in this case in order to define the "practice of law."

3. The court enjoined NLPA from continuing to engage in the unauthorized practice of law and further ordered NLPA to refund all fees paid on behalf of Cash Whitmore and King S. Burden. In addition to these consequences, non-lawyers who engage in the unauthorized practice of

law can be subject to contempt or criminal conviction. Do you think such an approach benefits the legal profession and the public in general?

SATTERWHITE V. STATE
Court of Criminal Appeals of Texas (1998)
979 S.W.2d 626

McCormick, Judge

Appellant was indicted for violating V.T.C.A. Penal Code, Section 38.122 which makes it an offense for a person, with intent to obtain an economic benefit for himself, to hold himself out as a lawyer unless he is currently licensed to practice law in this State, another state, or a foreign country, and is in good standing with the State Bar of Texas. The indictment alleged that the offense was committed on or about December 13, 1993. On November 15, 1995, a jury found appellant guilty as charged in the indictment and assessed appellant's punishment at confinement in the Institutional Division of the Texas Department of Criminal Justice at a term of four and one-half years, and assessed a $7,500.00 fine.

On direct appeal, the Corpus Christi Court of Appeals affirmed appellant's conviction, rejecting appellant's contention that the evidence was legally insufficient to sustain the jury's verdict. *Satterwhite v. State,* 952 S.W.2d 613 (Tex.App.–Corpus Christi, 1997). The majority held that, "[t]he retroactive effect of the payment of past-due State Bar dues had no effect on appellant's conviction for falsely holding himself out as an attorney while not in good standing with the State Bar." *Id.* at 618. To the contrary, the dissent concluded that appellant's payment of dues retroactively returned him to his former status and good standing with the State Bar and therefore the evidence was legally insufficient to show that appellant was not in good standing with the State Bar at the time of the commission of the offense. *Id.* at 621 (Hinojosa, J. dissenting).

The Court of Appeals' rendition of the facts is correct, therefore we take the liberty to recite them for the benefit of the bench and bar:

> On May 1, 1993, appellant was notified that his annual State Bar dues were due and payable by June 1, 1993. Prior to May 1, 1993, however, appellant was suspended for failure to meet the MCLE requirements. On July 1, 1993, the 30day "grace period" afforded attorneys to pay their bar dues had expired. Appellant was not sent a reminder notice because, as stated above, appellant was already on suspension for noncompliance with the MCLE requirements.

On September 1, 1993, a letter was mailed from the State Bar to appellant notifying appellant that his license to practice law was suspended for nonpayment of State Bar dues. In October 1993, appellant sent two checks to the State Bar. These checks were not written in the correct amount and were returned by the State Bar. Appellant sent another check in November 1993, which was also written for an improper amount and returned. On November 8, 1993 a check was received from appellant in the correct amount, but this check was not paid due to insufficient funds. It was not until January 4, 1994, that appellant finally paid his bar dues in the proper amount.

However, on December 13, 1993, at a time when appellant's license to practice law in Texas was suspended, appellant represented John Lemke as his attorney of record in seven felony criminal cases. For this conduct, appellant was indicted under section 38.122 of the Texas Penal Code for falsely holding himself out as a lawyer. *Satterwhite v. State*, 952 S.W.2d at 614.

In the case before us, a case of first impression, we are faced with the issue of whether a retroactive return to pre-suspension status via the payment of past-due State Bar dues excuses an attorney from prosecution for illegal conduct committed by an attorney during that attorney's period of suspension. We hold that it does not and affirm the decision of the Court of Appeals.

Appellant was convicted for violating Section 38.122 of the Texas Penal Code (Vernon 1994). Section 38.122 provides:

> (a) A person commits an offense if, with intent to obtain an economic benefit for himself or herself, the person holds himself or herself out as a lawyer, unless he or she is currently licensed to practice law in this state, another state, or a foreign country and is in good standing with the State Bar of Texas and the state bar or licensing authority of any and all other states and foreign countries where licensed.
>
> (b) An offense under Subsection (a) of this section is a felony of the third degree.
>
> (c) Final conviction of falsely holding oneself out to be a lawyer is a serious crime for all purposes and acts, specifically including the State Bar Rules."

The record before us reflects that appellant intentionally and knowingly violated Section 38.122. First, appellant intended to obtain an economic benefit for himself by representing Mr. Lemke. Second, appellant held himself out as a lawyer to Lemke. Thirdly, appellant was not in "good standing" with the State Bar at the time he represented John Lemke because he was in default in the payment of his bar dues resulting in the suspension of his law license. Since the language of Section 38.122 provided no exceptions, appellant's prosecution and subsequent felony punishment under the statute was proper.

However, appellant argues that the retroactivity clause of Article III, section 7(A) of the State Bar Rules affects a lawyer's "good standing" insofar as liability under Section 38.122 is concerned. We disagree. Paying delinquent bar dues does not suggest that the attorney is absolved from prosecution for illegal conduct committed during the period of suspension.

Article III, Section 7(A) of the Texas State Bar Rules provides:

> When a member, who has been suspended for nonpayment of fees or assessments, removes such default by payment of fees or assessments then owing, plus an additional amount equivalent to one-half the delinquency, the suspension shall automatically be lifted and the member restored to former status. Return to former status shall be retroactive to inception of suspension, but shall not affect any proceeding for discipline of the member for professional misconduct."
>
> TEX STATE BAR R. art. III, Section 7(A), *reprinted* in TEX. GOV'T CODE ANN., Title 2, subtitle G. app. (Vernon 1983) (emphasis added).

We find that the emphasized language of section 7(A) only affects appellant's ability to resume the status of an active member of the State Bar. Upon payment of his delinquent bar dues, appellant does not have to be readmitted to the Bar, nor does he have to show his qualifications or competence to practice law. At most, the retroactivity clause places appellant in his previous position of being a licensed attorney authorized to practice law in Texas. The language of section 7(A) also indicates that appellant may still face possible administrative discipline by the State Bar for any conduct which occurred prior to the lifting of his suspension. Appellant is still subject to prosecution for illegal conduct committed by him during the period of suspension and any attempt by the State Bar to enact a rule which would alter or negate the Legislature's creation of a criminal offense would be unconstitutional. *See McDonald v. Denton*, 63 Tex. Civ. App. 421, 132 S.W. 823 (1910), *error denied* 104 Tex. 206, 135 S.W. 1148; *Brown Cracker & Candy Co. v. City of Dallas*, 104 Tex. 290, 137 S.W. 342 (1911)(If an executive agency or a local government should take action in the suspension of a law, independently of any delegation by the Legislature, that action could be nullified under Article 1, Section 28 of the Texas Constitution without a consideration of the question of legislative declaration of power.) Therefore, we hold that the retroactivity clause of section 7(A) does not affect appellant's criminal prosecution, but is strictly applicable to administrative proceedings conducted by disciplinary officials with the State Bar.

To support his position, appellant relies upon *Hill v. State*, decided by this Court almost three decades before the adoption of Section 38.122 by the Texas Legislature. Texas Penal Code, Section 38.122, added by Acts 1993, 73rd Leg., ch. 723, Section 5, eff. Sept. 1, 1993. This Court, in *Hill v. State*, 393 S.W.2d 901 (Tex.Cr.App.1965) dealt solely with the issue of whether a defendant who was represented by an attorney during the period of time that the attorney's license was suspended for failure to pay bar dues was entitled to a new trial because of ineffective assistance of counsel. In *Hill*, this Court concluded that the status of a delinquent attorney not being a member of the State Bar of Texas does not place him in the position of being unlicensed to practice law in this State. *Id.* at 904. We further noted that "he [a delinquent attorney] only has to pay his dues to resume his status as a "practicing lawyer." Such attorney does not have to again show his fitness or qualifications to practice law." *Id.* at 904. This Court also concluded that such attorney "does not have to be re-admitted to the practice," and that "[h]is competency as an attorney has not been diminished." *Id.* at 904. Finally, we stated that the attorney faces no future disbarment proceedings, and he "automatically resumes his status as an active member of the State Bar of Texas." *Id.* at 904.

However, our holding in *Hill* and in another case recently decided by this Court, *Cantu*, can be distinguished from the instant case. Unlike the case at bar where this Court is deciding the issue of whether an attorney's payment of delinquent bar dues and his acts during the period of suspension were validated because his membership in the State Bar was "revitalized" retroactively, *Hill* and *Cantu* deal with whether a criminal defendant received effective assistance of counsel when represented by an attorney not in good standing with the Texas State Bar.

Therefore, we conclude that the Court of Appeals did not err in holding that the evidence was sufficient as a matter of law to sustain the jury's finding that appellant was not in good standing with the State Bar. The retroactive effect of the payment of past-due State Bar dues has no effect on appellant's conviction for falsely holding himself out as an attorney while not in good standing with the State Bar. The judgment of the Court of Appeals is hereby affirmed.

MANSFIELD, Judge, concurring.

I join the opinion of the Court. It is clear from the record that appellant, knowingly and intentionally, falsely held himself out as a lawyer in violation of Texas Penal Code §38.122. The State met its burden of proving, beyond a reasonable doubt, appellant continued to practice law despite having knowledge that he was not in good standing with the State Bar of Texas for failure to pay his dues.

Concern has been expressed that our holding in this case might lead to criminal liability for, potentially, thousands of attorneys who inadvertently send their bar dues in a few days late, whose checks are "lost in the mail" or who, accidently, send a check for the wrong amount. Another situation, quite common, is where the check is returned for insufficient funds when the remitter, in good faith, believed there were sufficient funds in his account to cover the check. I believe this concern is misplaced. The State must prove intentional, knowing or reckless conduct on the part of the accused to obtain a conviction under Texas Penal Code § 38.122; such would rarely be provable in the instances cited in the two previous sentences. In any event, anyone indicted under section 38.122, where such circumstances existed, would have available the defense of mistake of fact under Texas Penal Code § 8.02. With these comments, I join the opinion of the Court.

PRICE, Judge, filed a dissenting opinion joined by BAIRD, OVERSTREET and MEYERS, Judges.

Because I find the majority's statutory analysis flawed, I dissent.

Appellant's State Bar dues were due and payable on June 1, 1993. Following a thirty day grace period, appellant was suspended for failing to pay his bar dues.1 Between October and January, appellant sent a total of four checks to the State Bar, as payment of his dues. However, three of the checks were not written for the correct amount, and one was for the correct amount, but was not paid due to insufficient funds. Finally, on January 4, 1994, appellant paid his bar dues in the proper amount.

On December 13, 1993, appellant represented one John Lemke in seven felony cases. As a result of this, an indictment was filed against appellant on May 27, 1994, and he was subsequently re-indicted, the latter filed on October 17, 1995. Appellant was eventually convicted under Tex. Pen. Code Ann. §38.122 (Vernon 1994), titled "Falsely Holding Oneself Out as a Lawyer."

Ultimately, this is a case of statutory interpretation, based on the interaction between Tex. Pen Code Ann. §38.122 and Tex, State Bar. R. art. III, § 7, reprinted in Tex. Gov't Code Ann., tit. 2, subtit. G app. (Vernon 1988). As we have previously stated, when interpreting a statute, we look to the literal text for its meaning, and we ordinarily give effect to that plain meaning. *Boykin v. State*, 818 S.W.2d 782, 785 (Tex. Crim. App.1991). The only exceptions to this rule are where application of the statute's plain language would lead to absurd consequences that the Legislature could not possibly have intended, or if the plain language is ambiguous. *Id.* §38.122(a) provides that:

> A person commits an offense if, with intent to obtain an economic benefit for himself or herself, the person holds himself or herself out as a lawyer, unless he or she is currently licensed to practice law in this state, another state, or a foreign country and is in good standing with the State Bar of Texas and the state bar or licensing authority of any and all other states and foreign countries where licensed. (emphasis added)

Two things are immediately discernible from the language of the statute. First, the term "currently" only modifies "licensed to practice law"; that is, it does not modify "good standing." Also, the use of the phrase "is in good standing with the State Bar of Texas" indicates that this provision of the penal code fully incorporates, without modification, the State Bar concept of "good standing."

Art. III, § 7(A) of the State Bar Rules provides that:

> When a member, who has been suspended for nonpayment of fees or assessments, removes such default by payment of fees or assessments then owing, plus an additional amount equivalent to one-half the delinquency, the suspension shall automatically be lifted and the member restored to former status. *Return to former status shall be retroactive to inception of suspension, but shall not affect any proceeding for discipline of the member for professional misconduct.* (emphasis added)

It is clear from the language of the rule that an attorney's former status is returned once payment is made, and that it is deemed to apply from the initial date of suspension. However, this retroactivity does not apply in regard to disciplinary measures.

Reading the penal statute and the State Bar Rule together, then appellant's conduct certainly did not fall under the prohibition of § 38.122. When appellant paid his dues on January 4, 1994, his former status of good standing was reinstated and was deemed to go back to July 1, 1993. As a result, appellant does not fit within the prohibition of § 38.122, since on the date that the alleged criminal conduct took place, December 13, 1993, he was deemed, retroactively, to have been in good standing with the Bar.

***

Based on the above, I would hold that the evidence was legally insufficient to sustain the jury's finding that appellant was not in good standing with the State Bar, an essential element of § 38.122. Therefore, I would reverse the judgment of the Court of Appeals and set aside appellant's conviction.

For the foregoing reasons, I dissent.

Questions and Comments

1. The *Satterwhite* case demonstrates how a suspension may have a severe effect on a lawyer's career and even his life. Do you think the magnitude of punishment imposed on the lawyer was justified?

2. Four judges filed a dissent in *Satterwhite*. The dissent opinioned that construing the Texas Penal Code and the Texas State Bar Rules together show, "[i]t is clear from the language of the rule that an attorney's former status is returned once payment is made, and that it is deemed to apply from the initial date of suspension." 979 S.W.2d 626, 631 (Tex. Crim. App. 1998). Therefore, upon payment, the evidence was legally

insufficient to show Satterwhite was not in good standing with the state bar. Do you find the dissent's position to be persuasive?

3. If a lawyer is delinquent in bar dues or continuing legal education credits and is thereafter suspended, do you think honoring that suspension may be more harmful than protective to her client or the public in general? Even if the suspension and resulting consequences are justified, what sort of punishment do you consider appropriate? Would your answer be different if, unlike in *Satterwhite*, an individual attempting to practice law without a valid license was never an attorney to begin with?

D. DISCUSSION QUESTIONS

1. Who disciplines judges when they violate the rules of judicial conduct? Many states have a commission on judicial performance where an individual, lawyer, or another judge may file a complaint against a state court judge. Complaints against federal judges are filed with the clerk of the court of appeals for the specific circuit where the judge is seated, or the chief judge of that circuit may bring a complaint against a judge. These proceedings are filed under the Judicial Conduct and Disability Act. *See* 28 U.S.C. §§351-364.

2. The Model Rule against the unauthorized practice of law has two prongs: (1) a lawyer is subject to discipline for practicing in a jurisdiction where she is not admitted to practice, and (2) a lawyer is subject to discipline for assisting a non-lawyer to engage in the unlicensed practice of law. *See* ABA Model Rule 5.5(a). Are there any options for lawyers when they need to represent clients who are sued in a jurisdiction to which they are not admitted? How does a lawyer file a *pro hac vice* motion and what does it allow her to do? Must the lawyer always gain court approval to practice in another jurisdiction? If court approval is required, does the approval also allow the law partner's subordinate associates to practice law in that jurisdiction?

3. Even when a lawyer is licensed to practice in a particular state, she must consider her relationships with non-lawyers employees and their contact with clients. The Model Rules specify that a lawyer must not assist a non-lawyer in practicing law. Can you think of a scenario when a lawyer's failure to adequately supervise her paralegal would constitute "assisting" him to engage in the unauthorized practice of law?

Theories of Malpractice
Liability

CHAPTER 12:
Malpractice Liability:
Regulating from Outside the
Disciplinary System

Difference in Malpractice
Liability and ABA
Model Rules

Chapter 12:
Malpractice Liability—Regulating from Outside the Disciplinary System

A. INTRODUCTION

The ABA Model Rules of Professional Conduct state, "[a] lawyer, as a member of the legal profession, is a representative of clients, an officer of the legal system and a public citizen having special responsibility for the quality of justice."[1] Although the discussion of whether law practice is a business or profession is ongoing, many would agree it is a combination of both. Similar to medicine or accounting, legal practice is certainly a profession. Practicing law requires a lawyer to put her client's interests ahead of her own. This idea of professionalism and zealous representation of one's client supports the concept of lawyers needing an internalized code of conduct and self-regulation.

The preceding chapters of this book discussed lawyer self-regulation through a licensing board's administration of the rules of professional conduct; however, disciplinary action for failure to follow the code of conduct is not the exclusive avenue for regulating the legal profession. In addition to disciplinary proceedings, lawyers may also find their conduct regulated by judicial decisions over legal malpractice claims.

Legal malpractice claims began to peak in the 1960s and have since become a routine practice in the legal field.[2] Statistically, *every lawyer will be subject to three malpractice claims during her career*.[3] Every year, more than 20 percent of attorneys in private practice are faced with having to defend against legal malpractice actions.[4] Generally, legal malpractice claims are based on allegations of an attorney's tortious conduct or negligent act. To prevail, a client must show that an attorney-client relationship existed, the attorney owed a duty to the client, the lawyer breached that duty, and the breach caused the client injury. *See Smith v.*

---

[1] Model Rules of Prof'l Conduct, Preamble ¶ [1] (2016).
[2] Robert E. Mallen & Jeffrey M. Smith, *Legal Malpractice,* §1:6, at xiii (2014 ed.).
[3] *Id.*
[4] Paul E. Kovacs, *Legal Malpractice Claims, Avoidance and Defense: If an Attorney Who Represents Himself Has A Fool for A Client, Who Are You Representing?*, 61 J. Mo. B. 142 (2005).

McLaughlin, 769 S.E.2d 7, 13 (Va. 2015). "Typically, a legal malpractice claim involves a case within a case, because the legal malpractice plaintiff must establish how the attorney's negligence in the underlying litigation proximately caused the legal malpractice plaintiff's damages." *Id.* at 10. In addition to traditional malpractice claims, various complaints can be brought against attorneys by a former client or by a third party. Examples of such theories include allegations of a lawyer's breach of fiduciary duty, aiding and abetting a client's breach of fiduciary duty, third party beneficiary and others.

The materials in this chapter demonstrate instances in which an attorney's alleged conduct gave or could give rise to a claim of legal malpractice. As you read, consider what changes in our legal system have increased legal malpractice exposure. For example, consider a client's attitude and expectations and how they change with public perception of the profession. In the end, how much responsibility does or should a lawyer take? Also, should we, the lawyers, get defensive about this potential flood of accusations against us or should we practice defensively? Can we think of a way to stay proactive and preempt any possible claims?

B. CASES AND ADDITIONAL READING

BUTLER V. MAYER, BROWN & PLATT
Appellate Court of Illinois (1998)
704 N.E.2d 740

Cahill, Justice.

Plaintiff Frank Butler appeals the trial court's dismissal of his legal malpractice suit against defendant Mayer, Brown & Platt under section 2–619 of the Code of Civil Procedure (735 ILCS 5/2–619 (West 1996)). The trial court ruled that plaintiff's suit was barred by the two-year statute of limitations for claims against attorneys. See 735 ILCS 5/13–214.3(b) (West 1996).

Plaintiff makes two arguments on appeal: (1) the statute of limitations did not begin to run until the appellate court affirmed the adverse judgment against him in the case defendant was hired to try; and (2) even if the statute of limitations began to run when the trial court entered judgment, defendant is estopped from invoking the statute of limitations because of postjudgment reassurances. We find that a question of fact remains about when the statute of limitations began to run and remand for further proceedings.

Plaintiff's verified amended complaint alleges the following. In July 1986, plaintiff and his brother and sister signed an agreement to govern the division of shares they had inherited in six corporations. In a separate shareholder agreement, they created a "put" procedure: each shareholder could require the other shareholders to either purchase the interests of the shareholder who exercised the put or sell the corporation. In April 1989, plaintiff exercised a put for one of the corporations. Plaintiff's brother and sister elected to buy plaintiff's interest, but they failed to do so.

Plaintiff sued his brother and sister to enforce the shareholder agreement. Shortly after a complaint was filed, he hired defendant to represent him in the case. Plaintiff's complaint sought a single remedy: specific performance under the shareholder agreement. The complaint was never amended to add a breach of contract claim for damages. The trial court first granted summary judgment for plaintiff on his right to enforce specific performance of the shareholders' agreement, but set the matter for trial to determine: (1) whether the liability of plaintiff's brother and sister was joint and several; and (2) what the net fair market value of plaintiff's shares was.

Plaintiff alleges that at trial Mayer, Brown & Platt relied on the testimony of only one expert, who had advised the firm that some matters on which he was being asked to testify were outside his expertise.

On January 15, 1993, the trial judge ruled that plaintiff was not entitled to specific performance because he had failed to prove the net fair market value of the shares by clear and convincing evidence. The trial court opined on the record that, given the heightened standard applicable to specific performance cases, a breach of contract suit, where "clear and convincing" proof of damages is not required, might have been more appropriate. But the court suggested that plaintiff could still seek damages under a breach of contract theory.

Plaintiff then sought leave to amend his complaint to add a breach of contract claim. On February 19, 1993, the trial court granted this motion. Plaintiff's brother and sister moved to reconsider. At a June 3, 1993, hearing on the motion to reconsider, the trial court said that it found it "inexplicable *** why there was not a second count filed for breach of contract in addition to specific performance" in the original complaint and noted that allowing plaintiff to amend would create a "grossly inefficient result" because there had been a lengthy trial on the specific performance count involving the same set of facts. The trial court then vacated the February 19, 1993, order and denied plaintiff leave to amend the complaint. The trial court later awarded attorney fees to plaintiff's sister and entered a final judgment on February 1, 1994. The judgment was appealed and affirmed on September 13, 1995. *Butler v. Kent*, 275 Ill. App. 3d 217, 211 Ill. Dec. 737, 655 N.E.2d 1120 (1995).

Plaintiff alleges that he learned of the January 15, 1993, order through the press, before the law firm sent a copy of the trial court's opinion by facsimile. The firm did not tell plaintiff about the judge's oral comments or give plaintiff a copy of the transcript. Attorneys from the firm called plaintiff within a few days and told plaintiff that the court erred and that he would likely prevail on appeal.

Defendant continued to represent plaintiff on appeal. Plaintiff alleges that he spoke with his attorney at the firm at least six times between January 15, 1993, when specific performance was denied, and the date of the appellate court decision. His attorney repeatedly expressed confidence, orally and in writing, that plaintiff would prevail on appeal. Plaintiff alleges that the firm relayed the same opinion through "friends with whom [the firm] regularly communicated about the case." Plaintiff further alleges that the law firm told plaintiff "he would be unable to obtain the services of any other attorneys to represent him [in the case] because *** the law firm would be able to depict [plaintiff] in a manner which would dissuade other attorneys from agreeing to represent and advise [plaintiff]."

Plaintiff filed his complaint against defendant on March 7, 1997, three years and one month after the final trial court judgment. One year and seven months elapsed between the final judgment of the trial court and the appellate affirmance. We address the lapse of time between the trial court judgment and the appellate affirmance later in this opinion to dispose of plaintiff's claim of estoppel.

Plaintiff's complaint alleges legal malpractice, breach of contract and breach of fiduciary duties. The complaint was later amended. The firm moved to dismiss the verified amended complaint under section 2–619 of the Code of Civil Procedure, arguing that plaintiff's claims were barred by the two-year statute of limitations for claims against attorneys. 735 ILCS 5/13–214.3(b) (West 1996). The trial court granted the motion. The court ruled that plaintiff reasonably should have known that he was injured and that the injury was wrongfully caused when final judgment was entered on February 1, 1994. The trial court also ruled that the firm was not estopped from relying on the statute of limitations because the alleged reassurances were opinions, not intentional misrepresentations of fact.

***

A legal malpractice suit must be brought within two years from the time when the plaintiff "knew or reasonably should have known of the injury for which damages are sought." 735 ILCS 5/13–214.3(b) (West 1996). In *Garcia v. Pinto*, 258 Ill. App. 3d 22, 195 Ill. Dec. 795, 629 N.E.2d 103 (1993), we held that "[s]ection 13–214.3 statutorily accepts the discovery rule which serves to trigger a statute of limitations period at the time the injured party knows or reasonably should know that he has suffered an injury which was wrongfully caused." *Garcia*, 258 Ill. App. 3d at 24, 195 Ill. Dec. 795, 629 N.E.2d 103. When a plaintiff should have discovered his injury is ordinarily a question of fact, and judgment as a matter of law should only be entered where the undisputed facts allow for only one conclusion. *Jackson Jordan, Inc. v. Leydig, Voit & Mayer*, 158 Ill. 2d 240, 250, 198 Ill. Dec. 786, 633 N.E.2d 627 (1994); *Nolan v. Johns–Manville Asbestos*, 85 Ill. 2d 161, 171, 52 Ill. Dec. 1, 421 N.E.2d 864 (1981).

The trial court held that the undisputed facts supported only one conclusion: that plaintiff knew or should have known no later than February 1, 1994, that he was injured and his injury was wrongfully caused. Plaintiff argues that he could not have known he had been injured because "he only faced a possibility of damages which could be eliminated by a reversal" until *Butler v. Kent* was affirmed on appeal. But we rejected this argument in *Belden v. Emmerman*, 203 Ill. App. 3d 265, 270, 148 Ill. Dec. 583, 560 N.E.2d 1180 (1990), and in *Zupan v. Berman*, 142 Ill. App. 3d 396, 399, 96 Ill. Dec. 889, 491 N.E.2d 1349 (1986). We held a plaintiff is injured at the time an adverse judgment is entered, even if the amount of damages is uncertain or the judgment might be later reversed. *Belden*, 203 Ill. App. 3d at 270, 148 Ill. Dec. 583, 560 N.E.2d 1180; *Zupan*, 142 Ill. App. 3d at 399, 96 Ill. Dec. 889, 491 N.E.2d 1349. We noted in *Belden* that damages result from an adverse judgment whether or not it is reversed on appeal. *Belden*, 203 Ill. App. 3d at 270, 148 Ill. Dec. 583, 560 N.E.2d 1180. For instance, plaintiff here was assessed attorney fees and hired another attorney to represent him in "anticipation of *** litigation *** to enforce the judgment." But as plaintiff notes, our inquiry does not end with the determination that plaintiff should have known of his injury. We must also address plaintiff's argument that he did not know his injury was wrongfully caused.

Plaintiff argues that even if he was on notice of injury because of the judgment, he could not have known that the adverse ruling by the trial court was wrongfully caused until the appellate court "disproved the law firm's consistent assurances that the trial court, not counsel, had erred." Alternatively, plaintiff argues that a question of fact remains about when he knew or should have known his injury was wrongfully caused.

As plaintiff stresses, we held in *Goodman v. Harbor Market, Ltd.*, 278 Ill. App. 3d 684, 689–90, 215 Ill. Dec. 263, 663 N.E.2d 13 (1995), that a layperson is presumptively unable to discern malpractice as it occurs. Yet a professional opinion that legal malpractice has occurred is not required before a plaintiff is charged with knowing facts that would cause him to believe his injury was wrongfully caused. *Cf. Dancor International, Ltd. v. Friedman, Goldberg & Mintz*, 288 Ill. App. 3d 666, 673, 224 Ill. Dec. 302, 681 N.E.2d 617 (1997). The discovery rule "delay[s] commencement until the person has a reasonable belief that the injury was caused by wrongful conduct, thereby creating an obligation to inquire further on that issue."

Dancor, 288 Ill. App. 3d at 673, 224 Ill. Dec. 302, 681 N.E.2d 617. "At some point the injured person becomes possessed of sufficient information concerning his injury and its cause to put a reasonable person on inquiry to determine whether actionable conduct is involved. [T]his is usually a question of fact." *Knox College v. Celotex Corp.*, 88 Ill. 2d 407, 416, 58 Ill. Dec. 725, 430 N.E.2d 976 (1981). See also *Betts v. Manville Personal Injury Settlement Trust*, 225 Ill. App. 3d 882, 896, 167 Ill. Dec. 1063, 588 N.E.2d 1193 (1992).

We note that in *Belden* and *Zupan*, the trial court judgment marked the point when the plaintiffs should have known they were injured and that the injury was wrongfully caused. But *Belden* and *Zupan* do not hold that an adverse judgment alone always signals a client that legal malpractice has occurred. In *Belden*, the client had reason, beyond the judgment itself, to suspect negligence—the defendant firm told the client it had a conflict of interest, withdrew as counsel, and yet continued to advise the client. See *Belden*, 203 Ill. App. 3d at 267, 148 Ill. Dec. 583, 560 N.E.2d 1180. And in *Zupan*, the client admitted that she was "reasonably aware that defendant had wrongfully caused her injury at the time judgment was entered." *Zupan*, 142 Ill. App. 3d at 399, 96 Ill. Dec. 889, 491 N.E.2d 1349.

The adverse ruling here was the trial court's denial of plaintiff's motion for leave to amend his complaint. Whether a plaintiff may amend his complaint is a matter within the discretion of a trial court. See *Loyola Academy v. S & S Roof Maintenance Inc.*, 146 Ill. 2d 263, 273–74, 166 Ill. Dec. 882, 586 N.E.2d 1211 (1992). The trial court's exercise of that discretion, standing alone, does not suggest that the ruling was caused by legal malpractice rather than the merits of plaintiff's case.

The trial court did orally suggest, at the hearing on damages and at a hearing on plaintiff's motion for leave to amend, that failure to amend the complaint earlier was fatal to plaintiff's case. But plaintiff alleges that he was not in court and that the firm did not tell him about the judge's comments. We do not know when plaintiff first learned of those comments. Plaintiff alleges that firm attorneys then assured plaintiff that the trial court had erred.

Further, plaintiff alleged that Mayer, Brown & Platt was negligent, not only for failing to amend the complaint, but for using an expert witness that the firm knew was not qualified to answer the questions necessary to establish net fair market value at the hearing on damages. Nothing in the January 15, 1993, order or the February 1, 1994, judgment signaled to plaintiff that the firm called an expert witness that it knew lacked the expertise to establish plaintiff's damages.

Mayer, Brown & Platt argues that plaintiff should have known his injury was wrongfully caused when he consulted new attorneys in 1993.

Plaintiff relies on the affidavit of Lee Abrams, one of the firm's attorneys. The affidavit states:

***

"[Plaintiff] retained the services of two new attorneys to provide advice and counsel in connection with the Litigation, Frederic Brace of Chicago and Larry Mesches of Palm Beach, Florida.

In October 1993, Mr. Brace met with [defendant's] attorneys *** to review and discuss the status of the Litigation, [defendant's] performance, the trial court decision, the general strategy and Butler's options going forward.

From late 1993 through the prosecution of the appeal, Mr. Mesches from time to time reviewed and commented on defendant's work and offered his views on how defendant should proceed with the Litigation."

The affidavit does not specify that either attorney reviewed work performed before January 15, 1993, when the alleged negligent conduct occurred. The affidavit can be read as consistent with Butler's affidavit, which states that the attorneys were hired to assist Butler in matters arising after the January 15, 1993 order, such as the fee dispute between Butler and the firm, the firm's work on subsequent motions and on the appeal, and the separate judgment collection proceedings in Florida.

We detect several points in time where a fact finder could conclude plaintiff should have known his injury was wrongfully caused. But the facts are not undisputed and do not point to only one conclusion. Since the facts could support more than one conclusion, we must remand for further proceedings. See *Jackson Jordan*, 158 Ill. 2d at 251, 198 Ill. Dec. 786, 633 N.E.2d 627.

Plaintiff also argues that the firm is estopped from relying on the statute of limitations. If, after a trial, a jury finds the statute of limitations did not commence until the appellate court affirmance and plaintiff's suit was timely filed, plaintiff's estoppel argument need not be addressed. But if the jury finds the statute of limitations began to run more than two years before plaintiff filed suit, plaintiff's estoppel argument becomes relevant. Because the issue may arise again on remand, we address it here. Plaintiff alleges that the firm caused plaintiff to delay filing a malpractice suit by concealing the trial court's oral comments at the January 15, 1993 hearing, reassuring plaintiff that an appeal would be successful, and threatening to interfere with plaintiff's efforts to obtain new counsel.

Jackson Jordan makes clear that the continuous reassurances of one's lawyer after an adverse result may toll the statute. *Jackson Jordan*, 158 Ill.

2d at 253, 198 Ill. Dec. 786, 633 N.E.2d 627. But equitable estoppel is unavailable to plaintiff because he failed to sue within a reasonable time after defendant stopped offering the reassurances that plaintiff alleges lulled him into not filing suit.

Under Illinois law, equitable estoppel does not give a plaintiff the entire limitations period measured from the date the defendant discontinues the conduct that lulled the plaintiff into inaction. Equitable estoppel will not apply if the defendant's conduct ended within ample time to allow a plaintiff to avail himself of his legal rights under the statute of limitations. *Barratt v. Goldberg*, 296 Ill. App. 3d 252, 259, 230 Ill. Dec. 635, 694 N.E.2d 604 (1998); *Serafin v. Seith*, 284 Ill. App. 3d 577, 589, 219 Ill. Dec. 794, 672 N.E.2d 302 (1996). We have held that as little as six months remaining in a statute of limitations period is "ample time" for a plaintiff to bring suit. See *Smith v. Cook County Hospital*, 164 Ill. App. 3d 857, 866, 115 Ill. Dec. 811, 518 N.E.2d 336 (1987). See also *Serafin*, 284 Ill. App. 3d at 588–89, 219 Ill. Dec. 794, 672 N.E.2d 302 (plaintiff had "ample time" to file suit where approximately six months remained under statute of repose). We believe the logical extension of this rule is that where ample time does not remain under a statute of limitations, the plaintiff will be allowed a reasonable period to bring suit. To allow the full limitations period would be to inconsistently allow a plaintiff less time when "ample" time remains in the limitations period and significantly more time when "ample" time does not remain.

Plaintiff does not dispute that any conduct that caused his delay in filing suit ended on September 15, 1995, when *Butler v. Kent* was decided by this court. Almost five months remained under the statute of limitations measured from the date of the trial court judgment. Yet plaintiff waited 18 months to file suit. We cannot conclude under *Smith* and *Serafin* that plaintiff's 18-month delay was reasonable.

Reversed and remanded.

Questions and Comments

1. *Butler* discusses the general rule stating legal malpractice claims must be brought within two years. However, a plaintiff can overcome this limitation period if he can show the facts supporting the cause of action for malpractice were concealed by affirmative misrepresentations. This rule is sometimes referred to as the "concealment rule." See *DeLuna v. Burciaga*, 857 N.E.2d 229 (Ill. 2006). Can you think of a scenario where such a rule would be applicable?

2. The statute of limitation in a legal malpractice case begins to run when the plaintiff *knows* or *should have known* facts leading him to believe his attorney likely wrongfully caused the injury. Does this mean that a professional opinion as to whether legal malpractice has occurred is

needed before a plaintiff may be charged with knowledge, triggering the statute of limitations?

3. The court in *Butler* found facts indicating several points in time, which could have been viewed to trigger the statute of limitations. What facts did the court rely on when arriving at its final determination on this issue?

CONT'L CAS. CO. V. LAW OFFICES OF MELBOURNE MILLS, JR., PLLC

United States Court of Appeals for the Sixth Circuit (2012)
676 F.3d 534

Rogers, Circuit Judge.

This case involves whether a malpractice liability policy is properly rescinded for incomplete responses to questions on the applicable insurance applications. After lawyer Melbourne Mills, Jr., was successfully sued for millions of dollars for legal malpractice, his ostensible malpractice insurance carrier, Continental Casualty Company, sought a judicial declaration that it was entitled to rescind Mills's insurance policy for the time period covered by the class action. The district court granted Continental summary judgment, holding that Mills's failure to disclose an ongoing state bar association inquiry constituted a material misrepresentation when the policy renewal application specifically asked if "any attorney [was] subject to any disciplinary inquiry . . .during the expiring policy period." On Mills's appeal, there are two alternative bases for affirming the judgment in favor of Continental: (1) Mills's negative response to a different question constituted a material misrepresentation in light of the ongoing bar association inquiry which ultimately led to Mills's disbarment, and (2) the policy's dishonesty exclusion clause bars coverage of any claim arising out of a "dishonest, fraudulent, or . . . malicious act or omission." In 2010, the Kentucky Supreme Court issued an order which permanently barred Mills from the practice of law in Kentucky. This order constituted a sufficient "regulatory ruling" under the dishonesty exclusion clause to bar coverage. Each of these two bases supports upholding the district court's grant of summary judgment.

Continental sued below to rescind a malpractice insurance policy for the Law Offices of Melbourne Mills, Jr., after Mills and other attorneys allegedly breached their fiduciary duties during the negotiations of a large class action settlement. Mills and others, including Shirley Cunningham and William Gallion, represented a group of over 400 plaintiffs in a class action suit against American Home Products for injuries related to the use of the diet drug Fen-Phen. At the outset of the suit, it was agreed that the lawyers' fees would be determined by contingency fee contracts, limited to 30% of the clients' gross recovery. In May 2001, American Home Products agreed to settle the class action for almost $200 million. The plaintiffs in the action together received only $74 million, or 37% of the settlement, while the lawyers received the following: Mills received $23 million; Cunningham received $26 million; Gallion received $30 million; Stan Chesley received $20 million; and consultants and other counsel received $7 million. The remaining $20 million was used to establish The Kentucky Fund for Healthy Living, Inc. Mills served as a member of the Fund's Board of Directors, for which he allegedly received a monthly compensation of $5,350.

In early February 2002, Mills learned that the Kentucky Bar Association ("KBA") was investigating complaints filed against him in connection with the Fen-Phen class action. The Inquiry Commission Complaint stated that Mills was under "investigation" for "fees obtained in settlement of certain [claims regarding the use of Fen-Phen and other pharmaceuticals] . . . [that] were divided with other counsel not in your firm," as well as allegations concerning a paralegal in Mills's office who was "conducting the unauthorized practice of law" as part of the work on the class action.

In August 2003, Mills applied to renew his professional liability insurance with Continental for the 2003-2004 year. Continental had insured Mills's law office for many years prior to this application.

Question 3 of the application asked: "Are there any claims, or acts or omissions that may reasonably be expected to be a claim against the firm, that have not been reported to the Company or that were reported during the expiring policy period?" In response, Mills checked "NO," but made a notation to "See Schedule 2." Schedule 2, entitled *E & O Claims*, stated: "In addition to Melbourne Mills, Jr., the lawyers currently serving in the firm include two of counsel partners, David L. Helmers and E. Patrick Moores. The information regarding the of counsel attorneys is contained on the attached attorney information sheet."

Question 4 of the 2003 application read: "Has any attorney been disbarred, suspended, formally reprimanded or subject to any disciplinary inquiry, complaint or proceeding for any reason other than nonpayment of dues during the expiring policy period?" Again, Mills checked "NO," but wrote that Continental should "See Schedule 3." Schedule 3, entitled *Disciplinary Proceedings*, stated:

> During the current year no attorney has been disbarred, suspended, formally reprimanded or subject to any disciplinary inquiry, complaint or proceeding. In prior years, attorneys in the Firm have responded to inquiries filed by all jurisdictions exercising jurisdiction and control over attorney conduct. There have been no adverse findings regarding any attorney or other party's conduct.

According to Mills, at the time of the 2003 application, he did not know the status of the 2002 KBA investigation; in his own words, the case "lay in limbo for years at a time. Just nothing was done."

In August 2003, Continental granted an insurance policy, entitled Lawyers' Professional Liability Policy, to the Law Offices of Melbourne Mills, Jr. The policy contained various exclusions, including a Dishonesty Exclusion, which stated:

> This Policy does not apply . . . to any claim based on or arising out of any dishonest, fraudulent, or criminal or malicious act or omission by an Insured except that this exclusion shall not apply to personal injury. The Company shall provide the Insured with a defense of such claim unless or until the dishonest, fraudulent, criminal or malicious act or omission has been determined by any trial verdict, court ruling, regulatory ruling or legal admission, whether appealed or not. Such defense will not waive any of the Company's rights under this Policy.

In 2005, the Fen-Phen class action members asserted legal malpractice claims against Mills and others in *Abbott, et al. v. Chesley, et al.* The Boone County Circuit Court determined that the attorneys "breached their fiduciary duties to the Plaintiffs when they paid themselves fees over and above the amount to which they were entitled to under their fee contracts with their clients." As a result, the class plaintiffs were awarded $42 million. Continental initially provided Mills a defense in this case; however, Continental also fully reserved its rights, including the right to rescind the policy.

Continental sought a judicial declaration that it was entitled to rescind the insurance policy granted to the Law Offices of Melbourne Mills, Jr., for the period covering August 21, 2003 to August 21, 2004. The district court granted summary judgment in favor of Continental, holding that Continental was entitled to void the policy because Mills's 2003 application included material misrepresentations and omissions regarding the ongoing KBA ethical inquiries. Because the district court found that "Mills knew that a bar complaint had been filed against him in early 2002," and the "KBA's investigation was ongoing," the district court held that Mills's response to Question 4 constituted a material misrepresentation under section (2) of K.R.S. §304.14-110. This section provides that a misrepresentation prevents recovery under a policy if it is "[m]aterial either to the acceptance of the risk, or to the hazard assumed by the insurer." The district court noted that the "ongoing KBA inquiry into Mills's actions with respect to the Fen-Phen Action is precisely the type of information Continental needed to evaluate its potential for current and future risk." The district court also determined that Mills's response to Question 4 satisfied section (3) of K.R.S. §304.14-110, which provides that a misrepresentation shall bar coverage if "[t]he insurer in good faith would either not have issued the policy or contract, or would not have issued it at the same premium rate . . . if the true facts had been made known to the insurer as required . . . by the application for the policy." In doing so, the district court relied heavily on the testimony of a Continental employee who stated that disclosure of the investigation would have led Continental to take "one of several potential restrictive underwriting actions in order to address potential exposure." Holding that Mills's response to Question 4 entitled Continental to rescind the policy, the district court determined that it was not necessary to address whether Mills's answer to Question 3 was a material misrepresentation or whether Continental was entitled to summary judgment based upon exclusionary language in the policy.

In addition to the grant of summary judgment to Continental, a money judgment for $233,674.49 was entered against Mills, which was the amount of the defense costs Continental paid on his behalf in the initial class action. On June 10, 2010, the same day that the money judgment was entered, the district court also granted Continental leave to file supplemental authority, namely: (1) the May 20, 2010 Order of the Kentucky Supreme Court which disbarred Mills from the practice of law in Kentucky, and (2) the August 27, 2009 Findings of Fact and Conclusions of Law of the Trial Commissioner, which the Kentucky Supreme Court used to reach its decision to disbar Mills. The district court held that it could take judicial notice of the Order of the Supreme Court disbarring Mills and the Findings of Facts because the documents came under Fed. R. Evid. 803(8), the public records exception to inadmissible hearsay. In the alternative, the district court determined that the documents had the "guarantees of trustworthiness" which allowed them to be admitted pursuant to Fed. R. Evid. 807. In allowing these documents to be included in the record, the district court noted that it did not reach the issue of whether the dishonesty bar in the policy voided Mills's insurance, and "[s]hould an appellate court have reason to review the additional grounds upon which Continental moved for summary judgment, these documents could be essential to a complete record."

Mills and the class members, who intervened to protect their ability to recover against Mills, now appeal. They argue that Mills did not make a material misrepresentation on the 2003 insurance renewal application, and thus the policy should not have been rescinded. Mills and the class action plaintiffs also maintain that the district court erred by allowing Continental to file supplemental authority that was both a finding of fact and hearsay after the court had already granted summary judgment.

Because Mills made a material misrepresentation in his malpractice insurance application with Continental, the policy was properly voided under Kentucky law. Though the district court determined that the policy was void due to Mills's response to Question 4 of the 2003 application, Mills's answer to Question 3 represented a material misrepresentation, and provides an alternative basis for affirmance. According to K.R.S. §304.14-110, a misrepresentation voids an insurance policy if the misrepresentation is "material" to the acceptance of risk or if the insurance company would not have issued the policy if the true facts had been made known. Though this standard is disjunctive, Mills's response to Question 3 was both a misrepresentation that was material to Continental's acceptance of risk and, if Continental had known of the investigation against Mills, Continental would not have issued the policy or would not have issued the policy at that rate.

Mills's answer to Question 3 of the 2003 application was a material misrepresentation. Question 3 of the application asked: "Are there any claims, or acts or omissions that may reasonably be expected to be a claim against the firm, that have not been reported to the Company or that was reported during the expiring policy period?" In response, Mills checked "NO," but made a handwritten notation to "See Schedule 2." Schedule 2, entitled *E & O Claims*, stated: "In addition to Melbourne Mills, Jr., the lawyers currently serving in the firm include two of counsel partners, David L. Helmers and E. Patrick Moores. The information regarding the of counsel attorneys is contained on the attached attorney information sheet."

Mills's answer to Question 3 was a misrepresentation because in August of 2003, when he was filling out the application, Mills knew of not only the ongoing KBA investigation, initiated in February 2002 but unresolved at that time, but also all of the acts surrounding the Fen-Phen class action settlement negotiations, which reasonably could have—and ultimately did—lead to a malpractice claim. Even though the class action members did not bring the legal malpractice suit until 2005, in August 2003 Mills still knew that, collectively, the lawyers in the Fen-Phen class action paid themselves over $126 million. According to one uncontested document put forth by the class members, the lawyers were limited to fees of a little over $60 million. Mills knew that the clients had not been told all of the pertinent facts regarding the settlement offer and the fee splitting arrangement, and that the KBA had subpoenaed the financial records from the case as a result of the 2002 inquiry. In sum, Mills was aware that he had engaged in conduct that led to the disbarment of him and two of his co-counsel. Mills knew that his conduct was egregious and that his "acts" and "omissions" could have "reasonably be[en] expected" to lead to "a claim against the firm." Mills was unquestionably required to disclose this information to Continental when filling out the policy renewal application.

Mills's failure to disclose his actions in response to Question 3 was also material to Continental's acceptance of risk, K.R.S. §304.14-110(2), and had an impact on Continental's decision to issue the policy at the rate that it did, K.R.S. §304.14-110(3). Mills incorrectly argues that K.R.S. §304.14-110 requires that the insured make an *intentional* misrepresentation; the plain language of the statute requires only that the misrepresentation be "material." According to Kentucky case law, a misrepresentation is material if "the insurer, acting reasonably and naturally in accordance with the usual practice of . . . insurance companies under similar circumstances, would not have accepted the application if the substantial truth had been stated therein." *Mills v. Reserve Life Ins. Co.*, 335 S.W.2d 955, 958 (Ky.1960). A misrepresentation is material if there is sufficient evidence that the insurance company would not have issued the policy or would have issued a different policy if it had knowledge of Mills's actions and omissions under K.R.S. §304.14-110(3). Therefore, many of the reasons that support a determination of "materiality" under K.R.S. §304.14-110(2) also support a holding that Mills's misrepresentation satisfied section (3) of the statute as well.

Mills's failure to disclose the circumstances surrounding the Fen-Phen class action and the ongoing KBA investigation was material to Continental, which likely would not have issued the policy, or would have issued a different policy, had it known of Mills's acts and omissions during this time. Because Continental has a duty to defend all claims against its insured, including non-meritorious claims, Continental has an interest in all potential claims. This is "precisely the kind of information that Continental [sought and] would need to evaluate its potential for current and future risk." *Cont'l Cas. Co. v. Lampe & Hamblin, PLLC*, No. 3:03CV604–H, 2004 WL 5708261, at *4 (W.D. Ky. Nov. 1, 2004) ("*Lampe*"). In this case, that risk was amplified by the enormity of the $200 million class action settlement. Mills had a duty to disclose this information in response to Question 3, and when he did not, he affected Continental's opportunity to consider and weigh its options when issuing the Policy.

Peter Brinkman, underwriter for Continental, also testified that he could "state without hesitation or qualification that an affirmative response to Question 3 . . . of the 2003 application would have been material to Continental's underwriting of policies issued to the Firm." Though the class members argue that the testimony of the insurance company's own employee is not sufficient for a finding of materiality, this is not correct. In *Lampe* the district court applied Kentucky law and determined that a misrepresentation was material solely on the basis of commonsense assumptions regarding what would have an impact on the decision making process of a reasonable insurance company. Underlying documents or employee testimony was not necessary to support this determination. *Id.* at *2.

Both Mills and the class action members dispute the district court's finding and argue that an answer to Question 3 reflects the "subjective state of the applicant's mind," and thus the question of materiality should be determined by a jury. However, in reviewing a policy under K.R.S.

§304.14-110, this court has not hesitated to declare that a misrepresentation was "plainly material." *See Cook v. Life Inv. Ins. Co.*, 126 Fed. Appx. 722, 724 (6th Cir. 2005). In addition, while Question 3 is subjective, the ongoing investigation by the KBA, as well as the circumstances surrounding the class action settlement, meant that Mills knew that there was the potential for a "claim" against him, and thus the only possible answer to Question 3 was "YES." The purpose of K.R.S. §304.14-110 is to "encourage honesty . . . on the part of potential insureds and to dissuade misrepresentations," *Progressive*, 891 F. Supp. at 381; therefore, even if Mills did not "know" that the Fen-Phen class action members would initiate a lawsuit against him, he should have let Continental know of the *possibility* of a claim in light of the complaints and inquiry. Mills's reference to Schedule 2, which does not answer Question 3 at all, further suggests that Mills understood and was trying to get around Continental's clear attempt to learn of any current and potential future risk.

Mills resurrects an argument raised in *Lampe*, comparing malpractice coverage to Kentucky's universal automobile liability insurance coverage and arguing that the "expressed public interest" in legal malpractice insurance "outweighs any right of an insurer to rescind an insurance contract." *Lampe*, 2004 WL 5708261, at *3. The district court in *Lampe* considered this argument carefully but rejected it, concluding "that a Kentucky court would not find public policy of the state so strongly in favor of lawyers liability insurance coverage that it could outweigh an insurer's right to rescission as is the case with automobile liability coverage." *Id.* at *3-4. In any event, Mills did not make this argument during the proceedings before the district court and this court will not review issues raised for the first time on appeal, because "[o]ur function is to review the case presented to the district court, rather than a better case fashioned after a district court's unfavorable order." *DaimlerChrysler Corp. Healthcare Benefits Plan v. Durden*, 448 F.3d 918, 922 (6th Cir.2006). Accordingly, we need not consider this new argument on appeal. *See Post v. Bradshaw*, 621 F.3d 406, 415 (6th Cir.2010).

As a final argument, the Fen-Phen class action plaintiffs suggest, as best we can understand, that if Continental had known of Mills's ongoing investigation, and as a result had cancelled or not renewed the 2001-2002 policy, Mills could have purchased a three-year extended reporting period ("ERP"), thus covering Mills during the time frame encompassing the claims of the class action plaintiffs. However, this argument makes little sense, as the opportunity for Mills to purchase the ERP would have expired 60 days after the hypothetical non-renewal or cancellation in 2002, and thus would have occurred almost ten months prior to the 2003 misrepresentation that is at the crux of this case.

Though not argued on appeal, the class action plaintiffs made a similar argument below with regard to a potential ERP after the cancellation or non-renewal of the 2002-2003 policy. However, in addition to not being adequately raised, this claim suffers from the following weakness: such an ERP would have had to been purchased at 175% of the premium rate. Thus, even under this speculation, Continental was deprived of the ability to charge a higher premium due to Mills's misrepresentation. Therefore, the hypothetical existence of the ERP does not change the materiality analysis.

In sum, Mills's response to Question 3 failed to disclose the circumstances surrounding the Fen-Phen class action and the ongoing KBA investigation, and this information was material to Continental's risk assessment. These conclusions are sufficient to uphold the district court's grant of summary judgment.

In addition, the policy could have been rescinded under the plain terms of a clause in the policy excluding coverage for dishonest acts. The clause provides:

> This Policy does not apply . . . to any claim based on or arising out of any dishonest, fraudulent, or criminal or malicious act or omission by an Insured except that this exclusion shall not apply to personal injury. The Company shall provide the Insured with a defense of such claim unless or until the dishonest, fraudulent, criminal or malicious act or omission has been determined by any trial verdict, court ruling, regulatory ruling or legal admission, whether appealed or not. Such defense will not waive any of the Company's rights under this Policy.

Although Kentucky law states that an insurance policy "should be liberally construed" and "all doubts [should be resolved] in favor of the insureds," this does not mean that the clear terms should not be interpreted "according to their 'plain and ordinary meaning.'" *K.M.R. v. Foremost Ins. Group*, 171 S.W.3d 751, 753 (Ky. App. 2005) (citing *Nationwide Mut. Ins. Co. v. Nolan*, 10 S.W.3d 129, 131–32 (Ky.1999)). *See also Scottsdale Ins. Co. v. Flowers*, 513 F.3d 546, 564 (6th Cir.2008). Policies should reflect "the parties' mutual understanding at the time they entered into the contract and '[s]uch mutual intention is to be deduced, if possible, from the language of the contract alone.'" *K.M.R.*, 171 S.W.3d at 753 (quoting *Nolan*, 10 S.W.3d at 131–32).

In this case, the dishonesty exclusion clause can only be interpreted to mean that the parties did not intend for the policy's legal malpractice coverage to include acts that were objectively fraudulent or dishonest. To the extent that the clause requires a court or regulatory ruling, the requirement is satisfied by the May 20, 2010 Order of the Kentucky Supreme Court which disbarred Mills from the practice of law in Kentucky. *Ky. Bar Ass'n v. Mills*, 318 S.W.3d 89, 93 (Ky. 2010). After granting Continental's motion for summary judgment, the district court properly granted Continental leave to file the disbarment order as supplemental authority.

The Kentucky Supreme Court ruling is within the plain language of Fed. R. Evid. 803(8), the public records exception, and thus is not inadmissible hearsay. Moreover, the class action members concede that the Disbarment Order may be considered as part of the record, and that this court may take judicial notice of it as part of our de novo review on summary judgment. The Kentucky Supreme Court's ruling determined that Mills had committed "dishonest" and "fraudulent . . . act[s] or omission[s]," and thus is sufficient to bar coverage under the dishonesty exclusion clause of the policy. In addition to other violations, the Kentucky Supreme Court found that Mills violated S.C.R. 3.130-8.3(c) by *deceiving* his clients into accepting the individual settlement amounts devised by a fraudulent method; *misrepresenting* to the Boone Circuit Court that his clients had agreed to donate a substantial portion of the total settlement received to charity; failing to inform the Boone Circuit Court that he had contingent fee contracts with all of his clients which set a specific fee; *providing, or assisting in providing, false or misleading information* to the Boone Circuit Court about the fees and expenses . . . ; and *misappropriating, or participating in the misappropriation of*, his clients' funds and the subsequent cover up. *Id.* (emphasis added).

As the court found that Mills's "participat[ed] in the misappropriation of . . . clients' funds," Mills's argument that he did not *personally* misappropriate funds, and thus did not act fraudulently, is not persuasive. Even if he did not himself engage in the misconduct, the Kentucky Supreme Court found that Mills's acted dishonestly "by failing to exercise professional judgment independent of his cocounsel." *Id.* This omission is covered by the dishonesty exclusion clause. Similarly, Mills's assertion that he did not act fraudulently because, unlike his colleagues, he was acquitted of criminal charges, also fails because the dishonesty exclusion clause does not require a criminal conviction to bar coverage. Therefore, the May 20, 2010 Order of the Kentucky Supreme Court disbarring Mills from the practice of law is a sufficient basis for precluding coverage under the policy's dishonesty exclusion clause.

Because it is not necessary to rely on the August 27, 2009 Findings of Fact and Conclusions of Law of the Trial Commissioner to affirm the district court's grant of summary judgment, we do not address whether this document was inadmissible hearsay and whether the district court erred by allowing Continental to file it as supplemental authority. We also do not address whether Mills's response to Question 4 warranted rescission of the policy.

The judgment of the district court granting summary judgment to Continental is affirmed.

Questions and Comments

1. Oregon is the only state that requires lawyers to carry legal malpractice insurance, although several states require disclosure of whether a lawyer carries professional insurance to clients or to her licensing board upon completion of her annual registration statements. *See* ABA Standing Committee on Client Protection, State Implementation of ABA Model Court Rule on Insurance Disclosure, 2015. Many policies include dishonesty exclusion clauses and only cover problems that arise from rendering or failing to render professional legal services. Lauren Schulz & Michael Hunter Schwartz, *Lawyer, Know Your Safety Net: A Malpractice Insurance Primer for New and Experienced Lawyers*, J. Kan. B. Ass'n, March 2013, at 22.

2. Specifically, legal malpractice insurance policies commonly exclude "any dishonest, fraudulent, criminal, or malicious act or omission." *Conner v. Transamerica Ins. Co.*, 496 P.2d 770 (Okla. 1972). When should this exclusion apply? Can an insurer refuse to defend any suit where a plaintiff claims dishonesty or fraudulent acts? What standard would likely be applied in such instances?

3. The mass tort case discussed in *Cont'l Cas. Co. v. Law Offices of Melbourne Mills, Jr., PLLC* included a fee agreement between William Gallion, Shirley Cunningham, Melbourne Mills, and Stanley Chelsey. The case settled for just over $200 million, however only $74 million was paid to the clients. The judge approved an attorneys' fee award of 49% of the gross settlement, and an additional 10% of the settlement went into a charitable trust, with the judge appointing Gallion, Cunningham, and Mills as its initial directors. The trust fund, however, never made any charitable contributions. Chelsey received over $20 million, Cunningham received over $21 million, Gallion received almost $31 million, and Mills received close to $24 million. In the aftermath, Gallion and Cunningham were convicted of wire fraud and were sentenced to 25 and 20 years in prison, respectively. Mills, Chelsey, and the judge were all disbarred for their conduct in the case. *See* Sheila B. Scheuerman, *Mass Tort Ethics: What Can We Learn from the Case Against Stanley Chesley?* 23 Widener L.J. 243, 245–57 (2013). What is your assessment of such an outcome?

HOW TO OUTSOURCE LEGAL WORK—ETHICALLY: AUTHORITIES WEIGH IN
The New York Law Journal (Online), August 24, 2011
By Devika Kewalramani

It's Sunday night in New York, Monday morning in New Delhi. When the New York lawyer opens her laptop the next morning, the project will be complete and the documents will be in her inbox. Legal process outsourcing maximizes speed, saves costs and manages overflow work. But is it ethical? And if it can be ethical, what must the lawyer do to keep it ethical?

Ethics Authorities

Yes, outsourcing legal work is ethical. Indeed, it is old wine in a new bottle. Lawyers have long been associating other counsel in matters and obtaining nonlawyer services from third parties. The ABA Commission on Ethics 20/20 recently took up the subject and, in its May 2011 report (ABA Report) to the ABA House of Delegates, concluded that it did not need to make any changes in the Model Rules of Professional Conduct to accommodate outsourcing.

> However, the delegation of legal tasks to other lawyers, in the United States and abroad, has highlighted concerns about:
>
> • Client awareness of who is doing the work;
> • Confidentiality;
> • Competence of lawyers and supervision of their work;
> • Unauthorized practice of law by out-of-state or foreign lawyers;
> • Conflicts.

The dramatic growth of legal process outsourcing has prompted ethics authorities around the country to examine it. The 2011 ABA Report and a 2009 report by the Committee on Professional Responsibility of the New York City Bar (City Bar Report) are the most recent papers from the ABA and the city bar.

In addition, in 2006, the Committee on Professional and Judicial Ethics of the city bar issued an advisory opinion that a New York lawyer may ethically outsource legal support services offshore provided that the New York lawyer (i) rigorously supervise the nonlawyer to avoid aiding in the unauthorized practice of law and to ensure competent representation of the client; (ii) take steps to ensure the preservation of client confidential information; (iii) attend to conflict checking to avoid conflicts of interest; (iv) bill appropriately for the services provided; and (v) obtain advance client consent when appropriate.

In 2008, the ABA Standing Committee on Ethics and Professional Responsibility issued an opinion approving outsourcing of legal services, and concluding that "[t]here is nothing unethical about a lawyer outsourcing legal and nonlegal services, provided the outsourcing lawyer renders legal services to the client with the 'legal knowledge, skill, thoroughness and preparation reasonably necessary for the representation,' as required by Rule 1.1 [of the Model Rules]."

Key Concerns

The 2011 ABA Report offers general guidance on outsourcing; the 2009 City Bar Report offers specific procedures. There are no universally applicable rules yet, but a consensus may be emerging as to how to handle the specific areas of concern. The unifying theme is that the outsourcing lawyer remains responsible for the work.

Client consent. The ABA Report said that the client's informed consent should "ordinarily" be obtained before lawyers outside the retained firm provide legal services. Proposed Comment 6 to Model Rule 1.1 ("Competence"). Likewise, the 2009 City Bar Report stated that client consent should be obtained for substantive legal work performed by foreign firms, such as legal research and brief writing. The 2006 advisory opinion by the city bar, analogizing to previous opinions about temporary lawyers, said that client consent should be obtained in some circumstances, but did not clearly define those circumstances.

Confidentiality. The ABA Report concluded that Model Rule 1.6, the rule protecting client confidences, applied to legal outsourcing, but that no new Comment was required. The City Bar Report, on the other hand, required substantial scrutiny of the degree of risk to client information in the outsourced jurisdiction, including review of the laws there, instructing the outsource provider on U.S. ethical obligations, putting protection of confidentiality in the outsourcing contract, and several other specific procedures.

Competence. The ABA Report said that the outsourcing lawyer must satisfy himself that the outsourced lawyer will contribute to the competent and ethical representation of the client and must ensure that the outsourced lawyer's work is performed in a manner consistent with the outsourcing lawyer's own duty of competence. The City Bar Report required checking of the outsourced lawyer's credentials and supervision and review of the outsourced lawyer's product, and imposed a number of other specific supervisory requirements.

Unauthorized practice of law. The ABA Report considered unauthorized practice to be a matter of avoiding the outsourced lawyer's violating his own local unauthorized practice rules. In contrast, the City Bar Report considered unauthorized practice to be a matter of avoiding the New York lawyer's violating New York's unauthorized practice rules, and required the New York lawyer to adequately supervise the outsourced lawyer's work and retain complete responsibility to avoid such violation.

Conflicts. The ABA Report observed that a number of outsource providers themselves use conflicts checking procedures like those of large American and U.K. law firms. That report concluded that the existing Model Rules on conflicts of interest were sufficient. The City Bar Report generally placed responsibility for conflicts checks on the outsourced lawyer (and law firm), but said that the outsourcing firm must ensure that the outsourced firm understands its obligations concerning conflicts and has satisfactory procedures in place.

The ABA Report

Without recommending changes to the text of the Model Rules, the 2011 ABA Report proposed amendments to some Comments to the Model Rules ("Proposed Comments"): Model Rules 1.1(Competence), 5.3 (Responsibilities Regarding Nonlawyer Assistants), and 5.5 (Unauthorized Practice of Law; Multijurisdictional Practice). The Proposed Comments in the ABA Report cover both outside lawyers and nonlawyers. Following are some of the highlights of the ABA Report.

Terminology: "Retain" vs. "Outsource." The most striking feature of the ABA Report is that the term "outsourcing" is not used anywhere. The ABA Ethics Commission concluded this would "create unnecessary confusion," as lawyers are already familiar with the concept of "retaining" or "contracting with" rather than "outsourcing," a relatively new term which may become outdated. Consequently, the commission retained the original terminology on the theory that legal process outsourcing is conceptually identical to the retention of nonfirm attorneys or outside nonlawyer services.

Client Consent. The ABA Report states that client consent will usually be required and will almost always be advisable before retaining a nonfirm lawyer on a client matter. An exception is made when a nonfirm lawyer is hired to perform a discrete and limited task not requiring disclosure of confidential client information.

"Assistants" vs. "Assistance." The ABA Report also addressed outsourcing of non-legal work. Proposed Comment [3] to Model Rule 5.3 focuses on the use of nonlawyers who work "outside" the firm to remind lawyers to use reasonable efforts to ensure that those outside services are provided in a manner that is compatible with the lawyer's professional obligations. The prescribed standard depends on factors that parallel those recited in Proposed Comment [6] to Model Rule 1.1, regarding nonfirm lawyers.

To clarify that "outside" nonlawyer services are not only performed by individuals but also by entities, the ABA Report recommended a title change for Model Rule 5.3. In the title, "Responsibilities Regarding Nonlawyer Assistants," the word, "Assistants" is to be replaced with "Assistance." For the same reason, Proposed Comment [3] to Model Rule 5.3 expressly includes emerging new technologies, such as cloud-based providers, as examples of entity services.

"Monitor" vs. "Supervise." With respect to nonlawyer services, the ABA Ethics Commission draws a distinction as to the level of quality control required. It says that if a client selects the nonlawyer service provider, the lawyer should ordinarily consult with the client regarding the structure of the outsourcing arrangement and the person responsible for "monitoring" the performance of the nonlawyer service provider.

The word "monitoring" was selected by the commission to emphasize that the lawyer may have a duty to remain aware of how the nonlawyer service provider is performing its services, even if the lawyer has not personally chosen the nonlawyer service provider and may not have direct supervisory duties. If it is the lawyer who selects the nonlawyer service provider, the lawyer (or firm) would shoulder the monitoring responsibility, in which case there would likely be no reason for the lawyer to discuss the responsibility for monitoring with the client.

Unauthorized Practice of Law. Model Rule 5.5 prohibits a lawyer from engaging in the unauthorized practice of law, whether through the lawyer's direct action or by aiding another person. The unauthorized practice issue raised by outsourcing is not whether the outsourced lawyer is practicing in the outsourcing jurisdiction, but rather whether the outsourced lawyer is keeping within the unauthorized practice rules in his or her own jurisdiction.

Proposed Comment [1] to Model Rule 5.5 says that "a lawyer may not assist a person in practicing law in violation of the rules governing professional conduct in *that person's* jurisdiction" (emphasis added). Thus, the laws of the outsourced jurisdiction must be considered in determining whether the outsourced lawyer may provide the services. Note that, at least in New York, "nonlawyer" includes foreign country lawyers or out-of-state lawyers, as well as laypersons.

City Bar Report

Unlike some state bar ethics opinions that address only the propriety of legal process outsourcing, the 2009 City Bar Report offered specific procedures to deal with five ethical issues in four outsourcing scenarios. In each scenario, the foreign lawyers are licensed in the foreign jurisdiction only. The ethical issues are client disclosure and consent; confidentiality; competence and supervision; unauthorized practice of law; and conflicts.

In **Scenario 1**, a New York law firm retains a foreign law firm through an intermediary to conduct patent searches for its clients. The New York firm would be required to take two actions: (1) disclose to the client the foreign firm's role in conducting patent searches; and (2) obtain advance client consent if confidential data will be disclosed, or the client will be billed on a basis other than actual cost, or if the foreign firm will play a significant role in the representation.

In terms of confidentiality, the New York firm should consider the following steps: (1) assess the level of risk posed to client data by the foreign jurisdiction's laws on data protection, security and privacy, and whether the levels of protection are equivalent to those in the U.S. lawyer's jurisdiction, (2) review the data security procedures of the intermediary and the legal services provider and require notice of any security breach in their contracts, (3) minimize the amount of data shared with the intermediary, especially if there is a significant risk of governmental seizure of data (in which case store data on the U.S. firm's servers with limited access), (4) instruct the intermediary and the legal services provider on relevant ethical/legal obligations of the U.S. lawyer and require compliance with confidentiality obligations (and breach provisions) in their contracts, and (5) advise the client about the risks and advantages of the outsourcing relationship and obtain its informed consent.

Regarding competence and supervision, in Scenario 1, the New York firm should consider the following measures: (1) interview the intermediary and the foreign professionals, check the intermediary's references, require the intermediary to provide foreign worker references and sample work product (for highly sensitive matters, the firm may retain a private investigator for additional background checks on the foreign firm and its personnel), (2) understand the professional credentialing scheme and disciplinary regime in the foreign jurisdiction for legal support work and the business/ethical practices of the foreign firm, (3) supervise the foreign professional's understanding of the assignment and ensure quality of work in a manner compatible with New York's ethical standards, and (4) establish procedures to appropriately communicate with the foreign firm's personnel.

In **Scenario 2**, a New York firm directly hires a foreign firm for legal research and brief writing in a pending matter. Advance client consent is necessary because substantive legal work will be performed.

Confidentiality requirements would be similar as in the first scenario, except that since the outsourcing agent is the legal services provider, depending on the volume of work, the U.S. lawyer may request segregation of its client data from that of the provider's other customers.

In **Scenario 3**, a legal department of a New York company uses an intermediary to hire a foreign firm to perform due diligence for its transactions. In **Scenario 4**, a legal department of a New York company directly retains a foreign firm to draft contracts with vendors.

Since in Scenarios 3 and 4 the client is itself outsourcing its legal work, the legal department may inform the company's business unit of its outsourcing plans.

For purposes of confidentiality, Scenario 3 is analogous to the first scenario, except that the legal department should enter into a retention agreement with the foreign firm, covering the nature and scope of the engagement. In Scenario 4, which is comparable to the third scenario, the legal department should follow its guidelines for retention of foreign counsel.

Scenarios 2, 3 and 4 are similar to the first scenario on competence and supervision, except that in Scenario 3, the in-house lawyers may need to travel to the offshore location to observe the work firsthand or spot-check it.

On the question of unauthorized practice of law, in Scenarios 1 to 4, the New York firm should provide adequate supervision of, and retain complete responsibility for, the work of foreign licensed professionals (not admitted in New York) in order for the New York firm to avoid engaging in the unauthorized practice of law under New York's rules on unauthorized practice.

Regarding conflicts, in Scenarios 1, 3 and 4, if the intermediary and/or the foreign firm acts as co-counsel to the New York lawyer, the intermediary must ensure that the foreign professional (i) has a conflicts checking system that is compliant with New York's conflicts rules and (ii) completes a conflicts questionnaire (to ensure that it's not adverse to the client in the matter or in related/unrelated matters; it does not represent the adverse party in related/unrelated matters; and it did not previously represent the adverse party in substantially related matters). However, if the intermediary acts as a temporary attorney agency and the foreign professional acts as a temporary employee retained to supplement the New York lawyer's staff, the New York lawyer must conduct a conflicts check and obtain a conflicts questionnaire from the intermediary and the foreign professional, listing recent matters, clients and adverse parties to identify matters substantially related to the New York lawyer's ongoing representations.

In Scenario 2, where the New York firm hires a foreign firm for legal research and brief writing, the conflicts check must be performed directly by the foreign firm, but the New York firm must ensure that the foreign firm understands the obligation to check conflicts and has procedures to confirm that its professionals are not engaged in representations that are adverse to the New York firm's clients such that it would be impermissible for them to work on the matter. Note: under New York Rule of Professional Conduct 1.10(a), if any professional at the foreign firm is conflicted from working on a matter, then all professionals at the firm are also barred.

Conclusion

Legal process outsourcing is ethical, and a consensus is beginning to develop regarding the particular ethical issues it involves. The unifying theme is that the ethical obligations of the outsourcing lawyer remain unchanged regardless of who performs what work, where and when. At the end of the day (whatever the time zone), it is the supervising lawyer who is responsible for the work.

Endnotes omitted (See Devika Kewalramani, How to Outsource Legal Work-Ethically: Authorities Weigh In, New York Law Journal, (2011) for full article version.) Reprinted with permission from the August 2011 edition of the "New York Law Journal" © 2016 ALM Media Properties, LLC. All rights reserved.

Questions and Comments

1. What is your assessment of the current viewpoints on outsourcing? Do you envision a long-term increase in malpractice claims against American lawyers based on the outsourcing-related issues? Will this possibly lead to the creation of global or international legal malpractice standards and claims? Explain your position.

2. Must a client's informed consent be obtained before outsourcing work? Does it depend on the nature of the work being outsourced? How can/should an attorney protect herself and her clients when outsourcing documents that may contain confidential information?

3. Should lawyers who outsource legal work to other countries be subject to malpractice liability under a theory of strict vicarious liability? If a foreign provider's conduct gives rise to a malpractice claim, is the United States lawyer automatically subject to liability even when outsourcing was done with her client's consent and in order to limit costs?

METADATA & LAWYERS: AN ISSUE THAT WILL NOT DIE
New York Legal Ethics Reporter, New York Professional Responsibility Report Archive, June 1, 2007
By Lazar Emanuel

[Author's Note: I am indebted for much of the technical material in this article to my son David, IT consultant, who has guided me, as he always does, through the maze of technology surrounding computers.]

A March 14, 2007, Opinion of the Alabama State Bar Disciplinary Commission confirms that the issues created for lawyers by metadata remain essentially unresolved. The Alabama opinion cites and relies upon two Ethics Opinions of the New York State Bar and ignores an essentially contrary Opinion of the ABA. Recent opinions from Florida and Maryland have added to the confusion. [See, Florida Opinion 06-02; Maryland Opinion 2007-09.]

The New York view is two-pronged: (1) a lawyer has a duty to purge from an electronic document he intends to send to the opposing attorney all metadata which might disclose a client's secrets or confidences [NYSBA Opinion 782]; and (2) a lawyer who receives an electronic document from his adversary may not make use of computer software applications to "mine" (i.e., search for metadata in) the document [NYSBA Opinion 749]. The ABA, on the other hand, concludes as follows [Formal Opinion 06-442 (Aug. 5, 2006)]:

> This opinion addresses whether the ABA Model Rules of Professional Conduct permit a lawyer to review and use embedded information contained in e-mail and other electronic documents, whether received from opposing counsel, an adverse party, or an agent of an adverse party. The Committee concludes that the Rules generally permit a lawyer to do so.

***

At this juncture, therefore, we are left with the following issues:

1. Does a lawyer who sends a document electronically have an obligation to exercise reasonable care to ensure that the document does not inadvertently disclose a secret or confidence of her client through metadata? If so, what constitutes "reasonable care"?

2. Does a lawyer who receives an electronic document from opposing counsel have an obligation: (a) to refrain from researching, reviewing and using metadata embedded in the document; and/or (b) to notify the sender that he knows or suspects that the document contains metadata which she appears to have forwarded inadvertently?

***

Definition of Metadata

***

In the word "metadata," the term "meta" connotes the data in an electronic file (the electronic record behind a finished document). It is generally referred to as "data about data." As ABA Formal Opinion 06-442 (Aug. 5, 2006) advises: "E-mail and other electronic documents often contain 'embedded' information. Such embedded information is commonly referred to as metadata."

A more extended definition of the term is supplied by the ABA publication, "What's the Meta with Metadata?" by Peter H. Geraghty, Director, ABA Ethic Search (e-news for members, January 2006):

> Metadata may reveal who worked on a document, the name of the organization that created or worked on it, information about prior versions of the document, recent revisions, and comments inserted in the document during drafting or editing. ... The hidden text may reflect editorial comments, strategy considerations, legal issues raised by the client or the lawyer, or legal advice provided by the lawyer...

ABA/BNA Lawyers' Manual on Professional Conduct 21 Current Rep. 39 (2004).

***

Inherent Metadata Risks

The risk for a lawyer is that, however careful he may have been, a document transmitted by him electronically is apt to contain metadata which is inimical to his client's interest or, in the worst case, reveals the client's secrets or confidences. My limited research leads me to conclude that many solo practitioners and many lawyers in small or medium-sized firms don't know what metadata is or don't understand its potential for damage.

In the process of preparing a final document, a lawyer who uses all the word- or data-processing tools on his computer will have gone through several steps, all of them ostensibly buried in the document and invisible to anyone but the lawyer himself. The reality, however, is that the document's history is embedded in his files and is in fact available to anyone—including opposing counsel—who receives the document electronically.

Here's one example of metadata's potential impact. A partner in a law firm, too busy to write a memo of law requested by his client, assigns the memo to his associate. The associate writes the memo and the partner reviews it. With minor changes, the memo goes out to the client, together with the firm's bill, reciting the partner's hourly rate. Buried in the document, traceable by the client, is the name of the original author of the memo — the associate — as well as the time spent by each lawyer on the memo.

***

Recommended By ABA

In a 41-screen slide show, the ABA has constructed a dramatic and instructive review of metadata and its inherent problems. [See, "Metadata (and other things that go bump in the night)," by Catherine Sanders Reach, Director, American Bar Association Legal Technology Resource Center (July 27, 2006).] After describing metadata, the slides encourage law firms to "get the facts, understand the implications, and establish firm policies to protect yourself and your clients." The slides then proceed through a series of illustrations showing how metadata becomes lodged in documents and offering access to ABA Ethics Opinions devoted to metadata.

One slide in the series lists and describes various software programs that are designed to work with Word, WordPerfect and PDF to eliminate metadata. The list includes all the following:

- Payne's Metadata Assistant (*www.tinyurl.com/e2zef*). The Assistant is designed to be used with Microsoft Word, Excel and PowerPoint. It comes in two versions, Retail and Enterprise (for multiple users). The program can analyze/clean files attached to outbound e-mail messages and convert them to PDF format for extra protection.
- iScrub (Esquire Innovations, Inc.) (*www.tinyurl.com/28e38p*). iScrub is also designed for use with Microsoft products. iScrub removes the visible document properties and scrubs the more-difficult-to-reach file elements, such as the list of past authors (all document authors) and Deleted Text.
- ezClean (Kraft, Kennedy & Lesser) (*www.tinyurl.com/34asd2*). This product is also limited for use with Microsoft products. Its website offers a review of metadata and some Microsoft bugs that have to be considered when using the program. It also gives detailed installation instructions.
- Workshare Protect (Workshare) (*www.tinyurl.com/2ornnp*). This product offers real-time warnings when your outgoing e-mail contains passwords, social security and credit card numbers, or a history of deleted texts or comments. It removes metadata with the click of a button, or automatically with no interaction from the user.
- Out-of-Sight (Softwise) (*http://tinyurl.com/2cn6mr*). Out-of-Sight offers compatibility with Office 2007 in its next release, and an evaluation license good for 30 days.

***

Endnotes omitted (See Lazar Emanual, Metadata & Lawyers: An Issue That Will Not Die, New York Legal Ethics Reporter, New York Professional Responsibility Report Archive, (June 2007) for full article version). Reprinted with permission from the 2007 edition of the "New York Legal Ethics Reporter" © 2016 New York Legal Ethics Reporter. All rights reserved.

Questions and Comments

1. Lawyers may be allowed to protect themselves from mistakenly producing confidential information in metadata. The common trend, however, is to require the production of electronic information in a native format with metadata intact. Does a lawyer violate any ethical rules by "scrubbing" metadata? Would your answer depend on specific circumstances?

2. It is likely that many lawyers refuse to use any "new technology" in their individual practice and defer computer-related discovery production or safekeeping to others in their law firm. Do these lawyers violate their ethical duties? Should the lawyer actually be or is she already

required to become familiar with, if not make use of software, relating to metadata?

3. Obtaining and interpreting metadata can be very costly. Who will bear such costs? Will such an issue be addressed during the discovery process? Have you heard of e-counsel and what they do?

C. DISCUSSION QUESTIONS

1. Statistically, *a lawyer will be the subject of three claims of malpractice before finishing a legal career.*[5] Negligence theory makes up about ¼ of all legal malpractice suits.[6] Liability to non-clients makes up about 20% of all suits.[7] Fee disputes concerning the quality and value of legal services make up about 20% while about 40% have some relationship to how the fee arrangement was handled/communication about the value of services.[8] Do you find this data surprising? Why or why not?

2. What is the burden of proof in malpractice cases? Does the defendant lawyer lose even if she wins? Is this fair? If not, what is a better alternative?

3. May a judgment and findings of fact against an attorney in a disciplinary action be introduced in a malpractice suit against the same attorney? Does a ruling in favor of an attorney bar a civil lawsuit for the same or similar conduct alleged in the disciplinary action?

4. Successful malpractice claims generally result in the lawyer paying money damages. When a lawyer is disciplined under the rules of professional conduct, however, the lawyer can be sanctioned. These sanctions can be in the form of disbarment, suspension, reprimand or other disciplinary measures. Do you see any correlation between these separate proceedings and results?

5. Do grievances and malpractice claims involving allegations against the same lawyer and involving the same conduct need to be filed together, separately, or can the claimant even choose which one to pursue? If the claimant gets to choose, what would he consider in making such a determination?

---

[5] *See* Mallen & Smith, *Legal Malpractice, supra* note 14, at xiii.
[6] *Id.* at §1:1.
[7] *Id.*
[8] *Id.*

Chapter 13:
Lawyers and Their Role in Protecting Human Rights

A. INTRODUCTION TO LAWYER ETHICS AND RIGHTS OF THE ACCUSED

A lawyer will encounter challenges in her legal career on a daily basis. However, there is no doubt that one of the most difficult challenges is balancing ethics with the rights of another human being. When a client hires a lawyer for any matter he is putting his full trust in his lawyer to protect his rights. The difficulty for lawyers in this situation is finding the perfect balance between adhering to legal ethics principles while at the same time protecting the rights of their clients. This is especially the case when a criminal lawyer is representing someone who stands the chance to spend several years in prison or even be subject to the death penalty. Criminal lawyers are not the only group that must encounter human rights issues. As the articles suggest, government lawyers and lawyers who work in the military also face issues regarding this topic.

Articles and cases included in this chapter will address the balance between duties of the government lawyer and individual rights of the accused. In addition, the chapter will lead to discussions of numerous issues relating to lawyers and human rights, including the level of responsibility a lawyer should take for the actual, real-life consequences of her legal advice. Although the Model Rules of Professional Conduct do not specifically touch upon these issues, human rights concepts have many connections to legal ethics and profession. Do lawyers, especially when involved in major human rights cases, find themselves in conflict between their own morality and rules of professional conduct? Should morality even be considered and, if so, who decides what is moral and what is not? Where does the balance lie? As you read the remainder of the chapter, try and answer these questions for yourself.

B. RULES

In preparation, read carefully the following sections of the Model Rules of Professional Conduct along with any relevant comments listed below.

- Rule 3.8 Special Responsibilities of a Prosecutor
  - Comment [7], [8], & [9]
- Rule 3.4 (a) (b) & (c): Fairness to Opposing Party and Counsel
  - Comment [2]

C. CASES AND ADDITIONAL READINGS

ETHICAL ISSUES RAISED BY THE OLC TORTURE MEMORANDUM
1 J. Nat'l Security L. & Pol'y 455 (2005)
By Kathleen Clark

Introduction: A Tale of Two Memos

In the fall of 2001, the Bush administration was looking for a place to imprison and interrogate alleged al Qaeda members away from the prying eyes of other countries and insulated from the supervision of United States courts. The Defense Department believed that the Naval Base at Guantánamo Bay, Cuba might work, so it asked the Justice Department's Office of Legal Counsel (OLC) whether federal courts would entertain habeas corpus petitions filed by prisoners at Guantánamo, or whether they would dismiss such petitions as beyond their jurisdiction. On December 28, 2001, OLC responded with a thorough and balanced analysis of how the federal courts were likely to resolve the jurisdictional question. The memorandum prepared by OLC explained the arguments against such jurisdiction, but it also explored possible strengths in the opposing position. The memorandum predicted that federal courts would not exercise jurisdiction but explained the risk of a contrary ruling. Acting in reliance on this memorandum, the government started imprisoning and interrogating alleged al Qaeda members at Guantánamo the following month, cognizant of the risk that a federal court might find habeas jurisdiction.

In 2004, the Supreme Court considered habeas corpus claims by prisoners at Guantánamo, and reached a result contrary to that predicted by the Justice Department memorandum, ruling that the district court did have jurisdiction. The fact that the Court came to a different conclusion than that advanced by OLC does not, however, mean that the OLC attorneys failed to fulfill their professional obligations to their client. The authors appropriately explained the risk of an adverse decision, and they provided enough information for the client to understand that risk and make decisions accordingly.

Whenever a lawyer offers a legal opinion, there is always a possibility that other legal actors will take a contrary view. If that risk is substantial and the lawyer apprises the client of the magnitude of that risk, the lawyer has adequately advised and informed the client. The authors of the Guantánamo Memorandum certainly met that standard.

During the summer of 2002, CIA officials had grown frustrated with the interrogation of al Qaeda member Abu Zubaydah, who had stopped cooperating with his interrogators. The CIA wanted to use harsher interrogation techniques against Zubaydah, and it sought the imprimatur of the Justice Department for those techniques. In particular, agency officials were concerned that certain harsh techniques might violate the international Convention Against Torture and implementing federal legislation, which makes it a crime to engage in torture under color of law outside the United States. White House Counsel Alberto Gonzales commissioned OLC to provide legal advice about the scope of the torture statute. Gonzales specifically asked that OLC explore two of the elements of the crime of torture: (1) infliction of severe pain or suffering and (2) specific intent. Deputy Assistant Attorney General John Yoo drafted a memorandum that was signed in August 2002 by Assistant Attorney General Jay Bybee, and which will be referred to here as the "Bybee Memorandum." The memorandum defined torture narrowly, developed defenses that might be raised in any future torture prosecution, and asserted that the President could authorize torture despite the treaty and statute prohibiting it. The government apparently acted in reliance on this memorandum in setting interrogation policies for alleged al Qaeda members.

The Bybee Memorandum purported to provide objective legal advice to government decision makers. Nevertheless, its assertions about the state of the law are so inaccurate that they seem to be arguments about what the authors (or the intended recipients) wanted the law to be rather than assessments of what the law actually is. The following section will describe the substantive inaccuracies in the memorandum. Section II will examine the legal ethics implications of those inaccuracies, with particular attention to the distinction between legal advocacy and legal advice.

I. The Substantive Inaccuracies in the Bybee Memorandum

The Bybee Memorandum consists of 50 pages of text supporting three assertions: (1) the federal criminal statute prohibiting torture is very narrow in scope, applying only where an interrogator specifically intends to cause the kind of extreme pain that would be associated with organ failure or death; (2) an interrogator who is prosecuted for violating the torture statute may be able to use an affirmative defense to gain an acquittal; and (3) the torture statute would be unconstitutional if it interfered with the President's war-making powers, including the power to detain and interrogate enemy combatants as he sees fit. The memorandum's claims about the state of the law in each of these areas are grossly inaccurate.

The first major inaccuracy is in the memorandum's assertion that the federal criminal statute prohibiting torture applies only where a government official specifically intends to and actually causes pain so severe that it "rise[s] to . . . the level that would ordinarily be associated with . . . death, organ failure, or serious impairment of body functions." This claimed standard is bizarre for a number of reasons. In the first place, organ failure is not necessarily associated with pain at all. In addition, this legal standard is lifted from a statute wholly unrelated to torture. It comes from a Medicare statute setting out the conditions under which hospitals must provide emergency medical care. That statute mentions severe pain as one possible indicator that a person is in a condition calling for such care. The statute goes on to define emergency medical condition" as one in which failure to provide medical care could result in "serious jeopardy" to an individual's health, "serious impairment to bodily functions," or "serious dysfunction of any bodily organ or part." The Bybee Memorandum twists this legal standard, and asserts that "severe pain" occurs only in connection with a "serious physical condition or injury such as death, organ failure, or serious impairment of body functions." It purports to give interrogators wide latitude to cause any kind of pain short of that associated with "death, organ failure, or serious impairment of body functions."

A second major inaccuracy is found in the memorandum's discussion of defenses available to those who might be prosecuted for violating the federal torture statute. The Bybee Memorandum discusses two affirmative defenses—necessity and self-defense—that could justify an interrogator's decision to torture a prisoner in order to extract information about al Qaeda's plans to attack other Americans. The memorandum's analysis of the self-defense option is somewhat measured. It acknowledges that the self-defense option would be unconventional in two ways. First, the interrogator would not engage in torture to prevent harm to the interrogator himself. Rather, he would be preventing harm to other Americans who could be injured by a terrorist attack. Second, the prisoner to be tortured would not actually be in a position to harm anyone at all. Instead, it is assumed that he would have information about an attack plan that would be carried out by others. The Bybee Memorandum asserts that a government official charged with violating the torture statute could make a self-defense (or defense of another) argument, but it does not assert that such an affirmative defense would necessarily succeed. The memorandum also asserts that an interrogator charged with torture might well be able to gain an acquittal using the necessity defense. Yet as David Luban has noted, the memorandum never mentions the fact that the Convention Against Torture itself seems to proscribe such a defense when it declares that "[n]o exceptional circumstances whatsoever, whether a state of war or . . . any other public emergency, may be invoked as a justification of torture." At a minimum, the Bybee Memorandum leaves the reader with the false impression that it is likely that an interrogator will be able to avoid a torture conviction by claiming the necessity defense.

A third major inaccuracy is found in the memorandum's discussion of presidential authority. The Bybee Memorandum asserts that the President can, at least under some circumstances, authorize torture despite the federal statute prohibiting it. This position is based on an expansive view of inherent executive power, but the memorandum does not even mention —let alone address—*Youngstown Sheet & Tube Co. v. Sawyer*, the leading Supreme Court case on this aspect of separation of powers. *Youngstown*, colloquially known as the Steel Seizure Case because it invalidated President Truman's seizure of the nation's steel mills during the Korean War, seriously undermines any claim of unilateral executive power. The Bybee Memorandum does not even acknowledge that the Constitution explicitly grants to Congress the powers to define "Offences against the Law of Nations; . . . make Rules concerning Captures on Land and Water; . . . [and] make Rules for the Government and Regulation of the land and naval Forces," all of which suggest that Congress was well within its constitutional authority in banning torture.

On each of these three points—the threshold of pain that constitutes torture, the necessity defense, and unilateral executive power—the Bybee Memorandum presents highly questionable legal claims as settled law. It does not present either the counter arguments to these claims or an assessment of the risk that other legal actors—including courts—would reject them. Despite these obvious weaknesses, the memorandum apparently became the basis for the CIA's use of extreme interrogation methods, including "waterboarding," and shaped Defense Department interrogation policy. In fact, much of the memorandum was used verbatim in an April 2003 Defense Department Working Group Report on interrogation methods, which then became the basis for Defense Department policy.

The legal analysis in the Bybee Memorandum was so indefensible that it could not—and did not—withstand public scrutiny. Press reports about and excerpts from the memorandum began to surface in early June 2004, and there was a wave of criticism. The Justice Department resisted congressional pressure to turn over the memorandum, insisting that the

President had a right to confidential legal advice. When *The Washington Post* posted the complete text of the memorandum on its website, the wave of criticism turned into a flood. Eight days later, the Bush administration disavowed the memorandum. Six months later, in December 2004, OLC issued a new torture memorandum that offered legal analysis that was more accurate, repudiating the Bybee Memorandum's analysis of "specific intent" and "severe pain," adopting a broader definition of torture, and omitting the troublesome sections claiming inherent presidential power to disregard the torture prohibition and the ready availability of criminal defenses to torture charges.

II. Ethical Analysis of the Bybee Memorandum

The substantive inaccuracies in the Bybee Memorandum are so serious that they implicate the legal ethics obligations of its authors. In analyzing the legal ethics implications, it is important to make three preliminary observations. First, lawyers who work for the federal government are subject to state ethics rules. In the late 1980s and early 1990s, Attorneys General Richard Thornburgh and Janet Reno asserted that the Constitution's Supremacy Clause gave the Justice Department the authority to exempt its lawyers from state ethics rules. In 1998, however, Congress passed the McDade Amendment, making it clear that federal government lawyers must comply with state ethics rules in the states where they represent the government. Both Jay Bybee and John Yoo were subject to the D.C. Rules of Professional Conduct. Bybee is licensed by the District of Columbia and thus was and is directly subject to those rules. Yoo is licensed by Pennsylvania but was subject to the D.C. Rules by operation of the McDade Amendment, because he practiced in D.C. when he worked for the Office of Legal Counsel.

Second, these OLC lawyers had as their client an organization—the executive branch of the United States government—rather than any individual officeholder. Although White House Counsel Alberto Gonzales requested the Bybee Memorandum, he was not the client. Instead, he was simply a constituent of the organizational client. Ordinarily, lawyers must accept the decisions made by such constituents when those constituents are authorized to act on behalf of the organization. But where a lawyer knows that a constituent is acting illegally and that conduct could be imputed to the organization, the lawyer must take action to prevent or mitigate that harm. Where the constituent can exercise control over the lawyer's future career, taking such action may jeopardize the lawyer's advancement. Nevertheless, the legal ethics rules require lawyers to take action to protect entity clients from harm committed by their constituents.

Third, in analyzing the performance of the lawyers who wrote the Bybee Memorandum, it is important to analyze whether they were acting as legal advisors or as legal advocates. Different ethics rules apply to these two distinct functions. The role of the lawyer as an advocate before a tribunal is a familiar one. In that role, the lawyer may make any legal argument as long as it is not frivolous. She does not need to give the court her honest assessment of how the law applies in the case. Her only obligation of candor regarding legal argument is that if her opponent fails to mention directly adverse controlling authority, she must bring it to the tribunal's attention.

When a lawyer gives legal advice, on the other hand, she has a professional obligation of candor toward her client. One finds this obligation in Rule 2.1, which states that in representing a client, "a lawyer shall . . . render candid advice." In advising a client, the lawyer's role is not simply to spin out creative legal arguments. It is to offer her assessment of the law as objectively as possible. The lawyer must not simply tell the client what the client wants to hear, but instead must tell the client her best assessment of what the law requires or allows. Similarly, Rule 1.4(b) requires a lawyer to explain the law adequately to her client, so that the client can make informed decisions about the representation.

David Luban has described this obligation of candor in the following way: In many areas of law, there is not absolute agreement among lawyers about the state of the law. In those situations, knowledgeable lawyers' opinions about the law usually fall somewhere in a range similar to the familiar bell curve. If a lawyer advises a client that the law is at an extreme end of that bell curve (rather than that the state of the law is where most knowledgeable lawyers would view it), then the obligation to give candid legal advice requires the lawyer to inform the client that the lawyer's interpretation is at the extreme end and not shared by most knowledgeable lawyers.

In giving legal advice, a lawyer may provide advice that is contrary to the weight of authority, spinning out imaginative, even "forward-leaning" legal theories for the client to use. When doing so, however, the candor obligation requires the lawyer to inform the client that the weight of authority is contrary to that advice, and that other legal actors may come to the opposite conclusion. A lawyer who fails to warn a client about the possible illegality of proposed conduct has violated her professional obligations.

If a lawyer fails to candidly advise a client, she harms the client and may harm others affected by the client's actions. A lawyer who inaccurately advises a client that a proposed *legal* action is illegal may be foreclosing an option that should be open to the client's consideration, usurping the client's role in an attempt to limit the client's options. Similarly, a lawyer who inaccurately advises a client that proposed *illegal* action is legal also harms the client. On one level, a client may want to hear that conduct she wants to engage in is legal, since that makes it easier for the client to engage in the desired activity. But the client may face serious long-term consequences for such illegal conduct. While a client can choose to act illegally, the consequences of illegal conduct should not come as a surprise to the client. Just as a patient can take action that is contrary to medical advice, a client can take action even though it is against the law. But such a decision should not be accompanied by his lawyer's false assurance that the conduct is legal.

The harm to the client from failing to advise about the illegal character of proposed conduct may be even greater when the client is an entity rather than an individual. Indeed, a lawyer working for an entity client has an enhanced obligation to guard the interests of the entity against wrongdoing by the entity's constituents.

The Bybee Memorandum purports to offer legal advice. Its authors, Jay Bybee and John Yoo, had an obligation to be candid with their client, the executive branch. The constituent who requested the Bybee Memorandum, then White House Counsel Alberto Gonzales, may have wanted a particular answer to his questions about the torture statute. But the OLC lawyers had a professional obligation to give accurate legal advice to their client, whether or not the client's constituent wanted to hear it. Based on the available facts, it appears that Bybee and Yoo failed to give candid legal advice, violating D.C. Rule 2.1, and that they failed to inform their client about the state of the law of torture, violating D.C. Rule 1.4.

Because of the secrecy surrounding the Bush administration's torture policy, we do not know exactly what techniques have been used against prisoners, or whether CIA interrogators or managers were informed of the Bybee Memorandum. With Congress controlled by the President's party and no Independent Counsel statute in place, it is unclear how or when the facts surrounding the torture policy will be revealed.

If bar disciplinary authorities investigate Yoo and Bybee, these two attorneys will have an opportunity to explain or defend their actions. In that setting, they might assert that the ethical obligations of candor and adequately informing their client did never intended as legal advice in the traditional sense. In fact, David Luban and other scholars have speculated that this Bybee Memorandum was not intended as legal advice at all, but instead as an immunizing document, to ensure that CIA officials who engage in torture would not be prosecuted for that conduct. Indeed, the Bybee Memorandum might prove helpful torturers in avoiding domestic criminal accountability. It is unlikely that even a future administration would prosecute government officials who relied on an OLC memorandum for the legality of their actions, because to do so would undermine future government officials' reliance on OLC opinions more generally.

But if the authors of the Bybee Memorandum intended to immunize torturers in this way, they might have violated a different ethical rule, D.C. Rule 1.2(e), which prohibits an attorney from assisting a client's criminal conduct. So even if their memorandum successfully immunizes torturers from criminal prosecution, it might jeopardize its authors' licenses to practice law.

Conclusion

Why would otherwise competent and skilled lawyers ever risk violating the ethics rules that require candid legal advice and adequate informing of clients? Yoo has publicly defended the Bybee Memorandum in general terms but has not addressed its substantive inadequacies. Bybee, now a judge on the United States Court of Appeals for the Ninth Circuit, has remained silent. Perhaps Yoo and Bybee thought that they would never have to explain their legal advice because the Bybee Memorandum would never be made public. Perhaps they thought that Bush administration actions based on their advice would never come to light. Perhaps this advice reflected what they sincerely believed the law should be.

Bybee and Yoo are not the only government lawyers for whom the Bybee Memorandum may raise ethical concerns. News reports indicate that several White House lawyers reviewed drafts of the Bybee Memorandum. Did the White House lawyers object to the flawed analysis in the memorandum, or did they instead actually insist that the memorandum include such analysis? Still other Bush Administration lawyers, DOD General Counsel William Haynes and Department of the Air Force General Counsel Mary Walker read the final Bybee Memorandum and insisted that it become the basis of Defense Department interrogation policy, despite the glaring legal inaccuracies apparent on its face. The Defense Department's Working Group on Detainee Interrogations adopted the Bybee Memorandum nearly verbatim in its April 2003 report. The Defense Department withdrew that Report in March, 2005, three months after the Justice Department issued a replacement of the August 2002 Bybee Memorandum.

Not all government lawyers accepted the patently inaccurate claims of the Bybee Memorandum. Career military lawyers who were involved in developing Defense Department interrogation policy objected to the Bybee Memorandum, and they went up the chain of command to register their objections. The contrast between the career military lawyers, who objected to the Bybee Memorandum, and most of the politically appointed lawyers, who championed it, is quite striking, and it is worthy of more detailed study as more facts become public.

This article's conclusion—that John Yoo and Jay Bybee apparently failed to comply with their ethical obligations to provide candid legal advice and to adequately inform their client— might seem somewhat insignificant compared to the serious human rights violations that have occurred in Guantánamo, Afghanistan, Iraq, and at secret CIA interrogation sites. There will likely be long delays before any government officials are held criminally or otherwise accountable for those human rights violations. But bar disciplinary authorities have a responsibility to examine the conduct of the high-level Bush administration lawyers who wrote and propagated the Bybee Memorandum, and to hold them accountable if they violated their professional obligations.

Reprinted with permission from the July 2005 edition of the "Journal of National Security Law" © *2016 Kathleen Clak. All rights reserved.*

Questions and Comments

1. The U.S. Department of Justice Office of Professional Responsibility initiated an internal investigation of John Yoo and Jay Bybee and concluded in July 2009, that both attorneys had "engaged in professional misconduct by failing to provide 'thorough, candid, and objective' analysis in the memoranda regarding the interrogation of detained terrorist suspects."[1] However, the associate deputy attorney general then concluded that professional misconduct was not committed and Yoo and Bybee would not be subject to discipline by the state bar. Do you agree with either of these findings?

2. If the government requests an objective opinion from an attorney and reasonably relies on the legal advice to construct a policy, but following such legal advice would result in criminal activity, should the advising attorney be accountable? If so, in what way? Do lawyers need to consider the practical consequences of their legal advice? If yes, how far are you willing to extend this responsibility/liability?

3. Could the lawyers be implicated in war crimes? Lawyers assisted the Nazis in the enactment, interpretation, and enforcement of laws meant for the persecution of the Jewish and Polish populations. Five of the top Nazi leaders on trial at the first of the 12 trials at Nuremberg, held between 1945 and 1949, were lawyers, including: Hans Frank, Hitler's personal lawyer, who was found guilty of war crimes and crimes against

---

[1] *See* Robert Bejesky, *An Albatross for the Government Legal Advisor Under MRPC Rule 8.4*, 57 Howard L.J. 181, 183 (2013).

humanity and executed; Wilhelm Frick, a judge and author of the Nuremberg Laws, who was found guilty for war crimes and crimes against humanity and executed; and Konstantin von Neurath, who was also found guilty of war crimes and sentenced to 15 years imprisonment. A common excuse was "following orders" or doing what the government expected of them. Is that a sufficient explanation or defense to misconduct? Bernhard Loesener, a lawyer and "Jewish expert" in the Third Reich's Ministry of Interior drafted portions of the Nuremberg Laws. In his memoir, Loesener claimed that he personally wanted to mitigate the severity of the Nuremburg Laws, wording legislation in such a way that would limit the number of Jews affected by the Laws.[2] He also testified in the Nuremburg Trials against his former Interior Ministry boss. Do you believe he should have been tried as well? It is possible he took the position to draft the law to lessen the number of Jews affected or did he willfully take the position for ulterior reasons?

THE ETHICAL DUTIES OF PROSECUTORS OF DETAINEES WHO APPEAR BEFORE MILITARY COMMISSIONS
18 Temple Pol. & Civ. Rts. L. Rev. 69 (2008)
By John M. Burman

Military Commissions were established in November of 2001 to try persons charged with crimes against the United States as part of the "War on Terror."

While many of the persons detained as part of the struggle have not been charged or tried, they will be charged and tried before the commissions, or they will be released. While the structure, standards and procedures of Military Commissions are unique, they are, ethically, just another tribunal. The lawyers who appear before the commissions, whether prosecutors or defense attorneys, have the same ethical obligations as any other lawyer.

Given the unique natures of Military Commissions and standards and procedures used to hold and interrogate detainees, prosecutors before Military Commissions face difficult, and sometimes insurmountable, hurdles in the prosecution of detainees.

***

---

[2] *See* Karl A. Schleunes & Carol Scherer, Legislating the Holocaust: The Bernard Loesener Memoirs and Supporting Documents 1 (2001).

I. The Ethical Framework for Prosecutors Practicing Before Military Commissions

[I]t is fundamental that the prosecutor's obligation is to protect the innocent as well as ... to enforce the rights of the public.

As originally established by Executive Order, the rules of the Appointing Authority (the Secretary of Defense) specified that while practicing before a Military Commission, lawyers remain subject to "[s]tate and branch specific armed forces Rules of Professional Conduct." In addition, lawyers were required to comply "with all rules, regulations, and instructions applicable to trials by military commission... [and they] shall be deemed a professional responsibility obligation for the practice of law within the Department of Defense." Though the United States Supreme Court subsequently found the Military Commission system unconstitutional, the system was reinstated by Congress with few changes. Nothing in the new system changes the ethical framework for prosecutors—it is common that military lawyers have to abide by branch specific, state, and American Bar Association rules of ethics.

The Manual for Military Commissions (the "MMC")—the guidelines for the Military Commissions promulgated by the Secretary of Defense—addresses lawyers' ethics expressly. Rule 109 is titled "Professional Responsibility Rules for Military Judges and Counsel." It applies to military judges and all lawyers, military and civilian, who participate in proceedings before Military Commissions. As a general matter, such lawyers must comply with "[s]tate and service-specific Rules of Professional Conduct." Additionally, lawyers practicing before Military Commissions "shall adhere to any rules of professional responsibility prescribed by the Secretary of Defense [there are none] and shall... apply state, service-specific and commission-specific rules of practice and professional responsibility consistent with the provisions of this Rule.

A lawyer who fails to follow the applicable rules of professional conduct "may be subject to appropriate action by the military judge, the convening authority [the Secretary of Defense], the Judge Advocate General of the appropriate armed force, or the General Counsel of the Department of Defense." While there is no express authority for a state licensing authority—the highest court in the jurisdiction—to take disciplinary action based on a lawyer's conduct before a commission, such authority is invariably part of the rules of that jurisdiction. "Appropriate action" may include "permanently barring an individual from participating in any military commission proceeding . . . and any other lawful sanction." Disciplinary action by a state licensing authority generally ranges from disbarment to admonition, also known as a private reprimand.

A major problem for lawyers in general, and prosecutors in particular, who appear before Military Commissions is that they are often licensed in different jurisdictions and military lawyers may be members of different branches of the service. Not surprisingly, conflicts among the rules abound. Despite the differences, some general principles are fairly constant and permit generalizations that apply to most lawyers who appear before the commissions.

***

The ethical standards for prosecutors, "trial counsel," who appear before a Military Commission vary considerably among the various licensing jurisdictions and branch-specific rules. Most jurisdictions, and the branch-specific rules for the Air Force, the Army, and the Navy, define the "special responsibilities of a prosecutor [or trial counsel]." The provisions of that rule, however, vary.

In most jurisdictions, the standard for prosecutors is similar. ABA Rule 3.8(a), a version of which is in effect in most jurisdictions, states: "The prosecutor in a criminal case shall ... refrain from prosecuting a charge that the prosecutor knows is not supported by probable cause." The rules of the various military branches contain somewhat different language.

The Air Force Rules of Professional Conduct ("the Air Force Rules") "are directly adapted" from the ABA's Model Rules, "with important contributions" from the Army'' rules. Air Force Rule 3.8 "was modified to conform to military practice." The modification reflects that the "trial counsel," who may be the prosecutor, or "other persons involved in a prosecution such as, for example, the Staff Judge Advocate and Chief of Military Justice," may make charging decisions. Thus, the prosecutor still has an important duty to ensure that persons are not improperly convicted. "The trial counsel in a criminal case shall . . . recommend that the convening authority withdraw any charge not warranted by the evidence.

The Army also has Rules of Professional Conduct ("the Army Rules"). The Army Rules apply to all "Army lawyers, military and civilian, and . . . nongovemmental lawyers appearing before Army tribunals." The Army Rules also use the term "trial counsel" in place of "prosecutor."

Army Rule 3.8(a) is virtually identical to its Air Force counterpart. Unlike the Air Force Rules, the Army Rules contain Commentary, which appears to be modeled on the ABA's. As the Comment to Rule 3.8 notes, "[a] trial counsel is not simply an advocate but is responsible to see that the accused is accorded procedural justice and that guilt is decided upon the basis of sufficient evidence." Finally, "[a]pplicable law may require other measures by the trial counsel . . . ."

Rule 3.8 in the Navy Rules of Professional Conduct ("the Navy Rules") is nearly identical to both the Air Force's and Army's: "A trial counsel shall . . . recommend to the convening authority that any charge . .

. not warranted by the evidence be withdrawn." The Comment to Navy Rule 3.8 is similar to the Commentary to Army Rule 3.8:

> [A] trial counsel has the responsibility of administering justice and is not simply an advocate. This responsibility carries with it specific obligations to see that the accused is accorded procedural justice and that guilt is established on the basis of sufficient evidence . . . . [T]rial counsel does not have all the authority vested in modem civilian prosecutors. The authority to convene courts-martial, and to refer or withdraw specific charges, is vested in convening authorities. Trial counsel may have the duty, in certain circumstances, to bring to the court's attention any charge that lacks sufficient evidence to support a conviction. . . . Applicable law may require other measures by the trial counsel.

The potential difficulty of a lawyer complying with both jurisdictional and branch-specific rules is clarified in the Navy Rules, which also require lawyers to do both, and may, at times, be impossible. A Navy lawyer must comply with the Navy Rules, and remain "in good standing . . . with the licensing authority admitting the individual to the practice of law."

In sum, the overriding ethical standard for prosecutors, whether civilian or military, is reasonably clear. Prosecutors are not simply advocates. They have special duties to ensure procedural justice and to ensure that guilt is based on sufficient evidence. They are, in the words of the ABA's commentary, "minister[s] of justice." Accordingly, prosecutors are held to the highest ethical standards of any lawyer, in contrast to criminal defense lawyers or lawyers who are engaged in civil practice.

Some of a prosecutor's obligations are a result of the constitutional protections afforded criminal defendants, which may not apply to detainees tried before Military Commissions. Others are separate ethical obligations, which "may subject a prosecutor to professional discipline regardless of whether the underlying conduct violates a defendant's constitutional right."

"Probable cause," the ABA's standard for prosecutors filing criminal charges, is not defined by the rules. It has, however, been the subject of innumerable court opinions, many of which address the Fourth Amendment's "probable cause" requirement for issuing search warrants. While it is not possible to read all of the relevant cases, it is clear that "probable cause" is "a standard well short of absolute certainty." Rather, "probable cause" for a search warrant exists if "a reasonable person [would] believe that the entry was necessary to prevent physical harm to the officers or other persons." Transplanted to filing criminal charges, "probable cause" means that a prosecutor should not file charges unless "a reasonable" prosecutor would believe that there is an evidentiary basis for doing so that can be proven beyond a reasonable doubt.

The reason that prosecutors are held to a higher standard is simple. They are not just advocates with "a duty to use legal procedure for the fullest benefit of the client's cause." Rather, "[a] prosecutor has the responsibility of a minister of justice and not simply that of an advocate." Accordingly, a prosecutor has an ethical obligation "to see that the defendant is accorded procedural justice, [and] that guilt is decided upon the basis of sufficient evidence."

Paragraph (a) of ABA Rule 3.8 uses the term "knows." A "prosecutor in a criminal case shall . . . refrain from prosecuting a charge that the prosecutor knows is not supported by probable cause. "Knows" is a defined term: "'[K]nows' denotes actual knowledge of the fact in question. A person's knowledge may be inferred from circumstances."

The reference to "actual knowledge" means that "knows" is subjective. A prosecutor must actually know whether the charge is "supported by probable cause." The last clause, which states that such knowledge may be "inferred from circumstances," means that a prosecutor may not close his or her eyes to the obvious facts that he or she has been presented with, since in considering "knowledge" for criminal purposes, a law firm's "deliberate ignorance constituted the equivalent of knowledge of the truth. The only way a prosecutor can have "actual knowledge" about the legitimacy of a criminal charge is if he or she has investigated the law and the facts involved.

The ABA has established additional standards for prosecutors and defense attorneys in criminal cases. While the standards, unlike a jurisdiction or service's Rules of Professional Conduct, are not binding, they reflect generally accepted norms for lawyers who engage in either the prosecution or defense of criminal cases, and they have been so acknowledged by the United States Supreme Court, which described the Standards for the Defense Function as "guides to determining what is reasonable."

"The duty of the prosecutor," according to the ABA standards, and consistent with the ABA's Rules of Professional Conduct and the service-specific rules of the armed services, "is to seek justice, not merely to convict." Furthermore, "[i]t is an important function of the prosecutor to seek to reform and improve the administration of criminal justice." The reason for these responsibilities is that "[a]lthough the prosecutor operates within the adversary system, it is fundamental that the prosecutor's obligation is to protect the innocent as well as . . . to enforce the rights of the public." Far too often, the former obligation gets lost in the rush to judgment, especially in the cases of alleged terrorists.

Among the standards for prosecutors is an investigative function, particularly relevant to the situation of prosecuting detainees who have been mistreated during their captivity. While a prosecutor normally relies on investigative agencies to gather evidence of a crime, a "prosecutor has an affirmative responsibility to investigate suspected illegal activity when it is not adequately dealt with by other agencies." Similarly, "[a] prosecutor should not knowingly use illegal means to obtain evidence or to employ or instruct or encourage others to use such means.

The standards echo the Model Rules' prohibition on a lawyer offering false evidence. "A prosecutor should not knowingly offer false evidence . . . ." The commentary clarifies the scope of this duty. "This obligation applies to evidence that bears on the credibility of a witness as well as to evidence on issues going directly to guilt."

In short, prosecutors are different. In the words of the United States Supreme Court, the prosecutor is:

> the representative not of an ordinary party to a controversy, but of a sovereignty whose obligation to govern impartially is as compelling as its obligation to govern at all; and whose interest, therefore, in a criminal prosecution is not that it shall win a case, but that justice shall be done.

While the words were written about an Assistant United States Attorney, the rules do not distinguish between civilian and military prosecutors, and there is no reason to do so, at least ethically. Although there may be a difference in who decides to initiate criminal charges, any difference ends at that point. At trial, both the civilian and military prosecutors should strive for justice, not for victory.

The ethical standards that apply to prosecutors are particularly important given the apparent mistreatment of detainees while in the hands of the Department of Defense, the Central Intelligence Agency, or a third party.

Ideally, a "trial counsel" before a Military Commission should investigate the conditions under which the detainee was held, and the procedures that were used to obtain the information which will be used as evidence against the detainee. If the investigation reveals that the conditions and procedures fall far short of fair and humane, the prosecutor should not proffer charges against the detainee. If charges have already been filed by someone else, such as an appointing or convening authority, trial counsel should recommend that they be withdrawn because of the absence of sufficient evidence. If the matter goes to trial, trial counsel should not seek to convict a detainee using false or inherently unreliable evidence.

The same should apply to prosecutors bound by the Air Force, Army or Navy Rules of Professional Conduct, not just jurisdiction- or service-specific rules. While the charges before a Military Commission may have been filed by someone else, as the Army's Rules declare: "A trial counsel shall . . . recommend to the convening authority that any charge . . . not warranted by the evidence be withdrawn." The reason for this obligation, according to the Comment, is that "a trial counsel is not simply an advocate but is responsible to see that the accused is accorded procedural justice and that guilt is decided upon the basis of sufficient evidence."

The Navy goes further: the Comment to Rule 3.8 acknowledges that "trial counsel does not have all the authority vested in modem civilian prosecutors," and that "[t]he authority to convene courts-martial, and to refer and withdraw specific charges, is vested in convening authorities," but that difference does not eliminate trial counsel's duty. "Trial counsel may have the duty, in certain circumstances, to bring to the court's attention any charge that lacks sufficient evidence to support a conviction."

A military prosecutor, therefore, has the following duties: First, to advise the appointing or convening authority if the charge is not warranted by the evidence, which was obtained properly. Second, to ensure "procedural justice" for the accused. And finally, to ensure that findings of guilt are based on "sufficient evidence." The only way to competently discharge these duties is to investigate, so the lawyer will know the legal and factual bases for the charges. This is especially true when any reasonable lawyer knows that the conditions under which detainees have been held, and the procedures that have been used to elicit information from them, including "confessions," have been and continue to be inhumane, and in violation of international law. Any claim to ignorance to the contrary is "deliberate," and deliberate ignorance is the same as knowledge.

While the words used in the ABA's Model Rules, and in many other jurisdictions, may be different from those used by the Air Force, the Army, or the Navy, all relevant or potentially applicable rules of professional conduct have a similar theme. Prosecutors are not just advocates. They have a higher duty, a duty to ensure that justice is done, not just that the government "wins" the case and obtains a conviction.

In addition to their special duties as prosecutors, lawyers who appear before a court or any other tribunal, have certain duties. Those duties are essentially the same for all lawyers, whether military or civilian, prosecutors or defense attorneys, or lawyers in civil practice.

The highest duty every lawyer owes is to the tribunal before which he or she appears. Rule 3.3 defines the extent of that duty. It is substantially similar in all sets of rules of professional conduct that are relevant to lawyers who appear before Military Commissions.

Rule 3.3 of the ABA Model Rules is entitled "Candor Toward the Tribunal." Among other things, it provides that "[a] lawyer shall not knowingly . . . offer evidence that the lawyer knows to be false." If the lawyer unknowingly does so, and the evidence is "material . . . and the lawyer comes to know of its falsity, the lawyer shall take reasonable remedial measures, including, if necessary, disclosure to the tribunal."

This obligation is so important that it will "apply even if compliance requires disclosure of information otherwise protected by Rule 1.6," the rule which requires attorneys to maintain client information in confidence. "This duty [of candor] is premised on the lawyer's obligation as an officer of the court to prevent the trier of fact from being misled by false evidence." Not only do most civilian jurisdictions adhere to this rule, the Air Force, Army, and Navy do as well.

The Air Force Rule is virtually identical to the ABA's. "A lawyer shall not knowingly . . . offer evidence that the lawyer knows to be false." Further, if material evidence has already been offered, and the lawyer learns it is false, "the lawyer shall take reasonable remedial measures." Overall, the rule contains the same principle as the ABA's. A lawyer's highest duty is to the tribunal, not the lawyer's client, so the obligation not to offer false evidence applies "even if compliance requires disclosure of information otherwise protected by Rule 1.6."

The Army Rules similarly provide that "[a] lawyer shall not knowingly . . . offer evidence that the lawyer knows to be false." As with the ABA rule on which it is based, the Army Rule requires a lawyer who has offered material evidence and comes to learn of its falsity, to "take reasonable remedial measures." Also, in conformity with the ABA, a lawyer must comply with the foregoing "even if compliance requires disclosure of information otherwise protected by Rule 1.6." Because of this rule, a lawyer's duty as an advocate "is qualified by the advocate's duty of candor to the tribunal." The Navy Rule is substantially similar in all respects." Further, this rule is similar to a prosecutor's obligation not to offer false evidence.

Therefore, regardless of a prosecutor's special duties, all lawyers, including military or civilian lawyers who appear before Military Commissions, have a duty to not knowingly offer false evidence to the tribunal (the Military Commission). This duty comes sharply into focus when a detainee is prosecuted using evidence, either from the detainee or others, which was elicited by coercive means, in violation of international law.

***

Under the Military Commissions Act ("the MCA"), trial counsel has a limited obligation to disclose exculpatory information to detainees accused of crimes. That "obligation" is potentially too narrow to allow trial counsel to meet their ethical obligation. "Where exculpatory evidence is classified, the accused shall be provided with an adequate substitute . . . ." As noted below, "classified information" is defined broadly and the determination of whether information is classified appears to be entirely up to the discretion of the President. Further, it seems unlikely, if not impossible, that there can be an "adequate substitute" for truly exculpatory information that has been deemed "classified." Finally, whether the substitute is "adequate" should be a decision for the defense attorney, not the prosecutor.

One can argue that the ABA and the service rules limit the disclosure obligation in a way that allows trial counsel in Military Commissions to comply with both the MCA and their professional responsibility. The argument is that the ABA rule does not require disclosure "when the prosecutor is relieved of this responsibility by a protective order of the tribunal." The problem in the Military Commission context is that the prosecutor has not been "relieved of this [disclosure] responsibility by a tribunal." Rather, the MCA has given the President virtually blanket, unreviewable authority to decide what is "classified," and need not, therefore, be disclosed. Instead of that decision being made by an independent tribunal, it is made by the executive-through classifying the evidence-a person who can hardly be said to be independent; he apparently subscribes to the view that the Guantanamo Bay detainees are "the worst of the worst." The odds of getting a fair or independent determination of whether something should be "classified" appear to be nonexistent, and the exception should not apply. The result is that by not providing complete disclosure of exculpatory information, trial counsel is at best walking on ethical thin ice.

One can also argue that the Army and Navy Rules, which allow for withholding exculpatory evidence pursuant to a "regulation," provide a basis for at least some military prosecutors to withhold information. There are three problems with this argument.

First, why would a prosecutor want a detainee to be found guilty when there is exculpatory evidence that may have exonerated the accused? After all, a prosecutor's duty is to see that justice is done, not simply that accused persons are wrongly convicted. He or she has an obligation to ensure that "guilt is decided upon the basis of sufficient evidence, including consideration of exculpatory evidence known to the prosecution."

Second, very few, if any, military prosecutors will not also be bound by the rules of the jurisdiction in which they are licensed. Most jurisdictions follow the ABA's lead, allowing only for non-disclosure when a protective order has been issued by a tribunal. Few, if any, of those jurisdictions allow a "regulation" to create an exception. A military prosecutor may, therefore, be in compliance with the branch-specific rules, but in violation of the rules of his or her licensing jurisdiction.

Third, acting in accordance with a law may not be ethical. It is clear, for example, that obeying orders or following the law will not always be a defense. If the Nuremberg trials decided nothing else, they "clearly demonstrate[] that there are times when moral responsibility supersedes legal duty." Further, it is well established in this country that a government official is entitled to "qualified immunity" if his or her actions do not violate a "clearly established" legal right. If they do, by contrast, the official may be liable. Just as a government official should not be able to deprive anyone of a clearly established legal right, neither should a prosecutor be allowed to deprive a detainee of a clearly established right.

III. Acting at the Direction of Another Is Not a Defense to Unethical Conduct

A lawyer is bound by these rules [of professional conduct] notwithstanding that the lawyer acted at the direction of another person.

Every potentially relevant set of rules of professional conduct that might apply to prosecutors ("trial counsel") appearing before Military Commissions eliminates acting at the direction of another as a defense to misconduct.

The ABA Rule, which has been adopted in most jurisdictions, contains the general principle: "A lawyer is bound by the Rules of Professional Conduct notwithstanding that the lawyer acted at the direction of another person." In language particularly apt for military prosecutors who are, by definition, commissioned officers subject to the authority of one or more commanding officers, the commentary to the rule explains that "a lawyer is not relieved of responsibility for a violation by the fact that the lawyer acted at the direction of a supervisor." The Air Force Rule is identical. The Army and Navy Rules use slightly different language, though they are substantially similar.

Whatever a lawyer's experience or position in a law firm or law office, every "lawyer is bound by the Rules of Professional Conduct notwithstanding that the lawyer acted at the direction of another person." Although following the orders of a supervisory lawyer is not a defense to misconduct, "that fact may be relevant in determining whether a lawyer had the knowledge required to render conduct a violation of the Rules."

In sum, it does not matter who tells a lawyer what to do, or what that lawyer is told. The lawyer must comply with the applicable rules of professional conduct, or the lawyer has committed "misconduct," for which the lawyer may be sanctioned.

***

The name "Guantanamo Bay" has come to symbolize inhuman treatment and unwarranted and indefinite imprisonment of detainees, persons arrested and imprisoned indefinitely, and often never charged with crimes, as alleged participants or supporters of the War on Terror. Rumors about what has occurred and what is still occurring at Guantanamo abound, though little is known for sure as the Bush Administration has gone to great lengths to prevent anyone, even international human rights groups, from investigating or reporting on conditions at Guantanamo Bay.

Those rumors have brought demands for the base's closure. The situation is so bad that Guantanamo Bay has, in the words of the *The New York Times*, "become a lightning rod for international criticism." According to a February 2006 United Nations report, "[t]he Government of the United States should close the Guantanamo Bay detention facilities without further delay."

Despite the attempts of the Bush Administration to shroud Guantanamo Bay and the activities that occur there behind a veil of secrecy, the sordid story of how the United States has treated and continues to treat Guantanamo Bay detainees has leaked out. It is now beyond dispute that the treatment of detainees has been inhumane, at best. It now appears that the treatment of detainees at Guantanamo Bay represents one of the sorriest chapters in the history of the United States. Many Americans would find the conduct approved and even mandated by the President intolerable if engaged in by other countries, yet this conduct is somehow justifiable as part of our War on Terror.

Almost lost amid the controversy over the treatment of detainees is the ethical effect on the prosecutors ("trial counsel") who are or will be responsible for prosecuting cases against those detainees actually charged with crimes, as opposed to the vast majority of detainees, imprisoned indefinitely without criminal charges ever being filed. Holding detainees without charging them and without allowing them to challenge their confinement is a clear violation of international law. The ethical consequences of a lawyer prosecuting detainees based, entirely or substantially, on evidence derived from coerced confessions from the defendant, coerced information acquired from other detainees, or both, are profound and disconcerting. Such prosecutions are, quite simply, unethical, and the lawyers who present them are committing misconduct, which, in some cases, may be mandated by the Bush Administration. As discussed above, the so-called "Nuremburg Defense," acting at the direction of a third person, is not a defense to unethical conduct. Prosecutors need to stand up and refuse to be a part of such unethical proceedings.

Even if the detention facility at Guantanamo Bay is closed, which seems inevitable, though the UN's call for immediate closure is well over two years old, the ethical issues regarding trials of detainees will likely still remain. Nothing, not even their release, can make up for the hardship the Guantanamo detainees have endured, and the years that have been stolen from their lives. Any attempt to prosecute the detainees, at Guantanamo Bay or elsewhere, either outside the boundaries of the United States or inside, will raise the same ethical issues.

Summary

The procedures of Military Commissions are unique, but that uniqueness does not change the ethical responsibility of the lawyers who appear before them. When all is said and done, military lawyers practicing before Military Commissions are bound both by the rules of the jurisdiction or jurisdictions in which they are licensed, and the rules of the branch of the military in which they serve.

Complying with two or more sets of rules of professional conduct, as well as the MCA, and the MMC, may be, and at times is likely to be, impossible. The only safe course for a lawyer to take in such a situation is to follow the more restrictive of the potentially applicable rules. Further, following the "safe" course will also be an important step to correcting the systemic wrongs that have been done to detainees, though it will be impossible to completely right the wrongs that have been perpetrated on hundreds of innocent detainees.

In the case of criminal charges filed against a detainee, a prosecutor appearing before a Military Commission has an ethical duty to conduct a reasonable investigation into the facts and the law, an investigation that will often reveal that the charge is based on a coerced confession by the defendant, coerced statements from other detainees, or both. In such circumstances, the trial counsel has ethical duties to: (1) recommend that the convening authority withdraw the charges; (2) completely disclose exculpatory information regarding guilt or mitigation of any possible sentence; and (3) not offer evidence that he or she knows is false. Finally, a prosecutor appearing before a Military Commission may not hide behind the orders of superior officers, even those of the President as Commander-in-Chief, or congressional directives, as an excuse for engaging in unethical conduct. The "Nuremberg defense" is invalid. Every lawyer is responsible for his or her ethical conduct, notwithstanding that the lawyer acted at the direction of a third party.

In the final analysis, a prosecutor is not simply an advocate for the government, using the legal system to gain a result favorable to his or her client. Rather, a prosecutor must seek justice, and "it is fundamental that the prosecutor's obligation [be] to protect the innocent as well as to enforce the rights of the public."

Endnotes omitted (See John M. Burman, The Ethical Duties of Prosecutors of Detainees Who Appear Before Military Commissions, 18 Temple Pol. & Civ. Rts. L. Rev. 69 (2008) for full article version).

Questions and Comments

1. A military prosecutor may be in compliance with her branch-specific rules, but in violation of the rules of her licensing jurisdiction. Should she be immune from discipline if her respective state disciplinary board finds she violated a rule? Should a lawyer seek an advisory opinion from her state bar association before proceeding?

2. Several civilian attorneys have represented Guantanamo Bay detainees before military commissions. Is this, in and of itself, a violation of the Model Rules? In 2003, the National Association of Criminal Defense Lawyers opined that defense attorneys could not ethically participate in the military commissions because the "conditions imposed upon defense counsel before these commissions make it impossible for counsel to provide adequate or ethical representation." See Nat'l Ass'n of Crim. Def. Lawyers, Ethics Advisory Comm., Opinion 03-04 (2003).

IN RE DIAZ
Supreme Court of Kansas (2012)
288 P.3d 486

This is an original proceeding in discipline filed by the office of the Disciplinary Administrator against the respondent, Matthew M. Diaz, of Forest Hills, New York, an attorney admitted to the practice of law in Kansas in 1995.

On October 20, 2010, the office of the Disciplinary Administrator filed a formal complaint against the respondent alleging violations of the Kansas Rules of Professional Conduct (KRPC). The respondent filed an answer on November 8, 2010. A hearing was held on the complaint before a panel of the Kansas Board for Discipline of Attorneys on October 19, 2011, where the respondent was personally present and represented by counsel. The hearing panel determined that respondent violated KRPC 1.6(a) (2011 Kan. Ct. R. Annot. 480) (confidentiality) and 8.4(b) (2011 Kan. Ct. R. Annot. 618) (commission of a criminal act reflecting adversely on the lawyer's honesty, trustworthiness or fitness as a lawyer). The panel made the following findings of fact and conclusions of law, together with its recommendation to this court:

"Findings of Fact . . .

"22. In December, 1994, the Respondent received a commission from the United States Navy to serve as a judge advocate. The Respondent was admitted to the practice of law in the State of Kansas on April 28, 1995. [Footnote: The Respondent's license to practice law in the State of Kansas has been temporarily suspended, due to his convictions, for more than three years.]

"23. In July, 2004, the Respondent, a deputy staff judge advocate, was assigned to the Joint Task Force in Guantanamo Bay, Cuba. The Respondent remained at Guantanamo Bay, Cuba, until January 15, 2005.

"24. On June 28, 2004, the United States Supreme Court issued its opinion in *Rasul v. Bush*, 541 [542] U.S. 466 [124 S.Ct. 2686, 159 L.Ed.2d 548] (2004). In that case, the United State Supreme Court held that the habeas corpus statute, 28 U.S.C. §2241, entitled the Guantanamo Bay detainees to challenge the validity of their detention. [542 U.S.] at 483 [124 S.Ct. 2686]. The Respondent read *Rasul* on his way to Cuba.

"25. On December 17, 2004, Barbara Olshansky, the Deputy Legal Director for the Center of Constitutional Rights sent a letter to the Honorable Gordon R. England, the Secretary of the Navy. The Respondent and his immediate supervisor, Lt. Colonel Randall Keys were sent copies of the letter.

"26. In her letter, Ms. Olshansky stated:

'As you know, the United States presently acknowledges detaining approximately 550 individuals at the Guantanamo Bay Naval Base, Cuba. Approximately 63 of those individuals have filed habeas corpus petitions with the D.C. district court. We intend to take any legal action necessary, including filing habeas petitions on behalf of the remaining detainees, in order to ensure that every detainee at Guantanamo has the opportunity to avail themselves of the decision in Rasul.

Accordingly, we are writing to request that you provide us with the names and other identifying information about each person held at Guantanamo who[se] identity has not yet been made known and who has not yet filed a petition for a writ of habeas corpus ("unidentified detainee" or "detainee").'

"27. After Ms. Olshansky's letter was received, the Respondent understood that the government's response was to not release the requested information.

"28. The Respondent had strong feelings about a prisoner's right to habeas corpus proceedings. When the Respondent was sixteen years old, his father, a nurse, was arrested and charged with 12 counts of murder for injecting patients with a lethal dose of Lidocaine. Later, the Respondent's father was convicted and sentenced to death. The Respondent's father's death sentence was not carried out because of a pending habeas corpus action. In fact, the Respondent's father's habeas corpus proceeding remained pending until he died in prison of natural causes in August, 2010.

"29. For a period of three weeks, the Respondent contemplated what he could do to comply with the law and follow his orders.

"30. During that time, the Respondent failed to seek or obtain guidance regarding his conflict between his ethical duties and military duties. Pursuant to § 13, Rule 1.13 of JAG Instruction 5803.1C, the Respondent could have sought and obtained guidance, but did not. Additionally, the Respondent failed to seek or obtain a formal ethics opinion pursuant to § 10(b) of JAG Instruction 5803.1C. The Respondent also failed to seek or obtain an informal ethics opinion pursuant to §12(a) of JAG Instruction 5803.1C. Further, at his courtmartial, the Respondent testified that he could have gone to Lt. Col. Keys, General Hood, the Chief of Staff, the Inspector General, or a Congressperson regarding this issue. Moreover, at the hearing on this matter, the Respondent testified that he could have gone to Admiral Gouder or Admiral Hudson for guidance. Finally, the Respondent testified that he could have contacted the Disciplinary Administrator for guidance.

"31. From December 23, 2004 through January 4, 2005, Lt. Col. Keys was on Christmas leave and away from the office.

"32. During the evening hours on January 2, 2005, the Respondent returned to the staff judge advocate office and printed a list of detainees from the Joint Defense Information Management System from the secret computer. The list that the Respondent printed contained each detainee's full name, their internment serial number, their country of origin, their country of citizenship, and other identifying information including ethnicity, source identification number, and information regarding the detention or interrogation team assigned to each detainee. The list contained classified information.

"33. While contemplating what to do with the list, the Respondent maintained the list in a safe in the staff judge advocate's office.

"34. The Respondent purchased a large Valentine's Day card. The Respondent cut the list into strips and placed the strips into the card. The Respondent did not sign the card. The only return address listed was 'GTMO.' On January 14, 2005, the Respondent sent the card to Ms. Olshansky. Ms. Olshansky did not have a security clearance and was not authorized by the government to access detainee information.

"35. The Respondent knew that if he had the list in his belongings it would be found when he was leaving the island because his belongings were subject to search.

"36. When Ms. Olshansky received the list, she believed that it might be a hoax or a practical joke. She immediately contacted the federal judge handling the detainee litigation. The judge requested that the list be secured from Ms. Olshansky. An agent came to Ms. Olshansky's office, secured the list, and provided it to the judge. The judge realized that it was an actual list of detainees and should not have been released to Ms. Olshansky in that fashion. Thereafter, an investigation ensued.

"37. On March 3, 2006, the Respondent was interrogated and fingerprinted. Additionally, at that time, the Respondent provided writing samples.

"38. In August, 2006, the Respondent was charged in a three count complaint. The first charge alleged that the Respondent violated a lawful general regulation by wrongfully mailing classified secret information. The second charge alleged that the Respondent wrongfully and dishonorably transmitted classified documents to an unauthorized individual. The third charge alleged three different specifications, (1) that the Respondent made a print out of classified secret information with the intent to use the information to the injury of the United States or to the advantage of a foreign nation, (2) that the Respondent knowingly and willfully communicated classified secret information relative to national defense to a person not entitled to receive the information that could be used to injure the United States or to the advantage of a foreign nation, and (3) that the Respondent knowingly removed materials containing classified information without authority and with the intention to retain such materials at an unauthorized location.

"39. On May 17, 2007, a court-martial consisting of senior officers convicted the Respondent of the crime of [1] violating a lawful general regulation by wrongfully mailing classified secret information, [2] wrongfully and dishonorably transmitting classified documents to an unauthorized individual, [3] knowingly and willfully communicating classified secret information relative to national defense to a person not entitled to receive the information that could be used to injure the United States or to the advantage of a foreign nation, and [4] knowingly removing materials containing classified information without authority and with the intention to retain such materials at an unauthorized location.

"40. The court-martial acquitted the Respondent of the most serious charge which was printing out the information with the specific intent to harm national security or to provide an advantage to a foreign government.

"41. On May 18, 2007, the Respondent was dismissed from the Navy and sentenced to serve six months confinement. The Respondent served six months' confinement in 2007.

"42. On August 8, 2007, counsel for the Respondent reported the Respondent's convictions to the Disciplinary Administrator.

"43. On August 31, 2007, the Respondent submitted a clemency request. After reviewing the matters submitted in clemency, the Convening Authority approved the sentence.

"44. On September 17, 2007, Captain H.H. Dronberger wrote to the Disciplinary Administrator regarding the Respondent. In the letter, Captain Dronberger stated:

'The Judge Advocate General permanently revoked Lieutenant Commander Diaz' certification under Article 27(b) of the Uniform

Code of Military Justice, 10 U.S.C. § 827(b), thereby disqualifying him from representing members of the Naval Service before any forum in the Department of the Navy. The Judge Advocate General also revoked Lieutenant Commander Diaz' authority to provide legal assistance and prohibited him from providing any other legal services or advice in any matter under the cognizance and supervision of the Judge Advocate General.

'The Judge Advocate General found that Lieutenant Commander Diaz violated the "Rules of Professional Conduct of Attorneys Practicing Under the Cognizance and Supervision of the Judge Advocate Genera'" by:

   a. committing a criminal act that reflects adversely on Lieutenant Commander Diaz' honesty, trustworthiness, and fitness as an attorney in other respects, and

   b. revealing confidential information relating to representation of his client without his client's consent.'

***

Conclusions of Law

"47. Based upon the findings of fact, the decision of the Judge Advocate General, and Kan. Sup.Ct. R. 202, the Hearing Panel concludes as a matter of law that the Respondent violated KRPC 1.6(a) and KRPC 8.4(b), as detailed below.

"48. KRPC 1.6(a) provides:

A lawyer shall not reveal information relating to representation of a client unless the client consents after consultation, except for disclosures that are impliedly authorized in order to carry out the representation, and except as stated in paragraph (b).'

The Respondent revealed confidential client information without authorization. If the Respondent disagreed with the actions taken by his client, the Navy, then the Respondent was duty bound to so inform those with decision making power within the Navy. The Hearing Panel believes that the Respondent could not publicly announce his disagreement, or his reasons therefor, as such a public disavowment would harm the interests of his client. The actions taken by the Respondent to disclose the confidential information being protected by his client violated his fiduciary responsibility to that client. Accordingly, the Hearing Panel concludes that the Respondent breached the trust of his client and violated KRPC 1.6(a).

"49. 'It is professional misconduct for a lawyer to . . . commit a criminal act that reflects adversely on the lawyer's honesty, trustworthiness or fitness as a lawyer in other respects.' KRPC 8.4(b). In this case, the Respondent committed four crimes. The Respondent violated a lawful general regulation by wrongfully mailing classified secret information. The Respondent wrongfully and dishonorably transmitted classified documents to an unauthorized individual. The Respondent knowingly and willfully communicated classified secret information relative to national defense to a person not entitled to receive the information that could be used to injure the United States or to the advantage of a foreign nation. And, the Respondent knowingly removed materials containing classified information without authority and with the intention to retain such materials at an unauthorized location. The crimes which the Respondent was convicted of adversely reflect on the Respondent's trustworthiness. Accordingly, the Hearing Panel concludes that the Respondent violated KRPC 8.4(b).

***

Recommendation

"61. The Disciplinary Administrator recommended that, based upon the Respondent's convictions, the conclusions of the Judge Advocate General, and the conclusions of the military courts, the Respondent be disbarred. Counsel for the Respondent argued that the Respondent has been disciplined enough and that no further discipline should be imposed.

"62. The act of printing and sending classified and confidential information to an unauthorized person warrants significant discipline. The furtive nature of the Respondent's actions aggravate the malfeasance. Not only did the Respondent print the list which contained classified information from the secret computer, he also cut the list into pieces and placed the pieces into a Valentine's Day card so that the package appeared innocuous. Further, the Respondent's timing aggravates his conduct. The Respondent mailed the card the day before he left the island so as to reduce his chance of facing consequences for his actions.

"63. The United States Court of Appeals for the Armed Forces also noted the Respondent's method of disclosure:

'. . . [The Respondent] copied classified material and sent it to a person not authorized to receive it. The clandestine method of disclosure-by sending it through the postal system cut up in a Valentine's Day card-suggests that [the Respondent] knew at the time his actions warranted concealment. His failure to adhere to presidential directives and departmental regulations, including those regarding classified information and for addressing differences of legal views within the Department, demonstrates that [the Respondent] was not legally permitted to disregard the classified nature of the protected information.'

"64. Accordingly, based upon the findings of fact, conclusions of law, the conclusions of the Judge Advocate General, the conclusions of the military courts, and the Standards listed above, the Hearing Panel unanimously recommends that the Respondent be suspended for a period of three years. The Hearing Panel further recommends that the suspension be made retroactive to the date of his temporary suspension. Accordingly, the Hearing Panel recommends that the Respondent be immediately reinstated to the practice of law.

"6[5]. Costs are assessed against the Respondent in an amount to be certified by the Office of the Disciplinary Administrator."

Discussion

In a disciplinary proceeding, this court considers the evidence, the findings of the hearing panel, and the arguments of the parties and determines whether violations of KRPC exist and, if they do, the discipline to be imposed. Attorney misconduct must be established by clear and convincing evidence. *In re Foster*, 292 Kan. 940, 945, 258 P.3d 375 (2011); see Supreme Court Rule 211(f) (2011 Kan. Ct. R. Annot. 334). Clear and convincing evidence is "evidence that causes the factfinder to believe that "the truth of the facts asserted is highly probable." *In re Lober*, 288 Kan. 498, 505, 204 P.3d 610 (2009) (quoting *In re Dennis*, 286 Kan. 708, 725, 188 P.3d 1 [2008]). When the court assesses the existence of clear and convincing evidence, it refrains from weighing conflicting evidence, assessing witness credibility, or redetermining questions of fact. See *In re B.D.-Y.*, 286 Kan. 686, 699, 187 P.3d 594 (2008).

Respondent was given adequate notice of the formal complaint, to which he filed an answer, and adequate notice of both the hearing before the panel and the hearing before this court. He filed no exceptions to the panel's final hearing report. The panel's findings of fact are thus deemed admitted, and we adopt them. See Supreme Court Rule 212(c), (d) (2011 Kan. Ct. R. Annot. 352).

The evidence before the hearing panel establishes the charged misconduct of the respondent by clear and convincing evidence and supports the panel's conclusions of law. We therefore also adopt the panel's conclusions.

The only remaining issue is the appropriate discipline to be imposed. We have held that "[t]he panel's recommendation is advisory only and shall not prevent the court from imposing a different discipline." *In re Harding*, 290 Kan. 81, 90, 223 P.3d 303 (2010); Supreme Court Rule 212(f). At the hearing before this court, at which the respondent appeared, the office of the Disciplinary Administrator recommended that the respondent be disbarred. The respondent requested that no discipline be imposed beyond that assessed by the military courts. As referenced above, the hearing panel recommended that respondent be suspended from the practice of law for 3 years and that the suspension be made retroactive to the date of his temporary suspension.

We begin our analysis by recognizing that in apparent support of respondent's position that the military courts have sufficiently disciplined him, he repeats an argument he made before those tribunals. Respondent essentially argues that while his actions were wrong his motive was virtuous. In short, he disclosed the information to protect the Guantanamo Bay detainees' habeas corpus rights declared in the United States Supreme Court opinion of *Rasul v. Bush*, 542 U.S. 466, 124 S.Ct. 2686, 159 L.Ed.2d 548 (2004). During the general court-martial proceedings, that tribunal excluded respondent's motive evidence showing his purported honorable intent in disclosing the classified information. As noted by the hearing panel, the United States Navy–Marine Corps Court of Criminal Appeals affirmed, finding his motive argument "nonsensical and dangerous." *United States v. Diaz*, No. 200700970, 2009 WL 690614, at *5 (N.M.Ct.Crim.App.2009) (unpublished opinion).

The United States Court of Appeals for the Armed Forces found that while the motive evidence might be relevant to respondent's charge of conduct unbecoming an officer, its exclusion was harmless error. It observed that supporting a harmlessness determination was respondent's knowledge that his "actions warranted concealment." *United States v. Diaz*, 69 M.J. 127, 137 (2010). An additional consideration supporting a harmlessness determination was the "absence in *Rasul* of any indication the Supreme Court intended its ruling to supersede in some manner counsel's other legal and ethical obligations," including his obligation to adhere to presidential and naval directives regarding the handling of classified information. 69 M.J. at 137.

According to the record before us, respondent was asked during his general court-martial proceedings why he chose to disclose the classified information surreptitiously. He replied, "Selfish reasons, I was more concerned with self-preservation, I didn't want to get—make any waves and jeopardize my career." When asked why he did not share with his superior officers his concerns about the Navy's then-refusal to release the information to Ms. Olshansky, Diaz replied, "I was worried about the effect it would have on me . . . . I wasn't really to put—willing to put my neck on the line and jeopardize my career at the time . . . . [So], I did it anonymously." On this latter point, the hearing panel held that "[I]f the Respondent disagreed with the actions taken by his client, the Navy, then the Respondent was duty bound to so inform those with decision making power within the Navy." The panel did not cite a KRPC provision in support of its holding. But subsection (b) of KRPC 1.13 (2011 Kan. Ct. R.

Annot. 513), which sets out the rules for an attorney whose client is an organization, contains supportive language. It states:

> If a lawyer for an organization knows that an officer, employee or other person associated with the organization is engaged in action, intends to act or refuses to act in a matter related to the representation that is a violation of a legal obligation to the organization, or a violation of law which reasonably might be imputed to the organization, and is likely to result in substantial injury to the organization, the lawyer shall proceed as is reasonably necessary in the best interest of the organization. In determining how to proceed, the lawyer shall give due consideration to the seriousness of the violation and its consequences, the scope and nature of the lawyer's representation, the responsibility in the organization and the apparent motivation of the person involved, the policies of the organization concerning such matters and any other relevant considerations. *Any measures taken shall be designed to minimize disruption of the organization and the risk of revealing information relating to the representation to persons outside the organization.* Such measures may include among others:
>
> (1) asking for reconsideration of the matter;
>
> (2) advising that a separate legal opinion on the matter be sought for presentation to appropriate authority in the organization; and
>
> (3) referring the matter to higher authority in the organization, including, if warranted by the seriousness of the matter, referral to the highest authority that can act in behalf of the organization as determined by applicable law." (Emphasis added.) 2011 Kan. Ct. R. Annot. 513–14.

We continue our discipline analysis by referring to the ABA Standards for Imposing Lawyer Sanctions. As the hearing panel pointed out, suspension is generally appropriate when, as here, "a lawyer knowingly reveals information relating to the representation of a client not otherwise lawfully permitted to be disclosed, and this disclosure causes injury or potential injury to a client." ABA Standards, Section 4.22. And as the panel further pointed out, suspension is also generally appropriate when, as here, "a lawyer in an official or governmental position knowingly fails to follow proper procedures or rules, and causes injury or potential injury to a party or to the integrity of the legal process." ABA Standards, Section 5.22. But here, we have much more.

Under ABA Standards, Section 5.11, disbarment is generally appropriate when:

> "(a) a lawyer engages in serious criminal conduct, a necessary
> element of which includes intentional interference with the
> administration of justice, false swearing, misrepresentation, fraud,
> extortion, misappropriation, or theft . . . ; or

"(b) a lawyer engages in any other intentional conduct involving dishonesty, fraud, deceit, or misrepresentation that seriously adversely reflects on the lawyer's fitness to practice."

Respondent's intentional actions—resulting in four felony convictions, 6 months' actual confinement, and dismissal from the naval service—undeniably qualify as serious criminal conduct under Section 5.11. And some of his criminal acts easily meet several of the specific "necessary element[s]" for disbarment, *e.g.*, theft—of his country's classified information.

As the hearing panel additionally noted in its quotation from the United States Navy– Marine Corps Court of Criminal Appeals that reviewed respondent's general court-martial, "'One who elects to serve mankind by taking the law into his own hands thereby demonstrates his conviction that his own ability to determine policy is superior to democratic decision making.'" *Diaz*, 2009 WL 690614, at *5 (quoting *United States v. Cullen*, 454 F.2d 386, 392 [7th Cir.1971]). Accordingly, respondent's reviewing court later concluded that he "negatively impacted public trust in the fidelity of our military personnel *but, more fundamentally, the appellant's conduct strikes directly at core democratic processes.*" (Emphasis added.) Diaz, 2009 WL 690614, at *6. We agree.

On this general issue of harm, the hearing panel acknowledged that in determining the appropriate level of respondent's discipline, the ABA Standards call for considering as a factor "the potential or actual injury caused by the lawyer's misconduct." It correctly concluded that the respondent's misconduct "caused potential serious injury to the public." We independently observe that the particular information respondent disclosed about which detention or interrogation team was assigned to each detainee was labeled as classified. *Diaz*, 69 M.J at 133. That court concluded that if publicly disclosed, this and other information such as the detainee internment serial numbers and the source identification numbers also could "be used to the injury of the United States." 69 M.J. at 133. In addition to potential injury to the public and the United States, we also recognize the possibility of serious injury to particular persons. Simply put, the disclosure of the classified information about which team was assigned to each detainee could increase the chances of their individual members being publicly identified. Given the nature of their work, such identification could put them at personal risk by any Guantanamo Bay detainee's supporters around the world.

Based upon the number and nature of respondent's violations and criminal convictions, the conclusions of the military courts, the decision of the Judge Advocate General permanently revoking respondent's certification as a lawyer in the naval service, respondent's admitted selfish reasons for the clandestine disclosure of classified information, and the standards listed above, we conclude disbarment is the appropriate sanction. A minority of this court would impose the lesser sanction of indefinite suspension.

Conclusion and Discipline

IT IS THEREFORE ORDERED that MATHEW M. DIAZ be disbarred from the practice of law in the state of Kansas, effective on the filing of this opinion, in accordance with Supreme Court Rule 203(a)(1) (2011 Kan. Ct. R. Annot. 280).

***

Questions and Comments

1. Prior to the actions described in the disciplinary proceeding above, Diaz had 18 years of highly distinguished service in both the Army and Navy.[3] In his request for clemency after his conviction, Diaz stated he had "a moral obligation" to act, based upon "my upbringing, my experiences, my father's experiences, my own sense of justice and what looks like injustice, and what I've been trained as a Soldier and a Sailor."[4] Do you think the Supreme Court of Kansas should have considered this more when determining the appropriate level of discipline imposed? Do believe Diaz's disbarment was appropriate? Why or why not?

2. Two months before Diaz's court-martial case, the government released a list of detainees held at Guantanamo Bay pursuant to a lawsuit under the Freedom of Information Act filed by the Associated Press.[5] How then, could the Kansas Supreme Court find Diaz's misconduct "caused potential serious injury to the public"? Was there additional information in what Diaz released than that of the government, that made the determination of "potential serious injury to the public" less difficult for the panel and the court?

3. Do you believe Diaz had an ethical duty to report the possible criminal misconduct or illegal behavior of his client, the government? If so, whom should he have reported his concerns to? Does fear of retaliatory action or general career concerns excuse a lawyer's misconduct that adversely affects her client?

---

[3] Tim Golden, *Naming Names at Gitmo, The New York Times Magazine,* Oct. 21, 2007, at 78, 80-81.

[4] Ellen Yaroshefsky, *Military Lawyering at the Edge of the Rule of Law at Guantanamo: Should Lawyers Be Permitted to Violate the Law?*, 36 Hofstra L. Rev., 563, 576 (2007).

[5] *Id.*

D. DISCUSSION QUESTIONS

1. What is "moral consciousness" and do lawyers need to consider morality? If one's morality creates a conflict with the principles of legal ethics stated in the Model Rules, which of the two guidelines should the lawyer abide by? Does one lawyer's decision affect the ethical image of many, if not all, lawyers?

2. Is a governmental lawyer a public servant or executive branch advocate? Should there be different Model Rules for advisors and for advocates? If government lawyers are public servants, is it possible for them to breach a duty to the public? At the end, who is their actual client?

3. Should a lawyer represent an unpopular client and, if so, how can she defend against the public's projection of that client's values, character and actions upon his attorney?

Chapter 14:
Balance in the Legal Profession—
Contemplative Law and Mindfulness

A. INTRODUCTION

As with any profession, a lawyer's career may have many ups and downs. Lawyers face countless challenges: long hours, time away from their family, pressure to build a client base, ethical considerations, and managing a profitable business. These and other stressors sometimes make it difficult for lawyers to find balance in their personal and professional lives. Beginning in law school, lawyers frequently loose a sense of personal well-being with as many as 20 to 40 percent of students suffering from anxiety or depression.[1] Sending recently licensed attorneys into the profession without the skills to balance their work lives with their personal lives may lead to attorney mistakes or misconduct when practicing as lawyers. For these reasons, numerous law schools now teach skills courses in well-being and Mindfulness.[2]

The following excerpt is from this textbook author's article: Katerina P. Lewinbuk, *Lawyer Heal Thy Self: Incorporating Mindfulness Into Legal Education & Profession*, 40 J. Legal Prof. 1 (2015).

> Mindfulness represents a Westernized secular version of the ancient meditation practices. According to Dr. Kabat-Zinn, the pioneer of Mindfulness, it is non-judgmental awareness, paying attention

---

[1] *See* Connie J.A. Beck, Bruce D. Sales & G. Andrew H. Benjamin, *Lawyer Distress: Alcohol-Related Problems and Other Psychological Concerns Among a Sample of Practicing Lawyers*, 10 J.L. & Health 1 (1995-96).

[2] Mindfulness in law relates to the integration of mindfulness meditation skills into the law school classroom and the legal profession as a whole. Schools offering mindfulness classes that either introduce students to mindfulness or integrate it into the curriculum include, among others, Berkeley Law School, Florida International University Law School, Georgetown Law school, Houston College of Law, Phoenix Law School, Roger Williams University School of Law, University at Buffalo Law School, University of Miami School of Law, University of Missouri School of Law, University of Florida Levin College of Law, University of San Francisco Law School, Vanderbilt University Law School, and Washburn University School of Law. *See Bar Associations Involved in Mindfulness and the Law,* Mindfulness in Law at http://mindfulnessinlaw.org/page1/index.html (last visited Aug. 25, 2016).

deliberately, moment to moment, without judgment, to the workings of the mind and body. Mindfulness can improve the functions of the immune system and conditions such as chronic pain, heart disease, anxiety, and depression. Other benefits include improved concentration, mental clarity, and sensory processing. As a consequence, Mindfulness is becoming mainstream in America with the National Institute of Health spending $100 M on research pertaining to its benefits, *60 Minutes* presenting a segment on it, *Time* magazine featuring it on its cover and many more. Pentagon leaders, Silicon Valley entrepreneurs, Google and General Mills employees, and many law schools and bar associations now practice Mindfulness.

The effect of heightened clarity and focus from Mindfulness allows attorneys to produce more efficient work and empathetically represent clients. Through Mindfulness meditation, the lawyer has an increased awareness of any possible bias or prejudice and can overcome these barriers in mediation, negotiation, and litigation. Mindful lawyers are overall better equipped to deal with the unexpected in both their legal careers and lives.

***

This chapter discusses law student cognitive health and the application of Mindfulness to the legal profession, which intends to enhance the lawyer's skills in coping with daily challenges of the profession, while remaining ethical, and providing high quality legal service for her clients.

B. CASES AND ADDITIONAL READINGS

MINDFULNESS MATTERS IN LAW SCHOOL
Texas Bar Blog (Online), February 23, 2015
By Katerina Lewinbuk

Just as I finished answering a student's question, another hand went up. When I gave that person the floor, he asked the exact same question I just answered. Some of his classmates giggled while others rolled their eyes. The student, however, gave me a surprised look, observed the class's reaction, and then whispered, "What?" I tried to suppress my frustration, but part of me really resented his presence "in body only" and his lack of desire to pay attention.

Or was it a lack of ability to stay focused?

I went on with my day and never thought about the student again until I was in my car driving home. In my head, I engaged in a conversation with him, venting about how I take my teaching seriously and the least he could do was to follow along and pay attention. My internal dialog, which felt so real, escalated as the topic changed to faculty meetings and how our law school should approach new American Bar Association directives. The next thing I knew, I was standing in front of my house trying to open the door with my office key. *What route did I take home?*

Unfortunately, this is not an uncommon scenario. I believe many of us are ruminating about the past or worrying about the future while being present "in body only" as we walk through our daily lives with the mind living a life of its own. Many of us are as disconnected from reality as my student, but we cannot see it in ourselves, just as he could not understand why his classmates were giggling. Maybe if our names were called out in the middle of the day, we would also say, "What?"

One's mind is the biggest asset of a law student and practitioner. If the mind is not working, there are no legal studies and no lawyering. Yet we don't seem to address this in law school. We worry about proper training in legal doctrine and skills but seem to be missing the big picture. How will it all come together if the mind is spinning out of control, over stimulated, and exhausted, and if not treated well, can become anxious, depressed, or just plain miserable?

If it refuses to listen, the mind brings pictures from the past, plans for the future, or engages in texting, email, or online shopping—all the while "in" law school class. Is it rational to spend so much time and money on a legal education but spend one's time in class thinking about other things? Of course not, but the mind chooses to do so and the physical body obeys.

In fact, the mind is like an untamed puppy that runs wherever it chooses to go with the body following along, all without any awareness of what is happening. So we need to wake up (literally) and refocus. We need the mind to coordinate with us, stay on track with what we are asking it to do, or at least let us know when it is unable to do so. Easier said than done, isn't it?

"Mindfulness," which is a Westernized version of ancient meditation practices, can help us with that challenge. Research has shown that practicing mindfulness regularly reduces stress and leads to increased attention and focus and improved physical and mental wellbeing.

***

With numerous professionals writing on it in different fields, Mindfulness has also made its way to legal academic scholarship.

The gist of the practice is attention training, which helps us establish a connection between our intent and action at the moment. The meditative practices center around learning to stay focused on our breathing, and when distracted, acknowledge the distraction and redirect our attention back to the breathing in a non-judgmental way. If we learn how to do this with breathing, then we can keep our attention on any object, such as a law school lecture. We need to help our students develop the ability to better focus and minimize distraction.

***

"I think a lot of students, not just in law school, would really benefit from mindfulness seminars or classes," one law student wrote. That view was shared by almost 1,800 university professors, schoolteachers, scientists, and graduate students who gathered in Boston for the 2014 International Symposium for Contemplative Studies. The ISCS featured four days of numerous multidisciplinary sessions addressing the issues of training the mind through meditative practices to understand and enhance cognitive and emotional balance and overall health.

We don't know where this journey will ultimately take us, but at least we are aware that being present in our daily lives and lawyering tasks should not be taken for granted. Through Mindfulness practices, students can learn how to bring their attention back to the present moment. After all, great lawyering is about paying close attention.

Reprinted with permission from the February 2015 edition of the "Texas Bar Blog" © 2015 Matthew Bender & Company, Inc., a LexisNexis company. All rights reserved.

Questions and Comments

1. What are you doing right now? As you hold this textbook in your hand, are various thoughts running through your mind? Perhaps you are thinking about a looming deadline for a project in another class, or an upcoming final exam, or even the Multi-State Professional Responsibility (MPRE) Exam? You may also be thinking about the chores you need to complete or what you need to pick up at the grocery store for dinner tonight. STOP. Sit back in your chair. Inhale three times. Pay attention and count your breaths. Try to focus on only this breath, then only on the next, and so on. When your mind wonders, acknowledge it nonjudgmentally and bring your attention back to your breathing. Center your attention to the breath with your eyes closed and just merely observe those concerns your mind was spouting out earlier. Relax your shoulder blades downward. Enjoy the quiet, the stillness, and the release of your worries. Do that for five minutes in the morning and five minutes at night and you will feel a lot calmer.

2. The exercise in comment one is designed to show you a simple way to incorporate Mindfulness practice into your workday. You can bring this practice into your day by taking five or ten minutes to sit in a quiet place and repeat the steps discussed above. Also, it can be helpful to listen to a guided recording, download a meditation app to your cell phone with a

built-in timer, and practice pausing, breathing, and becoming aware of your emotional responses when you detect that you are becoming agitated or stressed throughout your day.

ON ENGAGEMENT: LEARNING TO PAY ATTENTION
36 U. Ark. Little Rock L. Rev. 337 (2014)
By R. Lisle Baker & Daniel P. Brown

Abstract:

In an age of electronic and mental distraction, the ability to pay attention is a fundamental legal skill increasingly important for law students and the lawyers and judges they will become, not only for professional effectiveness, but also to avoid error resulting from distraction. Far from being immutable, engaged attention can be learned. More specifically, with an understanding of how the attention system of the brain works, carefully designed mental practice can, over time, enhance an individual's capacity for focused attention, not only psychologically, but also apparently gradually altering the physical structure within the brain itself.

***

"[A]ttention must be paid."

I. Introduction: Paying Attention Matters

The ability to pay attention, especially to other people, is vital to success for law students and for the lawyers and judges they will become. Jeanne Nakamura and Mihaly Csikszentmihalyi wrote the following about the importance of attention:

> Information appears in consciousness through the selective investment of attention. People's *subjective experience*, the content of consciousness from moment to moment, is thus determined by their decisions about the allocation of limited attention. . . . Attention may be divided or undivided; indifferent or caring. The quality of the attention paid to the world affects the nature of people's interactions and the quality of their subjective experience.

Consider the following example of one such interaction:

> [Malcolm] Smith, a Democrat, was the New York State Senate Majority Leader who famously fiddled with his BlackBerry, checking e-mails, while billionaire Thomas Golisano, a major independent political player in New York, was trying to talk to him. Golisano, who had made a special trip to Albany to meet with Smith, was furious. "When I travel 250 miles to make a case on how to save the state a lot

of money and the guy comes into his office and starts playing with his Blackberry, I was miffed," he told reporters.

As a response, Mr. Golisano "went to the Republicans and told them he'd be happy to unseat Smith, perhaps in the hopes of having him replaced with someone who could pay attention for a few minutes." Golisano was successful, and Smith was unseated.

Few law students or lawyers imagine themselves acting like Smith, but in fact, law students often find themselves distracted by less important matters, and readers may recall their own examples. It can be a serious problem:

> Few things affect our lives more than our faculty of attention. If we can't focus our attention—due to either agitation or dullness—we can't do anything well. We can't study, listen, converse with others, work, play, or even sleep well when our attention is impaired. And for many of us, our attention is impaired much of the time. . . . Our very perception of reality is tied closely to where we focus our attention. Only what we pay attention to seems real to us, whereas whatever we ignore—no matter how important it may be—seems to fade into insignificance. The American philosopher and pioneer of modem psychology, William James, summed up this point more than a century ago: "For the moment, what we attend to is reality." Obviously, he wasn't suggesting that things become nonexistent when we ignore them; many things of which we are unaware exert powerful influences on our lives and the world as a whole. But by ignoring them, we are not including them in *our* reality. We do not really register them as existing at all. Each of us chooses, by our ways of attending to things, the universe we inhabit and the people we encounter. But for most of us, this "choice" is unconscious, so it's not really a choice at all.

According to Steve Bradt, "[p]eople spend 46.9 percent of their waking hours thinking about something other than what they're doing," and this he attributes to a wandering mind. But if law students are like those individuals whom Bradt surveyed, they are using almost half their time thinking about something other than what they are doing. If, instead, they could focus on more of what they intended, it would help them save not only scarce time for work, but also use that time more effectively, as well as perhaps even avoid error, which can be more serious when they graduate and begin representing clients and the problem were to become severe.

Indeed, if we think of lawyering skills, two overarching "meta-skills" involve careful preparation and paying attention to what matters. Preparation is something that law schools attempt to teach throughout the curriculum, but what about paying attention? Can law schools do better?

II. Paying Attention As Part Of Doing "Good Work" In Law School And Law Practice

While his research does not focus specifically on the legal profession, Professor Howard Gardner of the Harvard School of Education has written generally about what he called "GoodWork" and its three aspects: excellence, ethics, and engagement. First, to constitute good work, it needs to be *excellent* in the sense of technical competence, something that takes time to learn and develop. Second, good work needs to be *ethical*, by way of serving others; principally, the community in which the person is involved, but also the larger society of which the individual is a part. Third, in order to be good, work must be *engaging*. As Nakamura and Csikszentmihaly state, "vital engagement [is defined] as a relationship to the world that is characterized by both experiences of flow (enjoyed absorption) and by meaning (subjective significance)."

How can law schools help to vitally engage their students and lay the groundwork for similar vital engagement in their studies and ultimately their law practice? That is not to say that law schools do not attempt to do at least two of the things of which Professor Gardner speaks: providing for the study of professional excellence and ethics. Law schools try to develop professional competence in law students—that is, the knowledge of the law sufficient to understand the dimensions of a client's problem—and then the analytic skill to use that knowledge to help solve it appropriately. They also instruct students on ethics, the code of professional conduct applicable to lawyers, and urge students to serve others above self, such as through participation in pro bono programs. But what can law schools do to teach vital engagement, including the ability to pay attention? This challenge is significant, because paying attention often is presumed to be an innate ability, and therefore not worthy of learning in its own right, or otherwise inherent and incapable of further development once a student reaches post-graduate education.

Psychologist William James first noted the mind's propensity for distraction, which results in what he referred to as "a wandering attention." James elaborated:

> [T]he faculty of voluntarily bringing back a wandering attention, over and over again, is the very root of judgment, character, and will . . . .
> An education which should improve this faculty would be the education par excellence. But it is easier to define this ideal than to give practical directions for bringing it about.

This article attempts to provide some of those "practical directions," which can help bring about that "education par excellence." This objective is consistent with one of the positive aspirations of psychology, which is "to nurture genius, to identify our most precious resource—talented young people—and find the conditions under which they will flourish." This objective is also consistent with viewing the genius of attention as available to everyone and not to just the gifted few, as Alan Wallace writes about focus and creativity:

Just think of the greatest musicians, mathematicians, scientists, and philosophers throughout history—all of them, it seems, have had an extraordinary capacity to focus their attention with a high degree of clarity for long periods of time. A mind settled in such a state of alert equipoise is a fertile ground for the emergence of all kinds of original associations and insights. Might 'genius' be a potential we all share—each of us with our own unique capacity for creativity, requiring only the power of sustained attention to unlock it? A focused mind can help bring the creative spark to the surface of consciousness. The mind constantly caught up in one distraction after another, on the other hand, may be forever removed from its creative potential. Clearly, if we were to enhance our faculty of attention, our lives would improve dramatically.

The distraction problem is significant. Some studies have indicated that students in certain aspects of higher education may experience lapses in attention as early as the first thirty seconds of a lecture with additional lapses occurring in ever-shortening cycles throughout the lecture segment. Yet student success in law school requires intense and sustained attention. Law students "[engage] in every level of knowledge, from the simplest, memorization, to the most complex, reasoning." Attention is needed to process and commit this knowledge to memory.

As a consequence, a few law professors have started to pay attention to attention. As M. H. Sam Jacobson explains, "[a]ttentional control . . . is an essential skill for a person to successfully engage in the higher-order cognitive tasks required of legal analysis and reasoning. A person must be able to shut out distractions, including other cognitive work, when attending to cognitively complex tasks." Professor Leonard Riskin, a pioneer in the use of insights from psychology in legal education, wrote, "[f]or instance, if, while we are interviewing a client, we become aware that our mind has wandered off to thoughts about next week's football game, we can swiftly bring our attention back to the client." Finally, Professor Darshan Brach of the University of California, Hastings College of Law, has written in the context of negotiation:

> Maintaining attention for any length of time is a difficult feat. Often, in both life and negotiation, our body is in one place but our attention is elsewhere, and while we appear to participate in a conversation on one topic, we are often thinking about something quite different (our next meal, for example).

> This lack of mental discipline can have an extremely deleterious impact on the success of our negotiations for several reasons. As discussed previously, a first casualty of inattention can be losing sight of our real goals. Additionally, when our thoughts are elsewhere, we miss

information and cues, both verbal and nonverbal. Further, with a mind easily distracted, we lose mental acuity and are less able to take quick and appropriate action as needed when the tides of a negotiation shift.

It seems that in addition to preparation, an important component of success as a law student or as a lawyer is simple: pay attention. Also, it is important to remember the relationship between limiting one's attention to the task at hand and achieving maximum performance. Thus, it should come as no surprise that "the ability to control attention against competing demands is a major predictor of how well a person will perform on complex working memory tasks" or, in other words, those tasks requiring our persistent, undivided attention.

So how may law students learn to better attend toward what they want? Defining the problem is helpful, as well as the advice to try to minimize distractions and be present more consciously. But while offering useful ideas, even these helpful sources offer limited guidance on how to learn how to pay attention more successfully. Jacobson advises that students attempt to eliminate distractions, or when that proves impossible, to limit the effects of unavoidable distractions by processing information in a way that is easier to recall after an interruption. Hammerness et al., advise, "[l]earning how to meditate is all about learning to pay attention to the present moment and may be one of the best investments you can make." Hammerness et al., do not, however, elaborate further on how such meditation would help remedy this attention deficit.

Therefore, to learn more specifically how to enhance the capacity for focused attention, we must explore: (1) what is attention and how is it achieved; and (2) can our capacity to pay attention be enhanced, and if so, how?

III. Understanding Attention As Mental Activity

A. Orientation, Then Engagement

From a brain science perspective, the actual process of paying attention is a "remarkably involved task, requiring work from many distinct brain areas." In a broad sense, attention is "the ability to attend to desired or necessary stimuli and to exclude unwanted or unnecessary stimuli." This ability to attend to and/or exclude stimuli requires the brain to complete a two-step process, which is commonly referred to as the "attentional process."

The first step in this process is "to orient to the stimulus, whether it's the commercial on television, the teacher at the head of the classroom, or the red light flashing in the distance." During the orientation process, the brain "locks" on to the stimulus and, in a split-second, it identifies the stimulus and all of its characteristics. Below is an illustrative example of the orientation step:

> [L]et's imagine that the light flashing in the distance is the signal from a fire engine, racing down the street. You turn and look in the direction of that sound, as your brain locks in on it. . . . [I]n the blink of an eye, we have identified what the vehicle is, what direction it's coming from, and its probable purpose.

This example highlights the orientation step, whereby sensory modalities—auditory (hearing), visual (seeing), olfactory (smelling), tactile (touching), and gustatory (tasting)—enable the observer to quickly identify a stimulus. This period of orientation also provides other critical information regarding the stimulus, such as where the stimulus is, why or how it came to be, and if it is pleasurable or dangerous.

The "[n]ext step in the attention process is our engagement with that information." Using the fire engine example, the observer's brain first orients to the noise and sight of the truck, and during the engagement step it focuses on the details.

> You [might] notice it festooned with ladders and tanks, an impressive complement of modern firefighting equipment. You see the firefighters in their gear; you catch a fleeting glimpse of determined faces under their helmets. You read the lettering on the side of the truck and see which firehouse the engine has been dispatched from and recall that you've passed that building. Perhaps you even recall . . . a scene from the day your child's class visited the local firehouse or something you read in the local paper about the fire department requesting funds for new equipment. You are now attending to this "stimulus" fully, pulling in and synthesizing bits of information from various parts of the brain. You are homing in on the sound and bringing to it the full and awesome powers of sustained, focused attention. And yet it's all happening in a matter of seconds.

During this engagement step, you are attending to the fire engine with the "richness and breadth of [many] cognitive resources." Not only is the brain taking in the particularities of the fire engine currently in front of you, but it is recalling all past information that may relate in any way to fire engines, such as emergencies, loud noises, and bright lights. This process permits your brain to make the decision whether to exert sustained attention to the fire engine or to dismiss it and turn your attention elsewhere.

B. The Two Types of Attention: Goal-Directed and Stimulus-Driven

In addition to understanding how attention works, it is also helpful to understand the two different types of attention. These types are goal-directed attention (also known as controlled attention or top-down processing) and stimulus-driven attention (or bottom-up processing). Goal-directed attention "involves conscious awareness and requires significant cognitive effort to maintain focus without interruption or interference." This type of attention is "driven from within, voluntarily by our goals and aspirations . . . [and] is consistent with our own unique life, our specific interests or aims of the moment." Through goal-oriented attention, we are able to exert cognitive control. This ability allows a person to remain focused on a specific task while faced with competing demands for attention. An example of goal-directed attention is when a student uses mental effort to remain focused on classroom discussion while e-mails and instant messages are popping up on a neighboring student's computer screen.

On the other hand, stimulus-driven attention is instinctual and automatic. Another part of our brain constantly polls our environment for disturbances and causes our brain to fixate on certain ones. This region of the brain has evolved to notice rapid visual and auditory changes in our environment that may indicate danger or pleasure. For this reason, our attention is grabbed by novel or sudden changes in our surroundings. Our stimulus driven attention "can be captured by someone yelling fire, a pop-up screen on your computer, a flash of lightning on the horizon or the sound of a power chord on a guitar." While at times this "information can be life-saving, often, it is innocuous and arbitrary," serving only as a distraction to the person from the goal at hand. Under optimal conditions, our brains can strike the right balance between attending to our internal goals and the external environment.

To this end, our goals are key factors in helping us determine what is worthy of our attention and what, in the end, will prove unproductive to attend to. Hammerness et al., explain:

> What research is now telling us is that what "hooks" our attention is usually something consistent with our goals. That's more important than how "loud" or salient the stimulus is. We can process a lot of information about that fire engine, attend to it briefly and then get back on task. But if your cell phone vibrates and you see that it's your spouse, your boss or your physician, well, you're cognitively adept enough to block out the sirens and flashing lights and hook your attention to the phone call, the stimulus that really matters to you.

In other words, while part of our brain allows us to remain concentrated on a particular activity, another part continually determines which sensory information in our environment deserves our attention. Consequently, parts of the brain are in constant competition for the same resource: our attention. This is problematic because a person's cognitive capacity to pay attention is a limited resource. As Hammerness et al., observe, "[d]espite all of the brain's impressive attention hardware, there is indeed a limit to what it can deal with and for what duration."

Unfortunately, the "basic unit of attention is very brief," especially for those with attention deficit disorder. Psychologist William James said that the ordinary mind can stay focused on one thing for only a few seconds. In recent years, advanced brain scanning technology has confirmed that "[a] person's attention is a limited resource." So how do we add to the capacity for goal-oriented attention, or what might be called, "intentional attention?" How then can we help law students best direct their attention toward what they want to attend?

***

Endnotes omitted (See R. Lisle Baker & Daniel P. Brown, On Engagement: Learning to Pay Attention, 36 U. Ark. Little Rock L. Rev. 337 (2014) for full article version). Reprinted with permission from the 2014 edition of the "U. Ark. Little Rock L. Rev." © 2016 U. Ark. Little Rock L. Rev. All rights reserved.

Questions and Comments

1. Many commentators suggest that the biggest complaint about lawyers is that they do not return their clients' phone calls promptly and do not pay enough attention to their cases. In other words, lawyers ignore their clients. Having the mental discipline to pay attention and not become distracted could lessen complaints about lawyers and their representation. It could also allow lawyers to better connect with their clients.

2. Learning the skill of "paying attention" is vital to becoming an effective lawyer. In client interviews, the lawyer must listen attentively so that she can ask appropriate questions of the client. The lawyer must actively listen, remain in the present moment and respond appropriately to what the client says. Multitasking makes one's mind wonder away from the conversation while a client describes his problems thereby causing distraction and missed opportunities to gain insightful information about the case. Can you think of a situation where you attempted to listen attentively to someone, but continued in another task and did not even realize your attention was not in focus? Do you even know whether you missed something important the other person said? Were you thinking about something else at that time?

THE ART OF BEING MINDFUL IN THE LEGAL WORLD: A CHALLENGE FOR OUR TIMES
Fla. B.J., Apr. 2016, at 16
By Judge Alan S. Gold

You may be asking why a senior U.S. district judge is writing about mindfulness practice. That is a fair question. I will answer it directly. For me, it started in early 2001 when my cardiologist told me I needed open-heart surgery for a mitral valve repair. This surgery was not going to be a walk in the park. I wondered how in the world did I get into this situation, and what could I do to minimize future medical problems? It was at that point that I started to learn about mindfulness practice and meditation in earnest. It occurred to me that "heart surgery" was a metaphor for changing my life.

After I came back to the bench, I experienced a heightened awareness of the relationship between stress and civility. I found that mindfulness practice helped me do my job better, and also helped the lawyers relax and perform more effectively. No, I am not telling you that mindfulness is a silver bullet. It is not a pill you take once and you are cured. It is about purposely changing your way of living every day. Some days are better than others, but that is okay. I came to better appreciate that my job, as a judge, was to assist lawyers and others to do their jobs without my adding unnecessarily to their stresses. I am not here to tell you that I always have been successful. What I am here to do is pass on some important lessons that I have learned in the hope that my experiences may be of some benefit to you and to our profession.

The Relationship Between Mindfulness, Health, and More Effective Lawyering and Judging

My topic is the relationship between our health and mindfulness; that is, the ability to live in and enjoy the present moment in a civil manner. Why should this topic concern lawyers and judges? We constantly hear, both as lawyers and judges, about the "lack of civility" in the practice of law. The Florida Bar membership surveys continue to reflect that, besides earning money, the most significant concerns that face us as lawyers and judges are balancing family and work, high stress, and lack of professionalism and ethics. In June 2013, the Florida Supreme Court recognized that "[s]urveys of both lawyers and judges continue to reflect that lack of professionalism is one of the most significant adverse problems that negatively impacts the practice of law in Florida today."

What have we done about it as a profession? First, the Florida Supreme Court amended the Oath of Admission "to recognize the necessity for civility in the inherently contentious setting of the adversary process." Now, as part of our oath, we pledge to opposing parties and their counsel, fairness, integrity, and civility...not only in court, but also in all written and oral communications.

Second, on June 6, 2012, the Florida Supreme Court adopted the "Code for Resolving Professionalism Complaints." The code creates a structure for "affirmatively addressing unacceptable professional conduct." Violators can be sent to ethics school, professionalism workshops, stress management workshops, or, in serious cases, the Attorney Consumer Assistance and Intake Program may forward a complaint to The Florida Bar's Lawyer Regulation Department for further consideration.

I do not take issue with what the Florida Supreme Court has adopted and implemented. I just do not think it goes far enough to address the *root causes* of lack of civility and professionalism. My premise is that the root cause of incivility and lack of professionalism is the extreme and cumulative stresses that we, as lawyers and judges, find ourselves coping with daily. This is especially true given our uncertain and challenging economic times, and the increased alienation we experience from each other because of our technology. I believe there is a more comprehensive way to deal with the problem, and, in this article, I offer three specific recommendations.

First, let me be clear. In offering my recommendations, I am not asking you, as lawyers or as judges, to do anything to diminish your effectiveness or to give up your edge. To the contrary, in addition to managing stress, improving health, and increasing civility, my recommendations are directed to enhancing your skills and effectiveness. Does this sound too good to be true? Not so. What I am suggesting to you is no more than how martial arts masters deal with moments of intense conflict; that is, from the center, flowing with the breath. We can apply these same martial arts skills to the practice of law and achieve an energized calm, and with it, a proactive and focused choice that adds to our power to tread through the turbulent storm.

Recommendation 1:
Teach Lawyers and Judges About the Medical and Physiological Effects of Stress So We Can Become More Self-Aware

Problem? What problem? Let us acknowledge that we are adrenaline junkies. We are drawn to a profession that, at times, gives a rush by challenging us often in dramatic ways. Therefore, some degree of stress is inherent in what we do, and many of us can cope pretty well most of the time. But, what are the medical effects of extreme, cumulative stress? We all have seen them in action or experienced them. They include inappropriate anger, impatience, overreaction, anxiety, fear, irritability, and resentment (just to name a few). People under extreme and cumulative stress are overloaded with more than they can cope. They may be unable to concentrate or think clearly. They may be constantly active but accomplish little.

Yes, we, as judges, are susceptible, too. As noted by author Isaiah M. Zimmerman, "Judges work at the convergence of powerful demands...heavy dockets; restrictions on speech and behavior, intense media exposure; public ignorance of the role of the courts, and the relative isolation of the judicial position...." May I also add that, in Florida, our state colleagues face elections, bar polls, grievance procedures, never-ending pro se cases, and peer pressure to dispose of cases quickly. These challenges create unique stresses, personally and professionally. Lawyers are sometimes surprised that a judge's life is not so easy as it appears.

Here is what the medical literature says about the effects of extreme stress. There has been a revolution in medicine concerning how we think about diseases of the body and mind. It begins with recognizing the interaction between the body and mind and the ways in which emotions and personality can have a tremendous impact on the functioning and health of virtually every cell in our body. It is about the role of excess stress in making us more vulnerable to disease, including psychological impairments, or making diseases that we are coping with that much worse. We have come to recognize the vastly complex intertwining of our biology and our emotions, the endless ways in which our personalities, feelings, and thoughts both reflect and influence the events in our bodies.

Put simply, excess stress can make us sick or sicker. Perhaps it is more correct to say that excess stress increases our risk of getting diseases that make us sick, or if we have such a disease, excess stress can increase the risk of our bodily defenses being overwhelmed by the disease. Medical research has shown that chronic stress is linked to six leading causes of death: heart disease, cancer, lung ailments, accidents, cirrhosis of the liver, and suicide. Besides fatalities, when we become exhausted, the visible effects are evidenced by bad behavior that we label as "incivility."

A large body of evidence suggests that stress-related disease, both physical and emotional, emerges, predominantly, out of the fact that we so often activate a physiological system that has evolved for responding to acute physical emergencies, but we turn it on for months on end, worrying about our clients, our cases, our economics, our careers, and our families. We worry about how to be the "best" at all of our endeavors, and are confounded as to how to balance them.

What makes things worse is that the stress response may be mobilized not only in response to physical or psychological pressures or insults, but by the *expectation* of them. If we repeatedly turn on the stress response, or if we cannot turn it off at the end of a stressful event, our stress-related problems simply compound and grow worse.

Another feature of the stress response is that, with sustained stress, our perceptions of pain become blunted. We numb ourselves and are not even aware of what we are doing, how we are doing it, or why we are doing it. It becomes habitual. In fact, a well-known Johns Hopkins study has found that lawyers are more prone to depression than members of any other profession. Given all of the scientific explanation, is there any wonder that lawyers and judges often can be "uncivil" to each other and exhibit behaviors in court and in life that are unacceptable and unproductive?

Recommendation 2:
Teach Lawyers and Judges How to Better Cope with Stress
Before **We Fall Over the Cliff**

The key question: Are there available tools we can use *before* extreme stresses take over and affect our health and well-being? According to *Time Magazine*, "Scientists have been able to prove that *meditation and rigorous mindfulness* training can lower cortisol levels and blood pressure, increase immune response and possibly even affect gene expression." In fact, "Scientific study is also showing that meditation can have an impact on the structure of the brain itself." One answer to better health, then, lies with meditation and rigorous Mindfulness techniques.

What then is "Mindfulness" and how does it work? Simply put, Mindfulness is mental training of the brain. It is the ability to pay attention in a particular way in the present moment and without self-judgment. It is about obtaining a mind of calmness and clarity, with a good self-attitude, regardless of the situation. It is an indispensable tool for coping—both emotionally and practically—with the daily onslaught. It is about silencing that nattering voice in your head and cutting off that internal dialogue that is negative and self-referential.

What is your reaction to this information? Does it all sound too "new age"? Is your gut reaction that if you learn Mindfulness you will be seen as "weak" by your partners, your clients, or the courts? "Law practice," you say, "is dog eat dog. I have to earn a living. That is my reality."

Here is my response: Whether you realize it or not, mental training tied to meditation and Mindfulness practice is happening in Fortune 500 companies, with Silicon Valley entrepreneurs, and even with Pentagon chiefs. It is a revolution in process. Would it surprise you to learn that in 2012, there were 477 scientific papers published on Mindfulness and more each year that has followed? Would it surprise you that even a U.S. Congressman, Tim Ryan, has published a book, *A Mindful Nation: How A Simple Practice Can Help Us Reduce Stress, Improve Performance, and Recapture the American Spirit*? New age sounding or not, Mindfulness practice is becoming mainstream and is taking root even in the practice of law.

Here is what I am suggesting. I am not asking you to change your reality or to diminish your earning capacity. I am suggesting that you have the *freedom to choose how you deal with your reality,* and, in turn, increase your effectiveness, health, and earning capacity. First, take a good look at your present-day reality. This alone is no easy feat. It is like taking a step backward and honestly observing, with some detachment, what you are doing and how you are doing it. Then, make a choice about what kind of life you want to live.

What do you choose? Every time you act or react, some choice is made. Sometimes, these choices are conscious, and sometimes they are not. I am talking about choosing to increase your awareness that you have the power to choose another way to deal with your stresses.

Yes, admittedly, we carry within ourselves many factors that we believe limit our freedom to choose and which obscure our awareness. There are layers of emotions and physiological tendencies that we have formed over a lifetime. Yet, through a rigorous mindful practice, it is possible to take responsibility for all that we are. We can come to the transformative recognition that we are always the one doing the choosing, and that our choice can be to change into a greater self, and to do this right here and right now. Granted, this is not easy. It takes real courage and effort to break old habits. Even then, we can slip back into our old ways. No problem. We simply refocus and plow ahead. It is really a moment-to-moment commitment.

It Is as Simple as Breathing

There are many techniques to help us change. At the heart of many of these techniques, there is one constant: the awareness of the breath through meditation. We are breathing continuously from the moment of birth to the moment of death. Breath and life are synonymous. It is the bridge between your mind and your body, but breathing is not continuous. There are gaps. The breath goes out, then for a moment, breathing pauses. Then breath comes in. In that gap between breaths, anything is possible. Sincere observation and attention will help you feel the gap. If you feel the gap, you can choose to use that moment to calm the mind and your turbulent emotions and interrupt your "mind-streaming"—that constant source of mental junk mail. You just do not have to believe your own thoughts. How do you do this? Simply focus on your breath and observe its passage. The point is this. If you can train yourself to keep attention on something as neutral as your breath, then you can keep your attention on anything else

You can achieve an amazing goal: By observing your body, your thoughts, and emotions in any stressful situation *before* you react, you can respond more effectively and go from compulsion to choice. In sum: stop, breathe, notice, reflect, and then respond. This is the formula for the more effective and mindful practice of law, whether you are arguing in court, sitting on the bench, or dealing with difficult clients, partners, or other lawyers. This is empowerment. When you act boldly, there will be pushback in different forms, so to complete what you started, you need to relax, reaffirm your original intention, and hold your seat.

Here are five steps to mindfulness meditation to help you become more effective and healthier. First, sit with a good posture and close your eyes. Second, notice your breathing, but focus on the sensation of air moving in and out of your lungs. Third, as thoughts come into your mind and distract you from your breathing, acknowledge those thoughts and then return to focusing on your breathing each time. Fourth, do not judge yourself or try to ignore distractions. Your job is simply to notice that your mind has wandered and to bring your attention back to your breathing. Finally, start by doing this five minutes a day for a week. Then try 10 minutes, and so on.

I grant you that it is challenging to maintain a mindfulness practice particularly when you are faced with stressful circumstances. One of your first thoughts will be, "I cannot do this." Staying with your breath and observing what is happening to you in the moment can seem impossible. It is not impossible. Do not be upset if thoughts come and go. Just observe them and how your body reacts. The more you meditate, the easier it will be to keep your attention where you want it.

You may say, "Thank you, Judge Gold, but I do not have time for all of this in my busy life. I do not want to take on yet another self-help project to feel guilty about." You may say, "I am perfect the way I am. I am doing just fine. Just ask anybody."

Maybe you are one of the lucky ones. If so, I offer my admiration. For the rest of us, I can understand your resistance. Old habits and patterns are hard to break. You may think you are just fine and see no need to change, but consider this: Everything in life is changing all the time, including you, whether you realize it or not. It is just that we look for ways to believe we are exempt from it. *So, I suggest you breathe as though your life depended on it. It does.* We are talking about a critically important priority for your health, your civility, and your well-being. You can do this. There are lots of ways to fit meditation into your busy life. With practice, it might just help you use your time better.

How do you reinforce your efforts to change? This question leads to my final recommendation.

Recommendation 3:
Take Control of Our Lives with the Help of Allies and Reclaim the Nobility of the Profession

We cannot easily make real changes alone. It takes courage to move against the ingrained resistance of our profession. The legal profession inherently discourages changes that may help us individually, but may be perceived by some as "weaknesses" potentially threatening the economic bottom line or how we are viewed as judges. Like it or not, our profession is already changing rapidly and significantly. Clients are unhappy paying legal fees based on billable hours; associates are unhappy with unreasonable professional demands; partners are unhappy with their compensation or status and readily move their "book of business" across the street. Everyone complains about the lack of a balanced life and the effects of practice on their health and relationships. The level of anger and frustration is readily evident by incivility and lack of courtesy that we experience on a daily basis.

It is time to speak the truth about such things. What has been missing in our profession is an organized means to join with others with an interest in the subject matter at issue. In response, the Miami-Dade County Bar Association, in conjunction with the Miami-Dade Federal Bar Association, has created a Task Force on the Mindful Practice of Law. There are three components. First, an information component that offers a website and newsletters, identifying mindfulness-related resources. Second, the associations have held conferences and workshops on health and mindfulness practice. Third, regular meetings are offered to interested judges and lawyers to meditate together and to discuss how to live and practice mindfully. One area of discussion is how we can acknowledge that all of us are in this together, and that we need to cut each other a break in court and in life. These issues can never be addressed too soon; law schools are introducing mindfulness into their curriculum, with the University of Miami's Mindfulness in Law Program serving as a model for schools across the country. Alongside courses offered to students as part of the curriculum, CLE programs are offered to members of the legal community.

Where will all this lead? Perhaps to redefining what it means to practice law. Perhaps to returning to those values that caused many of us to become lawyers in the first place. The invitation is hereby extended to other local bar associations, The Florida Bar, and to the various Florida judge's conferences to join in these efforts and to create a statewide network of mindfulness practitioners and resources.

Will mindfulness really work in a law firm? One major Florida firm says "yes." The Berger Singerman law firm has undergone a seven-week mindfulness training course similar to the one offered by Google to its employees. The firm leadership was so impressed with the results that it funded and sponsored its own conference for judges and lawyers that it called, "Raising the Consciousness of the Bench and Bar." When asked at the conference about its purpose, the firm's senior partner answered, "We want to share it; not keep it a secret. We yearn to do what we do in service of something larger than ourselves."

Can, and should, the experience of Berger Singerman be replicated elsewhere? Can we meet the challenge of serving something larger than just ourselves? The publication of this Florida Bar *Journal* offers reasons to believe that the potential to accomplish meaningful change is upon us. What follows are anecdotal experiences of practitioners who explain how mindfulness practice has affected them. Meanwhile, it comes back to you.

Are you ready for a change? It is like the famous saying from India: "Wisdom is not something you learn; it is something you become." So, come along for the ride. Let us see where we go.

Reprinted with permission from the April 2016 edition of the "Florida Bar Journal" © 2016 Judge Alan S. Gold. All rights reserved.

Questions and Comments

1. Consider the author's recommendations on making the legal profession more mindful. Which recommendation, if any, appeals to you? Which recommendation, if any, can you implement as a law student today in order to become a more mindful attorney in the future?

2. The author points out that the legal profession has been slow to recognize that the members of the field need to be more mindful. Why do you think that is the case? What are some ways in which law students can start early to recognize and address these issues?

3. Being able to remain mindful and develop an effective mechanism for coping with stress is important for each attorney's well-being, as well as the profession as a whole. However, a lawyer's ability to stay focused and centered also impacts others—such as her clients. Do you think a lawyer that practices Mindfulness can serve as a better advocate for her client than a lawyer who is merely reactive and unaware of her lack of self-control?

MINDFUL ETHICS—A PEDAGOGICAL AND PRACTICAL APPROACH TO TEACHING LEGAL ETHICS, DEVELOPING PROFESSIONAL IDENTITY, AND ENCOURAGING CIVILITY
4 St. Mary's J. Legal Mal. & Ethics 198 (2014)
By Jan L. Jacobowitz & Scott Rogers

I. Introduction

Aristotle spoke of virtue and ethics as practical wisdom, which one may develop by acquiring knowledge and engaging in habituation—an individual gains wisdom only after he combines his knowledge with personal experience. Perhaps one of the earliest proclamations of the value of experiential learning, the Aristotelian view, reappears throughout history and is captured once again by the Carnegie Foundation for the Advancement of Teaching's Report, Educating Lawyers: Preparation for the Profession of Law (Carnegie Report), which includes a call for instruction that provides practical skills and ethical grounding to complement the teaching of legal analysis.

The Carnegie Report continues to play a role in the ongoing discussion of legal education reform; a debate that is currently driven by market demand and a legal profession in the midst of dramatic realignment. The debate has given rise to suggestions for educational reform in the area of legal ethics that are supported by reference to theories of moral psychology, cognitive psychology, and various innovative educational strategies.

Mindful Ethics, a class that we teach at the University of Miami School of Law, which integrates mindfulness and professional responsibility, is an innovative approach to legal ethics. The short-term goals of Mindful Ethics are to better prepare law students to deal with the reality of practice, to assist in the development of professional identity, and to provide lawyers with additional tools for responding to the ethical challenges inherent in the practice of law. The long-term, overarching goal is to impact how the legal profession functions and plays its critical role in society as protectorate of the rule of law.

This Article will briefly explore the relevancy of Aristotle's work on ethics to legal education. Next, the Article will trace the development of legal education and the early role of experiential learning in the United States. Then, the Article will note some of the current legal education literature, which seeks to apply psychological theory to legal education. Finally, the Article will discuss and demonstrate the methodology by which Mindful Ethics integrates professional responsibility and mindfulness to help law students and lawyers gain a broader insight into their own ethical decision-making. The discussion will include neuroscience research to explore the decision-making process and the role of mindfulness on decision-making. This research suggests that when embraced both as a life skill and a legal-practice skill, Mindful Ethics dramatically assists an individual to anticipate and avoid the ethical pitfalls of legal practice and maintain civility and professionalism—especially in light of the increasing pace of the practice owing to rapidly evolving technologies. Indeed, Mindful Ethics may provide an individual with the ability to "entertain a thought without accepting it" and to modulate and channel emotions in a civil manner towards a productive outcome.

***

V. Mindfulness

An overview of mindfulness is helpful for laying a foundation for the discussion of Mindful Ethics and providing a fuller understanding of the integration of mindfulness into the law school curriculum. Because mindfulness is an experiential practice, it is not easy to define. Still, definitions provide context and several definitions of mindfulness have found their way into legal discourse. Professor Leonard Riskin, drawing upon the writing of Jon Kabat-Zinn, describes mindfulness as "paying attention deliberately, moment by moment, and without judgment, to whatever is going on in the mind and body." in the context of ethical decision-making, the most important word in this definition may be "deliberately," and indeed, the intentional attending to our moment-to-moment experience is fundamental to mindfulness. It also highlights what may well be the most challenging aspect of mindfulness practice—namely, maintaining one's attention on an object and noticing when attention wanders. This focus, as we shall see, is relevant to our ability to conduct ourselves with integrity amid challenging, stressful, and emotionally reactive situations.

As a practice, mindfulness involves placing one's attention on an object—most commonly the breath—and when one realizes that attention has wandered, gently guiding it back to the object. The breath, as the object of attention, serves a variety of purposes. As a designated focal point, it helps one realize when the mind has wandered, thereby creating the opportunity to direct attention back to the breath. Though the traditional practice of mindfulness involves much more than this mental exercise, the scientific research on mindfulness that is conducted most frequently (and the conversations about mindfulness taking place within the legal profession and across much of society) looks to this straightforward, yet challenging exercise, as a primary vehicle for the practice and cultivation of mindful awareness.

VI. Mindfulness in Law

In the past twenty years, mindfulness has become popular in Western culture across areas as diverse as education, medicine, leadership, psychology, art, spiritual life, therapy, management and business, prison systems, sports, and the military. The legal profession has also begun to embrace mindfulness. Mindfulness programs have been included in state and national bar conferences and events, and mindfulness has been infused into legal discussions on topics ranging from family law, mediation, negotiation, client services, ethics, trial practice, health and well-being, professional identity, civility, and judicial decision-making. Law firms and legal organizations are bringing in mindfulness teachers to introduce lawyers and legal staff to mindfulness practices that can be integrated into their professional and personal lives. Law schools and faculty are introducing students to mindfulness, infusing it into the curriculum, and integrating it across the law school experience. There have been two national "mindfulness in law" conferences: one for all members of the legal profession, and another for legal educators. Even organizations that offer bar review courses are exploring how mindfulness might be an important component of bar preparation.

The heart of much of the legal profession's interest in mindfulness rests in the ways that mindfulness practices have been found to be helpful for working with stress, avoiding depression relapse, improving focus and concentration, and enhancing overall well-being. A growing body of research is exploring these effects among students in higher education. In fact, the ongoing attention being given to mindfulness—at the highest echelons of industry, education, and government—is largely the product of the vast and growing body of neuroscience research exploring the ways that mindfulness practice may change the very structure and function of the brain--in areas associated with wellbeing and performance. Amishi Jha, a cognitive neuroscientist who researches the influence of mindfulness practices on the brain, defines mindfulness as "a mental mode of being engaged in the present moment without evaluating or emotionally reacting to it." Her research, as well as the research of many neuroscientists, is adding to the growing body of findings that mindfulness practices may lead to structural and functional changes to the brain. In this regard, mindfulness has been found to be associated with thicker regions in the prefrontal cortex relevant to our ability to, among other things, focus and engage in reflection prior to taking action. Mindfulness has been found to lead to greater neural gyrification (think crinkles and folds in the cortex that allow for a greater surface area, and with it speed of information processing), increased gray matter density (brain cells), a thicker insula (sensory input from the body to the brain), and a thinning of the amygdala (fear activation). Not surprisingly, research is finding that mindfulness practices are associated with improved focus, the capacity to regulate emotions, and enhanced working memory capacity. This research is animating a great deal of national and international conversation on the merits of mindfulness practice across many domains, and the law is no exception.

VII. Mindfulness, Neuroscience and Ethical Decision-Making

Because mindfulness is an awareness practice, ethicists exploring the connection between mindfulness and ethics frequently look to the role of awareness on ethical decision-making. Various ethical decision-making models posit that it is only after one is aware of an ethical dilemma that "moral reasoning [can be brought] to bear on the issue." So too, one's tendency to get away with minor ethical breaches—especially when no one is looking--is reduced when moral benchmarks are made salient. In their research, Ruedy and Schweitzer investigated the relationship between mindfulness and ethical conduct. They found that persons scoring high in mindfulness place more importance on upholding a high moral standard and were less likely to report a willingness to engage in unethical behavior. Moreover, in a paper and pencil task in which most people cheated, those scoring high in trait mindfulness did so to a lesser degree. Shapiro and her colleagues explored the effects of Mindfulness-Based Stress Reduction (MBSR) training on ethical decision-making, finding that mindfulness training led to improvements in moral reasoning and decision-making.

So too, legal commentators identify awareness as fundamentally important to promoting ethical behavior. Riskin notes that mindfulness practices lead to greater awareness of thoughts, the intentions underlying conduct, and the "emotions, body sensations and behaviors they precipitate." He suggests that as "we observe these phenomena at a psychological distance, their strength or power or influence tends to diminish and we [then] have a chance to consider their merit." He sums this up with the observation that "mindfulness allows us to insert a 'wedge of awareness' before we act."

The connection between mindfulness and ethics is one that interests not only ethicists and lawyers, but also mindfulness practitioners and scientists. For example, ethics plays a central role in a traditional Buddhist mindfulness practice, and thus, the philosophical conversation within this community of practitioners has become especially spirited, as mindfulness has been introduced into the military. Neuroscientists, using brain-scanning technologies that allow for the real-time measurement of brain activity when subjects are engaged in decision-making scenarios, are finding that different areas of the brain may be involved depending upon whether an individual has a meditation practice and the nature of the moral or ethical decision at hand. One of these studies found that, when treated unfairly, the decision-making of meditators was more rational and less influenced by emotional reactivity than was the decision-making of those who did not meditate.

Thus, mindfulness practices offer the promise of playing an important role in how students relate to challenging situations, and how they recognize and respond to ethical dilemmas. As Daniel Goleman observes:

Self-awareness, then, represents an essential focus, one that attunes us to the subtle murmurs within that can help guide our way through life. And, . . . this inner radar holds the key to managing what we do—and just as important, what we don't do. This internal control mechanism makes all the difference between a life well lived and one that falters.

VIII. Mindful Ethics in the Classroom

William James, the father of modern psychology, penned a phrase that is among the most widely repeated amid mindfulness circles, especially those oriented around education. It is a phrase that speaks to one of the primary aspects of mindfulness practice and links it directly to ethics. He wrote, "[T]he faculty of voluntarily bringing back a wandering attention over and over again is the very root of judgment, character, and will."

The practice of mindfulness, in the form that is taught today and the subject of much scientific research, involves little more than following James's instruction. James is explicit in linking this simple (to articulate, challenging to practice), exercise to our ethical fiber—"judgment, character, and will"—and, with an anticipatory nod to the Carnegie Report, further states: "No one is compos sui if he have it not. An education which should improve this faculty would be the education par excellence."

Mindful Ethics, one of the first law school courses in the country to integrate mindfulness, is responsive to James's call to action. It also draws upon Aristotle's insights in fashioning a curriculum to help develop a law student's capacity for practical wisdom and the intuition that allows him or her to "assess situations correctly and act appropriately." Mindful Ethics first appeared in the Miami Law curriculum in Spring 2010 and has been offered every semester since. Two attributes of the course are worth noting at the outset. The first is that mindfulness is a core component of the class, as opposed to a stand-alone element introduced periodically to enrich the overall student learning experience. The second is that while students are taught mindfulness exercises, the primary exploration of mindfulness in the classroom is as an element embedded in the ethics conversation. Importantly, a decision was made to not use a casebook, but instead to create an integrated curriculum with class readings and assignments so that the mindfulness and ethics components would be more finely woven together.

The idea of teaching mindfulness with professional responsibility was essentially an academic experiment. The hypothesis was that if students could infuse a heightened sense of awareness into an engaged application of the rules of professional conduct then implicit learning might occur; much like Alan Lerner suggested, students might internalize a contextual application of the rules as opposed to just memorizing the rules for an exam. Because of the natural link between mindfulness and ethical decision-making, a professional responsibility class offered an ideal laboratory. Additionally, the semester-long exposure offered an ideal environment for learning mindfulness, as it is a skill that is developed through regular and ongoing practice.

The class, titled "Mindful Ethics: Professional Responsibility for Lawyers in the Digital Age," not only includes mindfulness exercises, but also has students draw upon mindfulness practices and insights in their analysis of a legal hypothetical—in other words, an applied mindfulness curriculum. The context of ethics for "lawyers in the digital age" focuses on cutting-edge issues involving the impact of technology and social media upon the legal profession. These issues lend themselves to an appreciation of the relevance of mindfulness given that digital technologies often trigger very quick, sometimes unfortunate impulsive reactions.

***

Endnotes omitted (See Jan L. Jacobowitz & Scott Rogers, Mindful Ethics—A Pedagogical and Practical Approach to Teaching Legal Ethics, Developing Professional Identity, and Encouraging Civility, 4 St. Mary's J. Legal Mal. & Ethics 198 (2014)) for full article version). Reprinted with permission from the 2014 edition of the "St. Mary's Journal on Legal Malpractice & Ethics" © 2016 St. Mary's Journal on Legal Malpractice & Ethics. All rights reserved.

Questions and Comments

1. Violations of ethical rules and unprofessional conduct can be caused by emotionally charged situations, and take place during moments of high stress. It has been shown that practicing Mindfulness leads to increased self-awareness and reduced levels of stress. Accordingly, practicing Mindfulness can help lawyers engage in ethical decision-making and analysis.

2. It is well-known that litigation practice may turn into uncivil and fuel impulsive reactivity causing lawyers to cross ethical lines without recognizing it. In addition, availability of social media further allows for impulsive and reactive action that can violate the boundaries of professional responsibility rules. A growing number of ethics advisory opinions and disciplinary actions stem from instantaneous emotional expression in a blog post or on Facebook. Practicing Mindfulness will allow an attorney to put pause between impulse and action, thereby providing an appropriate response to the situation instead of pure reaction.

3. Law students are trained to spot issues in a given set of facts and to think critically, including finding faults in one's legal arguments. However, it is not uncommon for law students to dwell in pessimism and ruminate on their potential inability to pass the Bar Exam or succeed professionally. Resilience, however, is not commonly taught in law school. Should it be?

A Lawyer's Guide to Dealing with Burnout: Does Burnout Mean I Should Leave My Job or the Law Altogether
Lawyers with Depression (Online) Blog, Guest Articles, May 16, 2016
By Amiram Elwork

When individual lawyers seek the help of a counselor, it is not unusual for the conversation to start with: "I have been thinking about quitting my job or law altogether, but I am not sure what I should go into." My usual advice on such matters is "slow down. While quitting your job or the law may in fact be the right thing to do, given the risks and costs involved, these should be options to consider only after you truly understand what has happened to you."

I give this advice because by the time many lawyers seek professional help, they are often "burned out." People who are experiencing burnout commonly want to make drastic decisions, but they are usually driven by desperation rather than inspiration. Because their thinking often lacks clarity, I ask them to take some time to just ponder.

"Burnout" is a term used to describe professionals engaged in people-oriented services who are experiencing emotional exhaustion, depersonalization, and a reduced sense of accomplishment. A typical symptom is feeling drained and unable to give to others, wishing that "they would all just go away." Sometimes this can result in callous, rude, and inappropriate responses toward clients, colleagues and staff. The person may also feel inadequate and lacking in personal achievement and purpose.

It should be noted that although mental health professionals use the term "burnout" regularly, it is not an official mental health diagnosis. However, people who are seriously "burned out" usually exhibit the symptoms of at least a mild form of depression (e.g., pessimism, sadness), which is a mental health disorder. And so, it may be more accurate to think of "burnout" as a form of depression.

Causes

Although not all of the problems that lawyers encounter can be blamed on their line of work, the fact that they experience particularly high rates of burnout suggest that certain stressful characteristics of being an attorney must have at least a contributory effect.

The most stressful occupational demands of attorneys include: time pressures, work overload, competition, the need to keep up with a wide range of legal topics, balancing a personal life with professional obligations, and dealing with difficult people. Another stressor relates to the fact that the American system of justice is highly adversarial. Some lawyers also experience conflict and ambiguity about their roles, such as when they are forced to hurt people or to advocate for what they know are unjust results.

In addition to these external stressors, there are several personality characteristics among lawyers which may make them less prone to withstand the demands of their profession. The most significant one is "perfectionism."

Because law requires objective logical analysis and close attention to details, the legal profession attracts perfectionists. These are people who live by the rule: "If I don't do a perfect job in every detail, I will fail." Perfectionists tend to be workaholics who are often viewed as inflexible, uncomfortable with change, and obsessed with control but unconvinced that they have it. Since perfection can't be achieved, striving for it can cause constant dissatisfaction.

Another reason that some lawyers experience burnout is that their core values are not aligned with their own behaviors. Sometimes this problem reflects an internal psychological conflict, whereas at other times it is a conflict between the lawyer's values and those of the organization at which he or she works. Either way, when what you do is in conflict with what you think you should be doing, that triggers chronic feelings of guilt and unhappiness.

Solutions

If you have experienced burnout for a long time or the symptoms are severe, it is best to seek professional help. However, if the symptoms are not severe enough to warrant professional intervention, there are a number of self-help techniques that are worth trying. All I can do here is to describe a few of them very briefly.

First, you must understand that the human stress response goes through a sequence of four events:

Stimulus > Thought > Emotion > Behavior

There is usually a triggering incident or stimulus that causes you to respond. Your initial response comes in the form of a conscious or unconscious mental appraisal. The thought causes an internal physiological response that results in one or more emotions. The emotions drive your external behaviors.

Using this model, your first attempt should be to try to change the external environmental demands that cause you stress. For example, if you are constantly being put under the stress of unreasonable deadlines, go to the person(s) involved and attempt to change the time lines. Or, if you don't have enough support in the office, ask for additional support.

One would think that such advice is obvious, but I find that too many lawyers don't even try these simple steps because they suffer from the illusion that it is a sign of weakness to do so. Their thought is that a "real lawyer can handle anything and if I can't take what is handed to me, I must not be good enough for this job." Typically, this sort of misguided logic is a sign that the lawyer is a "perfectionist."

This brings us to the second level of intervention one should try, namely to reduce one's level of perfectionism. You do that by first becoming aware of how your perfectionism plays itself out on a daily basis, and then by interrupting your automatic thought patterns until you change them.

For example, let's assume that you are a perfectionist and your senior managing partner asks you to take on a particularly difficult project (stimulus). Furthermore, let us assume that you are given an unreasonable deadline (stimulus), given all of the other matters for which you are responsible. Your initial reaction might be to think, "I have no choice. I must take on this case. I must accept this deadline. To do otherwise would be to show that I am incompetent." In the eyes of perfectionist, being less than perfect or just plain human is a equivalent to being incompetent.

Inwardly, you might also be thinking: "If I don't take this on without any hesitation, I will expose myself as being inferior. I don't want anyone to find out who the real me is—that I'm just an imposter and that I am not as good as others think I am." Such thoughts will trigger emotions like fear of failure and rejection, as well as guilt. As a result, your outward response will probably be to reflexively say "yes" and to take on the project without any hesitation.

These reactions create a vicious cycle. Your inability to say "no" causes more stress because it creates an impossible workload and increases your chances of making sloppy mistakes. It reduces your ability to have a personal life and eventually leads you to feel burned out.

In order to improve your predicament, you must start by becoming fully aware of types of thoughts and emotions outlined above and by slowing them down. The best way to do this is to keep a daily log of them for two weeks and break all stressful experiences down into four elements: stimuli, thoughts, emotions and behaviors.

Once you are fully aware of your perfectionistic thoughts and emotions, you need to force yourself to begin interrupting them. The problem is that because so many of our dysfunctional thoughts and emotions are products of years of repetition, they tend to be driven by an internal automatic pilot. By continually interrupting such thoughts and emotions, however, it is possible to regain conscious control of them. Once you have done this, you need to begin cross-examining the validity of your automatic thoughts and emotions and considering other choices.

For example, using the scenario outlined above, you might ask yourself the following questions: "Would it be possible for me to suggest that someone else take on this project given the other things I have on my plate? Is it possible for me to delegate some of my other work to other attorneys? Is it really true that if I legitimately can't do everything, I must take on this work anyway or be labeled a failure? Are my colleagues that unreasonable? Isn't it true that I am the one who is being unreasonable with myself?"

Of course, it is possible that the realistic and true answers to the questions just posed would suggest that your organizational culture is fully to blame for your stress and burnout—that you are not imagining it and there is nothing you can do about it, except leave. On the other hand, if perfectionism is responsible for much of your problem, then you should come to the realization that no matter where you go, you will still be you. The stresses that perfectionism cause will emerge on any job. Leaving your current job because you feel burned out may not be the long term answer to your problems after all.

Another intervention to try is to assess the extent to which your stress is caused by the fact that your work life is not in alignment with your values. Some misalignments are caused by internally conflicted or mutual exclusive values (e.g., high ambition vs. family). Other misalignments are created by the fact that there is a conflict between your values and the values of the organization for which you work (e.g., financial success at any cost versus ethical behavior).

If your value misalignments are internal, they must be resolved internally. Again, leaving your job or the law will usually not resolve such conflicts. If, on the other hand, your values conflict with those of your organization, then you are "a fish out of water" and a separation may be in order.

The interventions I have described are simple to comprehend, but they could be among the most difficult tasks you will ever undertake. Rather than running from your job or the law altogether, they require you to examine the issues that cause you stress more deeply before making any major moves, and to consider less drastic changes. You might still decide to leave your job or the law, but at least it will be for valid reasons.

Questions and Comments

1. The article indicates that when most lawyers are confronted with burnout and the feeling of being depressed, they have this thought in mind: a "real lawyer can handle anything and if I can't take what is handed to me, I must not be good enough for this job." Why do you think so many lawyers have this mentality? What are some possible solutions to prevent those entering the legal profession from developing this type of thought process? Consider the solutions, if any, and how law students can start implementing them.

2. Think about your law school experience thus far. It is likely most of your classmates have felt tired and unmotivated at times. However, hopefully you have not experienced the type of burnout discussed in this article as a second or third year law student. Where does one draw the line between the usual daily struggle of having a demanding and busy career and experiencing a severe burnout? Do you think it is easy to confuse constant exhaustion with severe burnout?

3. Does the article propose a way of coping with burnout? Do you think practicing Mindfulness on a daily basis would lead to lowering or eliminating burnout? For a reminder of what Mindfulness is, look back at some of the articles in this chapter and apply the principles underlying the Mindfulness practice to this specific scenario.

C. DISCUSSION QUESTIONS

1. Feelings of unhappiness and dissatisfaction may impair a lawyer's productivity. It is frequently understated that the legal profession is a *people's business*. Lawyers frequently have to deal with unhappy and stressed out clients, while often a client's needs cannot be fully addressed even through litigation or other means. Also, one's concentration becomes impaired under stress. Mindfulness meditation can help lawyers develop an ability to pay attention, calmly, in each moment, while its benefits can also be applied to all aspects of life. Studies show that daily meditation leads to improvement in concentration and a sense of calm, along with a decline in anxiety, hostility, and depression. It also can help a lawyer make more discerning decisions about how to respond to difficult behavior from an opposing lawyer, a judge, or even her own client. To learn more about Mindfulness in the legal profession, *see* http://www .mindfulnessinlaw.org. Numerous other sources are also available on the subject.

2. Numerous professionals in different fields, including legal educators and practitioners, have cultivated Mindfulness training in tandem with escalating public interest. For example, mediators for the U.S. Court of Appeals for the 9th Circuit have attended a daylong session

on Mindfulness at Spirit Rock Meditation Center; the Boston office of the 160-lawyer firm Nutter, McClennan and Fish, LLP offered lawyers Mindfulness meditation training; the ABA Journal Senior Editor Steven Keeva authored a book about Mindfulness practices for lawyers; the Center for Contemplative Mind in Society (CCMS) organizes a five-day contemplative practice retreat for law students from Yale and Columbia; Harvard Law School regularly leads a six-week workshop on stress reduction, meditation, and yoga since 2002. Also, Google, General Mills, Pentagon Leaders, and Silicon Valley entrepreneurs have all consistently used Mindfulness in their training and work skills courses. Knowing the widespread usage of Mindfulness and the reported benefits, would you consider incorporating Mindfulness practice in your workday?

3. Mindfulness is not a quick fix and it can be best understood as a "practice" rather than "technique." The full benefits of Mindfulness are only achieved with a regular, long-term practice. So how does one practice Mindfulness? For beginners, find a quiet place, set the time, close your eyes, and focus all your attention on your breathing for only one minute, although it can seem much longer. Breathe normally. Be ready to catch your mind when it wanders off, acknowledge the distraction nonjudgmentally, and return your attention to your breathing. The goal is to train your attention to stay in one place as directed and the breath is just an anchor we are using for such practice. Over time, you can gradually extend the duration of this exercise into longer and longer periods. You will feel much calmer overall after having practiced for some time.